D0948809

The Cockfight

Balinese wood carving in the collection of W. M. C. and Donna Dickinson. Photograph by Gene Prince.

Edited by Alan Dundes

The Cockfight

A Casebook

The University of Wisconsin Press

The University of Wisconsin Press
114 North Murray Street
Madison, Wisconsin 53715

3 Henrietta Street
London WC2E 8LU, England

Library of Congress Cataloging-in-Publication Data
The Cockfight: a casebook / edited by Alan Dundes.
302 p.   cm.
Includes bibliographical references and index.
ISBN 0-299-14050-4.   ISBN 0-299-14054-7 (pbk.)
1. Cockfighting.   I. Dundes, Alan.
SF503.C68   1994
791.8—dc20   93-30545

Contents

Preface

The cockfight, in which two equally matched roosters—typically bred and raised for such purposes and often armed with steel spurs (gaffs)—engage in mortal combat in a circular pit surrounded by mostly if not exclusively male spectators, is one of the oldest recorded human games or sports. It is at least 2500 years old, and it appears to have originated somewhere in southeast Asia. The cockfight may be brief—it can be over in a matter of minutes or even seconds, but it can also last much longer, e.g., up to half an hour or more, if the two roosters are both able to avoid serious injury. Banned in many countries on the grounds that the cockfight constitutes inhumane cruelty to animals, the activity nevertheless continues to flourish as an underground or illegal sport. The cockfight is by no means universal, as it is not reported from native North and South America, Sub-Saharan Africa, and northwestern Europe (e.g., Germany and Scandinavia). Still, in those areas of the world where cockfighting thrives, it is virtually the national (male) pastime, e.g., the Philippines, Bali, Puerto Rico.

The aim of this casebook is to sample some of the scholarship which has sought to describe and analyze the cockfight. Sources selected range from chapters in fictional novels to analytic essays which first appeared in professional anthropology and folklore journals. The goal is to give the reader some idea of the nature of cockfighting in a wide variety of cultural contexts as well as possible clues as to the meaning(s) of the cockfight as a traditional game/ sport. As these eighteen essays were written at different times (from 386 to 1993) and directed to vastly different audiences, one should expect a lack of consistency in terms of theoretical orientation. But that is precisely the point. The reader should come away from the casebook with an appreciation of the fact that there are numerous ways of analyzing the same data. Because these diverse essays were written independently of one another for the most part, it was not possible to avoid some overlap of content and detail. This repetition of ethnographic material should not be deemed undesirable. That a cockfighting practice in the Philippines is also reported in India may tell us something important about the possible historical relationships between these two cock-fighting traditions.

We begin the volume with St. Augustine's fourth-century musings on why cocks fight in the barnyard and why men are so fascinated by such cockfights. We then present a short essay from the Ming Dynasty, which again attests man's attraction to natural cockfights but which raises the question of whether or not man should intervene in such events. We then proceed to consider the cockfight proper, in which the "natural" cockfight has been taken over by humans so that cocks may act as human surrogates. The first of these essays gives an account of the rules of cockfighting. While each area of the world or, for that matter, each arena or "gallodrome" may have its own local rules, the general principles governing this event are discernible, and it is the purpose of this essay to familiarize the reader who may never have seen an actual cockfight with these principles. The next six essays consist of different descriptions of cockfights. The contexts include early nineteenth-century London, late nineteenth-century Puerto Rico, and twentieth-century Tahiti, southern California, Ireland, and the Texas-Mexico border. Although several of these accounts are literary, they do have the advantage of being vivid and well-written.

Then follows an essay describing the cockfighters themselves and their attitudes towards their sport, and how they defend themselves against the charges made by the Society for the Prevention of Cruelty to Animals. A second essay in this vein speculates not only about the pros and cons of cockfighting, but also about whether or not cockfighting should be the legitimate subject of study by scholars.

The final seven essays in the casebook all seek to analyze (as opposed to describe) the cockfight. The first of these, by anthropologist Clifford Geertz, is unquestionably a turning point in the history of cockfighting scholarship. First published in 1972, it has stimulated an interest in cockfighting outside of the relatively small world of cockfighters and cockfight fans. Almost all serious scholarship since 1972 takes Geertz's memorable commentary on the Balinese cockfight as a point of departure. Anthropologists Guggenheim, Marvin, Affergan, Leal, and Cook analyze the cockfight in the Philippines, Spain, Martinique, Brazil, and Venezuela, respectively. Each provides valuable ethnographic detail as well as an attempt to decipher the meaning of the cockfight in a particular cultural context. The final essay, by this volume's editor, seeks to examine the cockfight as a cross-cultural phenomenon from the vantage point of a psychoanalytic perspective.

The reader may agree with one, or some, or none of the authors represented in this casebook. In the latter instance, he or she may be inspired to propose a new interpretation of the cockfight, an interpretation not found in this sampling of cockfight scholarship. At least, the reader will have an advantage over most of those who have written on the cockfight in the past, the advantage of having a knowledge of some of the standard sources devoted to the subject. Many of the writers of the essays included in this volume appear to have known only the one cockfighting tradition they discussed.

While some individuals may adjudge the cockfight to be a cruel "male" game or sport, and as such unworthy of scholarly consideration, the fact is that the cockfight does exist and has existed for hundreds and hundreds of years. Folklorists are obliged to study *all* traditional materials, even those which may seem unpleasant or inhumane to some. Certainly there is no doubt that the cockfight is traditional. We cannot possibly hope to understand human behavior if we arbitrarily exclude any part of it from study. The cockfight may be "illegal," but it is perfectly legal to seek to explain its undeniable appeal to a substantial segment of the world's population.

Acknowledgments

I thank the indefatigable staff of the Interlibrary Borrowing Service of Doe Library at the University of California, Berkeley, for their remarkable expertise in locating hard-to-find obscure publications on cockfighting. I am also indebted to Rafaela Castro Belcher and Margot Winer for their bibliographical surveys of cockfighting compiled in my folklore theory seminars in 1976 and 1986 respectively. Thanks to Antonella Johnston for assisting me with the translation of Francis Affergan's essay into English. For valuable references, I am grateful to Jim Anderson, Stanley Brandes, Dan Melia, and Rodney Needham. For a careful reading of the entire manuscript, I thank Marcelo M. Suarez-Orozco. I must also express my appreciation to all the authors and publishers who were kind enough to allow me to print or reprint their essays in this casebook. Finally, I must praise my daughters Alison and Lauren, my son David, and my forbearing wife Carolyn for seeing me through what is likely to be the last part of the "chicken phase" of my academic career as a folklorist.

Balinese farmer with his fighting cock, 1956. Photograph by W. M. C. Dickinson.

The Cockfight

A Barnyard Cockfight
of the Fourth Century

It may come as a surprise to some readers to learn that perhaps the first great mind to ponder the possible meaning of the cockfight was St. Augustine (354–430), one of the leading Christian thinkers of all time. To be sure, the cockfight he described was a "natural" one, occurring in the barnyard rather than one arranged or coordinated by men. Nevertheless, the probing questions he asked, "Why do cocks fight?" and, equally important, "Why are men so fascinated by cockfights?" remain critical.

St. Augustine's ruminations on the cockfight occurred in one of his philosophical dialogues entitled De Ordine, *which can be dated in the year 386. The dialogue consists of two separate books, each of which has a passage referring to cockfights. Both passages are presented below.*

To appreciate St. Augustine's discussion of the cockfight, one must realize that De Ordine *("About Order") was primarily concerned with the vexing problem of theodicy. In other words, how can man reconcile the existence of evil in the world with the idea of a beneficent or good deity. If God is good, how could He have created evil or cruelty? Finding a satisfactory answer to this perplexing paradox is not easy, but the gist of it seems to be that there is order throughout creation, and that includes evil components of creation. Moreover, it is precisely the existence of evil or ugliness which confirms the existence of good or beauty. In the absence of evil, there could be no good; in the absence of ugliness, there could be no beauty. In folkloristic parlance, one might say that "It is the exception which proves the rule."*

In any event, in the present context, it is worth remarking that cockfighting is discussed in tandem with prostitution and "ugly" animal sexual parts by St. Augustine. His own personal struggle against the temptations of the flesh and sin in general are graphically described in his celebrated Confessions *(390). For more about his life, see Gerald Bonner,* St. Augustine of Hippo, Life and Controversies *(Philadelphia: Westminster Press, 1963), and Peter R. L. Brown,* Augustine of Hippo: A Biography *(Berkeley: University of California Press, 1967).*

Reprinted from Robert P. Russell, *Divine Providence and the Problem of Evil: A Translation of St. Augustine's* De Ordine (New York: Cosmopolitan Science & Art Service, 1942), pp. 49, 51, 91, 93, 95, 97.

Thereupon I also arose. And when our daily prayers to God had been said, we began to go to the baths; for that place was comfortable and suitable for our disputation, whenever we could not be in the field on account of inclement weather. Suddenly we noticed barnyard cocks beginning a bitter fight just in front of the door. We chose to watch. For what do the eyes of lovers [of truth and beauty] not encompass; where do they not search through to see beauteous reason signaling something thence?—reason which rules and governs all things, the knowing and the unknowing things, and which attracts her eager followers in every way and wherever she commands that she be sought. Whence indeed and where can she not give a signal?—as was to be seen in those fowls: the lowered heads stretched forward, neck-plumage distended, the lusty thrusts, and such wary parryings; and in every motion of the irrational animals, nothing unseemly—precisely because another Reason from on high rules over all things. Finally, the very law of the victor: the proud crowing, the almost perfectly orbed arrangement of the members, as if in haughtiness of supremacy. But the sign of the vanquished: hackles plucked from the neck; in carriage and in cry, all bedraggled—and for that very reason, somehow or other, beautiful and in harmony with nature's laws.

We asked many questions: Why do all cocks behave this way? Why do they fight for the sake of supremacy of the hens subject to them? Why did the very beauty of the fight draw us aside from this higher study for a while, and onto the pleasure of the spectacle? What is there in us that searches out many things beyond the reach of the senses? And on the other hand, what is it that is grasped by the beckoning of the senses themselves?

We were saying to ourselves: Where does law not reign? Where is the right of commanding not due to a superior being? Where is there not the shadow of consistency? Where is there not imitation of that beauty most true? Where is there no limit? And thus admonished that there should be a limit to our watching the chickens, we went whither we had purposed to go; and there, as best we could, we garnered into this part of the notebook all the points of our nocturnal discussion—carefully indeed, for the points were recent; and at any rate, how could such striking things escape the memory of three diligent inquirers? In order to spare my strength, nothing more was done by me that day, except that it was my custom to go over half a book of Virgil with them before the evening meal. And we were everywhere giving careful attention to moderation, which no one fail to approve. But to observe it when one is pursuing something eagerly, is extremely difficult and rare.

. . .

But let us get back to order, for Licentius may at any moment be returned to us. For the present, I ask you this question: Does it seem to you that the unwise man acts according to order, no matter what he does? But mark what snares the question contains. If you say that he acts according to order, then, if even the unwise man always acts according to order, what will become of that definition: *Order is that by which God governs all things that are?* And if there is no order in the things that are done by the unwise man, then there will be something which order does not embrace. But you are not willing to accept either alternative. See to it, I beg you, lest in your defense of order you throw everything into disorder.

At this point Trygetius answers again, for the other boy was still absent:

"It is easy," he says, "to reply to this dilemma of yours. For the moment, however, I cannot call to mind an analogy by which my opinion ought, I know, to be declared and illustrated. I shall simply state my impression; for you will do what you did a little while ago. Certainly that mention of the darkness has brought us a great deal of light on what has been put forward very obscurely by me. Indeed the entire life of the unwise, although it is by no means consistent and by no means well regulated by themselves, is nevertheless necessarily included in the order of things by divine Providence; and certain places having been arranged, so to speak, by that ineffable and eternal law, it is by no means permitted to be where it ought not to be. Thus it happens that whoever narrow-mindedly considers this life by itself alone, is repelled by its enormous foulness, and turns away in sheer disgust. But if he raises the eyes of the mind and broadens his field of vision and surveys all things as a whole, then he will find nothing unarranged, unclassed, or unassigned to its own place."

What great and wonderful responses does not God Himself—and, as I am more and more led to believe, also that unfathomable order of things—send to me through you! Verily, you speak things of such import that I cannot understand either how you discern them or how they can be spoken unless they are discerned. And for that reason I believe that they are both true and from on high. Now you were looking for just one or two illustrations for that opinion of yours. To me there occur already countless illustrations which bring me to complete agreement. What more hideous than a hangman? What more cruel and ferocious than his character? And yet he holds a necessary post in the very midst of laws, and he is incorporated into the order of a well-regulated state: himself criminal in character, he is nevertheless, by others' arrangement, the penalty of evil-doers. What can be mentioned more sordid, more bereft of decency or more full of turpitude than prostitutes, procurers, and the other

5

pests of that sort? Remove prostitutes from human affairs, and you will unsettle everything on account of lusts; place them in the position of matrons, and you will dishonor these latter by disgrace and ignominy. And therefore this class of people is by its own mode of life most unchaste in its morals; and by the law of order, it is most vile in social condition.

And is it not true that in the bodies of animals there are certain members which you could not bear to look at, if you should view them by themselves alone? But the order of nature has designed that because they are needful they shall not be lacking, and because they are uncomely they shall not be prominent. And these ugly members, by keeping their proper places, have provided a better position for the more comely ones. What more agreeable to us—because it was quite an appropriate sight for field and farmyard—than that contest and conflict of the barnyard cock, which we have related in the preceding book? But what have we ever seen more abject than the deformity of the vanquished one? And yet, by that very deformity was the more perfect beauty of the contest in evidence.

So it is, I think, with all things; but they have to be seen.

A Cock Fight
from the Ming Dynasty

Not everyone realizes that the cockfight has long been popular in China. The first recorded cockfight in China occurred in 517 B.C. There is some consensus that the cockfight may have originated in either Asia or Southeast Asia several millennia ago.

The following anecdotal account was written by Yuan Hung-tao (1568–1610), who came from Kungan County in Hupeh province. He and several of his brothers founded a school of writing, the Kungan School, during the Ming dynasty (1368–1644). The cockfight described is, like the one observed by St. Augustine centuries earlier, a natural one. Because the participants were not of equal size or strength, this natural cockfight appeared "unfair" to observers. The critical question was whether to intervene or to let nature take its course. It is, after all, human intervention into "natural" cockfighting that ultimately led to the human institution of the cockfight as we know it.

In this short essay, a cockfighting incident is presented as a parable which criticizes "do-nothing" academics who disparage activism. The distinction between pure research and "applied" knowledge remains relevant today. For a detailed discussion of the history of the cockfight in China, see Robert Joe Cutter, The Brush and the Spur: Chinese Culture and the Cockfight *(Hong Kong: The Chinese University Press, 1989). For commentary on this particular essay by Yuan Hung-tao as well as an alternative translation (entitled "Record of a Cockfight When I Dwelled in the Mountains"), see pp. 123–126.*

When I lived in the hills one of my neighbours to the south was a man named Chin, a minor official who lived a quiet life and whose hobby was keeping beautiful fowl. Another neighbour, Chiang, lived a quiet life as a merchant. Once Chiang brought back a huge cock from the north. All northern fowls are large, but this one was a monster with legs over a foot long, coarse feathers and a sharp beak. It moved with the unhurried gait of a stork and had a delightful dignity about it. Other cocks seeing it kept out of its way, all but one of Chin's

Reprinted from *Chinese Literature* 2 (1966): 70–72. By permission of the Chinese Literature Press, 24 Baiwanzhuang Road, Beijing 100037, China.

cocks, which strutted about and foraged for food as usual. With white feathers and a golden comb, this bird was even more handsome than the huge cock, but only one-fifth the size. The big cock, meeting it one day, expressed its contempt by casually pecking at it. But small as it was, the handsome cock had its pride. It leapt up and challenged the other. The big cock spread its wings and glared, preparing to pounce; but the handsome cock stood its ground so steadily that it dared not attack too rashly. Both showed their mettle then, advancing, retreating and warding each other off for a considerable time. Once when the huge cock swooped down and the handsome cock knew it could not withstand the attack, it hid itself between those great legs, skilfully avoiding the onslaught; then, while the huge cock was wondering where it had gone, it leapt up from behind to catch it off guard. The big cock, thus assailed, turned furiously to swoop down on its opponent, and, quick though the handsome cock was, it could not escape a mauling. I had watched the fight from the start, rejoicing each time the handsome cock got the upper hand and waiting eagerly to see it score again—but it failed to do so. As it never occurred to me to help, however, the handsome cock was being worsted.

I was on tenterhooks when a boy coming from the east stopped to watch the fight. He soon felt indignant and seized the big fowl to let the other peck it as it pleased; then he himself dealt the big one several heavy blows. Thus humbled, the big cock fled, and the handsome cock followed up its advantage by pursuing it all the way home. Then the big cock turned and chased it back to the scene of their battle, the boy intervened as before, and so it went on several times.

Two scholars who saw how seriously the boy took this said with a laugh, "We've never seen anyone attach such importance to a cock fight before."

The boy retorted, "Isn't this better than helping petty tyrants to bully humble folk, as do those who study the classics and wear the black gauze cap of an official?"

The two scholars slunk away.

I had been too unwell for some time to go out much, and had therefore not seen any gallant men chastising the powerful to help the weak; and this sight impressed me so much that I told the story to everyone I met. When they laughed, I joined in; when they kept a straight face, I still laughed. As I tell the story I laugh and leap for joy, and I revel in it all day.

JIM HARRIS

The Rules of Cockfighting

The "human" cockfight—as opposed to cockfights which occur naturally—like any other traditional game or sport is governed by rules. The rules of cockfighting vary over time and from place to place. However, there is a kind of hard-core set of regulations which are fairly consistent. These have to do with how the cockfight is to commence, how the rounds or intermissions are to be measured, and how it is to end, that is, how to determine the winner of a cockfight. Whatever the local rules may be, these are absolutely binding upon the participants. Part of the unofficial code of conduct of cockfighters is not to argue with the decision of the referee—just as it is considered totally inappropriate and dishonorable to reneg on a bet made on a cockfight.

In order to acquaint the reader with the basic rules and terminology of cockfighting—at least as it is customarily practiced in the United States in the late twentieth century, we have chosen "The Rules of Cockfighting" by Jim Harris, Professor of English at New Mexico Junior College in Hobbs, New Mexico, which appeared originally in the Publications of the Texas Folklore Society in 1987. Readers familiar with cockfighting in other countries will notice differences between the rules presented in this essay and the rules prevailing elsewhere. As all folkloristic phenomena are manifested through multiple existence (existence in more than one place and time) and variation, it is to be expected that no two sets of cockfighting rules will be absolutely identical.

For a few representative samples of different rules for cockfights, see Edwin Oliver, "The Laws of the Cockpit," The Cornhill Magazine, *56 (1924): 610–618 (for 18th-century England); Tito Saubidet,* Vocabulario y Refranero Criollo *(Buenos Aires: Guillermo Kraft, 1952), pp. 354–356 (for 19th-century Argentina); R. Van Eck, "Schetsen uit het Volksleven (I. Hanengevecht),"* De Indische Gids *1 (1879): 102–118 (for 19th-century Bali); L. G. Marquez,* Reglamento del Club Gallistico de Caracas *(Caracas: Tip. Londres, 1954) (for 20th-century Venezuela); Steven L. Del Sesto, "Roles, Rules, and Organization: A Descriptive Account of Cockfighting in Rural Louisiana,"* Southern Folklore Quarterly *39 (1975): 1–14 (for 20th-century Louisiana).*

Reprinted from *Hoein' the Short Rows.* Publications of the Texas Folklore Society, no. 47, ed. Francis Edward Abernethy (Dallas: Southern Methodist University Press, 1987), pp. 101–111.

9

No one knows why or when man first put fowl into a pit and let the game male do as he had done in the wilds for thousands of years: fight brother against brother until one cock ruled. No one knows why or when man first intervened and institutionalized part of the natural process that enabled the fittest to survive: the killing of all the competing roosters and the mating with all the hens. No one knows when game fowl were first taken from the jungles and bred in pens for their gameness.

What we do know is that the fighting of cocks was first the experience of the folk, that it became the passion of princes, generals, and kings, and that now it is again the pastime of the ordinary peoples of the earth. Historian Page Smith writes, "In much of present-day India, cockfighting has passed from the sport of princes and rajahs to the ordinary people of the country, who engage in it avidly, following formulas for diet and training several thousand years old. . . ."[1] But throughout the sport's history, cockers have always been a curious cross section of peoples. In his eighteenth-century diary, Englishman Samuel Pepys wrote, "To Shoe Lane to see a Cockfighting at a new pit there . . . but Lord! to see the strange variety of people, from Parliamentmen . . . to the poorest 'prentices, bakers, brewers, butchers, dairymen, and what not; and all these fellows one with another cursing and betting."[2]

Seventeen hundred years before Pepys wrote of attending a cockfight in London, the Romans came to the British islands, after having spread cockfighting throughout northern Europe, and found the inhabitants raising chickens for amusement and sport.

Cockfighting came to the southwestern United States from two directions. From the south, the Spanish and Mexicans brought a long tradition of "slasher," or knife fights, the blades tied to the cock's feet resembling a curved, single-edged razor blade. Today knife fighting is done by Latin Americans, the Spanish, the Portuguese, and peoples in the southern Mediterranean countries, Asia, and the South Pacific. From the southeastern United States, cockers brought gaff fighting to the Southwest, the blades resembling a rapier with a sharpened point and a round body.

Biologists surmise that all domestic chickens come from the Red and Grey Jungle Fowl of India. The game chicken we know today is the chicken that most resembles in appearance and demeanor his fighting forefathers of the East. As in the wilds, he is combative with his fellow fowls, and this is what the cocker exploits when he puts two birds in a cockpit.

In the Southwest, owning, operating, or using a cockpit is legal in New Mexico and in Arizona, New Mexico being the only state with no laws covering the fighting of chickens in particular or cruelty to animals in general that might be applied to cockfighting. California has the strictest laws against cockfighting in the United States. There the sport flourishes. And in Texas, where cockfighting is also illegal, cockfights are held in clandestine and not-so-clandestine locations across the state.[3]

But whether they are fought illegally on the banks of Mill Creek outside Canton in East Texas, or legally at the elaborate Phoenix Game Club in Arizona, the birds are fought under some fairly uniform rules in several different types of fights passed down through the ages.

A *main* is a series of odd-numbered fights between two parties. The party with the most wins during the day or during a two-day period is declared the winner. In a main, cocks are matched according to designated weights.

A *tournament* is a method of fighting a predetermined number of cocks at specified weights by a specific number of contestants. Several entrants are involved instead of just two.

Not fought often anymore, a *Welsh main* is a single elimination tournament in which a cock continues to fight in a series of battles until he loses, the winners advancing to the next round. The Welsh main usually begins with eight pairs of chickens, although these tournaments have begun with as many as sixteen pairs. Very few of even the best cocks today could take this sort of punishment since intensive inbreeding and line breeding have made competition very tough.

A variation of a Welsh main is called a *concourse*, in which not one but several different chickens are fought in each round. Again, this is not seen very much today.

Another fight not likely to be seen is the *battle royal*, in which many cocks are thrown into the pit and the fight proceeds until only two cocks remain, which are to be fought by standard rules outlined below. In England the battles royal were often associated with what the English called *Shakebags*, matches in which the birds were leftover cocks not good enough to fight in regular competition. Today cockers call any birds over six pounds *Shakes*, and they are not fought in tournaments.

Still another type of fight is called a *hack*, an impromptu fight between two parties usually arranged at the pit, a fight fought, so to speak, on the spur of the moment. Hacks are fought before and following more organized forms of competition.

The most popular form of battle today is called the *derby*, in which many people are invited to enter cocks or stags (roosters before their first moult) which are secretly matched according to top and bottom specified weights. In a four-cock derby, for example, a cocker will have his four cocks secretly weighed, banded, and numbered. The birds will then be matched to others within two or three ounces. If there are thirty cockers entering the derby, 120 fights may follow, the winner being the one with the most victories. The actual number of fights will decrease considerably when cockers who have lost

11

enough battles to know they will not win the derby drop out of battles with other losers. If the entry fee is $200, the winner will take home $6000 less a small percent for the house at some clubs. There is much betting on each fight. Usually the cocker or pitter will place a bet with his opponent before each fight.

Different sets of rules have governed the fights throughout the history of cockfighting in America, but since the 1950s the rules of Henry Wortham, "Modern Tournament and Derby Rules," have dominated.[4] (The editor of *The Gamecock* magazine, Faye Leverett, tells me that these rules were actually the brainstorm of a Dave Marburger, who let Henry Wortham, a famous cocker and referee, review and revise them before they were published.)[5] Most often, house rules are added, but they are not supposed to conflict with the Wortham rules which relate to gaff fighting.

Although in other centuries or other countries the pit was consistently circular, the cockpit in America can be circular, square, octagonal, or any shape as long as it is a minimum of sixteen feet across.

There are three sections to the Wortham rules. Section one relates to matching the birds, the authority of the referee, the length of the heels, trimming, and banding. Cocks are matched, as stated earlier, at weights within two or three ounces of each other. The referee has final and irrevocable decision-making authority. Any length of heel that is round from socket to point is fair, although tradition and predetermined agreement may call for a short heel, 1¼ to 1½ inches, or a long heel, longer than 1½ inches. Trimming of the bird is allowed only with the tail, wing, and saddle feathers along with the feathers around the vent. All battle cocks and stags are "dubbed," i.e., have their combs and wattles trimmed to be less of a target for the opponent.

Section two of Wortham's rules deals with the actual fighting. Just before entering the pit, the referee weighs the cocks, checking the band numbers and examining the heels.

In the pit the handlers, called "pitters," are allowed to "bill" the birds, allowing them to peck each other a few times while being held in the pitters' arms.

At the command of "get ready," the pitters place their cocks' feet facing each other. The cocks are eight feet apart at the start. On the command of "pit" the cocks are released.

Beak-to-beak pitting, called for under "Count" and "Time" provisions explained below, is performed with one hand. With the get-ready call, the pitter must have only one open hand under the bird, holding him in position. The center lines for beak-to-beak pitting are only twenty-two inches apart. After pitting on the eight-foot lines when the match begins or on center lines for beak-to-beak pitting, the pitter must stay at least six feet back from the cocks until the referee calls "handle," when each pitter must pick up his chicken.

The call to handle comes when one or both of the cocks is hung with a gaff. A pitter cannot touch the opposing bird except to remove the gaff hung in his own bird, and then he must grasp the opposing cock only below the knee and not lift him from the ground. Birds must be handled immediately when the referee so orders.

Between pittings after a handling, twenty seconds are allowed for Rest. At fifteen seconds into the Rest, the referee commands the pitters to get ready, followed in five seconds by the command to pit.

When the chickens are pitted, both will begin fighting most of the time. However, if one does not fight—and fighting can be the show of the least bit of aggression, including striking, chasing, or pecking—the opponent that is fighting is given "Count." Count is a way of determining a winner and ending the match. To initiate the Count, the fighting bird's pitter says, "Count me," and the referee counts to ten three times and he counts to twenty one time, taking a Rest of twenty seconds between each counting. If the other chicken does not fight in that length of time, the fighting bird is declared the winner. Again, Count is one of several ways to end the fight.

During Count, if the opponent *does* start fighting again, the Count is broken, and a new Count begins when one bird refuses to fight and the opposing bird's pitter says, "Count me."

If the aggressive cock that has Count suddenly dies, the other chicken is declared a winner unless he is running away at the time. A runaway chicken is hated by all cockfighters, and a runaway can never be a winner.

When neither chicken is fighting, the referee has another way of ending the fight. Often they are just too weak to fight, or they just do not have the desire to fight anymore. When the referee decides neither chicken is fighting, he initiates "Time." This is a period in which he counts to twenty three different times, taking a Rest of twenty seconds between each counting. If neither cock fights during this period, the fight is declared a draw. If both chickens are running away at the end of the time period, each entrant loses a full fight; there are two losers.

When one cock dies, the other cock is declared a winner if he is not a runaway. If a cock dies during Rest, he must be pitted dead a final time before a winner is declared. If both cocks are mortally wounded and neither has Count, the referee may call a draw. If a cock leaves the pit, the remaining cock may have Count until he is declared a winner; but if the remaining cock is a runaway, Time is called.

A fight can last as long as the cocks can last. Usually, after twenty minutes the battle is moved to a drag pit, which may be only eight feet wide, where the contest is completed. This moving of the fight is to keep up the pace of the derby, and it may result in two or three battles occurring at the same time.

13

The final section of Wortham's rules concerns penalties. These are given for such violations as the use of unfair heels, not pitting when ordered, taking any action that will distract the birds, and the use of stimulants to revive the cocks. The referee has the authority to penalize a pitter with Count or to declare a winner when a pitter breaks a rule or commits a foul.

Again, rules may vary from place to place in the United States. At one time Sol P. McCall's "Rules of the Cock Pit" were most often used, especially in the South. And from time to time someone offers a new set of rules that have minor variations in them. But there is a remarkable similarity between the fighting of cocks at the present time and throughout the history of the sport.

In a 1937 WPA article in the archives of the Museum of New Mexico in Santa Fe, Reyes Martínez describes cockfighting in northern New Mexico before 1900 and relates a famous 1892 fight in Arroyo Hondo just north of Taos between two famous roosters, "El Giro" and "El Motas."[6] Although the pit was only a circle drawn in the dirt, the fight could have been conducted today in any small town in New Mexico or the Southwest. In one part of the narrative, Martínez describes the professional "amarradores," the "men who knew the art, for it truly was an art, of tying properly the knife to the rooster's leg. . . . "[7]

Halfway around the world in Bali villages, the tying of spurs is also a very special and honored job. Anthropologist Clifford Geertz writes of the tying of spurs, "This is a delicate job which only a proportion of men, a half-dozen or so in most villages, know how to do properly."[8]

Geertz related the importance of the cockfight to the communal life of the Bali villages, how it is an expression of male sexuality, how it reinforces the whole structure of the village, how it represents animality, how it is a release of violent impulses. But in the fights, he describes rules that are similar to Wortham's rules. The twenty-second division for Count, Time, and Rest occurs when a Balinese referee drops a coconut with a small hole in it into a pail of water. It takes the coconut twenty-one seconds to sink.

In the early part of this century, British sportsman Sir Herbert Atkinson wrote about cockfighting throughout English history and particularly about cockfighting in the eighteenth and nineteenth centuries when it was the rage in England. His book, *Cockfighting and Game Fowl*, describes battles beside English taverns and in the royal pits of kings—and in these descriptions the reader can find traditions of pitting and handling that are remarkably similar to those in the Southwest today.[9]

In the early 1960s, Haldeen Braddy published in a magazine, a newspaper, and a Texas Folklore Society publication a story of an exciting cockfight in Juárez between two famous cocks, "El Negro" and "El Blanco."[10] Although

Braddy does not concentrate on the rules followed, the battle sounds like one that might be fought in Altus, Oklahoma, or Jackson, Tennessee.

Throughout the history of the game, cockers have been good sportsmen. Rarely in the pits today will one see a discourteous pitter; hardly ever will one see arguments with the referee as in football or basketball or baseball. Though there are questions among cockers about rules, they accept these rules and the referee's judgment as authority and as part of the traditional comradery among a fraternity of game fowl lovers that has its roots in folkways established long before there were such things as masons or hockey teams. In a 1949 book called *The Art of Cockfighting,* famous American cocker Arch Ruport writes:

> The cocker's fraternity is one of the greatest in the world. It has no officers or by-laws, and its members pay no dues. Yet there are rules, and they are honored and respected by all true and honest cockers. The sportsmanship of the members of the fraternity is seldom equaled and never surpassed in any other branch of sport.[11]

One final note in conclusion from Page Smith in his inquiry into the rise and fall of *Gallus Domesticus:*

> we must certainly be aware by now of the fact that history contains no form of behavior relating to humans and their animal companions which is higher in symbolic meanings, or which penetrates more profoundly into the inner recesses of the masculine psychic life than the cockfight, almost everywhere forbidden and almost everywhere practiced.[12]

Notes

1. Page Smith and Charles Daniel, *The Chicken Book* (Boston: Little, Brown, 1975), p. 115.

2. Samuel Pepys, *The Diary of Samuel Pepys,* ed. John Warrington (New York: Dutton, 1953), p. 470.

3. Giles Tippette, "The Birds of Death," *Texas Monthly,* November 1978: 163–65, 271–277; Dick Reavis, "Texas Monthly Reporter," *Texas Monthly,* September 1977: 78–81.

4. *The Gamecock* magazine holds copyright to the Wortham rules and publishes regular articles on rules and interpretations. Copy machines have made possible many issues of the rules, and they can be found in other publications, including Arch Ruport's *The Art of Cockfighting* (New York: Devin-Adair, 1949), p. 149.

5. Letter from Faye Leverett, 4 January 1985.

6. Reyes Martínez, "Cock Fights," WPA writing in the archives of the Museum of New Mexico, Santa Fe, 25 May 1937.

7. Martínez, "Cock Fights," p. 1.

8. Clifford Geertz, "Deep Play: Notes on the Balinese Cockfight," *Daedalus* 101 (1972): 8.

9. Herbert Atkinson, *Cockfighting and Game Fowl* (1938; reprint, Surry: Saiga, 1981).

10. Haldeen Braddy, "Feathered Duelists," in Mody C. Boatright, Wilson M. Hudson, and Allen Maxwell, eds., *Singers and Storytellers*, Publications of the Texas Folklore Society 30 (Dallas: Southern Methodist University Press, 1961), pp. 98–106; Braddy, "Feathered Duelists," *Pass Word*, Spring 1962: 70–74; and Braddy "Cocks Aren't Chicken in Border Sport," *The Southwesterner*, January 1964.

11. Ruport, *Art of Cockfighting*, p. 3.

12. Smith and Daniel, *Chicken Book*, p. 124.

A London Cockpit
and Its Frequenters

In centuries past, England was a place where cockfighting thrived. To try to get some sense of that time period, we offer a portion of an essay on cocking included in Pierce Egan's Book of Sports, *published in 1832. The original essay quoted generously from various esoteric pamphlets and tracts devoted to cockfighting and other amusements, e.g.,* The Court and City Gamester, *but these details of the selection, breeding, and care of cocks have not been reprinted here. Instead, we have elected to feature quite a striking picture of a cockfight and some of those who were in attendance.*

Pierce Egan (1772–1849) was a collector of folklore well before the word "folklore" was coined in 1846. He recorded English social customs in his Life in London *(London: Sherwood, Neely, and Jones, 1821) and added numerous slang phrases to the 1823 edition Francis Grose's of 1785* Classical Dictionary of the Vulgar Tongue. *His career interest in acting is reflected in his collection of theater anecdotes,* The Show Folks *(London: M. Arnold, 1831).*

In the following extract, it is not altogether clear whether Pierce Egan is quoting someone else, "an amateur" attending his first cockfight, or whether the "amateur" is in fact Egan's own persona. In either case, the ensuing account is one of the best ever written about the atmosphere of a cockfight.

We shall now give a description of a London cockpit and its frequenters with some *touches* at character by an amateur:—

"I was sitting, some evenings ago, in my room, at the first coming of twilight, which in our Albany rooms is fond of paying early visits—my head was indolently hung back upon the red morocco top of my easy chair, and my hands were hung like two dangling bell ropes over each arm of my seat—and in this position I was ruminating on many things of little moment. I had thus leaned back in my chair, and resigned myself to the most luxurious idleness,—a kind of reading made easy,—when a knuckle, knocking at my door, intimated the

Reprinted from Pierce Egan, *Book of Sports, and Mirror of Life: Embracing The Turf, The Chase, The Ring, and The Stage* (London: T. T. and J. Tegg, 1832), pp. 147–148, 150–153.

arrival of some impatient visitor—and before I could muster voice enough to give Tate Wilkinson's direction of "Come in!" the tooth of my door-lock was wrenched, and Tom Owen, with a newspaper in his hand, dashed in—and at once stood astounded, with his white hat elevated on his forehead,—admiring my amazing stupor.

"Why Edward! Edward Herbert! Asleep, by all that's sublime! There he sits, deaf to time! Edward, I say! Come bolt up from the morocco! I have news for your two *no-thoroughfare* ears, which ought to make you as lively as an eel with half his waistcoat off! Here," said he, smacking a creased and dingy newspaper, with an air of vehement exultation—"here is that which will be life itself to *you!*" I closed my book-mind quietly, or doubled it up, as Tom would say, and raising myself with difficulty into an erect posture—rubbing my eyes, uncrossed my tingling legs (which were just beginning to wake out of a nap,) and begged, through the archway of a yawn, to know what this very sprightly piece of news consisted of. Tom pulled, or rather tossed off his hat, nodded to me a nod more eloquent than speech, and tipping an acute wink out of the left corner of his little impudent grey eye—proceeded at once to read aloud from the first column of the newspaper. He pronounced one word with an emphasis the most pointed—COCKING!—and then paused to let loose wink the second, which, if possible, was more charged with mystery than the former,— "*cocking!*—there Edward!" continued he—"there! cocking—at the Royal Cockpit, Tufton-street, Westminster!—there;" and then he went strictly through a formal advertisement,—touching—"200 the main,"—and "byes," and ."feeders"—and "gentlemen of Norwich," and "a deal of skimble-skamble stuff," which for the life of me I could not then retain, and therefore cannot now repeat.

"When Tom had finished his formal information, he very readily and clearly, at my request, divested the announcement of its technicalities, and explained to me, that on such a day, being the morrow, a grand main of cocks was to be fought at the Royal Cockpit, at which, for 5s. the head (certainly not the heart), a man might be present. It required little of my volatile friend's rhetoric to induce me to promise my attendance, as I had never been present at any thing of the kind, higher than a full-feathered blustering skirmish of a couple of huge-combed, red-ruffled, long-tailed dunghills, amid a wilderness of poultry, in a farm-yard. I had seen no clean fighting—no beautiful sparring in silver—no blood-match! as Tom earnestly describes it. I was the more induced to accede to his request of accompanying him, from learning that he could introduce me to Mr. D———, one of the principal breeders of game cocks—a gentleman of the most winning manners—and the one who could and would describe to me the characters present, and procure for me the sight of the coops and pens, where the birds were fed and kept previously to the day of battle.

. . .

Tom Owen called punctually on the day and at the appointed hour, dressed up dutifully for the sport, and well fitted to rival a horse-dealer or a groom— yet with a loose-hung gentility about him, that just left it a matter of doubt whether you ought to ask him into your drawing-room or your stable. We took our way across the park with hasty, eager feet, and were with very little difficulty soon conducted to the door of a dull, old-fashioned building in Tufton-street, Westminster, around which were sauntering a sprinkle of old gentlemen, old hackney-masters, old sportsmen, old leather-breeches, old top-boots, old canes, old nondescripts: all that was strange, and vitiated, and extravagant in age seemed collected about this spot; and I could not but remark how few I saw of the young, the rakish, and the depraved, present at a sport which was cruel enough for excitement, and uncertain enough for the purposes of gambling. One or two solitaries of a youthful appearance dangled about as half in shame and half in curiosity; but I detected none of the enthusiastic bustle, none of the wildness, spirit, and pleasure which light up "young bloods" at other of the ancient and rude sports of this country. One very respectable and aged gentleman on crutches struggled his way on the unmolested pavement to the door, as though the fires of youth would not go out, and accident or disease could not warn him to subside into the proprieties of his years. The doors were at length opened, and we paid our entrance money, and received the check for admission. This check was cast in pewter, and had the figure of a fighting-cock embossed upon it. But we entered the pit!

The cock-pit is a large, lofty, and circular building, with seats rising, as in an amphitheatre.* In the middle of it is a round matted stage, of about eighteen or twenty feet diameter, as nearly as my eye can measure it, and rimmed with an edge eight or ten inches in height, to keep the cocks from falling over in their combats. There is a chalk ring in the centre of the matted stage, of perhaps a yard diameter, and another chalk mark within it, much smaller, which is intended for the setting-to, when the shattered birds are so enfeebled as to have no power of making hostile advances towards each other. This inner mark admits of their being placed beak to beak. A large and rude branched candle-stick is suspended low down, immediately over the mat, which is used at the night battles.

*The Royal Cock-pit in St. James's Park has been taken down, and never again to be rebuilt. The Governors and Trustees of Christ's Hospital, to whom the ground belongs, met on the spot, the very day the lease expired; and gave directions for the immediate erasement of the building.

When we entered there were very few persons in the pit; for, as the gentleman of the match were not seated, the principal followers of the sport were beguiling the time at a public-house opposite the cockpit. A tall, shambling, ill-dressed fellow was damping the mat with a mop, which he constantly dipped in a pail of water, and sparingly, and most carefully sprinkled around him. This was to make it soft for the birds, and to prevent their slipping. We took our seats at the foot of a flight of stairs, that went up into one of the coops—judging that that would be the best spot for seeing as much as was to be seen. There are two "tiring rooms"—of course for the separate sides.— One room, or more properly, coop, is up the flight of stairs I have mentioned; the other is beneath it, and has its entrance without the pit. At this time my friend Tom's friend, Mr. D———, arrived, and I was introduced to him at once. He was a young man (I was almost sorry for this, because it untied a theory of mine, respecting the sport being a propensity of age only, owing, as I had settled it, to its being easy of enjoyment, a sedentary amusement, not troublesome to the beholders, cruel enough to stir the blood, and open to money-stakes like a game at cards: played in fact at a table, and under shelter. However, my theory is foolish). Mr. D———, as I said, was young, he was also lusty, fresh-coloured, cheerful;—open as day in his manners and in his conversation;—and free from that slang slyness which generally characterises the sporting man. Tom told him that I was anxious to see and know all I could; and he immediately opened to me the curiosities of the place, with a lively liberty, and a power of description, which I wish in my heart I could have caught from him. Seeing that he was thus so pleasantly minded, I began boldly at the beginning, and begged to know something of the rules and regulations of cocking. He turned-to at them, in high feather, on the instant.

The birds, Russell (I am saying after him), are weighed and matched—and then marked and numbered. The descriptions are carefully set down in order that the cock may not be changed; and the lightest cocks fight first in order. The key of the pens, in which the cocks are set and numbered, is left on the weighing-table on the day of weighing; or the opposite party may, if he pleases, put a lock on the door. The utmost possible care, in short, is taken that the matched birds shall fight, and no substitutes intruded.

Mr. D———, next gave me a very particular description of the modes of setting-to—of terminating difficult battles—and of parting the entangled birds; but as I really could not very clearly follow his rapid and spirited explanation, and as I am about to relate to you a battle as I myself saw it, I will not detain you here with my imperfect detail of his very perfect description.

But before the birds are pitted, Mr. D———'s account of a few of the characters must not be omitted. I cannot at all give you them in *colours*, as my new friend dashed them off: but I will follow him in a respectful *Indian-ink*, and at a distance; and you must make the most you can of what I am able to afford you.

"There was a tall, sallow-faced, powdered man standing below us. He took snuff industriously, wore very yellow leathern breeches,—very brown aged top-boots,—and a black coat of the *same* colour. He was sixty years of age if he was a month—and I never saw a dull man so enlivened as he was with this his *betting hour,* and the approaching warfare. He had a word for every one near him, and a restlessness which would not allow him to wait for answers. I found that he was a hackney-coach proprietor, and that cockfighting was his only amusement. He thought playing at cards a waste of time,—a disgraceful kind of gambling,—and he could not endure the barbarities of a man-fight, which he called "seeing two human creatures knock each other to pieces for other people's sport." Cockfighting was the only game! He was steady in his business, when no cockfight was on the carpet, and idle and tacit in a public-house parlour at nights. But in the pit he was at home. Sovereigns were golden dust, which blew about in the breath of his opinion; and he rose into perfect life only in the presence of 'a Shropshire Red,' or 'a Ginger Pile!'

"Nearly opposite to this person was a very orderly, quiet, respectably dressed man, with a formal, low-crowned, broad brimmed hat,—a black suit of clothes,—and a dark silk umbrella. He was trying to look demure and unmoved; but I was told that he was a clergyman, and that he would be 'quite up in the stirrups' when the cocks were brought in. He forced himself to be at ease; but I saw his small, hungry, hazel eyes quite in a fever,—and his hot, thin, vein-embossed hand, rubbing the unconscious nob of his umbrella in a way to awaken it from the dead:—and yet all the time he was affecting the uninterested incurious man! The *cloth* was half in his mind! He would fain still be a clergyman—but he had 'no *spur* to prick the sides of his intent!'

"Another person,—very small,—very dapper,—powdered like a gentleman of the old school,—with glossy grey silk stockings, high ancled shoes and buckles,—perked up against the pit,—affecting nothing,—caring for no one,—but living, revelling in the ancient sport. He bowed smartly around him, looked about with a couple of nimble bird-like eyes,—crowned one or two offered bets,—and sent the little white tip of his extremely thin pigtail from shoulder to shoulder, with an alacrity which showed that he was 'a hearty old cock' still; and had neither of his little silken legs in the grave!

"The lame old gentleman was seated close to the mat, and sat pillowed in fatness on a truss of straw, which one of the feeders had procured for him, to make his position less painful. He closed a bet quietly, with the end of his crutch touching the ferule of the umbrella of a tall, gaunt, white-faced man in bright blue (a tailor as I learned); and thus forcibly reminded me of the conjunction of the two horse-whip bets, in Hogarth's admirable picture of the Cockpit in *his* day:—except that this extended crutch gave me a more poignant moral—a more sorrowful and acute truth!

"In one part of the place I saw shabby old men, apparently wanting a meal, yet showing by their presence that they had mustered 5s. for an hour's sport here. In another spot I beheld blunt, sly, coarse Yorkshiremen, with brownish-red cheeks, short uneven features, thick bristly whiskers, and cold moist bleak-blue eyes—looking as though they were constantly out upon prey.

"I was continuing my enquiries into the characters around me, when a young man of very slang, slight, but prepossessing appearance, passed me, dressed in tight kerseymeres, with a handkerchief round his knee, neat white cotton stockings, small shoes, a blue check waiter-looking jacket, short about the waist, and a gay 'kerchief knowingly tied on his neck. He was really a clean handsome faced young fellow, with thin but acute and regular features, small light whiskers, and with his hair closely cut, and neatly and 'cutely combed down upon his forehead. He had scarcely passed me before I felt something rustle and chuckle by my elbow; and turning round, saw a stout plump old ostler-looking man carry a white bag past me, which by the struggle and vehement motion inside, I guessed to be one of the brave birds for the battle. The two men stepped upon the mat, and the hubbub was huge and instantaneous. 'Two to one on Nash!' 'A guinea on Nash!' 'Nash a crown!' only sounds like these were heard (for the bets are laid on the setters-to), till the noise aroused a low *muscular*-brooding chuckle in the bag, which seemed to show that the inmate was rousing into anger even at the voice of man!

From the opposite door a similar procession entered. The setter-to (Fleming by name) was dressed much in the same manner, but he appeared less attractive than young Nash (the name of the young man I have just mentioned.) He certainly was not so smart a fellow, but there was an honesty and a neatness in his manner and look, which pleased me much. The chuckle of the cock in the one bag was answered deeply and savagely from the other—and the straw seemed spurned in the narrow cell, as though the spirit that struck it would not be contained.

"Nash's bag was carefully untied, and Nash himself took out one of the handsomest birds I think I ever beheld. I must have leave to try *my* hand at a description of a game cock!

"He was a red and black bird—slim, masculine, trimmed—yet with feathers glossy as though the sun shone only upon his nervous wings. His neck arose out of the bag, snakelike,—terrible—as if it would stretch upward to the ceiling; his body followed, compact, strong, and beautiful, and his long dark-blue sinewy legs came forth, clean,—handsome,—shapely, determined,—ironlike! The silver spur was on each heel, of an inch and a half in length—tied on in the most delicate and neat manner. His large vigorous beak showed aquiline,—

22

eagle-like; and his black dilating eyes took in all around him, and shone so intensely brilliant, that they looked like jewels. Their light was that of thoughtful, sedate, and savage courage! His comb was cut close—his neck trimmed—his wings clipped, pointed, and strong. The feathers on his back were of the very glossiest red, and appeared to be the only ones which were left untouched; for the tail was docked triangularwise like a hunter's. The gallant bird clucked defiance—and looked as if he 'had in him something dangerous!' Nash gave him to Fleming, who held him up above his head—examined his beak—his wings—his legs—while a person read to him the description of the bird from paper—and upon finding all correct, he delivered the rich feathered warrior back to Nash, and proceeded to produce his own bird for a similar examination

"But I must speak of the senior Nash,—the old man,—the feeder. When again may I have an opportunity of describing him? and what ought a paper upon 'cocking' to be accounted worth,—if it fail to contain some sketch, however slight, of old Nash? He wore a smock-frock, and was clumsily though potently built; his shoulders being ample, and of a rotundity resembling a wool-pack. His legs were not equal to his bulk. He was unconversational almost to a fault—and never made any the slightest remark that did not appertain to cocks and cocking. His narrow, damp, colourless eye, twinkled a cold satisfaction when a bird of promise made good work on the mat; and sometimes, though seldom, he was elevated into the proffer of a moderate bet—but generally he leaned over the rails of a small gallery, running parallel with his coop, and, stooping attentively toward the pit, watched the progress of the battle. I made a remark to Tom and Mr. D———, that I thought him extremely like a cock. Tom was intent upon Fleming, and could not hear me; but Mr. D. was delighted at the observation, which seemed to him one of some aptitude. Old Nash's beaked nose drawn close down over his mouth,—his red forehead and gills,—his round body,—and blue thin legs; and his silver-grey, scanty, feathery hair lying like a plumage over his head—all proved him cocklike! This man, thought I, has been cooped up in pens, or penned up in coops, until he has become shaped, coloured, mannered like the bird he has been feeding. I should scarcely have been surprised, if Mr. D. had told me that old Nash crowed when the light first dawned over the ancient houses of Tutton-street, in a summer morning! I warrant me he pecked bread and milk to some tune; and perchance slept upon a perch!

"But Fleming lifted his bird from the bag, and my whole mind was directed his way. This was a yellow bodied black winged, handsome cock,—seemingly rather slight, but elastic and muscular. He was restless at the sight of his antagonist, but quite silent—and old Nash examined him most carefully by the paper, delivering him up to Fleming upon finding him answer to his description. The setters-to then smoothed their birds, handled them—wetted their fingers and moistened their bandaged ankles where the spurs were fastened—held them up opposite to each other—and thus pampered their courage, and prepared them for the combat.

"The mat was cleared of all persons except Fleming and young Nash. The betting went on vociferously. The setters-to taunted each the birds with other's presence—allowed them to strike at each other at a distance—put them on the mat facing each other—encouraged and fed their crowning and mantling until they were nearly dangerous to hold—and then loosed them against each other, for the fatal fight.

"The first terrific dart into attitude was indeed strikingly grand and beautiful—and the wary sparring, watching, dodging, for the first cut, was extremely curious. They were beak-point to beak-point,—until they dashed up in one tremendous flirt—mingling their powerful rustling wings and nervous heels in one furious confused mass. The leap,—the fire,—the passion of strength, the *certaminis gaudia,*—were fierce and loud! The parting was another kind of thing every way. I can compare the sound of the first flight to nothing less than that of a wet umbrella forced suddenly open. The separation was death-like. The yellow or rather the *ginger* bird staggered out of the close—drooping—dismantled—bleeding! He was *struck!*—Fleming and Nash severally took their birds, examined them for a moment, and then set them again opposite to each other. The handling of the cocks was as delicate as if they had been made of foam, froth, or any other most perishable matter. Fleming's bird staggered towards his opponent, but he was hit dreadfully— and ran like a drunken man, tottering on his breast, sinking back on his tail!— while Nash's, full of fire and irritated courage, gave the finishing stroke that clove every particle of life in twain. The brave bird, thus killed, dropped at once from the 'gallant bearing and proud mien,' to the relaxed, draggled, motionless object that lay in bleeding ruin on the mat. I sighed and looked thoughtful—when the tumult of the betters startled me into a consciousness of the scene at which I was present, and made me feel how poorly timed was thought amid the characters around me.

"The victor cock was carried by me in all his pride—slightly scarred,—but evidently made doubly fierce and muscular by the short encounter he had been engaged in. He seemed to have grown to double the size! His eyes were larger.

"The paying backward and forward of money, won and lost, occupied the time until the two Nashes again descended with another cock.

"Sometimes the first blow was fatal—at another time the contest was long and doubtful, and the cocks showed all the obstinate courage, weariness, distress, and breathlessness, which mark the struggles of experienced pugilists. I saw the beak open, the tongue palpitate—the wing drag on the mat. I noticed the legs tremble, and the body topple over upon the breast,—the eye grow dim,—and even a perspiration break out upon the feathers of the back. When a battle lasted long, and the cocks lay helpless near or upon each other,—one of the feeders counted ten, and then the birds were separated and set-to at the chalk. If the beaten bird does not fight while forty is counted, and the other pecks or shows signs of battle, the former is declared conquered.

"Such is cockfighting, Tom proposed showing me the coops; and I instantly accepted his proposal, and followed him up the stairs.

"A covering was hung before each pen; so that I *heard,* rather than saw, the cocks. But it was feeding time; and I beheld innumerable rocky beaks and sparkling eyes at work in the troughs—and the stroke of the beak in taking up the barley was like the knock of a manly knuckle on a table. Old Nash was mixing bread and milk for his feathered family. But I have done!"

WILLIAM DINWIDDIE

Cock-Fighting in Puerto Rico

Not all descriptions of cockfights are free from bias. Some clearly present a pro-cockfighting point of view while others display a distinct anti-cockfighting attitude. In the following account of cockfighting in Puerto Rico by William Dinwiddie (1867–1934) we have an excellent example of the latter. Phrases like "morally reprehensible" and "brutal" clearly reveal the author's ill-concealed views. Moreover, his somewhat patronizing and condescending attitude towards the spectators as "quiet, hard-working people . . . who enjoy their few simple pleasures" is also evident—though he does give praise for the apparent lack of "ugly swearing" and "rowdyism" at Puerto Rican cockfights. There is even a political critique expressed by the author when he refers to the government of Puerto Rico at that time (1890s) as a despotic one which may or may not have been remedied by the Spanish-American War, which resulted in Puerto Rico's being ceded to the United States in 1898.

The bias notwithstanding, it is true that cockfighting was—and continues to be—a major form of entertainment in Puerto Rico. For other accounts of the cockfight tradition in Puerto Rico, see Manuel A. Alonson, El Gibaro: Cuadro de Costumbres de la Isla de Puerto Rico *(San Juan: Instituto de Cultura Puertorriqueña, 1988, a facsimile reprint of the first edition published in Barcelona in 1849), pp. 77–93; Maria Cadilla de Martinez, "El Gallo y sus Peleas," in her* Raices de la Tierra *(Arecibo: Tipografia Hernandez, 1941), pp. 145–166; Gabriel Gonzalez Calderin, "El Gallo de Pelea,"* isla literaria *10–11 (June/July, 1970): 16–18; and Ledo. José Roberto Feijoó,* Apuntes Sobre El Arte de Castar Gallos De Pelea *(Puerto Rico: Taller Gráfico Gongolí, 1990).*

The only real recreation of the rural Puertoriqueños seems to be cock-fighting. Bull-fights have never gained a foothold in the island, though many of the Spanish-born citizens profess a profound regret that their national pastime seems not to have met with favor. The only reason given is that the people have always been too poor to indulge in the expensive luxury of importing any of the

Reprinted from William Dinwiddie, *Puerto Rico: Its Conditions and Possibilities* (New York and London: Harper & Brothers Publishers, 1899), pp. 175–179.

distinguished matadors from home, such experts being indispensable when it is desired to raise bull-fighting above the level of mere brutality.

As a matter of fact, cock-mains are more reprehensible morally than bull-rings, since in the former is displayed a brutal fight to the death between untrained but plucky birds, while the latter call for an exhibition of skill of hand and nerves of iron on the part of the human participants.

Every town in Puerto Rico has at least one cock-pit built and owned by some thrifty lover of the mains. They differ little in construction, consisting of an earth-floored ring some eighteen feet in diameter, surrounded by an outwardly-inclined, closely-boarded fence, with half a dozen hinged entrance gates, which may be closed fast when a fight is on. Back of this fence, board seats are built, sometimes rising three deep like circus benches, and in the ultra-fashionable places they are divided into numbered and reserved seats. Covering the ring is a square, open-sided, roofed shed, with a railed balcony having a row of benches some eight feet above the ring level. Outside of all is a high fence, built of clapboards from the great royal palm, which prevents intrusive glances.

It requires little provocation to start the inhabitants of the entire countryside to fighting their pet game-cocks. Sunday afternoon—after a hasty visit to the church in the morning—is always devoted to the island pastime, but a saint's day, a feast day, or any one of the many constantly recurring festive holidays brings out hundreds of country folk, who trudge along the narrow trails, bare-footed and lightly clad, with birds under the arms or jog along upon the cantering-gaited ponies with their legs hung over the wicker side-panniers from which valiant chanticleers thrust forth their heads and lift their strident voices in defiant challenge.

It is not to be supposed that game-bird fighting is followed by the entire population as a means of recreation, for the wealthier and commercial classes, while not eschewing the amusement of watching a main now and then, take no active part in the pit. The followers of the gaff are, however, not numbered entirely, as in our own country, among the tougher element, but it has as its devotees most of the poorer element, laborers or peons who work on the large plantations for hire, and have little garden plots of their own to supply their family needs. They are quiet, hard-working people when work is to be had, who enjoy intensely their few simple pleasures and go into ecstasies over their great sport of cock-maining.

Around the cock-pit are gathered two hundred jabbering peasants, in cotton clothes and loose blouses, with a sprinkling of the better-dressed and more opulent townsmen, clad in immaculate white duck, set off with starched bosoms, collars, and small flowing ties. The ring is crowded with men carrying their pet prize-cocks under their arms, all striving to secure wagers and vociferously proclaiming the virtues of their respective birds as fighters.

The first fight has been arranged, and the referee claps his hands as a signal for all gathered in the ring to move outside, as only the "handlers" are allowed within the enclosure. The birds are fought with their own gaffs, instead of with the metal, razor-edged blade which is strapped to the legs of cocks in the United States, and a great deal of preparatory scraping and polishing of the bone gaffs takes place, until they become needle-like in sharpness. Then all the crest or neck feathers are cut off with scissors, and sometimes the comb is trimmed low, but not often, as all the minor details of handling, so rigorously observed among our own gambling fraternity, seem here to be dispensed with.

The birds are teased into fighting humor while held in the hand, and viciously pluck at each other's heads; now they are dropped on the ground with a quick movement, and at the order of the referee they are at it. High up in the air they strike the first few plunges, and one dodges under, while the uppermost bird lands over his enemy with a surprised look, but whirls and grabs his opponent on the red comb with a strong beak, and plants his gaff fairly on the side of the other's head. A roar of approval goes up from the crowd who have backed this bird, and a counter set of suppressed "hi's" of fear rise from those wishing for the success of the other favorite. The fight is fast and furious.

At last the red cock sinks his head with blinded eyes, and the blood drips off upon the ground. His panting antagonist watches him a moment, as if not willing to take advantage of his desperate condition, and at the lull, each owner rushes forward and grabs his bird. One takes the bloody head and neck of his pet into his mouth and sucks the congealing blood, and then breathes new life into the sinking cock from his own lungs; the other resorts to a water-bottle from which he fills his mouth and blows it on the head and neck, and under the wings of his bird until the closing eyes brighten from the refreshing spray.

Time is called! In the center of the ring lies a small square, outlined with sunken wooden sticks, and on its opposite edges the birds are set. The mongrel-spotted bird goes for his game-colored enemy immediately, and strikes him three times to the other's once. Poor fellow! his fight is over! he turns and runs away, followed by his fierce tantalizer. Once more they are rubbed into shape. One vicious gaff, as they come together, and the red bird sinks dead, the bone lance going deep into his eye and brain.

The crowd surges into the ring and the money changes hands, while the owner of the dead bird gathers up the bundle of bloody feathers with some show of tenderness.

On and on it goes for hours, until the hundred contestants have been reduced by half, and the once bright-plumaged, bragging birds, who dared each other on from the balcony as they struggled at the end of their restraining bark

28

thongs, have changed to bedraggled, bruised fellows with hanging heads and bent legs, whose drooping eyelids tell the story of the desperate fight. They are only birds, but there is something very pathetic in witnessing their fight for life,—fighting to kill, if you prefer,—surrounded by a concourse of howling human beings who cheer on each stroke that draws another drop of vital blood. It is a brutal sport, this baiting of birds against one another, that fight with blinded, bloody eyes, not seeing their enemy at the finish, but striking wildly, unflinchingly, at the superior force as they die; but it is the one, the only amusement which these people could afford, the only one offered them by a nation which has crushed out human hearts and dwarfed human minds by three centuries of malicious officialism.

There was no drinking, no carousing among the spectators; no ugly swearing, no bad feeling engendered, and no taint of rowdyism such as we see in our own country at such gatherings. Instead, with one accord the people were out to enjoy their holiday in gay good humor, and, while excitement rose to a tremendous pitch, no harsh word was spoken and threatening looks were unknown. That the amusement was brutal and of low order seemed not to occur to anyone. They had been taught this form of pastime, and conscience did not trouble them.

Through the little entrance gate, built from the wood of the royal palm, the crowd moved from a cock-fight to a solemn Catholic ceremony to be held in the near-by cemetery, and in the lead strode a little black youngster, in one of our soldiers' cast-off campaign hats, his bare, black chest shining through the front of a dirty cotton coat; what cared he that the fight had cost him a silver piece, hardly gained by blacking the army's shoes? he was happy in the possession of a handful of copper centavos which did credit to his acumen as a bird-backer, and made him envied by his youthful playmates. His twinkling eyes and merry laugh sobered quickly to awe-stricken glance and solemn expression, as the black-garbed priest strode by.

Verily only such a mercurial race could have stood the blighting abuses of a despotic government with complacence.

A Cockfight in Tahiti

*From an island in the Caribbean to an island in the south Pacific, we find that cock-
fighting is as much at home in Tahiti as in Puerto Rico. In this case, we utilize a
chapter of one of the many novels written by the highly successful team of Charles Bernard Nordhoff (1887–1947) and James Norman Hall (1887–1951). In this literary vignette of life on Tahiti, we have a relatively brief account of a cockfight, but we
are rewarded by an engaging story of the events leading up to and following the cockfight. Of special interest is the involvement of entire families in cockfights as well as the
dire consequences of excessive betting on the outcomes. Somewhat unusual in this delin-
eation of a Tahitian cockfight is the involvement of women. Cockfights in most locales
in the world specifically exclude—or at any rate discourage—female participation.*

Nordhoff and Hall are probably best known for their novel Mutiny on the Bounty
*(Boston: Little, Brown, and Company, 1932) which was made into a classic Holly-
wood motion picture in 1935, starring Clark Gable and Charles Laughton. The film
won an Oscar for Best Picture. The same plot also inspired two later films:* Mutiny on
the Bounty *(1962) and* The Bounty *(1984).*

For more about these two authors, see Paul L. Briand, In Search of Paradise:
The Nordhoff-Hall Story *(New York: Duell, Sloan & Pearce, 1966). See also
Robert Leland Johnson,* The American Heritage of James Norman Hall, The
Woodshed Poet of Iowa and Co-Author of Mutiny on the Bounty *(Philadel-
phia: Dorrance, 1969), and Robert Roulston,* James Norman Hall *(Boston: Twayne
Publishing, 1978).*

It was half-past eleven when Jonas and his family came home from church. He
walked first, with Mama Ruau, followed by Ropati in his wheelchair, then the
others in indiscriminate fashion, the babies in arms, the small children kicking
up the dust with their bare feet, all of them seemingly determined, despite

Reprinted from Charles Nordhoff and James Norman Hall, *No More Gas* (Boston: Little
Brown and Company, 1940), pp. 88–100. Copyright 1940 by Charles B. Nordhoff and James
Norman Hall. By permission of Little, Brown and Company. I am indebted to Caroline
McCullagh of University of California, Santa Cruz, for calling this interesting essay to my
attention.

their elders, to soil their Sabbath clothes thoroughly before they reached home. The church was little more than a quarter of a mile beyond the Tuttle house, so that the family, Ropati excepted, always walked to service unless some special occasion demanded the service of the truck or the surrey. Ropati had been crippled for life in a fall from a coconut palm when he was ten years old; nevertheless, he was among the gayest and most useful members of the household. To their lighter hours he contributed his splendid bass voice, for singing, and his skill with the nose flute. In addition to these accomplishments, he was an expert net maker and repairer. He was as useful to the family as any of the boys. His wheelchair was one of Paki's mechanical masterpieces, supported on a pair of motorcycle wheels, and propelled by a lever which turned the axle through a connecting rod. Two small front wheels steered the vehicle.

Jonas was a sincerely devout man, in the Tuttle fashion. As an indication of the position he occupied in the affairs of his village and district, it may be said that, while he had never been made an elder of his church, he was, nevertheless, looked upon as such: an elder without portfolio. And although he had never been elected chief of the district, there was no man in it who was listened to in local matters with greater attention and interest. This position suited him; he had the rewards and none of the responsibilities of office. Had he been an elder of the church, chief, or even subchief of the district, he would have been compelled to assume an irksome dignity unsuited to him. Occupying no public position, he had greater influence with his friends and neighbors than those who did, with the added advantage that he was free to be himself. None of those who saw him trudging home from church at the head of his clan thought it at all unseemly that, later in the day, they would see him again at the cockpit in Vaipopo Valley. He was at home in either place, and belonged to both.

Sunday dinner, usually a long-drawn-out affair with the Tuttles, was quickly dispatched on this occasion. No man loved his food more than Jonas, but even he ate hastily and absent-mindedly. All of the family, his mother excepted, were in the same state of subdued, deeply stirred expectancy. Mama Ruau was no lover of cocks in their capacity as fighters. Egg-fertilizing cocks were among the most valuable possessions a family could have, but these others, treasured so highly by the men of her family, were worse than useless. They knew her feelings about them, but she had long since said all that could be said against Sunday matches or any other matches. Their infatuation with the sport was incurable. She could do nothing more except to insist that cocks and cockfighting should not be discussed in her presence. Effie was as bad as the men, which was Mama Ruau's one grievance against her only daughter.

It was generally known that the match to be held on this Sunday afternoon would be something out of the ordinary. Spectators began arriving, on foot and in vehicles, while the Tuttles were still at their noonday meal. Several char-

31

tered trucks, converted into coaches for the occasion, had already arrived from Papeete. They were crowded to capacity, their passengers, in holiday mood, singing as they came. Chinamen, appearing mysteriously from nowhere, set up their booths where watermelon, ice cream, cakes, and other refreshments could be had. Ah Sin, the Vaipopo bread baker, was there with a wagon of his own. While he entirely disapproved of the Tuttle love for cockfighting which kept the family continually in his debt for bread, he felt it all the more a reason why he should turn such occasions to account; and often he made more at these Sunday matches than a full week of breadmaking and distributing would produce.

Emily and her oldest son, Moa, were the first of the Taios to appear. They had come before the rest of their family to settle the preliminaries. Chairs and benches were brought to a shady spot, where Jonas refreshed his rivals with the cool liquor of freshly plucked green coconuts. It was an unwritten law on the island that there should be no drinking at a cockfight, and Jonas was as particular as Emily herself in observing the law, even to a point beyond what the spirit of it required.

When they had discussed other matters for some little time, Emily turned to her host.

"We agreed, Jonas," she said, "that the bets for this fight should be placed before we show the birds."

Jonas nodded. "It was your own suggestion, Emily. I agreed, as you say, and I'll stick to it."

"Very well. How much money do you wish to place on you cock?"

Jonas leaned back, gazing into the checkered shade of the mango tree above them. "We got a pretty good cock," he said, presently. "I warned you about that, Emily."

"*Maururu.* Well?"

"We got five thousand four hundred francs says he's a better cock than the Taios have or ever will have."

"Good. I'll cover it," Emily replied, quietly. "Cornelius, will you hold the stakes?"

Cornelius, the proprietor of the Bon Ton Bar, in Papeete, and a great follower of the sport, readily agreed to act. Emily took out a purse of finely woven pandanus leaf, and counted out the larger part of the sum in crisp five-hundred-franc notes. The Tuttle stake, of various denominations from five- to one-hundred-franc bills, took longer to count, but at last all was checked and placed in the barman's custody.

"You seem pleased with your bird, Jonas," said Emily.

"So we are," said Jonas.

"Pleased enough to bet something more on him? I'll cover anything you want to put up."

A murmur of astonishment went through the crowd that had gathered around the principals in this affair. Five thousand francs on a side was an extraordinary wager for island folk, even for such wealthy ones as Emily Taio. That she was willing to risk more, to the farthest limit of Tuttle-ma's capacity to bet, caused a stir. But all knew the somewhat tarnished quality of the Tuttle fortunes, and a moment of reflection convinced the spectators that Emily was, probably, safe enough in making this proposal. It was a mere gesture on her part, a way of showing off before her less wealthy neighbors.

Jonas gazed at his bare toes. What a pity, he thought. Here was the chance of a lifetime and he couldn't take it. Moa Taio spoke up.

"How about your accordion, Chester? Willing to risk it?"

Chester was so eager to accept that not a word would come. He looked appealingly at his father, who turned at once to Moa.

"What'll you put up against the accordion?"

Emily spoke for her son as Jonas had for his. "It's secondhand, of course," she said. "However, as Moa wants it, I'll stake three thousand francs against it."

Chester now found his voice.

"Th-th-th-three thousand?" he exclaimed, "I pu-pu-pu-paid two hundred and s-s-s-sixty-eight dollars for it in Frisco. That's better than eight th-th-thousand francs."

After a prolonged discussion, Emily agreed to raise the bet to four thousand, which was accepted. Then Effie took a sudden resolution, surprised that she had not thought of it before.

"You've still got money to bet, Emily?" she asked.

"As long as there's something worth having to put up against it."

"*Mea maitai!* You know my furniture. There's my brass bed, my wardrobe, my new bicycle, my Wilcox sewing machine. I'll bet the lot if you'll cover them for what they're worth."

A gasp went up from the spectators. This was to be a historic match and no mistake. Nat gave his aunt an enthusiastic slap in the middle of her broad back, and Jonas beamed approval. Effie's possessions were carefully appraised, and Emily pushed across the table to Cornelius a stack of bills from a seemingly inexhaustible supply.

No sooner had this latest wager been covered than a distant rhythmic booming was heard, far down the road, growing more and more distinct. It was the other Taios announcing their approach from Tarahoi with bass drums and bamboo drums. Effie, immediately stirred by the sound, sprang to her feet, facing Emily with her hands on her hips, her eyes challenging and scornful. She began to dance in time to the far-off drumming. Emily leaped from the bench to accept the challenge. She was no longer the dignified woman of business. With her head thrown back and her eyes shining, she danced her defiance in a way that brought cheers from the delighted audience. This was what they liked: good friends and good sportsmen on both sides, and their women dancing confusion to their opponents. The Taio truck turned into the drive and came to a halt, discharging a noisy band of men, women, and children, almost as numerous as the Tuttles. Tihoti Taio remained on guard beside a mysterious coop which was covered with a red cloth. Jonas stepped forward to greet the folk from Tarahoi.

The Vaipopo cockpit, where most of the important matches on the west coast of Tahiti were held, was on the Tuttle land, across the river and about two hundred yards from the house. A dense thicket concealed it from the road. Tuttles and Taios, in a mingled noisy throng, now took the short cut across the stream. An unusual number of devotees were already gathered in the hidden clearing. Some held cocks for the preliminaries which the crowd was inspecting while they waited. The cockpit itself was a circular space about twenty feet in diameter, floored with sand well packed, and enclosed by a low fence. The railing surmounting it offered good elbow rests for the spectators. There were a number of benches for participants and the more notable visitors.

Jonas and Emily strolled about, shaking hands and exchanging greetings with their friends. Announcement was made that the Tuttle and Taio cocks would not be shown until after the other matches were over. Ropati drove his wheelchair along the path at a smart clip, and a place was made for him next to the barrier. Jonas and Emily took their customary ringside seats, and the spectators, a crowd of between two and three hundred, gathered closely around. A preliminary match was being made, cautiously, and with true Tahitian disregard for time. The trainers, two young stevedores from town, subjected one another's birds to a scrutiny as deliberate as it was minute. The fight agreed upon, the betting began, each bettor privileged to examine the birds as long and thoroughly as he desired. At last the owners stepped over the barrier, billed the birds for a moment, and released them on the sand.

Match after match was fought to a decision while the shadows of the coconut palms lengthened farther and farther to the east. There came a pause in the proceedings. The last of the preliminaries was over. All eyes turned to the heads of the Tuttle and Taio clans. Emily smiled brightly as she regarded her rival.

"Time we were showing them, Jonas."

"Suits me," said Jonas.

He sat, relaxed and easy, his hands clasped around his belly. He signaled

Fana with a slight lifting and lowering of the eyebrows. Moa and Fana moved off briskly to fetch the two champions. Craning their necks and whispering amongst themselves, the spectators waited impatiently. Fana was the first to return. The crowd gathered around Jonas till they formed a ring three-deep. Emily waited complaisantly, with an air of indifference. At a sign from his father, Fana removed the covering of the little coop and permitted the Mortgage Lifter to step out. The cock shook himself, glanced about with fierce bright eyes as if in search of an antagonist, and crowed. A collective exclamation of wonder and delight rose from the spectators.

"*É aha ra!*"

Emily's smile faded as she stared at the bird. She turned to face the man at her side.

"Tubuai?" she exclaimed, accusingly. "That cock's from none of our islands! I know better! He's from Sydney!"

Jonas shook his head. "Frisco," he corrected, gently.

A louder murmur of interest rippled through the crowd. "Frisco! From California! *No te fenua popaa mai!*"

Fana took the Mortgage Lifter under his arm as Moa approached with the Taio warrior. Jonas moved slightly for a better view. His broad face wore an expression of interest more courteous and perfunctory than real. Squatting in the center of the ring, Moa opened the tiny coop he carried, and the Taio cock stepped into view. A second long-drawn "*É aha ra!*" went up from the spectators.

The bird was of about the same weight as the Tuttle cock, but of a different type: standing more upright, heavier in the leg, and with a look of cruelty about eyes and beak. He crowed. The Mortgage Lifter replied, struggling in Fana's grasp. Jonas's hands left his belly and gripped the bench; his eyes seemed to protrude slightly as he stared at Emily's bird. His jaw fell, but for a moment the evidence of such duplicity left him speechless.

"You can't fool me, Emily," he said, indignantly. "That ain't no Raiatea cock! Where'd you get him?"

"From Australia, Jonas," Emily replied. "I've had him these three months past."

The eyes of the two owners met. Jonas's great body shook with a soundless chuckle.

"Well, Emily, you thought of it first. Guess neither one of us is as smart as we thought we was."

"You'd like to back out now," Emily replied. "But it's too late."

"Me? Back out?" Jonas gave a snort. "That bird ain't got a chance with ours!"

The two trainers were circulating among the prospective bettors, permitting the birds to be examined and appraised. Emily looked thoughtful. The expression of Jonas's face did not betray the inner qualms and doubts stirred by the sight of the Taio cock. No match for the Mortgage Lifter, of course, but still . . . the fight wouldn't be quite the sure thing the Tuttles had counted on. There was a look of cold ferocity about the Australian cock that Jonas didn't like. Listening without appearing to listen, he was a little depressed to learn that the betting slightly favored the Taio bird, but the Tuttle morale received a great boost when Cornelius, an excellent judge of cocks, after much study, backed the Mortgage Lifter to the sum of three thousand francs. It stiffened yet more when Fana bet his guitar against Farani Taio's. Stirred into last-minute action, old Tupa bet all three of his mouth organs. Then voices were hushed and the trainers stepped over the barrier to bill the cocks. Jonas leaned forward, every faculty concentrated upon the birds. Emily, a tight-lipped smile on her face, sat motionless, chin in hand. The people pressed shoulder to shoulder around the barrier, and the trees above their heads were filled with boys, perched on every limb that would bear them. A long "Ah-h-h" went up as the champions were released.

Fitted for battle by generations of skilled selective breeding, the two cocks eyed each other warily, crouching beak to beak with hackles raised. The Taio bird attacked. They buckled in mid-air. They crouched, bloody and panting, only to leap together once more, to contend with a skill and pertinacity that brought low-voiced exclamations from the crowd. The battle was prolonged and evenly matched. Jonas seemed scarcely to breathe as he watched, clasping and unclasping his hands. Emily's small bare foot tapped the ground noise-lessly. A shout went up as the Australian bird, half-blinded, retreated totter-ingly from his foe. They squatted, regaining their strength, pecking at the sand beside them. As the Australian bird rose, the Mortgage Lifter made for him at a trot, but in a last weak buckle, Emily's cock drove his spur into a vital part.

"*Aué tatou é!*" Jonas exclaimed, in a voice of anguish.

The Mortgage Lifter fell on his side, struggled gamely to regain his feet, and went down for good. Fana and Moa sprang over the barrier, and Emily leaped to her feet with a shout of triumph.

Scarcely able to realize the full extent of his misfortune, Jonas sat staring at his feet, drawing in and expelling his breath in long inaudible sighs. The Mortgage Lifter, declared by experts to be invincible, was dead, and the Tuttle fortunes, so bright in prospect, had fallen with dizzy speed to an all-time low.

Jonas rose heavily. "Come over to the house, Emily."

The sun was near to setting and the spectators were straggling homeward in small gesticulating groups. As he walked across the brook, Jonas had a glimpse of his sister Effie on the way to her house on the beach. Her carriage, her gait, her whole general appearance of collapse, brought home yet more clearly to Jonas the nature of the disaster that had overtaken Tuttle-ma.

Tuttles and Taios assembled in the outdoor dining room. A stranger, seeing the two families at that moment, and for the first time, could have separated the members of one from the other without chance of a mistake. Jonas sank upon a bench. Virtue seemed to be oozing out of him, but not to be lost in the wide air. It was being sucked into Emily's substantial frame as fast as it escaped from that of Jonas.

"Well, Emily," he admitted. "You've cleaned us out this time."

Cornelius smiled wryly as he handed the winner her gains. "It ain't often I'm wrong in judging cocks," he said. "There's my three thousand to go along with Jonas's lot. I ain't complaining. It was worth it, to see such a fight as that."

Emily opened her capacious handbag and stowed her winnings neatly inside.

"Live and learn, Cornelius," she replied, briskly. "I'll be on hand, Jonas, when your vanilla's sold." She turned to her sons. "Get your instruments, boys; then we'll go down and pick up Effie's things."

Chester handed over his piano accordion.

"You got to give me lessons, Chester," said Moa, as he took the instrument.

"Lessons?" said Chester. "Nu-nu-not me! You can learn to p-p-play it yourself."

The Taios climbed aboard their truck. Jonas followed them down the drive and stood watching while the vehicle was backed up to Effie's veranda. The brass bed, polished to a dazzling splendor by Paki's hands, was taken apart and placed on the truck, followed by the wardrobe with its mirror of plate glass and the sewing machine. Farani Taio's wife took the bicycle to ride it home. Effie came down the steps of her sacked house and joined her brother by the mango tree.

In silence they watched the Taio truck return to the Broom Road and head toward Tarahoi. Moa was fingering the piano accordion with the hands of a novice, drawing from it sounds no more discordant than Chester's thoughts. The Taio drums struck up. Emily, who stood near the tailboard, gave a shrill whoop of triumph, grinned at Jonas and his sister, placed her arms akimbo, and began to dance. This was more than Effie could bear. She did a smart turn-about to present her back to Taios; then, leaning over, she flipped her skirts in a gesture of contempt and defiance that brought a shout of delight from the triumphant Taios.

Jonas turned his head slowly. Tupa was approaching from the other side of the road.

"Tea's ready," he announced, glumly. . . . "But they ain't no sugar for it."

California Cockfight

Another fictional account of a cockfight, this one set in southern California, comes from a chapter of The Day of the Locust *(1939) by Nathanael West (1903–1940). West, whose life was cut short by an automobile accident near El Centro, California, wrote four novels in the 1930s, of which the most memorable were* Miss Lonelyhearts *(1933) and the one containing the following depiction of a cockfight. It is not really necessary to identify all of the odd cast of characters mentioned. They include, among others, Tod Hackett, the central character of the novel, and his friend, a dwarf named Abe Kusich. There is also a cowboy, Earle Shoop, from a small town in Arizona, and a Mexican named Miguel who owned some gamecocks and who was waiting for a man from San Diego to bring his cocks to a garage belonging to Homer Simpson. When the San Diego cocker fails to turn up, the cockfight is cancelled. However, Miguel sells one of his cocks to a member of the group assembled and a cockfight materializes after all.*

Although this fight presumably occurs in the 1930s, cockfights have continued to take place throughout California up until the 1990s. Newspaper reports in March of 1992, for example, describe police raids on cockfights in Fresno, Sacramento, and Marin County. Cockfighting remains particularly popular among Mexican-Americans and Filipino-Americans in California.

For more about West, see James F. Light, Nathanael West: An Interpretive Study, *2d ed. (Evanston: Northwestern University Press, 1971), and Dennis P. Vannatta,* Nathanael West: An Annotated Bibliography of the Scholarship and Works *(New York: Garland, 1976).*

When Tod told Claude Estee about the cock fight, he wanted to go with him. They drove to Homer's place together.

It was one of those blue and lavender nights when the luminous color seems to have been blown over the scene with an air brush. Even the darkest shadows held some purple.

A car stood in the driveway of the garage with its headlights on. They could see several men in the corner of the building and could hear their voices. Someone laughed, using only two notes, ha-ha and ha-ha, over and over again.

Tod stepped ahead to make himself known, in case they were taking precautions against the police. When he entered the light, Abe Kusich and Miguel greeted him, but Earle didn't.

"The fights are off," Abe said. "That stinkola from Diego didn't get here."

Claude came up and Tod introduced him to the three men. The dwarf was arrogant, Miguel gracious and Earle his usual wooden, surly self.

Most of the garage floor had been converted into a pit, an oval space about nine feet long and seven or eight wide. It was floored with an old carpet and walled by a low, ragged fence made of odd pieces of lath and wire. Faye's coupe stood in the driveway, placed so that its headlights flooded the arena.

Claude and Tod followed Abe out of the glare and sat down with him on an old trunk in the back of the garage. Earle and Miguel came in and squatted on their heels facing them. They were both wearing blue denims, polka-dot shirts, big hats and high-heeled boots. They looked very handsome and picturesque.

They sat smoking silently, all of them calm except the dwarf, who was fidgety. Although he had plenty of room, he suddenly gave Tod a shove.

"Get over, lard-ass," he snarled

Tod moved, crowding against Claude, without saying anything. Earle laughed at Tod rather than the dwarf, but the dwarf turned on him anyway.

"Why, you punkola! Who are you laughing at?"

"You," Earle said.

"That so, hah? Well, listen to me, you pee-hole bandit, for two cents I'd knock you out of them prop boots."

Earle reached into his shirt pocket and threw a coin on the ground.

"There's a nickel," he said.

The dwarf started to get off the trunk, but Tod caught him by the collar. He didn't try to get loose, but leaned forward against his coat, like a terrier in a harness, and wagged his great head from side to side.

"Go on," he sputtered, "you fugitive from the Western Costume Company, you . . . you louse in a fright-wig, you."

Earle would have been much less angry if he could have thought of a snappy comeback. He mumbled something about a half-pint bastard, then spat. He hit the instep of the dwarf's shoe with a big gob of spittle.

"Nice shot," Miguel said.

This was apparently enough for Earle to consider himself the winner, for he smiled and became quiet. The dwarf slapped Tod's hand away from his collar with a curse and settled down on the trunk again.

"He ought to wear gaffs," Miguel said.

"I don't need them for a punk like that."

They all laughed and everything was fine again.

Abe leaned across Tod to speak to Claude.

"It would have been a swell main," he said. "There was more than a dozen guys here before you come and some of them with real dough. I was going to make book."

He took out his wallet and gave him one of his business cards.

"It was in the bag," Miguel said. "I got five birds that would of won easy and two sure losers. We would of made a killing."

"I've never seen a chicken fight," Claude said. "In fact, I've never even seen a game chicken."

Miguel offered to show him one of his birds and left to get it. Tod went down to the car for the bottle of whiskey they had left in a side pocket. When he got back, Miguel was holding Jujutala in the light. They all examined the bird.

Miguel held the cock firmly with both hands, somewhat in the manner that a basketball is held for an underhand toss. The bird had short, oval wings and a heart-shaped tail that stood at right angles to its body. It had a triangular head, like a snake's, terminating in a slightly curved beak, thick at the base and fine at the point. All its feathers were so tight and heard that they looked as though they had been varnished. They had been thinned out for fighting and the lines of its body, which was like a truncated wedge, stood out plainly. From between Miguel's fingers dangled its long, bright orange legs and its slightly darker feet with their horn nails.

"Juju was bred by John R. Bowes of Lindale, Texas," Miguel said proudly. "He's a six times winner. I give fifty dollars and a shotgun for him."

"He's a nice bird," the dwarf said grudgingly, "but looks ain't everything."

Claude took out his wallet.

"I'd like to see him fight," he said. "Suppose you sell me one of your other birds and I put it against him."

Miguel thought a while and looked at Earle, who told him to go ahead.

"I've got a bird I'll sell you for fifteen bucks," he said.

The dwarf interfered.

"Let me pick the bird."

"Oh, I don't care," Claude said, "I just want to see a fight. Here's your fifteen."

Earle took the money and Miguel told him to get Hermano, the big red.

"That red'll go over eight pounds," he said, "while Juju won't go more than six."

Earle came back carrying a large rooster that had a silver shawl. He looked like an ordinary barnyard fowl.

When the dwarf saw him, he became indignant.

"What do you call that, a goose?"

"That's one of Street's Butcher Boys," Miguel said.

"I wouldn't bait a hook with him," the dwarf said.

"You don't have to bet," Earle mumbled.

The dwarf eyed the bird and the bird eyed him. He turned to Claude.

"Let me handle him for you, mister," he said.

Miguel spoke quickly.

"Earle'll do it. He knows the cock."

The dwarf exploded at this.

"It's a frame-up!" he yelled.

He tried to take the red, but Earle held the bird high in the air out of the little man's reach.

Miguel opened the trunk and took out a small wooden box, the kind chessmen are kept in. It was full of carved gaffs, small squares of chamois with holes in their centers and bits of waxed string like that used by a shoemaker.

They crowded around to watch him arm Juju. First he wiped the short stubs on the cock's legs to make sure they were clean and then placed a leather square over one of them so that the stub came through the hole. He then fitted a gaff over it and fastened it with a bit of the soft string, wrapping very carefully. He did the same to the other leg.

When he had finished, Earle started on the big red.

"That's a bird with lots of cojones," Miguel said. "He's won plenty fights. He don't look fast maybe, but he's fast all right and he packs an awful wallop."

"Strictly for the cook stove, if you ask me," the dwarf said.

Earle took out a pair of shears and started to lighten the red's plumage. The dwarf watched him cut away most of the bird's tail, but when he began to work on the breast, he caught his hand.

"Leave him be!" he barked. "You'll kill him fast that way. He needs that stuff for protection."

He turned to Claude again.

"Please, mister, let me handle him."

"Make him buy a share in the bird," Miguel said.

Claude laughed and motioned for Earle to give Abe the bird. Earle didn't want to and looked meaningly at Miguel.

The dwarf began to dance with rage.

"You're trying to cold-deck us!" he screamed.

"Aw, give it to him," Miguel said.

The little man tucked the bird under his left arm so that his hands were free and began to look over the gaffs in the box. They were all the same length, three inches, but some had more pronounced curves than the others. He selected a pair and explained his strategy to Claude.

"He's going to do most of his fighting on his back. This pair'll hit right that way. If he could get over the other bird, I wouldn't use them."

He got down on his knees and honed the gaffs on the cement floor until they were like needles.

"Have we a chance?" Tod asked.

"You can't ever tell," he said, shaking his extra large head. "He feels almost like a dead bird."

After adjusting the gaffs with great care, he looked the bird over, stretching its wings and blowing its feathers in order to see its skin.

"The comb ain't bright enough for fighting condition," he said, pinching it, "but he looks strong. He may have been a good one once."

He held the bird in the light and looked at its head. When Miguel saw him examining its beak, he told him anxiously to quit stalling. But the dwarf paid no attention and went on muttering to himself. He motioned for Tod and Claude to look.

"What'd I tell you!" he said, puffing with indignation. "We've been cold-decked."

He pointed to a hair line running across the top of the bird's beak.

"That's not a crack," Miguel protested, "it's just a mark."

He reached for the bird as though to rub its beak and the bird pecked savagely at him. This pleased the dwarf.

"We'll fight," he said, "but we won't bet."

Earle was to referee. He took a piece of chalk and drew three lines in the center of the pit, a long one in the middle and two shorter ones parallel to it and about three feet away.

"Pit your cocks," he called.

"No, bill them first," the dwarf protested.

He and Miguel stood at arm's length and thrust their birds together to anger them. Juju caught the big red by the comb and held on viciously until Miguel jerked him away. The red, who had been rather apathetic, came to life and the dwarf had trouble holding him. The two men thrust their birds together again, and again Juju caught the red's comb. The big cock became frantic with rage and struggled to get at the smaller bird.

"We're ready," the dwarf said.

He and Miguel climbed into the pit and set their birds down on the short lines so that they faced each other. They held them by the tails and waited for Earle to give the signal to let go.

"Pit them," he ordered.

The dwarf had been watching Earle's lips and he had his bird off first, but Juju rose straight in the air and sank one spur in the red's breast. It went through the feathers into the flesh. The red turned with the gaff still stuck in him and pecked twice at his opponent's head.

They separated the birds and held them to the lines again.

"Pit 'em!" Earle shouted.

Again Juju got above the other bird, but this time he missed with his spurs. The red tried to get above him, but couldn't. He was too clumsy and heavy to fight in the air. Juju climbed again, cutting and hitting so rapidly that his legs were a golden blur. The red met him by going back on his tail and hooking upward like a cat. Juju landed again and again. He broke one of the red's wings, then practically severed a leg.

"Handle them," Earle called.

When the dwarf gathered the red up, its neck had begun to droop and it was a mass of blood and matted feathers. The little man moaned over the bird, then set to work. He spit into its gaping beak and took the comb between his lips and sucked the blood back into it. The red began to regain its fury, but not its strength. Its beak closed and its neck straightened. The dwarf smoothed and shaped its plumage. He could do nothing to help the broken wing or the dangling leg.

"Pit 'em," Earle said.

The dwarf insisted that the birds be put down beak to beak on the center line, so that the red would not have to move to get at his opponent. Miguel agreed.

The red was very gallant. When Abe let go of its tail, it made a great effort to get off the ground and meet Juju in the air, but it could only thrust with one leg and fell over on its side. Juju sailed above it, half turned and came down on its back, driving in both spurs. The red twisted free, throwing Juju, and made a terrific effort to hook with its good leg, but fell sideways again.

Before Juju could get into the air, the red managed to drive a hard blow with its beak to Juju's head. This slowed the smaller bird down and he fought on the ground. In the pecking match, the red's greater weight and strength evened up for his lack of a leg and a wing. He managed to give as good as he got. But suddenly his cracked beak broke off, leaving only the lower half. A large bubble of blood rose where the beak had been. The red didn't retreat an inch, but made a great effort to get into the air once more. Using its one leg skillfully, it managed to rise six or seven inches from the ground, not enough, however, to get its spurs into play. Juju went up with him and got well above, then drove both gaffs into the red's breast. Again one of the steel needles stuck.

"Handle them," Earle shouted.

Miguel freed his bird and gave the other back to the dwarf. Abe, moaning softly, smoothed its feathers and licked its eyes clean, then took its whole head in his mouth. The red was finished, however. It couldn't even hold its neck straight. The dwarf blew away the feathers from under its tail and pressed the lips of its vent together hard. When that didn't seem to help, he inserted his little finger and scratched the bird's testicles. It fluttered and made a gallant effort to straighten its neck.

"Pit birds."

Once more the red tried to rise with Juju, pushing hard with its remaining leg, but it only spun crazily. Juju rose, but missed. The red thrust weakly with its broken bill. Juju went into the air again and this time drove a gaff through one of the red's eyes into its brain. The red fell over stone dead.

The dwarf groaned with anguish, but no one else said anything. Juju pecked at the dead bird's remaining eye.

"Take off that stinking cannibal!" the dwarf screamed.

Miguel laughed, then caught Juju and removed its gaffs. Earle did the same for the red. He handled the dead cock gently and with respect.

Tod passed the whiskey.

MICHAEL O'GORMON

An Irish Cockfight

Two of the preceding cockfight descriptions were chapters in novels, but it should be pointed out that there are entire novels devoted to cockfighting. Clancy's Bulba, *published in 1983 but set in Ireland in the late 1920s, is a prime example of such a novel. The novel was written by Michael O'Gormon who was born on the outskirts of Ennis Town in County Clare and who certainly has an ear for the idioms of Irish-English.*

The story begins with three men from County Mayo asleep in a hotel room with their cock named Taurus Bulba. The men are Barra Diffy in his mid-thirties, Pagannini O'Leary in his early fifties, each of whom own one-fourth interest in the cock, and the third man, Milo Clancy, who owns a half interest. The men and cock have travelled more than 100 miles from home to participate in a cockfight. At the hotel, they encounter Stallion O'Casey, who joins forces with them and counsels them as to how to get better odds. The selection below consists of the first half of the second chapter of the novel.

For another, much briefer account of a cockfight in Ireland, see P. O. Crannlaighe, "Cock Fighting," The Bell *19 (1945): 510–513; and P. Beacey, "Prelude to a Cockfight,"* The Bell *11 (1945): 574–576.*

Turnpike Road ran along the back of the White Willow hotel. It ran as straight as a die for the first half mile before beginning its climb on to Patriot's Hill. The road on that fine summer's evening was choked with men on foot. Halfway up the hill on the right-hand side of the Pike stood a huge corregated barn. For the crowds on the road that balmy summer evening the barn was the only goal. By eight o'clock the Pike was clear of tramping feet and only a few abandoned cars were to be found scattered on its surface as twilight fell, brushing away the fading light of day.

In an outhouse behind the barn the thirty-two cocks that would fight that night were housed. Half of them would not see the morrow's dawn. Biding time with

Reprinted from Michael O'Gormon, *Clancy's Bulba* (London: Hutchinson & Co., 1983), pp. 19–28. Reprinted by permission of Random Century Group. I am indebted to Professor Dan Melia of the Rhetoric Department, University of California, Berkeley, for calling my attention to this novel.

the thirty-two cocks were their handlers; anxious men, all appearing busy, strain showing clearly on their faces. The first pair of cocks to enter the ring were already spurred, their two-inch slits of spiked steel gaitered and fastened sound to the stubs of their natural spurs. But their handlers still fussed over them, checking and rechecking good work already done.

Barra Duffy and Bulba kept themselves well away from the rest of the handlers and cocks. Duffy found himself a quiet corner once he had entered the outhouse and sat himself down on the wooden floor, legs outstretched and back up against the wall. Bulba was safely housed in his cage on the floor beside him. The cock was at ease and oblivious to the sounds and movement around him, but Barra Duffy was not. Duffy's cheeks were crimson with rage, as they had been since breakfast that morning. He had protested throughout the day that Bulba's dignity should not be violated. He had tried to argue his protest with logic, just as Milo Clancy always did, but they wouldn't listen to him, so his well-renowned temper had taken over. "But it'll damage him mentally! If ye bastards were to degrade a racehorse by slashing off its proud mane, the thing would die of shame right there on the racetrack and run the worst race of its life!" he'd screamed at them. "Bullshit!" Clancy had retorted. " 'Tisn't bullshit! Ya'll end up doin' him mental damage! He'll lose his fight from that vile treatment!" But for Barra it had been a battle lost right from the word go. Now, in the outhouse, with an hour to go before Bulba entered the ring, he was still fuming at his miserable day. Smart men, men with little dicks and heads full of horse shit. Put them all up against a fuckin' wall and shoot the fuckin' lot a 'em, that's what I say! raged Duffy to himself.

But when he watched the tranquil creature surveying his surroundings he had to smile. "Look at yarself Taurus Bulba! Ya should be swearin' like a trooper after all I've done ta ya. Half yar lovely belly feathers are in one of Aggie Carney's dustbins. There's enough self-raisin' fuckin' flour on yar coat to take the sheen off a prize bull's arse! As for yar entire general appearance, well let's just say that even a sex-starved hen that hasn't seen a prick in a month of Sundays would run a mile on seein' ya comin'! It doesn't affect ya in the least, does it? Just as long as I don't fool around with yar ol' rang-doo-rum. Now if I was to fuck about with that ya'd have somethin' to say, wouldn't ya! Ya'd be mentally disturbed then, me bucco, wouldn't ya?"

The door to the outhouse opened and every handler in the place turned to look. "Nice and Easy! Potato Merchant!" cried the figure at the open doorway. Two of the handlers got off their haunches with their fighters under their arms and followed the master of ceremonies. The door closed and everyone tried to relax again. But every now and again eyes turned and sneaked glances at the closed door. Conversations were in low and whispered tones and most of them were between man and cock. Each painful minute went slowly by.

Duffy checked his watch. He reckoned there was at least another hour to get through before Bulba's name was called. But he decided he had baby-sat long enough and so he took Bulba from his cage and procceded to dress him for the fight. Slowly and with infinite care Duffy wrapped pads of dampened cotton wool around both of Bulba's legs, then he slipped the alloyed shoes over the stumps of the cock's natural spurs. Next came the weapons of death—two two-inch slits of steel. These he slipped into the slots in the shoes, and over the shoes he fixed the leather gaiters. Long strands of the softest leather bound Bulba's armoury together. He checked and rechecked his handiwork, testing the rigidity and grip of the steel spurs. Satisfied at last, he gloved the spiked armoury in two strong cotton bags, and settled back cooing over the bird. "Ya've got to do it tonight me darlin'. Tonight's yar night, you have to eat the bastard right inta the ground because everything yar uncle Barra has is on yar back!"

Well over five hundred men were packed inside the barn that night. The platformed arena where the cocks would fight was in itself a perfect circle eight feet in diameter. It was surrounded by a grilled barrier high enough to prevent the combatants from jumping out. Above it was a big arc lamp pouring down light onto a sawdust ring. Just to the right of the ring was the judge's box, a plastic see-through hut which was also round. The spectators sat on wooden benches circling the ring. The wooden benches rose in tiers up and up, the topmost failing to make contact with the roof by a mere six feet.

The atmosphere was electric. Noise fairly bounced off the corrugated steel walls of the barn. Hundreds were on their feet shouting their bets and hundreds of takers shouted, eyeballed and nodded back at them. The air was already pungent with clouds of tobacco smoke, and the odours of whiskey, poteen and porter mingled and settled over the place like an unseen haze. Everyone was waiting for the master of ceremonies to come through the giant doorway bearing the first cocks of the evening. The fight was about to start.

Milo Clancy was right beside the ring. His hands were on the metal grille and his eyes were on the very surface where Bulba would do his fighting that night. He was impressed, to say the least. If there's a Mecca for bullfightin', then 'tis Madrid for sure, he thought. And for Gaelic football? Croke Park, in the heart of Dublin. And the place of the cock? Where the cock goes to seek out his destiny? His eyes didn't move from the ring, imagining the fights that had been fought there. Here, he told himself. Surely this has to be the place. He turned his back on the ring and looked around him. My God! There must be ten thousand men here and all of 'em lookin' down at meself! Jasus! But 'tis a wonder that the cocks don't come over all embarrassed and walk away.

47

He glanced down at his left lapel, at the bright green badge that marked him as a man of some importance. It has been given to him an hour earlier by no less a person than the judge himself, and it signified to all that he was a "presentor of the cock." This gave him additional rights: he could approach the judge's box, converse with the judge before and after the fight, and enter the ring and present his bird. But, most important of all, he, and only he, could pace the outskirts of the arena while his bird did combat and usher him on to victory. Everyone else had to remain by their seats. 'Tis civilization at work, thought Clancy to himself. To think of Pat Darcy's pigstye of a shack back there in the bogs of Mayo. With meself being shoved and hassled as I urge Bulba on to another victory, and Pagga standin' at the fuckin' broken doorway lookin' out for Sergeant O'Malley to come down on that crock of a bicycle of his and arrest us all. How the fuck can people live like that, I ask ya? Jasus, they won't believe us when we get back and tell 'em of the glories of this place.

"Milo!"

Clancy managed a smile as O'Casey drew level with him. "How's it goin'? Did ya manage to get it all down?"

Stallion rubbed his hands with satisfaction. "Everythin' is down except for the last hundred. I'll split that with Pagga just before Bulba makes his entrance. We'll lay it with the bookies proper if they'll give good odds."

"What about the stuff laid already?"

"Well, since we started this mornin' and with what we've laid tonight, Pagga and I reckon it works out at about six to one over all."

"That's good."

"That's good? That's fuckin' marvellous, Milo. Have ya ever known the outside of two cocks to fetch more than three to one?"

"Never."

"Then we're in heaven," Stallion smiled broadly. "Right!"

"Right," answered Clancy, his face straight as a poker.

"Worried about Bulba?" asked O'Casey, anxious himself.

"No," said Clancy simply. "Where's Pagga?"

"Checkin' up on Barra. Seein' if he needs a hand." O'Casey noticed a harshness in Clancy's eyes. Those eyes had been on him all afternoon. But then, he knew that Clancy was a cautious man.

"Clancy?"

"Wha'?"

"I can be good for you. Real good."

Milo looked at him closely. "Oh . . . in what way would that be now?"

"I can make ya rich, richer than yar wildest dreams."

" 'Tis a generous man ya are if ya could do it. But tell me, Mr. O'Casey, why would ya be bestowin' such generosity in my direction?"

48

" 'Tis a two-way thing," replied Stallion, ignoring the expression on Clancy's lips. "For me to be good to you, you'd have to be good for me."
"For you?"
"For me, and my son."
"Ya've dreams to fulfil, Stallion O'Casey. I can see that. Ya're a man of ambition to be sure."
"I have one dream," said O'Casey flatly. "I want to give my Colin a full expanse of life."
Milo looked at O'Casey steadily for a moment, as though choosing his words. "Only the Lord can do that, I'm afraid," he said at last.
If Stallion wanted to reply he hadn't a chance, for just then a great wave of shouting went up as the master of ceremonies entered the barn.

The presenters of the first fight of the evening stood in the centre of the ring, their fighters nestled in the cradles of their arms. The judge, alone in his box, just ten feet away from them, blew his whistle and the presenters faced each other. He gave a second blast on his whistle. This was the cue for the grand challenge to be made. They thrust their birds forward and the statutory angry contact was made. Both birds were willing to do battle unto the death.
The whistle blew for the third time, killing momentarily the tense silence that hung over the barn. The two men walked the few paces to the opposite gates of the ring. Then they turned and looked across at one another, each awaiting the other's nod. The owner and presenter of Potato Merchant got the ball rolling with the wink of an eye; the presenter of Nice and Easy followed at once with a nod of the head. The cocks were lowered to the ground, pointed straight at each other, and their minders left the arena.
Potato Merchant was as black as midnight except for his stubbed red comb. Nice and Easy was a deep copper except for his neck, which was a mixture of copper and bright yellow. He carried himself well, had a champion's chest and the money was on him. But the Merchant was an old hand, a veteran of seven fights. He knew his trade and carried some heavy scars on both his wings. In appearance he didn't look a winner. His chest, what there was of it, was all on the bone. There was no meat to spare on this wily fighter.
Nice and Easy took the baton straight away and showed the old hand the terrain on which the battle would be fought. Easy shifted his way round the ring in a clockwise direction. The Merchant immediately went the other way, his eyes never off his opponent. But suddenly, without a hint of warning, Easy shot high into the air, wings blasting hard to gain maximum height. The Merchant followed a split second later. Easy reached the peak first, feet up and the glinting shafts of steel ready. He was already descending while Merchant was still in his climb. Merchant saw the mortal danger coming down and whirled in

49

midair—but too late. There was an explosion of black, copper and orange feathers, and a second later both birds were back on the sawdust. There was a trickle of blood running down the Merchant's back as they started to manoeuvre for position once more. Outside the ring it was clear to all that Easy's spurs had not gone home. All he had done was to kiss a little of the Merchant's sparse flesh.

Thirty seconds passed with the birds just circling in opposite directions. But the width of that circle was decreasing rapidly. Finally their beaks met, and they pecked and stabbed and hacked away at each other, darting backwards and forwards as they tried to seek out the hidden flaws in each other's defence. It was soon clear to all that both birds were well matched. Then again without warning Easy was up off the ground and soaring, but Merchant went with him and, with a desperate effort of his scarred wings, got to his summit first, his legs positioned for a thrust at the oncoming Easy. His left spur caught Easy in the face. A squawk of piercing pain tore from Easy's throat as they exploded into each other. Feathers burst and splayed out over the arena, then both birds dropped like stones. Easy landed badly and staggered. His right eye had been plucked from his head. There was a black clotting hole where the eye had been and a fountain of blood was pouring out of the empty socket. Merchant's fall was a split second behind Easy's but his drop was true. He came down on his wounded prey with thunderous force, legs on point and slits of steel on target as they plunged deep into Easy's back. It was over without another squawk. Potato Merchant stayed put on the mound of bloody flesh and, head held high, crowed out his victory to the rafters.

Two hours later eight fights had been completed. Eight cocks were alive, cheered as the victors, and were being cradled away to have their wounds tended. The other eight were either being given a ceremonial burial by their grief-stricken owners, or were already being plucked and gutted and made ready for the stewing pot.

There was an hour's interval while spectators, owners and handlers got their breaths back and killed the rawness of their parched throats with bottles of stout, served up by the twenty-odd hawkers that now surrounded the ringside. It was the general opinion of all that the first and last fight of the eight were the ones that would be remembered for a long time to come. Potato Merchant had been sold straight after the fight to a publican for £60, a staggering sum to be sure. The publican reckoned that if Merchant could see off his next three challengers his reputation would be made. He could then retire the bird with honour, and put him on show in his establishment. He reckoned that would be good—very good—for business. The last fight of the set had turned out to be a marathon event. A fighter named Broadchest, which had been on the sawdust floor and apparently dead, came back to life, got to his feet and killed his aggressor, before an astounded audience.

The ninth fight of the night was under way and the crowd were on their feet. Bets and counter-bets were being screamed back and forth and the fight itself (inside the metal grille) was up for grabs.

Behind the judge's box, four men on their haunches surrounded their bird. With a wet sponge Clancy was busy dousing the bindings that held Bulba's steel armoury in place. Barra Duffy was fanning the cock with a makeshift cardboard fan. O'Casey and O'Leary were dragging hard on their cigarettes, ready to help out if needed.

"Someone in this fuckin' place should go and open a fuckin' door!"

"Aye, I agree with yarself there, Barra," replied O'Casey. " 'Tis like an oven in here."

"Not a good place for cocks at all," fussed Duffy. "Bulba'll sweat himself to death before he ever gets into the ring."

"Fan the fuckin' bird, Barra Duffy, and shut yar shaggin' gob!" hissed Pagga, rising to his feet. "Jasus, but the piles are playin' me up somethin' awful tonight."

"Do ya suffer from the piles then, Pagga?"

"That I do, Stallion. An army of brimstones burnin' their ugly fires on the lips a me arse."

"That can be a curse," O'Casey sympathized. But his eyes were fixed on Clancy and Duffy, checking to see that they were doing their job well. He had watched all three Mayo men throughout the day, willing to give advice. But no advice was required. They really knew their job, and that irritated O'Casey, for it meant that he needed them more than they needed him.

"Well, that's that. He couldn't be readier than he is now," said Clancy.

"Spurred, laced and all ready to go!" answered Barra, cradling Bulba in his arms.

"How's that pox of a fight goin', Pagga?" asked Clancy.

"They're still at it. They'll be at it for another hour or two the way they're carryin' on."

"All the same," continued Clancy, "why doesn't yarself and Stallion here go and lay the rest of the green stuff down?"

"Good idea, Milo," agreed O'Casey. "How about it, Pagga?"

"Age before beauty!" smiled Pagga.

O'Casey was already into the crowd, Pagga following, when Clancy called out, "Hey Pagga, just a minute!"

Pagga turned back, "What is it?"

"Don't let that bastard outa yar sight."

"Ya still don't trust him?"

"If he goes to the bog follow him. Wipe his arse if ya have to, but don't let him out a yar sight."

"Gentlemen, your attention. The tenth fight of the evening. On my left—four years old, nine fights, owner, Matthew Charles Patrick Finn—Randy Sheeba!"

A roar went up from the crowd. Sheamus Collins waited for silence. "Gentlemen! On my right—three years old, six fights, owner, Milo James Clancy—Taurus Bulba!"

A few scattered roars came back at Sheamus Collins's ears. He stepped down from his rostrum in front of the ring and turned towards Matti Finn. "Yar cock, please."

Matti Finn held his bird out for inspection. Collins checked Sheeba's spurs and beak and, satisfied, pointed towards the left gate of the arena. "Yar cock, please." He checked Bulba's armoury and sent Clancy and cock to the right gate.

The third blast of the judge's whistle signalled the end of the introductions. Milo Clancy bent down, got Finn's half nod, let Bulba go, and left the enclosure.

Taurus Bulba watched as the midnight cock began to make his circle, but refused to participate in the etiquette of cockmanship. All he did was shift his body and keep his eyes on the target. This baffled the well-mannered Sheeba, who stopped in his tracks, staring at this peculiar opponent. A roar of disapproval went up from the crowd. Randy Sheeba's eyes left Bulba for a second. It was his biggest mistake. Clancy's cock charged into a run, took off and climbed for the heights. Only when he heard the flapping of Bulba's wings did Sheeba take notice. Immediately he saw the mortal danger of the slanting soar and darted backwards. But Taurus Bulba had his legs at full stretch, and the steel spurs caught and bit deep into Sheeba's fleeing arse. Bulba crowed with rage as Finn's cock slipped from his grasp and took to the air in flight.

He did not follow, but stood his ground, looking up at the glinting spurs coming down at him. Swiftly he sidestepped out of harm's way, and when Sheeba met the sawdust he was on him like a shot. Sheeba's landing was heavy and Bulba's charge was true. Close-quarter fighting was his speciality and he did his work with great will and determination. He stabbed home time and time again with slashing beak, using it solely on his victim's head, while the spurs ripped and lanced at underbelly and wing. Sheeba had no chance of recovery, no chance of flight; the flaying wings of his aggressor blocked sight of all retreat. Sheeba's sap was ebbing away with the passing of each second. With one last, tremendous effort he managed to break free. But even while darting back he saw the beating wings of Bulba above him. Sheeba strained to climb and meet the challenge but his legs gave way. The cock keeled over, skidding in his own blood. Both of Bulba's two-inch spurs sank into Randy Sheeba's belly and scissored through the soft flesh. The dying cock's spilling guts tangled in Bulba's legs.

The gates opened and in came Sheamus Collins. Squatting on his haunches, he examined the stricken Sheeba while Bulba, in his frenzy, slashed and pecked away at his bloody, lifeless victim. Collins took a red handerchief from his pocket and waved it high in the air.

The Birds of Death

Our final "literary" description of a cockfight is set in Mexico, very near the Texas-Mexico border. The account provides gratifying detail of the preparation, training, and overall folk philosophy of cockfighting. Of special interest are the "tips," as to which drugs or vitamins can be utilized to stimulate the cocks to fight with greater ferocity.

The author, Giles Tippette, has also written The Trojan Cow: A Novel *(New York: Macmillan, 1971), and a mystery entitled* The Mercenaries *(New York: Delacorte Press, 1976). Fiction or not, it seems obvious that Tippette had to do some fieldwork on the Texas-Mexico border in order to elicit all the rich ethnographic detail he presents.*

For other accounts of cockfighting in the Texas area, see Wayne Gard, "Rooster Fight," Southwest Review *22 (1936): 65–70; and Haldeen Braddy, "Feathered Duelists," in Mody C. Boatright, Wilson M. Hudson, and Allen Maxwell, eds.,* Singers and Storytellers, *Publications of the Texas Folklore Society, vol. 30 (Dallas: Southern Methodist University Press, 1961), pp. 98–106.*

The four matches had been made for 5000 pesos each. They were between Fernando Solís and Antonio Chapa, the two best breeders in Nuevo Laredo. If it had been bullfighting it would have all seemed matter-of-fact. But it was not bullfighting, it was cockfighting and it was illegal.

The last fights of the season had been held in the interior of Texas, and now the only action a cockfighter could hope for until the fall was along the border. Which was not so unlikely: though Texas has perhaps more cockfighters and breeders than any other state, the headquarters is in the border country. It is looked upon there almost like a national sport, and the Mexicans and Texans fight their birds freely across the Rio Grande.

But the match had begun badly for "Nano" Solís, a young man of 28 who looks enough like a bullfighter to be one, with his slim size and handsome, sculptured dark face, his jet-black hair and flashing white teeth. It had begun badly because he had put his best bird, a purebred Spanish cock named Pepito, in the match in hopes of shaking his opponent's confidence. But Pepito was in

Reprinted with permission from *Texas Monthly* 6 (1978): 163–165, 271–272, 274, 276.

trouble. Three times the two cocks had been pitted, faced off across the line drawn in the hard-packed dirt of the little ring, and three times Nano's handler had had to take Pepito up lest the referee call a win for the opposing cock. Now Pepito had a broken left leg and his right eye was swollen almost shut. The handler walked around the ring with him, cradling him in both arms, taking mouthfuls of water and spraying them down Pepito's back, trying to cool him, to give him new life.

Outside the ring Nano looked worried. Even though he was a professional cockfighter, 5000 pesos was a great deal for a man of his poor means to bet on each match, and he had counted on Pepito winning this first one.

And it would be a hard thing indeed to lose Pepito. Pepito's sire was dead, killed in a fight at one of the big *ferias*, (fairs), and Pepito was the last of the pure Spanish stock he'd imported from Spain. Watching, he now regretted his decision to fight the little red cock, but there was bad feeling between him and the opposing breeder, Antonio Chapa, and he had wanted to embarrass him quickly.

But Chapa had countered with a pinto cock, a brown-and-white-speckled cock of mixed German and Spanish breeding that was jumping higher than Pepito and spurring him about the head. The pinto was, as some boxers are, a headhunter. He had several times dazed Pepito and had closed one eye. They were not fighting the cocks with the long, deadly steel gaffs that are attached to the natural spurs of the birds, nor with the swordlike inch and a half slashers, but with short, blunted steel spurs. It was late in the season and neither breeder had wanted to risk losing valuable battle stock. Nevertheless, a cock could be beaten to death with the short spurs unless the referee stopped the fight in time.

Now, as his handler still circled the ring with Pepito, Nano was considering whether to concede and save his cock or hope that Pepito would make a comeback. The little cock had fought three times before, but he'd won so easily each time that he'd never been really tested.

The crowd and the referee were beginning to yell for the fight to resume. "*Pelea, pelea!*"—"Fight, fight!"—they were shouting. And the referee was motioning to both handlers to bring their cocks forward. Chapa, who was handling his own cock, came forward readily, but Nano's man pretended not to have seen. He glanced over at Nano to see what the owner wanted to do, and Nano stared blankly back, thinking.

The fight was being held in an arena, if it could be called that, about ten miles outside Nuevo Laredo. It was reached from the highway over a dirt obstacle course that should have ruined every car that came there. The arena itself was nothing but a tin-roofed shack, open on all four sides. The ring was an enclosure twenty feet in diameter formed by a three-foot-high wall of canvas. Forty or fifty spectators sat just behind the canvas wall in old and rusted metal folding chairs, most of which were imprinted, from some long past time, with ads for Coca-Cola or Carta Blanca or Corona. Nearby, in a booth, a woman cooked *carne asada* and *fajitas* over an open fire, and those at the ring could smell the mesquite smoke and aroma of the meat. The impresario of the establishment, Miguel Martínez, sold soda pop and beer and Scotch whisky from his own booth. He was doing a lively business during the delay, though not so much on the Scotch because it cost 30 pesos (about $1.50 American), and, besides, as one spectator told his friend, it was too hot to drink whisky anyway. In the vicinity of the pit there stood a whitewashed ramshackle building that was referred to as the "rancho," and a couple of stripped, rusting trucks sat in the yard, looking as if they'd be there forever. Beyond that there was nothing but baked soil, dry mesquite trees, and chaparral.

Contrary to what most people think, cockfighting is not illegal in all of the United States. It *is* illegal in Mexico, except at the big fairs that are held on certain holidays. It is permitted at the fairs because there the government can collect a tax, or *impuesto*. Miguel Martínez, like all of the operators of the "brush pits," is in a difficult position. Since his business is illegal, he cannot pay the tax, but to exist he must pay the tax. So, instead, he pays a *mordida*, a bribe, in order to be able to pay his tax. He doesn't find it ironic or even unusual. Asked about it, he just shrugged, "Well, that is the way of the thing, so what can one do?"

Miguel had promoted this fight. It had taken some doing because it was so late in the season, but he knew that, if he could arrange it, it would draw a good crowd and he'd make money. To attend the fight cost 50 pesos, quite a sum for an afternoon of entertainment in Mexico. And then there was the food and the drinks. Miguel had already made his money and he didn't much care how the matches turned out. As is the custom in Mexico, he put up no prize money. The winnings consisted of bets made by the owners of the cocks. And then there was the betting among the spectators, which was also a private affair. The betting on the match had generally been 100 pesos to 70 in favor of Pepito, and the customers who had bet on him were incensed at the showing he had made. They were beginning to shout curses and insults at the handlers, which was why Nano never handled his own *gallos* (cocks).

"They yell bad things," he said, especially if they are losing. Certain insults and curses a man cannot well stand. Sometimes they get drunk and lose their heads and say too much. So I stay out of the ring because"—here he smiled slightly—"I have a little bit of a temper, and if the wrong thing is yelled at me it could be there would be more fights than just the one between the *gallos*."

Nano has been raising and breeding fighting cocks for about ten years, but fighting them himself for only four. He says he began fighting them himself to

56

better establish his reputation as a breeder. He presently has about two hundred battle cocks and battle stags (a cock under eighteen months), and he and his wife breed, train, and care for them. Of course not all two hundred of them are in fighting trim. During the regular season he will keep only about twenty *gallos* in training.

But now he had to make a decision, because the referee was growing angry, and that would not do. Also Chapa yelled across at him, with an insolent, triumphant look, *"Pelea o pagar!"*—"Fight or pay!"

Chapa is ten years older than Nano. He is a fair-complexioned man with reddish hair. He has big shoulders and a bit of a potbelly. He handles his own cocks in the ring because he doesn't care what the spectators shout. Sometimes he shouts insults back at them. He resents Nano because Nano has consistently beaten him.

He shouted at Nano again, and Pepito's handler, still cradling the cock in his arms, looked over at the breeder.

Fernando stared back for a long moment, then slowly nodded.

"Arriba!" the referee yelled, motioning both handlers forward. The small crowd yelled as the cocks were faced across the line. The big pinto, held by Chapa, strained forward, bristling his hackles. But Pepito barely had to be held. He sagged sideways toward his broken leg. It was not broken at the thigh, but lower, so that the leg was more or less held together by the tough sinew and skin. His eye was still closed, but his head was raised and his good eye gleamed maliciously at the other cock. The referee dropped his arms and the two handlers stepped back. The two cocks leaped at each other. The pinto went higher, vaulting with his back almost parallel to the ground, hitting Pepito with quick one, two, threes, each time they went up. But Pepito was slugging back, going to the body just below the wing, hitting hard with his good right leg and using his broken left more for a guide and a hold. They went up and up and up. Five, ten times. At first the pinto, looking bigger but not heavier, was forcing Pepito back. But the little rooster hung on, socking away with that right leg. Gradually the pinto dropped back until they were even across the line again. Finally they both stopped, squatting on the ground, pecking futilely at each other. The referee made a sign to the handlers to take up their cocks, and Nano's man rushed forward to pick up Pepito and do what he could to revive him. Outside the ring Fernando raised his eyes to the sky as if in prayerful thanks.

In cockfighting, on both sides of the border, the referee is an integral part of the fight. He is responsible for enforcing what few rules there are to the sport (primarily the weight matching), and his word is absolute law. He can, whenever he wishes, disqualify a cock, and bets are paid off on his decisions. He is especially important in fights that are not fought to the death, but to a decision, for the decision is his and his alone. Normally the handlers must instantly bring their birds to the line when he calls for them, but this referee, moving unobtrusively around the ring, was being especially lenient, for he knew that the two cocks had not had a sufficient training period and were tired and in poor condition.

Nano would, however, have to make another decision, though it seemed to him that Pepito had rallied somewhat and he was beginning to wonder if Chapa's cock had as much heart as he might need. But the bettors did not seem worried. Those who had bet on the pinto were now seeking to press their bets with Pepito's backers. There were few takers. In the break there was much laughing and going back and forth to the refreshment stands. Miguel Martínez seemed the most contented man there.

The Mexicans say that their cocks are far superior to those in the United States. American breeders clearly do not agree. A man we will call Morris, from a small Central Texas town, who, like his father before him, has been breeding and fighting cocks all his life, said: "Yeah, I've heard that old story and it makes me laugh. Tell you what, one time I took fifty chickens down to a big fair in Monterrey. Fought forty-seven times and won forty and that was against about as good as they got in Mexico. They say that because they got more foreign bloodlines than most of our cocks do, German and Spanish and Belgian. For some reason they think that makes them better."

Morris is a big, ambling, slow-talking man of some forty-odd years who wrinkles his brow in concentration as he tries to explain about cockfighting. He looks more like a farmer than a cockfighter.

"There are some other differences, too," he said. "We'll fight cocks within a three-ounce limit of each other, but they'll try to get them right on the nose and even squabble over half an ounce. Hell, I've give away as much as six ounces when I knew I had the best cock. Won with him, too."

Morris keeps some sixty prime fighting cocks on his place, maintaining careful breeding records on the cocks and the hens and leg-marking them so that his breeding lines are exact. He does not cage his cocks as many breeders do but keeps them staked out in a large field. Each cock is leashed by one leg to a twelve-foot cord on a swivel. "That way," he said, "they've got 450 square feet of movement and they're exercising all the time. It also lets them get grasshoppers and bugs and other natural foods that are good for them." Each cock has a tepeelike house with a high roost inside made of stacked-up rubber tires. To get on and off their roost requires some effort since roosters don't fly too well. Mostly they have to jump, which is good for their leg muscles.

The similarity between fighting cocks and boxers is astounding, both in their training and in the ring. In the ring, the slugging, though with spurs rather than fists, is obvious. So is the repeated pitting, which is similar to the system of rounds and which echoes the oldtime style of boxing when a man had to "come to taw" (return to a line at the center of the ring). Also, in the short-spur form of Mexican fighting, there is only occasionally a "knockout," and most fights are ended on a decision by the referee.

But it is in the training that the resemblance is most striking. Cocks do roadwork just like boxers. Depending on what type of card he is preparing for, a six-, eight-, or ten-match fight, Nano will begin training that many cocks plus a few more in order to have the required number ready at the time. Two to three weeks prior to the fight, he starts them with three minutes of roadwork, running them around an improvised ring he has on his property. Each day he increases the roadwork up to a maximum of twenty minutes.

"After that much time," he says, waving a hand, "you do not accomplish what you are after, which is the conditioning of the cock. All you are doing is tiring muscles that are ready to fight."

The cocks' legs are plucked up to their bellies, as are their posteriors. A straight line is also sheared down their backs for ventilation, since cocks get hot easily and lose strength by being overheated. During the training period, Nano rubs down the cocks' thighs with a mixture of glycerine and alcohol. He says it makes the muscles more supple. Morris does this, too, though he uses a different mixture, which he says is a secret. But he does not run his cocks. Instead he goes out each evening, when they are on their roosts, and gives their leashes just enough of a tug to make them fight and struggle to stay on their perches.

"See, that develops their legs and wings and wind at the same time. I'll give a half-dozen tugs on one leg then switch over to the other one. The good thing about this method is that it really makes them flap those wings and that develops breast muscle, which is important the way we fight in the U.S. with the gaffs. A cock will get hit in the head, but he'll get hit in the breast a lot more, and you want as much meat between that steel and his vitals as you can get.

"Another thing, you don't want any fat in the rear end. I'll take a cock up and feel his behind and if I can feel his gizzard I know he's in shape."

To hold a fighting cock is a surprise. They are hard—hard like well-conditioned muscle—much harder than you'd ever expect a bird to feel.

"Oh, it's muscle all right," Morris said. "You can maybe fry a stag if he's a young stag, but you get one of those three- or four-year-olds killed, all you can do with him is make chicken and dumplings. Always somebody around the pit ready to buy your dead birds for meat. They don't go to waste."

All breeders spar their cocks. They strap on the steel gaffs and on the end of each they stick a small cork ball, much as you would with a foil or an épée. They are sparred to test them for gameness, endurance, and general quickness.

"Sparring," Nano said, "is also very good for the conditioning. After all, the hardest work the *gallo* will do is in the ring, so the more fighting you can give him the better will be his condition. It is the same with boxers, is it not?"

Nano has cocks in a wide range of prices. They are somewhat cheaper in Mexico than in the United States, but they are still expensive as chickens go. His lowest-priced stags will cost a buyer at least $20, and those out of proven fighters will go up to $50 and even $100. He has a few cocks like Pepito that would cost $200 or more—if he were willing to sell them.

"You must not," he said, "sell too much of your best breeding stock or else you are out of the breeding business."

Of course the hens are sold, too. And some of these bring as large a price as the cocks.

"Most people do not understand," Nano said, "that the *gallina* is more important to the breeding than the cock. I test my hens, sparring them against each other just as I do the *gallos*. But the true test of a hen is in the performance of the *gallos* she brings. That is always the test, in the ring."

Morris' run-of-the-mill cocks bring about $50. After that the prices start upward rather sharply, going to $150, $200, and $250. Not all his cocks are kept in the field. Eight or ten are housed in a special shed. These are the expensive cocks, the ones that have won time and time again and have been or are about to be retired to stud.

But in one special run is the true cock of the walk on Morris' place. This is his cock that has fought eleven times and won every match. He is in a large, cool enclosure, surrounded by a little harem of hens. His fighting days are over.

"That cock," Morris said firmly, "is not for sale at any price. I wouldn't take two thousand dollars for that bird. Why should I? He's only four years old and God knows how many chickens I'll get out of him, the least of which will be worth a hundred dollars as stags. That cock is famous. Even if I wanted to fight him again I probably couldn't make a match. No cockfighter is going to put his bird in against that one."

The eleven-game winner does not have a name, nor do Morris' other cocks.

"No use naming them. I just go by their color and their leg markings. Tell you a story about that eleven-game winner. My boy who lives up in East Texas came down to get him, said he had a match for him. Well, at that time, he'd won ten fights, and I had firmly decided to retire him to stud. I said, 'Oh, son, don't fight that cock. Please don't fight that cock.' But he said, 'Dad, I've got a match made with this old boy who's got more money than he has sense and it's just too good a chance to pass up. There's not a cock in this part of the country can beat that bird. I've got to take him.'

"Well, of course I let him because I do with my boy just like my daddy done with me, let him use his own judgment. But, I tell you, I stood out in the front yard damn near with tears in my eyes watching that truck drive off.

"But he come back next day with the cock absolutely unmarked. Had a nice little chunk of money, too. But, I tell you, I took that cock out of the truck and said, 'Buddy, you are now retired!' Said it loud, too, so everybody could hear me."

Most matches are individually made. A handler takes as many cocks to a fight as he thinks he can match and then goes from breeder to breeder looking for a fight and a bet for his birds. Such matches are called "brush fights" because they usually take place out in the country on someone's private property. The other type of fight is the derby, where a promoter makes the match-ups and there are entry fees and prize money. There may be as many as two or three hundred spectators at a derby, and the betting is fast and heavy with wagers in the thousands.

Morris pointed out a white cock with a few brown markings. "Now this cock fought the longest fight I've ever been involved in or ever seen. I don't know exactly how long it took, but we started in the afternoon and was fighting in this little brush pit that didn't have no lights. Well, it come on and got dark and those birds were still going after it. Now my cock is white and the other bird can see him, but mine can't because the other cock is a dark brown. So all my rooster could do was counterpunch. Every time that other cock would hit mine, this little white cock would hit back. Pretty soon my cock got in a good lick and this other bird let out a squawk. Well, that done it. That other bird went to squawking and my bird was finding him by sound. Chased him over in the corner and killed him."

Morris, like most breeders, gives his cocks a shot of the male hormone testosterone 72 hours before a fight. He says it increases their gameness. He also gives them a shot of some secret preparation fifteen minutes before they go in the ring. He says it stimulates their hearts.

"I've been offered a hundred dollars for that formula, but I'm not about to tell anyone. It's not anything so really special. You can buy most of the ingredients from the drugstore. Course it helps if you know a friendly vet."

There is probably little mystery to the shot that Morris gives his cocks. It is common practice to give the birds a shot of digitalis to stimulate the heart just before they fight. Many of the more sophisticated breeders give their birds shots of vitamin K to make their blood clot faster, so that when they are wounded by the gaffs they will not bleed to death. And, of course, all breeders feed their cocks a high-protein diet. Their diet is quite different from that of ordinary chickens, even to the addition of vitamin supplements to their water.

Cocks fight their best during the breeding season, and most cockfighters capitalize on this by depriving the cocks access to the hens while they are in training.

"They get very fierce then," Nano said seriously. "Sometimes they get so tensed up they will try to peck me, which is almost unheard of. And there are some, who know about such things, who give their *gallos* some medicine that makes them desire the hens even more. But I don't do that. I do not have to."

It is not considered unethical to dope a bird. Even though there is an official cockfighting association, there is not a great deal of control. Anything goes that you can get away with. For instance, since the cocks peck each other about the head, some handlers will put poison on their cock's hackle feathers so that the other cock, pecking there, will become ill.

The gaffs are slightly curved surgical steel weapons that look like large needles. They are supposed to be perfectly round. "But some old boys," Morris said, "will file an edge on the bottom side. If that diamond-shaped gaff hits bone it will penetrate and likely break the bone, whereas if it's round it will just generally slide on off. You've got to watch for everything in this game."

The cockfighting season begins, depending on the climate of the locale, in late fall and usually ends in midsummer. This is because the cocks molt during the hot months, and the molting makes them feverish and weak and therefore unable to fight. Of course, some cocks do not shed as much and do not get as sick, and some breeders have a few cocks on hand that are available for hack matches, which are impromptu fights between two breeders.

Even though it exists freely in Texas, cockfighting is illegal here. Laughing, Morris explained how it works: "Well, we don't exactly rent the auditorium downtown to hold these things, you know. Mostly some old boy will have a pit out on his place in a barn or some such—a place that will maybe hold fifty or seventy-five spectators. Word gets around through our associations and we have a fight. Then a lot of our fights are scheduled ahead of time in our monthly newsletter.

"Course you've got to remember that the local law has more important things to do than run around chasing a bunch of old boys fighting chickens. Occasionally, though, some bunch will get all lathered up, and the sheriff will have to make a raid." He shrugged his shoulders. "When that happens you just pay your fine and charge it up to the price of doing business. No big deal."

Cockfighting is, however, legal in Louisiana. This is because there doesn't happen to be a law against it, a fact which was discovered when a sheriff once raided a pit and brought in fifty or sixty defendants and the judge couldn't find a statute against it. Louisiana is also where the "world championship" of cockfighting is held, in the little town of Sunset. It is a derby. In it a man will fight eight matches with eight different cocks. The entry fee is usually $150 per man, there are about thirty breeders who enter, and it is generally winner take all. The winner is the breeder who wins the most fights, which usually means winning all eight, a difficult thing indeed.

Morris said: "Best breeders and the best cocks in the country. A man has got to have an awful lot of birds to come up with eight of the best because all some hotshot has to have to knock you off is one topflight cock and you're a blowed-up sucker." He looked thoughtful for a moment. "I come close one time. Won seven out of eight. Of late they've started paying more than one person the money, but I'd rather just see the winner get it all."

Morris, like all breeders, has no feelings about whether cockfighting is cruel or not. He said: "I don't think about it one way or the other any more than that guy who raises meat chickens wonders if it's cruel when he goes to slaughter and process them. I won't deny I love it, and I won't deny I get a thrill out of seeing a game bird fight, but I'll leave the question of cruelty to others."

It is difficult to say if it is a cruel sport or not. On the one hand, a meat chicken, a capon, is slaughtered at anywhere from eight to ten weeks. On the other, a gamecock will not even be fought before he's one year old and, during that one year, he will receive excellent care. And then some cocks, like the eleven-game winner, are never killed, but die a natural death. Many are retired to stud after only three or four wins. The question seems to be whether it is less cruel for a cock to be killed by a man rather than by another cock.

Cockfighters say that the humane societies would like to see the breed outlawed so that it would vanish. To some this makes about as much sense as extinguishing that breed of men who have a penchant for dangerous sports. "The *gallos*," said Nano, "were fighting long before man took an interest in sparring them. It is their nature just as there are various natures of men."

A gamecock's aggression is directed only at another gamecock. A man can hold him, touch him, handle him, and he won't make the slightest attempt to peck. A dog or cat can play around him and the cock will ignore it. Several breeders said that a fighting cock will not even bother a barnyard rooster.

"Beneath his dignity," one said. "He'll just ignore him. Course, it damn near will scare the feathers off that barnyard rooster and he'll find business elsewhere in a hell of a big hurry."

Nano says that he does not feel anything personal for his cocks, that it is a business, the way he makes his living. Yet he does something few other breeders do—he names some of his birds. He named Pepito long before he had his first fight, naming him after his sire, Pepe. He said, "Even when he was young there was something special about him, something rare, and I knew he was going to be very good in the ring. Is it correct to say he had a look?"

But now Pepito did not look well. His right eye was swollen completely shut, and he seemed to almost sag down in the handler's arms. He would react a little when the handler sprayed him with water, but you could almost feel his fatigue. It was as before, the crowd yelling for the fight to go on, the referee motioning the two handlers forward, and Antonio Chapa glaring triumphantly at Nano.

Finally Fernando motioned his handler to bring the cock over. Nano stroked Pepito's head and looked at his good eye. It gleamed back. He studied him, then sighed. "I think he still wants to make a fight. Pit him."

They were at the line again, and this time even the pinto was too tired to strain forward. Yet, when the handlers released them, the pinto still jumped higher and spurred more viciously. But Pepito continued to fight back, slugging the pinto with his good right leg just under the wing, getting in sometimes as many as two or three hits as they went up in the air.

The momentum was slowing, and neither cock seemed able to gain an advantage. It even seemed that the head blows the pinto cock was inflicting were less severe. The two handlers hovered just in the background, ready to take up their cocks at the slightest signal from the referee. Outside the ring Nano looked on, his face impassive. But in the ring Chapa exhorted his cock urgently in Spanish.

They went up again and then again and then a third time. Finally, as if by agreement, they both settled to the ground in almost exactly the place they had been pitted. Pepito was listing slightly toward his damaged leg. But there somehow seemed something different about him. He did not seem so tired. His good eye gleamed and glinted as he glared across at the other cock. The referee motioned the handlers to take up their birds, and they had just started across the ring when Pepito suddenly darted forward and pecked the pinto on the head. Instantly they sprang into the air. But this time it was Pepito that hit first and hit the hardest. A few feathers came floating out from beneath the pinto's wing. The cocks went up again and the pinto did not rise above Pepito for a head shot and again Pepito hit the other with two hard breast blows.When they went up again it was Pepito who was on top, and he hit the pinto in the side of the head with the short, blunt spur. When they landed, the pinto did not jump and Pepito rose above him, spurring now even with his broken leg. Suddenly the pinto let out a loud squawk and turned and ran for the canvas wall. Pepito limped after him and cornered him against the canvas and leaped up, holding him with that left leg and slugging away with his right, jumping on top of him. Two, three, four, five, six times he hit, almost too fast to follow, holding himself in position with his wings, now on top of the pinto, pecking him on the head and slugging away with his spur. The pinto made no attempt to fight back.

The referee hovered over them. Suddenly he threw out his hands, like an umpire calling a runner safe, shouting, "*Se terminó!*" He reached down and picked up Pepito and held him aloft triumphantly. Those who had bet on the red cock cheered and yelled. Those who had not looked disgusted and blurted insults at Antonio Chapa. Money began to change hands. The referee circled the ring and handed the cock to Nano. He took him, smiling slightly. The cock's good eye still gleamed.

For a second Fernando stroked Pepito's head. Then he looked over at Antonio Chapa and began to laugh. Chapa glared back. Fernando laughed some more, then smiled and turned to put the cock in his carrying case.

It was anticlimatic after that. Nano won the second fight, lost the third, and won the fourth. Then it was over and the spectators vanished as quickly as they had come, jouncing back to civilization over the nearly impassable dirt road. Miguel Martínez began to put up his stock of Scotch and beer and soda pop. The woman who had cooked put out her fires.

Chapa had paid and left, but Fernando was slow to leave. He got Pepito out of his cage and examined the bird's damaged leg and eye. Someone asked if the injuries were very serious.

"Not so very," Nano said. "The leg will mend itself and the eye is only swollen shut, not harmed."

Someone else asked if Pepito would ever fight again.

Nano's white teeth suddenly flashed a large smile. "Oh, yes," he said, "he will fight again. Only now he will fight the hens only. I think he will like that very much." He laughed, enjoying the thought. "Yes. I think he will like that very much."

The Fraternity of Cockfighters:
Ethical Embellishments
of an Illegal Sport

With this essay, we begin our scholarly consideration of the cockfight. One of the most critical questions with respect to the cockfight has to do with the ethical or moral issue. To put it succinctly: Is the cockfight cruel and inhumane? How do cockfighters answer this inevitable question? To find an answer to this question, Charles H. McCaghy and Arthur G. Neal, both sociologists at Bowling Green State University, attended cock- fights in Virginia, West Virginia, and Ohio, where they interviewed cockfighters, refer- ees, and breeders. What they learned is presented in the following discussion of the cockfighting fraternity.

For a further consideration of the views of cockfighters, see Clifton D. Bryant and Li Li, "A Statistical Value Profile of Cockfighters, Sociology and Social Research *75 (1991): 199–209. For other sample considerations of both sides of the ethical issue— either attacking or defending cockfighting—see Samuel Pegge, "A Memoir on Cock- fighting,"* Archaeologia *3 (1775): 132–150; William E. A. Axon, "Cock-Fighting in the Eighteenth Century,"* Notes and Queries, *9th Series, 4 (1899): 62–64; Lionel James, "The Ancient Sport of 'Cocking,' "* National Review *92 (1928): 138–143; Haruspex, "Cockfighting,"* National Review *96 (1931): 517–525; C. S. Jarvis, "Blood-Sports and Hypocrisy,"* Cornhill Magazine *159 (1939): 358– 378; Anon., "Your Taxes Support Cockfights,"* The National Humane Review *40.11 (1952): 10–11, 25; Barrie Penrose, "Blood in the Suburbs,"* The Listener *95 (1976): 236; F. Frederick Hawley, "Cockfight in the Cotton: A Moral Crusade in Microcosm,"* Contemporary Crises *13 (1989): 129–144; and Clifton D. Bryant, "Deviant Leisure and Clandestine Lifestyle: Cockfighting as a Socially Disvalued Sport,"* World Leisure and Recreation *33 (1991): 17–21.*

Reprinted from the *Journal of Popular Culture* 8 (1974): 557–569.

A robin redbreast in a cage
Puts all Heaven in a rage. . . .
He who shall hurt the little wren
Shall never be belov'd by men
  William Blake, *Auguries of Innocence*

The more enthusiastic supporters of cockfighting claim it is the oldest sport in the world.[1] This is impossible to prove, but it seems safe to conjecture that the sport of fighting chickens was contemporaneous with their domestication, which may have occurred as early as 3000 B.C. Admiration for and even adoration of the gamecock unquestionably reaches far into antiquity. It was the object of worship among the Babylonians, ancient Syrians, and Greeks; in Rome it was idealized as the symbol of courage in battle.[2]

Data and even conjectures on the extent of cockfighting today are admittedly scarce. However, few sports can claim its breadth of geographical distribution: practically all of the western hemisphere (including Alaska), Hawaii, the Philippines, Indonesia, southeast Asia, India, and central China, at least in precommunist days. In western and southern Europe there is limited acceptance of the sport, although it was never popular in the East or North.[3]

In the United States, cockfighting occurs under a wide variety of circumstances ranging from Puerto Rican boys in New York City who tote their birds in shopping bags while seeking out matches to highly organized and nationally advertised "derbies." Fights are held in such diverse places as barnyards, abandoned sawmills, cornfields, forest clearings, or wherever a "pit" can be drawn. The human participants are of various ethnic and social backgrounds; it is particularly popular among Cajuns, Delta Blacks, Mexican-Americans, and rural whites.

The sport of fighting cocks is far more complicated than it appears. Very simply, it involves the breeding, training, and conditioning of birds to fight other birds who they sense are invading their territory. In the United States they are equipped with artificial steel spurs or "gaffs." The gaff's blade is perfectly round; it tapers and curves from the socket on the leg to an extremely sharp point, and its length may range from 1¼ to 3 inches. (A variation, known as a "slasher," has a sharp edge along its entire length but its use is limited in this country.)

Birds are matched by weight; usually they are within one ounce of each other if under five pounds, and within two ounces if over five pounds.[4] The fighting takes place within a pit, which may be simply a circle drawn in the dirt. Generally the pit is enclosed by a wall about a yard high and is about twenty feet in diameter.

At the fight's onset, the combatants are held by their handlers at the pit's center and allowed to peck one another. At a signal from the referee the birds are released to fight. The handlers remain in the pit but may not touch the birds until given permission by the referee, usually when the cocks become entangled because of the spurs. The battle most likely ends with the death of one of the birds, which may occur in seconds or several minutes. Should the fight be prolonged, the cocks are removed from the main pit to a smaller "drag pit" making room for new contenders.

Any accurate estimate of the extent of cockfighting in the United States is impossible to obtain since, as we shall see, the sport is illegal in most states. An editorial in *The National Humane Review* claims that cockfighting "in commercial terms . . . is at least a $10,000,000-a-year business."[5] In an issue of *Grit and Steel*, there are estimates of 70,000 "gamecock breeders" and 500,000 "cockers" in the United States.[6] A later issue asserts that there are "at least 250 cockfighting arenas" in New York City alone.[7]

The sport's popularity and wide distribution in the United States are evident from an examination of cockfighters' periodicals. The sport has no national organization or federation but its enthusiasts can rely for information about matches, results, and breeding advice on three nationally distributed monthlies: *Feathered Warrior* (published in De Queen, Arkansas), *Gamecock* (Hartford, Arkansas), and *Grit and Steel* (Gaffney, South Carolina), each with a paid circulation approaching six thousand copies.[8] Matches announced and reported in these magazines take place in pits with fixed operating schedules which attract participants from a wide geographic area. But the scope of cockfighting as represented by these magazines is biased and scarcely indicates the degree to which it takes place. On the other hand, they do provide evidence of the range of the sport. The various announcements and results of fights plus the advertisements selling birds, equipment, supplies, and medical products reveal that cockfighting occurs in practically every state.

Contemporary United States' laws prohibiting cockfighting generally are based on the principle of cruelty toward or ill use of animals, and are derived from Acts of British Parliament passed in the nineteenth century.[9] The earliest legal restrictions on the sport predated the Acts by five centuries and had nothing to do with the welfare of the birds. In 1365, Edward III ordered the sheriffs of London to forbid cockfighting and certain other amusements in order that leisure time be better spent on practicing shooting. During the reigns of Oliver Cromwell (1653–1658) and Charles II (1660–1685), prohibitions were also enacted, but for political, not humane, reasons: cockpits were seen as meeting places of riffraff and hence spelled potential trouble, not the least of which might be rebellion.

The benchmark for contemporary anti-cruelty statutes was "An Act to Prevent the Cruel and Improper Treatment of Cattle," enacted in England in 1822. The first such law in the United States was passed in New York in 1828. Both these laws were limited to larger domestic animals, thus did not include chickens. The first subsequent law specifically to prohibit cockfighting in either England or the United States was an 1830 statute in Pennsylvania.[10]

Today the laws of thirty-nine states and the District of Columbia contain specific statutes or references to the prohibition of the fighting of "cocks," "chickens," "birds," or "fowls." Three qualifications exist: in Kansas cockfighting is specifically banned only on Sunday, Alabama forbids only the keeping of a cockpit and the fighting of cocks in "any public place," and Kentucky prohibits dog or chicken fighting only "for profit."

In five states (Alaska, New Jersey, Oklahoma, South Dakota, and Wisconsin), the relevant statutes are not specific, referring only to the baiting or fighting of "animals" or "creatures." Oklahoma courts have ruled that gamecock fighting is not included under the law barring "instigating fights between animals." The laws of the remaining states (Arizona, Florida, Louisiana, Maryland, New Mexico, and Oregon) contain only broad prohibitions against cruelty toward animals which could apply to cockfighting. In Florida and New Mexico, the interpretations have been that the laws do not apply. The Florida interpretation contains provisos that sharpened or artificial spurs not be used and that there be no gambling on fight outcomes.

It appears that, certain restrictions aside, in only six states (Kansas, Alabama, Kentucky, Oklahoma, Florida, New Mexico) can cockfighting as a sport occur within legal bounds. Since betting and the use of gaffs are integral aspects of cockfighting in the United States, it is safe to assume that even within these states a great proportion of the fights are technically illegal.

Legislation concerning cruelty to animals is directed at preventing suffering from a variety of sources, of which fighting is but a minor one: lack of food, shelter, and water, trappings, inadequate transport facilities, etc. In the matter of fighting animals, the laws are not exclusively concerned with cruelty. There is also an underlying belief that the spectacle is demoralizing or can agitate in an undesirable way those attracted to the fights. As mentioned above, legislation in England prior to the nineteenth century was more political than humanitarian. The laws of such states as Kansas, Alabama, and Kentucky which respectively ban cockfighting only on Sundays, in public places, and for profit, were evidently motivated by factors other than the suffering of the animals.

Clearly, much of the disapproval of cockfighting stems from the belief that those who observe or participate will develop, if they do not already possess, traits adversely affecting their roles in society. This belief, which for convenience we will call the "riffraff assumption," is historically exemplified in William Hogarth's cartoon series, "The Stages of Cruelty" (1750), in which cockfighting is depicted as a source of brutality and immorality in English life. A later Hogarth work, "The Cockpit" (1759), shows the fighting birds surrounded by a rowdy collection of gentlemen, gamblers, pickpockets, and rogues.

A verse chanted by eighteenth-century cockers indicates the hooliganism that evidently accompanied many of the matches. Here are three stanzas:

> Ruff Mory bit off a man's nose,
> It's a wonder no one was slain,
> They trampled both cocks to death,
> An so they made a draw main.
> Raddle tum, &c.

> The cockpit was near to the church,
> An ornament to the town,
> On one side an old coal-pit,
> The other was well goss'd round;
> Peter Hadley peep'd through the goss,
> In order to see them fight;
> Spittle jobb'd his eye out with a fork,
> An cried, 'B——st thee, it served thee right.'
> Raddle tum, &c.

> Some people may think this is strange,
> Who Wednesbury never knew,
> But those who have ever been there
> Won't have the least doubt but it's true;
> For they are all savage by nature,
> And guilty of deeds the most shocking,
> Jack Baker whacked his own father,
> And so ended Wednesbury cocking.
> Raddle tum, &c.[11]

Contemporary versions of the riffraff assumption no longer emphasize the rowdiness of the participants but are built about the theme that the so-called "blood-sports" reflect humanity's callous indifference to suffering and death generally. Thus Van der Zee's description of a match in California:

> Violence, big money, blood lust are present among the walnut trees and the tidy rows of grapes . . . the warm sunlight and blue sky, all felt more strongly, clearly, keenly in the aftershock of beating heart and coursing blood and blinking eye . . . snuffed out. . . .

A spectator finishes a beer and throws the empty into a garbage drum; the refuse beneath it flutters. It is one of the losers, flung away. This is no place for sentiment.[12]

Cleveland Amory is reminiscent of Hogarth in his attack on those who engage in such sports:

You have to think what it would be like to be the baited bear, the stuck pig, the coursed hare, the wounded cock, the exhausted and terrified fox. The people who set one animal against another haven't got the guts to be bullies themselves. They're just secondhand cowards.[13]

The central moral issues thus revolve around definitions of cockfighting as cruel, brutalizing, and debasing to humanity. How do cockers react to these accusations? What justifications do they present for the sport in the face of its illegality and moral stigma? In short, what are the ethics supporting cockfighting? To answer these questions the authors attended cockfights in Virginia, West Virginia, and Ohio (our admissions to these illegal events was through the sponsorship of well-known cockers). From interviews with cockfighters, referees, pit managers, and gamefowl breeders, we were able to ascertain a uniform set of ethics generally agreed upon by those engaged in the sport. The recurring themes from the interviews can also be found throughout the gamecock journals and other written material.

The one issue which cockers must face squarely in the accusation that theirs is a cruel sport. This they do in two ways. The first can be described as *condemning the condemners:* those who denounce the sport are hypocritical and frequently violate their own moral codes. Cockfighting supporters argue that their critics are inconsistent when calling for the prohibition of the sport and yet permitting other forms of cruelty toward animals and even humans to continue.

Cooks plunge the living lobster or crab into boiling water and then side with people who vote to outlaw one of nature's most spectacular displays—the gamecock.[14]

A common point of comparison is that of boxing and other contact sports:

If you go to a prize fight you will see more blood than you would if you saw a hundred gamecocks fought.[15]

One only needs to listen to the audience at a boxing match in order to follow the contest. During the moment of poking, jabbing, weaving, ducking, and bobbing, a soft, whispering murmur prevails. But the shouting and screaming of the fanatic fans can only mean one thing—one of the boxers is undergoing a series of brutal smashes to his face. . . . Since man can think and reason, he considers it an undue cruelty to match two cocks against one another.[16]

Condemning the condemners is but one means by which cockers deal with the cruelty issue. A second type of justification rests on the denial that cock-fighting is cruel at all. This serves to reserve the argument by insisting that it is inhumane *not* to allow the birds to engage in battle, based on the premise that the gamecocks are natural born fighters who enter conflict voluntarily and with enthusiasm. It is a matter of *self-actualization:* By being victorious gamecocks attain their highest possible level of accomplishment. As Fitz-Barnard puts it:

> Where the agents are willing, there can be no cruelty; one man can put a cock in the pit, but fifty cannot make him fight. If the gamecock was not meant for fight-ing, why was he created? . . . Cockfighting is the most humane, perhaps the only humane, sport there is. The game-cock loves fighting, the joy of battle is his greatest joy; if he dies, he dies as all brave things wish to die.[17]

A more contemporary cocker expresses similar sentiments:

> A game cock does the battling whether in a place provided for the purpose or in his natural habitat—combat is by instinct, a way of life for a game cock.[18]

When confronted with the argument that the fighting "instinct" is altered by the inputs of breeding, conditioning, and use of artificial spurs, cockers re-spond that few creatures are raised under more humane conditions. The cocks receive the best of shelter and food. One breeder took great pains describing to us the cramped conditions and forced feeding of fowl commercially raised for their eggs or flesh, in contrast to the raising of gamecocks. The natural proclivi-ties of the birds are perhaps embellished and enhanced within the context of the sport but, claimed this breeder, nothing he does can force any gamecock to fight. Or, to quote Fitz-Barnard:

> As a chicken he is brought up with the tenderest care and attention; as a young cock he is kept in luxury and freedom, monarch of all he surveys; . . . he is given the joy of battle, and if he dies, what more could a brave heart ask?[19]

Still another proponent of the sport attempted to lay to rest permanently the issue of cruelty by combining a reference to man's own fight for existence with the self-actualization theme:

> To brand cock-fighting as a cruel and barbaric sport is absurd, when we know that man kills millions of living things daily to appease his hunger. Cocking is nothing but an organized natural sport, from which the onlookers derive moral profit tempering nerves for the daily struggle, and learning how to carry on upright in the constant mill of life. As both combatants are equally matched and fall on to fight guided by nothing but their own desire to do so, it is perhaps the only sport where a decision conforms to the most perfect honesty.[20]

Although the accusation that cockfighting is a cruel sport can be neutralized by condemning its condemners, and by claiming it provides self-actualization for the birds, the "riffraff assumption" remains—that fights attract disreputable elements and are a corrupting influence for those who participate, either as spectators or owners. Conversations with cockers and a review of gamecock publications leave no doubt of their awareness of the derogatory image cockfighting elicits in the mind of the public. Our respondents, without urging, would often emphasize that the human participants are "respectable folks" from a wide range of socioeconomic backgrounds—a statement confirmed by our experience and by others' research.[21] More to the point of refuting the riffraff assumption are statements from publications; one author describes the crowd at a fight he attended:

> Good farm-class churchgoers in a jovial mood who were as happy as if they were in the middle of a Sunday School picnic.[22]

Another writes:

> I only met a few cockfighters who were not gentlemen. . . . I've met all kinds of fine gentlemen at these fights including statesmen and members of the clergy both Protestant and Catholic, and all of them enjoyed the fights and regard the sport as one of the finest in existence.[23]

However, cockers do not rely solely on defending the character of contemporary participants. They have certain *precedents* on their side: the sport itself is old, and a host of important historical personages have been in one way or another connected with it. Its antiquity and its dispersion throughout the world are frequently alluded to when legitimizing the sport, particularly since it was popular in the seats of our civilization: Greece, Rome, and early England.

In addition, the sport's defenders cite many famous persons who have approved cockfighting—ranging from Genghis Khan to Helen Keller.[24] Those most frequently mentioned include Alexander Hamilton, Napoleon, Woodrow Wilson, Gustavus Adolphus, John Adams, Alexander the Great, Andrew

Jackson, Henry Clay, Hannibal, Caesar, and Thomas Jefferson. Among the elite in the cockfighters' pantheon are, not surprisingly, George Washington, who it is claimed bred and fought cocks; Benjamin Franklin, who allegedly supported the gamecock as our national bird, losing by one vote in favor of the bald eagle;[25] and Abraham Lincoln, who once served as a fight referee. (One respondent informed us that Lincoln's performance in this capacity earned him the nickname of "Honest Abe.") Lincoln is supposed to have responded, when asked about supporting an anti-cock fighting law,

> As long as the Almighty permits intelligent men created in His image and likeness to fight in public and kill each other while the world looks on approvingly, it is not for me to deprive the chicken of the same privilege.[26]

The argument from precedent is embodied in yet another form of justification: the gamecock as a *model* to emulate. The bird is seen as emblematic of courage, commitment, and a variety of other virtues which manifest themselves in the pit. In its earliest form this justification focused exclusively upon the martial values and inspirations which the cock could provide. An example from the nineteenth century is provided by Scott, who cites a letter published in a London newspaper in 1875:

> Pomponius Mela, the historian, asserted that the Roman Empire did not begin to decline until cockfighting had fallen into disrepute among its Governors. He proves that Severus was not able to conquer Britain until he had rendered his principal officers passionately emulous of glory by exhibiting a main of cocks every day before them. The soothsayers warned Mark Antony to take heed of Caesar, because his cocks were always beaten by him. The great Gustavus told the King of Denmark he had no cause to fear the Imperialists since they had given up cocking, and were devoted to drinking and dancing. Christian, King of Denmark, said: "Were I to lead an army against the great Infidel of Constantinople I would choose none but cockers for my commanders, and none but lovers of the sport for soldiers.[27]

More recently in American history, a gamecock was the mascot of Company H of the 3rd Tennessee Infantry during the Civil War. It died in 1864 and was buried with full military honors.[28] Today the gamecock still provides inspiration as a mascot on the athletic fields of the University of South Carolina.

Lest critics of the sport be confused about the exemplary values being transmitted, Fitz-Barnard points out that:

As to the brutalizing effect (which exists only in the imagination) . . . war today is more bloody and brutal than ever it was, and disregard for pain and contempt of death *is what we want* (italics in original).[29]

In an article reprinted from 1939, the author comments on the "fine estimation of values" in naming a game fowl magazine *Grit and Steel* since anything worth doing, whether by a successful gamecock or a man, requires grit:

Maybe we love a gamecock for the reason he has so many qualities we lack. Grit is fortitude, valor. . . . A real game-cock is loyal to his family and himself—and he has the grit to back that loyalty. He don't [*sic*] argue about the advisability of loyalty—he acts. Yes, it takes grit to be loyal—to your ideals, to your wife, to your husband, to your friends, to your country.[30]

Scott believes the courage-arousing justifications for cockfighting are being abandoned or at least soft-pedaled in England.[31] From our experience, such is not the case in the United States. Though we did not encounter instances of militaristic justification, patriotism was often found incorporated as a theme:

I believe that we cockers, and I mean every one of us who love and admire the gamecock for his gameness, fighting abilities, and beauty, are as "American" as they come. . . . Let us all fight together against this tyrant (Communism) with every means we can as Americans who, like our Gamecocks, will fight unto death for what we believe in—Freedom.[32]

The gamecock is thus viewed as more than a fighting chicken; its value transcends the fervor of betting around the pit. Instead it is a paragon which has been imitated to good results in the past and which should provide direction in the present. In short, cockfighting does not encourage humanity's baser nature but serves as a model for its finer potential.

Cockers also champion their sport by attributing to it an assortment of benefits which can be grouped under the category of *altruism*—there are additional advantages even beyond those already discussed. Some of these benefits are listed by a pit operator: (1) cockfighting is a sport that requires a small investment and is not overcrowded in comparison with hunting, fishing, and golfing; (2) the entire family can participate thus keeping the adults out of bars and children out of trouble; (3) since it does not require excessive physical strength or stamina it is a particularly appropriate sport for the aged and the handicapped; (4) it is healthy and educational because it encourages "early to bed and early to rise, lots of exercise" and requires a knowledge of nutrition; and

(5) cocking encourages prosperity because cockers must be gainfully employed to support the hobby.[33]

Others argue that the sport effectively perpetuates a species of animal which otherwise would be lost in history, and still others that it also gives existence to hundreds of birds who otherwise might not have been born, most of whom are never put into a pit.[34] Lastly, it is claimed that the sport supports charity by donations or a proportion of gate receipts to local fund raisers. Evidently, the losing chickens are occasionally given to institutions.

Collectively, the justifications expressed by cockfighters are a set of logically ordered propositions intended to neutralize the stigma associated with the illegality of the sport: (1) if the gamecock enters combat voluntarily; (2) if he is acting out his genetically endowed proclivities; (3) if his keep occurs under circumstances in which he is ideally treated; (4) if his conditioning and training are such that he is optimally prepared for entering battle; and (5) if by success in battle he attains his highest level of self-actualization, then it follows that cockfighting may not be appropriately viewed as a manifestation of cruelty or of the degradation of humanity. Instead, cockfighting is one of the most humane and exemplary of sports.

Such justifications are consistent with those used in defending other forms of illegality involving private morality. The law is not seen as the exclusive source of legitimacy; instead, authentic forms of legitimacy may transcend the formal law of any society. Following this line of reasoning, the legitimacy of cockfighting derives in part from its assumptions of a naturalistic order: the long-range evolutionary sequence is one of eliminating the weaker and ill-adapted members of a species. In cocking only the fittest survive. While man may interfere to some extent, his activity is consistent with the natural selection process of enhancing the birds' adaptive qualities.

Additionally, of course, grounds for disregarding legal prohibitions also derive from historical arguments. The existence of cockfighting in antiquity and its popularity among great men of the past provide traditional evidence of its social worth in promoting humanistic and competitive values.

From our observations these justifications are an integral aspect of the sport and serve not only to support its continuation but also to sustain the high degree of personal commitment characterizing individuals deeply involved in it. As with any sport, the cockfighter becomes successful only after considerable time and effort. To become a "professional"—making profit enough to sustain a livelihood—requires a great expenditure of money as well as years of trial-and-error experience. Consequently, winning or losing is not simply a contest between two gamecocks—it also symbolizes the success or defeat of the cockfighter.

While the outcome of a single battle may be viewed as fortuitous, a cocker's long-range success is considered as final proof of his adequacy in connecting theory with practice. Leading up to the confrontations in the pit are several alternative theories about breeding, feeding, and conditioning (or, put another way, theories of genetics, dietetics, and reinforcement). The outcomes of the battles themselves are regarded as the result of some winning combinations of practices based on these theories. Thus, the results represent more than the victories or deaths of chickens: they are both operational and symbolic indicators of the abilities of the cockfighter.[35]

Critics of cockfighting, who are scarcely sympathetic to either evolutionary or historical reasons for continuing the sport, would view the cockers' commitment as simply self-aggrandizement at the expense of helpless animals. However, the fundamental point of conflict between critics and proponents of the sport derives from the claim of voluntarism. While the cockfighters emphasize the courage and bravery of cocks who go into battle of their own free will, the critics condemn cockfighters for controlling the conditions under which the choice occurs. The pivotal issues are: first, to what extent should the natural attributes of gamecocks be exploited by humans; and second, what is "humane" and what is "cruel"?

These interrelated issues are involved in the cockfighters' belief that the birds are either incapable of experiencing pain in a human sense, or indifferent to pain when fighting. Since "cocks love to fight, and they don't care about death,"[36] a cockfight is considered as something quite different from situations in which men deliberately neglect or inflict pain upon animals. There is no evidence that cockfighters, as a group, countenance cruelty to animals in other situations. Furthermore, they regard cocks as possessed of qualities uniquely worthy of being refined and developed—qualities which can be perfected only in the crucible of the cockpit.[37] Thus cockfighters are committed to a course of action congruent with their assumptions about what gamecocks are and what they represent; in some respects it is a modern variation on the theme of totemism.

On the other hand, critics who are committed to suppressing the sport proceed from a different set of assumptions: Since the combat is artifically induced, the birds' suffering is needless, and the commercialization of the sport perpetuates callous indifference to the torment of living creatures.

Conflict over the sport may also be viewed as one of differing responses to the issue of public morality versus the permissible scope of private freedom. The cockfighter looks upon his economic investment as the allocation of discretionary income after family obligations have been met and the bills paid. He sees his involvement as a form of discretionary behavior: freedom in the use of leisure time, participation in an intrinsically rewarding activity, and a potential source of supplemental income. The critics, of course, view the sport as beyond the limits of individual freedom and ultimately detrimental to society. The differences between cockers and their critics have been formally resolved in most states through the enactment of legislation prohibiting the sport. For most people, however, it is an insignificant issue because of general indifference plus the sport's low visibility in our urban society. Not surprisingly, officials often assume a casual attitude toward the enforcement of the laws. In our experience attending fights we found precautions against possible discovery were minimal, and the participants expressed confidence in the pits' "protection." We found that policemen, sheriffs, and judges were not only spectators but sometimes had entries among the combatants.

Apathetic law enforcement combined with the non-negotiable assumptions of the conflicting interest groups, the elaborate system of justifications, and the high levels of commitment all contribute to the persistence of cockfighting as a multimillion-dollar sport. And we believe it is a growing sport, judging from the complaints over increased numbers of entries and overcrowding at the pits. The ultimate fate of cockfighting in the United States is, of course, impossible to predict, but the sport represents in miniature the continuing conflict between the value of autonomy in personal choice and the principles constituting public morality.

Notes

1. We would especially like to thank Van Cleve Wysong of Matoaka, West Virginia, for introducing us to cockfighting and for serving as our sponsor at numerous fights. We are also indebted to Bob Solomon, Austin T. Turk, and Roy D. Wright for their encouragement. Additionally, we thank Dawn McCaghy for her library assistance in locating what otherwise would have been overlooked publications. This is a revised version of a paper presented to the Southern Sociological Society meetings, April, 1973.

2. A thorough discussion of the gamefowl's origins and distribution will be found in C. A. Finsterbusch, *Cockfighting All Over the World* (Gaffney, S. C.: *Grit and Steel*, 1929). For histories of the sport see also: R. Brasch, *How Did Sports Begin?* (New York: David McKay, 1970), pp. 73–83; L. Fitz-Barnard, *Fighting Sports* (London: Odhams Press, 1921), pp. 3–9; and George R. Scott, *The History of Cockfighting* (London: Charles Skilton, 1957), pp. 87–92.

3. Fitz-Barnard caustically remarked, "It is a curious reflection that in Germany alone I know of no records of cock-fighting; it is the lack of such manly sports that makes the Germans what they are." Fitz-Barnard, p. 6.

4. Age is also a factor. There are matches involving only "stags" (less than a year old) and only "cocks" (more than a year old).

5. Cited in Scott, p. 124.

6. *Grit and Steel* 72 (October 1970): 20, 31.

7. *Grit and Steel* 74 (September 1972): 29.

8. Since 1879 there have been at least thirty-two cocking periodicals published in the United States. For listings see: Finsterbusch, pp. 469–471, *Grit and Steel* 74 (November 1972): 29–30, and *Grit and Steel* 74 (December 1972): 32.

9. For histories of legislation regarding cruelty to animals in the United States and England, see: Gerald Carson, *Men, Beasts, and God* (New York: Charles Scribners, 1972); George F. Dyche, "Comments on the Law," in Arch Ruport ed., *The Art of Cockfighting* (New York: Devin-Adair, 1949), pp. 168–187; and Emily S. Leavitt, "The Evolution of Anti-Cruelty Laws in the United States," in Emily S. Leavitt, *Animals and Their Legal Rights* (Washington, D. C.: Animal Welfare Institute, 1970), pp. 13–28. According to Leavitt, the first law by any nation concerning cruelty to animals was embodied in the Massachusetts Bay Colony's "The Body of Liberties," printed in 1641. Liberty 92 reads: "No man shall exercise any Tirrany or Crueltie towards any bruite Creature which are usuallie kept for man's use."

10. The wording of this statute (Act of 1830, March 12, Public Law 80, Section 1) indicates that its intent was less humanitarian than to serve as a means to control public nuisance: cockfighting was illegal only if betting was involved. See Dyche, p. 169.

11. Scott, pp. 142–143.

12. John Van der Zee, "A Flurry of Feathers, A Slash in the Air. . . . And Something Living Dies," *New York Times,* 24 September 1972, section 20.

13. J. Richard Munro, "Letter from the Publisher," *Sports Illustrated* (22 May 1970): 5.

14. *Grit and Steel* 73 (January 1972): 31.

15. *Grit and Steel* 74 (May 1972): 25.

16. *Grit and Steel* 74 (October 1972): 3.

17. Fitz-Barnard, pp. 11–12.

18. *The Gamecock* 34 (June 1971): 5.

19. Fitz-Barnard, p. 12.

20. Finsterbusch, p. 187.

21. Clifton D. Bryant, "Feathers, Spurs, and Blood: Cockfighting as a Deviant Leisure Activity," and William C. Capel and Bernard Caffrey, "Grit and Steel: A Study of Deviance Reflected in Attitudes of Cockfighters, Devotees of a Stigmatized Sport," papers presented at the 34th annual meeting of the Southern Sociological Society, May, 1971. Generally research in this area is lacking; see: Gerald E. Parsons, Jr., "Cockfighting: A Potential Field of Research," *New York Folklore Quarterly* 25 (December 1969): 265–288.

22. *Grit and Steel* 73 (Sept. 1971): 35.

23. *Grit and Steel* 74 (July 1972): 36.

24. *Grit and Steel* 72 (October 1970): 20; 74 (May 1972): 25.

25. *Grit and Steel* 72 (September, 1970): 32-C.

26. *Grit and Steel,* 32-A. This quotation was cited by Kansas State Supreme Court Justice John Fontron when that court ruled that cockfighting was not illegal under the state's laws concerning cruelty to animals: *Sports Illustrated* (5 February 1973): 50.

27. Scott, p. 151–152.

28. *Grit and Steel,* 74 (April 1973): 32.

29. Fitz-Barnard, 12.

30. *Grit and Steel* 74 (February 1973): 33.

31. Scott, p. 155.

32. *Grit and Steel* 73 (September 1971): 25.

33. *Grit and Steel* 72 (October 1970): 31.

34. Scott, p. 159; *The Gamecock* 34 (August-September, 1971): 40; *Grit and Steel* 73 (October 1971): 33.

35. According to Geertz, the relationship between cockfighters and their birds is particularly pronounced in Bali: "In identifying with his cock, the Balinese man is identifying not just with his ideal self, or even his penis, but also, and at the same time, with what he most fears, hates, and ambivalence being what it is, is fascinated by—The Powers of Darkness. . . . In seeking earthly analogues for heaven and hell the Balinese compare the former to the mood of a man whose cock has just won, the latter to that of a man whose cock has just lost." Clifford Geertz, "Deep Play: Notes on the Balinese Cockfight," *Daedalus* 101 (Winter 1972): 7.

36. Tim Pridgen, *Courage: The Story of Modern Cockfighting* (Boston: Little, Brown, 1938), pp. 146–147.

37. In a show of disparagement rare in cocking literature, Pridgen writes: "The cock may be a stupid bird. Certainly, measured by the wisdom which moves the cautious he is more than stupid. But should he be, he carries under his blazing plumage qualities which call to men in compelling voice, and they answer in hordes." Pridgen, p. 25.

LAURIN A. WOLLAN, JR.

Questions from a Study
of Cockfighting

The debate over the ethical nature of cockfighting continues in this thoughtful essay by a professional criminologist. Laurin A. Wollan, a professor in the School of Criminology & Criminal Justice at Florida State University, not only explores the morality issue, but also ponders the basic appeal of the cockfight. What is the fascination of the cockfight? Does it depend upon an underlying sexual component? Why is cockfighting so commonly banned? Why despite the ban is cockfighting permitted in so many states? It is these and other basic questions which Wollan poses, even if he cannot satisfactorily answer all of them.

Why study cockfighting? Well, why not? It's there—not exactly the Everest of social phenomena, but it's there. Or at least it was. Consider the Wickery, an emporium of gift items and antiques just north of Tallahassee. The large barn–like structure isn't very striking, until one notices its peculiarities: the large opening in the ceiling of its ground floor is not at all well suited to the storage of hay, but such an opening would serve nicely as a gallery. And the little coop-like structures out in back are precisely that: the remains of a string of chicken coops that stretched all the way to the road, eighteen of them in all. Yes, the Wickery was once a cockpit, back when Tallahassee was a capital of cockfighting twenty years ago and more. It drew cockfight buffs from hundreds of miles around.

Even now something is there—not the ghosts of the game at the Wickery, but something real. One senses this instantly in driving onto the twenty acres of Gerald Cruikshank of Jacksonville, President of the Florida Gamefowl Breeders Association, and observing—not quite as far as the eye can see, but over many of those pine-shaded acres—the twenty-foot rings worn into the earth by staked-out gamecocks, each tethered by a ten-foot line, some sixty or seventy of them. They are brilliantly colored even as they begin to molt, and

Reprinted from the *Bulletin of the Center for the Study of Southern Culture and Religion* 4, no. 2 (July, 1980): 26–32.

stand somehow taller, prouder than typical barnyard roosters. There are other breeders, Cruikshank says, with a good deal more than he "just up the road." And he himself has had over two hundred birds at various times.[1]

Just how much cockfighting is there? Mike Strecker of Oklahoma, President of the United Gamefowl Breeders Association, told me there are some three hundred thousand active gamecock breeders in this country, with about ninety percent of them engaged in cockfighting. Don Atyeo, in *Blood and Guts: Violence in Sports*, states:

> Although accurate figures are naturally hard to come by, it would not seem unreasonable to suppose that there are now roughly half a million practicing cockfighters operating in hundreds, if not thousands, of pits across the country, ranging from makeshift arenas in converted barns to air-conditioned, purpose-built stadiums complete with bleachers, snack bars and permanent coops for visiting chickens.[2]

Cruikshank says the three or four hundred members of the Florida Association are only three to five percent of the total; in other words, there are somewhere between 6,000 and 13,000 cockfighters in Florida.

Cruikshank estimates that there are between fifty and a hundred indoor pits in Florida of the sort either built or altered for cockfighting, as opposed to the shed or barn pressed into occasional use. Of course there are also countless "brush pits" like the one just a few miles northwest of Tallahassee, nestled in a grove of oaks a short walk from a country lane. Fred Hawley, a Florida State graduate student, is beginning a dissertation on cockfighters as a "deviant recreational subculture." He has attended cockfights at three pits in the Tallahassee vicinity and estimates from what he has been told that there are about ten within an easy drive of an hour or so.

How could the numbers be accurately determined? By survey? This past January a survey was conducted of students in an introductory course in criminology, which revealed that 10 percent of the males had attended a cockfight. Can one extrapolate from that to a thousand males at Florida State University?[3] Whatever the exact number, it is interesting that so many grown men and even a few women—a woman handled cocks in the Pavo pit near Thomasville recently—will devote so much energy and time to the breeding and training of a bird (up to two years) for the few minutes, sometimes only a few seconds, that it takes for it to kill or be killed in the pit.

What is it that fascinated Clifford Geertz, the anthropologist now at the Institute for Advanced Study at Princeton, who wrote of it in the prestigious journal *Daedalus*? Or the distinguished historian Page Smith, who devoted two chapters to the subject in *The Chicken Book*? What moved the novelist Harry

Crews, professor of English at the University of Florida, to write his "unfashionable view" for *Esquire*? Why did Charles Willeford of Miami write an entire novel, *Cockfighter*? Why did editors of *Saturday Evening Post, Southern Exposure, Crawdaddy,* and *Esquire* think their readers would be interested in articles on cockfighting, all within the last ten or twelve years? Several scholarly journals have also published articles on cockfighting within the last few years: *The Review of English Studies, New York Folklore Quarterly, The Journal of Popular Culture,* and *The Tennessee Folklore Society Bulletin*. A description of a Louisiana cockfight appears in Rushton's *The Cajuns*. Atyeo, quoted above, devotes several pages to cockfighting in his book. And, most recently of all, *Playboy* has presented a spread of LeRoy Neiman color drawings of scenes of and around the cockfight.[4]

What is so interesting about cockfighting? Perhaps there is a clue in the way cockfighting terms and phrases have become part of everyday usage: for instance, "game," "cocky," "cock of the walk," (from the cock that dominates a territory when permitted to range free) or "can't stand the gaff" (from the two-inch razor-sharp artificial spur attached to the cock's heel), or "pitting" one thing against another. What about the word "cock" itself, which of course means both the male bird and the human organ of intromission? Is it significant that so many languages have words with the same root? For instance, *kukkuta* in Sanskrit, *kokotŭ* in Old Slavic, *cucurio* (I crow) in Latin, *Kūchlein* (chick) in German, *kuiken* (chicken) in Dutch, *kok* in Old Teutonic, *kuku* in African Senga, *koko* in Wisa, and *kuku* in Kaffir.[5]

Is cockfighting interesting because there is something implicitly sexual about it? In his Balinese study, Geertz noticed that in groups of men "squatting idly in the council shed or along the road in their hips down, shoulders forward, knees up fashion, half or more of them will have a rooster in his hands, holding it between his thighs, bouncing it gently up and down to strengthen its legs, ruffling its feathers with abstract sensuality. . . ."[6] If that is the cocker at ease, Harry Crews comments about action and failure:

> when a man's Kelso or Blueface or Gray or Whitehackle or Allen Roundhead quits—when a man's cock quits in the pit, he suffers a profound humiliation. *When a man's cock quits.* Yes, that's part of the ritual, too. Perhaps the biggest part.[7]

Cockers in their conversations suggest nothing of this identification, although it may be unwittingly betrayed in their preference for the word "chicken" (as in "chicken fight" or "chicken man"), much as the priggish "rooster" came into American usage in the Victorian period, indicating some uneasiness with the sexual connotation of the word.

Does the link of sex and language point to a deeper connection of cockfighting and culture? Is there significance to the difference between cockfighting in the Cuban culture of Miami, where a lighter, more agile bird is preferred, and cockfighting elsewhere in Florida? Does the heavier "Anglo" chicken reflect a more ponderous, perhaps a "heavyweight" culture? The difference between East and West may be reflected in the styles of cockfighting, with Orientals preferring the natural spur, which prolongs the fight sometimes for several hours, in contrast with the Occidental preference for the artificial spur, which hastens the climax and multiplies the bouts. Page Smith relates these two styles to the cultural attitudes toward time itself: "The Western spirit is to crowd as much sensation into as short a period of time as possible, while the Eastern mode is to savor the moment and to draw it out in a way that is intolerable to the Western consciousness."[8]

The cultural aspects of cockfighting date back to ancient times. What insight into cockfighting is gained from knowledge of the practice of sacrificing cocks to various gods, such as Osiris in Egypt and Jove in Greece? Smith states that in the Greek culture, "the cock embodied three of the most powerful themes in nature—sexuality, the sun, and the theme of resurrection. It is small wonder that the cock has been among the most powerful and ambiguous symbols in the history of the race."[9] Not surprisingly the cock's symbolism has entered Christianity:

> Christians took over the bird as a symbol which had, as it had for the Greeks, a variety of meanings—the awakening to a new life of those converted to Christianity, the cock as a symbol of the resurrection, as the bird of Peter, who thrice betrayed Christ before the crowing of the cock. The cock, by the same token, announces Christ and is intimately connected with His crucifixion through the story of Peter. . . .[10]

How much of this symbolism is present in modern cockfighting, and how much of it would be understood by cockers themselves, is difficult to say. How to research the topic is equally puzzling. Conversation promises to yield little information about cockfighting as a symbol, and certainly nothing about its sexual dimensions. Hence, interpretation of a sort not commonly done, certainly not in fashion in the social sciences, would seem indispensable. Along with analysis of symbolic qualities, perceptions and attitudes have to be starting points.

What about perceptions? Do Southerners have a clear perception of cockfighting? Do many of them know more than the hundreds of thousands who learned a little of cockfighting in the account of a raid on a cockfight, as told to Johnny Carson on "The Tonight Show" by Sheriff Katherine M. Crumbley of Belmont County, Ohio, in July, 1979? Cockfighters, according to the survey of a thousand subscribers to *Grit and Steel* a half dozen years ago by Clifton D. Bryant of Virginia Tech and William C. Capel of Clemson, attribute opposition in part to lack of information.[11] How many have merely imagined a cockfight? How many have relied on Nathanael West's account of a cockfight in *The Day of the Locust*? How much of their imaginary cockfight is realistic? Does it really matter? After all, how many criminologists have ever seen or experienced a crime? Are opponents of cockfighting primarily those who have not seen a cockfight?

What *are* the attitudes of cockers and of the public toward cockfighting? We know something about the attitudes of cockers because Bryant and Capel surveyed them and found, among other things:

> When asked the twin questions, "What is the thing about cockfighting that you think most people in it like?" and, "What is the major thing that *you* like about cockfighting?" there was close agreement. Some 19 reasons were presented in answer to these questions, but three clearly presented the vast majority viewpoint. The leading thing most like about cockfighting was "Competition," an answer that received 26.5 percent of the votes. A close second was "Thrills and excitement," an answer that received 23.5 percent of the votes and "Cock husbandry" which received 12.8 percent. "Money" came in a distant fourth, with 8.8 percent of the sample selecting this as their main reason for liking the sport. The same rating was given for both questions, as to what cockers think others would like best and what they themselves liked best.[12]

As for the public at large, little is known beyond what one can infer from the widespread illegality of cockfighting: the public must oppose it generally or at least an active minority does so. Some of the public vigorously opposes it, as indicated by the response to Harry Crews' "unfashionable view" in *Esquire* (one respondent addressing him, ever so cleverly using his initials, as "Dear Horrible Creature").

Do women have a different attitude than men? The survey of the introductory criminology class suggests that they do: nearly twice as many women as men characterized themselves as opposed to cockfighting, while half again as many men as women characterized themselves as indifferent. Two women emphasized their opposition with gratuitously vehement responses to the question on voluntary attendance at a cockfight: "NO!" said one, and "No! and never will!" said the other. Do women have a more refined ethical sensibility than men? Or is the difference biological, based on a woman's responsibility for the gene pool? Do men, by contrast, have a biological impulse to sow their seed as widely as possible, while at the same time sensing their expendability, hence becoming reckless, more cavalier about danger and death? Do men transcend their animal nature by dreaming, building, battling, and conquering? Is any of this represented in cockfighting, to which men may respond at some deep psychic, if not phallic, level of their being? And by how much do cockfighters exaggerate in claiming that the character of the British in the nineteenth century was inspired by the spirit of the fighting cocks so many of them knew so well? Or that the American frontier spirit was likewise animated by acquaintance with these selfsame qualities of do-or-die? Our Jacksonville breeder, Gerald Cruikshank himself is of such stock. To build up the foundation of his chicken house in a drained swampy area, he and his wife moved 175 tons of earth by wheelbarrow.

Would Southerners, more than others, resonate to Harry Crews' observation that "there is something in man . . . that loves blood"?[13] Do Southerners have a different set of attitudes to account for the greater degree of activity in cockfighting? According to Bryant and Capel, over half of the cockfighters are in the Southeast and Southwest, with more than a quarter from Delaware to Florida. Do such attitudes relate as well to the apparently higher degree of criminal violence and the community's punitive response in the South, and more particularly of homicide and the death penalty? Might the "blood lust" if you will, account for the greater popularity in the South of football and auto racing? As Crews states it: "They go to see a car get out of shape and swap ends on a turn. It makes their own blood more precious to see another man's boiling in a fiery collision. Isn't football a blood sport?"[14]

Might the difference be attributable to life in the country? Bryant and Capel indicate that the majority of cockers (56 percent) live in towns or larger urban areas, but more than half grew up in rural areas (villages under 2500 or open country).[15] Might the Southerner, the cockfighter in particular, be more attuned to nature than his urban cousin? According to Bryant and Capel, cockers defend their sport mainly on the basis of its natural quality: "the idea that 'the Lord made gamebirds to fight. . . .' "[16] Indeed, when Cruikshank released one of his chickens and dropped it near another, both instantly and naturally went at each other. Crews describes it more sweepingly:

> With the coming of winter, and the fighting season, their color comes full and their feathers lie flat and they glow like a light. Their blood goes high, rising in them like sap in a tree, and they know instinctively their moment is at hand. The long line they've been bred out of has come to a point. And they are at that point. They're ready to work.[17]

Atyeo stated yet another popular rationale as man's natural fascination with death: "Others see the pit, in the best Hemingway tradition, as providing one of the few opportunities left in modern society to take a long, hard stare at death."[18] Geertz suggests an even more complete meshing with nature:

86

Drawing on almost every level of Balinese experience, it [the cockfight] brings together themes—animal savagery, male narcissism, opponent gambling, status rivalry, mass excitement, blood sacrifice—whose main connection is their involvement with rage and the fear of rage, and, binding them into a set of rules which at once contains them and allows them play, builds a symbolic structure in which, over and over again, the reality of their inner affiliation can be intelligently felt.[19]

Can there possibly be any value in such an activity? Over half of the respondents in the Bryant and Capel survey said the major things they liked about it were competition, thrills, and excitement. Might there be a useful release in that for some? Crews' description of the moment suggests just that:

The cocks were billed and placed on their lines. When the referee gave the word, they powered toward each other in a great flapping of wings, both highfliers, each trying to get over the other. They met in the air nearly four feet off the ground and locked up in a fury that was awesome and beautiful and dreadful. A single sustained roar came from the throats of men and women and children around the pit.

It was all over in less than three minutes. A great cathartic rush of sighs and groans went out of us as we watched the winning cock stand on top of his dead opponent in the middle of the pit and crow his victory into the cold morning air.[20]

This release-and-containment of the forces of violence may enable cockers to be so authoritarian, so law-abiding, at least in their stated values. Bryant and Capel found that cockers scored significantly higher than the general population on authoritarianism, including its elements of obedience and respect for law and order.[21] It may be that these values—as well as honor and integrity, which are recurring themes in cockfight conversations—are strengthened by cockfighting's outlet or sublimation function, releasing or transforming the forces of violence. Atyeo quotes what he calls an "unusually perceptive cocker" thus:

We exploit animals for our psychic existence—to provide the emotional outlet through which daily tensions can be relieved, thereby enabling man to exist in the world without those shocking outbreaks of violence such as occurred not so long ago in Dallas and Chicago. Man has a real need for activities which can channel those impulses left over from more primitive days into socially harmless modes and then dissipate them.[22]

Despite these redemptive qualities, cockfighting is illegal almost everywhere. In Florida there is some question about its criminalization, which seems to rest on the authority of an opinion of the Attorney General rather than an explicit statutory statement. It is curious that there has been no litigation to resolve the ambiguity. An attempt to accomplish this legislatively was defeated, with an amendment striking cockfighting from a bill banning the use of dogs, bulls, and bears. Cruikshank attributes the defeat to his petition of 1300 signatures (obtained in two weeks). The attempt persists, with a bill introduced in the Florida House this spring, but beaten in the Senate Agriculture Committee. The ambivalence of the public and its lawmakers on this point no doubt explains why law enforcement is so indulgent, permitting cockfights to take place untroubled by "the law" as long as they don't get out of hand. This is a classic instance of the dissonance between "law on the books" and "law in action," or a *de facto* permission of what is prohibited *de jure*, presenting all the issues entailed in the perennial law-and-morals debate.

What is the basis of its prohibition? Ordinarily there is a precipitating event that catalyzes public opinion and galvanizes interests in support of legislation. This happened in England when the enormously popular pit sports, supported by plebians and patricians alike (as indicated in *Roots*), were quickly banned. Bear-baiting (pitting several dogs against a bear), bull-baiting, badger-baiting, dog-fighting and cockfighting were banned after the scandal of the pitting of the bulldog Physic against the human dwarf Brummy in 1866—oddly so, however, since Brummy won. Only ratting, or the pitting of a terrier against dozens or even hundreds of rats (Tiny, at 5½ pounds, killed 300 rats in 54 minutes, 50 seconds), lasted much beyond that, until 1912. In this country, the journalistic exposé of dogfighting, mainly in Illinois and Florida, led to a federal law, the Animal Welfare Act Amendments of 1975.

More broadly, if less directly, influential was the humanitarianism that swept Europe and America in the wake of the Enlightenment. This movement, coupled with the growing influence of women on public policy, culminated in nineteenth-century reforms of all sorts in fields as diverse as mental health, corrections, education, industry and politics.

But, more specifically, why prohibit cockfighting? Is the reason economic—chickens are needed for food? Not likely. If it is moral, what precisely about cockfighting is wrong? The gambling, which accompanies cockfighting? That can't be, given the prevalence of gambling on football and other sporting events. Cruikshank observes with some justifiable bitterness that singling out cockfighting for its attendant gambling makes little sense since more money is bet in Jacksonville at a single Gator Bowl than changes hands in a year of cockfighting.

Or is the real reason that death invariably ends the combat, with one or both birds dead in the pit? A bird that "runs," by the way, is almost always killed immediately by the handler, lest it sire a line of cowardly offspring. If it is death, which comes to us all, what precisely is it about the death of a bird in battle that is so offensive? What is it about this death at fairly even odds (cocks are matched by weight, like prizefighters) that revolts so many? Is it that death itself is evil? Or is it the "unnatural" quality of death before its time? Cruikshank admits to feeling quite badly at the death of a chicken by hawk or dog, but not in the least when it dies in the pit. Is it that the death is at the hands, so to speak, of man? Or for his pleasure? Or is it the pleasure itself, as Macauley thought: "The Puritan hated bear-baiting, not because it gave pain to the bear, but because it gave pleasure to the spectators." Is it the suffering that accompanies the death of the chicken? Cruikshank acknowledges that some suffering must be experienced, although, given the simpler nervous system of a bird, its suffering cannot be much—and in any event it doesn't linger long, for generally only a few seconds elapse from fatal plunge of spur to final expiration.

Is it the indignity of such a death? Is it that dead gamecocks are usually flung aside into a heap? But isn't there vastly more dignity in the death of a fighting cock than in the no less fatal death of a factory chicken destined for a frying pan?

> All parts of the chicken abattoirs are, of course, automated. In the Perdue plant the chickens are taken from the trucks at six-thirty in the morning at Accomac, Virginia, and hung upside down by their feet on a conveyor belt. The belt then moves through an electricially charged solution, which . . . "shocks almost all of them senseless. From there they move to the Kill Room where a knife-like instrument cuts their throats; then down the "bleed tunnel" where their blood drains away. . . ."[23]

Compared with such fryers, Cruikshank's birds are pampered indeed. Some of them live on without ever fighting; others, after two or three fights, live out their lives for ten or twelve years.

Is the opposition to cockfighting rooted in its brutality? Is it the effect on the humans? Compared with football, cockfighting is safe for humans (although I read a report recently of a cocker in the Philippines, I believe, who was slashed by a cock and bled to death!). The brutalizing of humans of course must not be physical but psychological. Cruikshank, however, is kind with his birds to the point of tenderness, knowing each one like a child, nursing sick ones back to health as assiduously as a mother. He even defies the conventional wisdom that the chicken that runs must be killed; he says such a bird may simply not feel well (a sensible view, to be sure), and proves his point with a cock that ran but thanks to his solicitude, lived to fight—and win!—another day.

In any event the brutality point is one of some ethical subtlety. But the times they are a-changing. "Animal liberation" as Peter Singer writes of it in his book of that title will no doubt influence many politically as well as philosophically.[24] And the cruelties of trapping, coon-baiting, and greyhound training (with live jackrabbits) are not long for this world. Watch the reformers, though: they will *not* prohibit the practice of snapping a show horse's tail that it may be reset in that distinctively prancy look that is so right in the show ring; nor will they ban the sale of goldfish, ninety-five percent of which do not go home bowl-bound for little boys and girls, but rather for the feeding of Jack Dempseys and other monsters of the aquarium.

And so we have prohibited cockfighting and will continue to do so. In doing so, however, do we make it a more, or less, serious offense? A felony, or a misdemeanor, or a mere infraction? Do we attach to it a prison sentence, a jail sentence, or a fine? Do we make the sanction mandatory, or do we permit the sentencing authority to set the penalty—or withhold it altogether? Should such authority be vested, for folk crimes of this sort, in the judge or in the jury? If not in the jury, should the jury recommend a sentence? Should the judge be empowered to increase the recommmended sentence? Lower it? Should the offense—or the sentence—be affected by aggravating and mitigating circumstances, such as age of the accused, diminished responsibility due to intoxication, and so forth? Should such factors be spelled out by statute or left to the judge and jury to find?

Should cockfighting be a civil offense rather than a criminal offense, carrying fines and injunctive relief? Should prior restraint be permitted to the authorities? And to which authorities? Sheriff, or county commissioners, or whom? Should the sale or possession of gamecocks be banned? Only in large numbers? If so, what? What about paraphernalia as peculiar to cockfighting as burglary tools are to burglary—gaffs, sparring muffs, dubbing shears (for trimming the comb), leg bands, tie-out cords, cockers scales, match sheets, call sheets, weight and band cards.

Should the prohibition be absolute or relative? If relative, dependent on what conditions? Should it be allowed in private clubs, with adults only, by permit, as long as gambling is not allowed, so long as there is no public disturbance, no public nuisance; or barred to out-of-state participants; or forbidden within the city limits, or within urbanized areas? Or should such rules be left to the determination of local authorities, the county commmission or the city council? If so, should that delegation of authority be absolute or relative, with the state setting outer limits of the tolerable? Should discretion be left relatively unconstrained by formal rules, left—in other words—to the common sense judgments of the enforcement agencies locally, the police chief, the sheriff, or even more locally to the deputy sheriff or the patrolman? Or should it be left mainly to the informal educative influence of moral suasion? Or does this bring us full circle to where we are today?

Has the tension between the prohibition *de jure* and the permission *de facto* been resolved in what is in effect a reconsideration of the reform itself, along the lines implicit in—and for the reasons stated in—Smith's concluding observation:

> What it suggests most specifically is that the "modern spirit," the spirit of improvement and reform, of psychotherapy and group dynamics, of social manipulation designed to rid us of our aggressions, may be going at things from the wrong end. . . .
>
> Banning public cockfights in the more "advanced" countries failed signally to diminish violence. Nor would I wish to suggest that legalizing cockfighting would at all reduce it. The opposition to cockfighting is a rather revealing quality of mind. One suspects that it has something to do with the notion—common to enlightened societies—that evil can be legislated out of existence. Devoted civil libertarians who are horrified at the thought of forbidding liquor or pornography see nothing contradictory in trying to legislate out of existence a sport that quite clearly reaches to the deepest levels of the human psyche. Perhaps this is the very point. The spectacle of public cockfighting is a reminder of those dark forces of nature that the Balinese—painfully aware of them as elements of their world— seek to exorcise; whereas we—members, as many of us feel, of a more advanced society—prefer to pretend that they do not exist.[25]

That is a possible, indeed a persuasive, but by no means an inevitable, conclusion. The subject is vast enough for many conclusions without exhausting its capaciousness to inquiry. Smith is no doubt right that "history contains no form of behavior relating to humans and their animal companions which is richer in symbolic meanings, or which penetrates more profoundly into the inner recesses of the masculine psychic life than the cockfight, almost everywhere forbidden and almost everywhere practiced."[26] So, why study cockfighting? Well, why not?

Notes

1. Information attributed to individuals is, unless otherwise indicated, from personal interview or conversation.

2. Don Atyeo, *Blood and Guts: Violence in Sports* (New York: Paddington Press, 1979), p. 98.

3. Such a figure, which seems so high, brings to mind the story Herman Kahn likes to tell to illustrate what he calls "educated incapacity," or the ignorance that comes from limited exposure to the facts of the world. This affliction especially strikes the upper-middle class, members of which are disproportionately represented in the policy-making circles of American government. When Kahn visits Ivy League class-

rooms, he likes to ask how many of the men own guns (not a gun but guns), and finds invariably that a third or more do own guns—to the surprise and consternation of their classmates. They acquired them in a sequence of .22 rifle, shotgun, and deer rifle at roughly the ages of twelve, fourteen, and sixteen, just as if in a rite of passage. Kahn's point is that gun control, which the upper-middle class assumes is so simple (after all, if it doesn't bother *me* to be unable to buy or own a gun without difficulty or embarrassment, why should it bother *you*), is up against deeply ingrained beliefs and experiences, to say nothing of numbers. See "Misunderstanding America: An Interview with Herman Kahn," *The Washington Post,* 1 July 1973, Outlook Section.

4. Clifford Geertz, "Deep Play: Notes on the Balinese Cockfight," *Daedalus* 101 (1972): 1–37; Page Smith and Charles Daniel, *The Chicken Book* (Boston: Little, Brown, 1975)—I assume the historical chapters are by Smith rather than his biologist collaborator; Harry Crews, "Cockfighting: An Unfashionable View," *Esquire,* April 1977: 8–14; Charles Willeford, *Cockfighter* (New York: Crown, 1972); Peter S. Beagle, "Cockfight," *Saturday Evening Post,* 24 August 1968: 28–31; Harold Herzog and Pauline B. Cheek, "Grit and Steel: The Anatomy of Cockfighting," *Southern Exposure* 7.2 (1979): 36–40; Courtenay Beinhorn, "Death in the Cockpit," *Crawdaddy,* March 1978: 38–40; Richard Rhodes, "Death All Day in Kansas," *Esquire,* November 1969: 148, 189–198; René Graziani, "Sir Thomas Wyatt at a Cockfight, 1539," *The Review of English Studies* 27.107 (1976): 299–303; Charles H. McCaghy and Arthur G. Neal, "The Fraternity of Cockfighters: Ethical Embellishments of an Illegal Sport," *Journal of Popular Culture* 8.3 (1974): 557–569; Gerald E. Parsons, "Cockfighting: A Potential Field for Research," *New York Folklore Quarterly* 25.4 (1969): 265–288; Steven L. Del Sesto, "Roles, Rules, and Organization: A Descriptive Account of Cockfighting in Rural Louisiana," *Southern Folklore Quarterly* 39.1 (1975): 1–14; Charles R. Gunter, Jr., "Cockfighting in East Tennessee and Western North Carolina," *Tennessee Folklore Society Bulletin* 44.4 (1978): 160–169; William Faulkner Rushton, *The Cajuns* (New York: Farrar Straus Giroux, 1979); and "LeRoy Neiman Sketchbook: Cockfighting in the Philippines," *Playboy,* June 1980: 186–187.

5. Smith and Daniel, p. 51. The double meaning evidently does not apply in the Semitic languages, although in Hebrew the word "cock" is occasionally applied to a young man. The English usage is nicely illustrated by Long John Silver's words with Jim in Stevenson's *Treasure Island:* "I've always liked you, I have, for a lad of spirit, and the picter of my own self when I was young and handsome. I always wanted you to jine and take your share, and die a gentleman, and now, my cock, you've got to" (New York: Holt, Rinehart and Winston, 1957), p. 212.

6. Quoted in Smith and Daniel, pp. 120–121.

7. Crews, p. 8; emphasis his.

8. Smith and Daniel, p. 115. A recent article, commenting on the difference between northern bred cocks for "short heel" (short spur) fighting and southern "long heel" cocks, suggests nothing less than differences between the Union and Confederacy in the fighting of the War between the States: "The Southern Speed cocks were bred to fight fast, shuffle long and hard, fly high and were deadly cutters. . . . [Northern cocks] are tougher, gamer, hit harder, and have much more endurance than [Southern

cocks]. However, they lack the fighting, smartness, and cutting ability of our southern speed strains as well as speed and shuffling ability." See Edward Bentley, "One Strawshaker to Another," *Grit and Steel*, July 1980: 28.

9. Smith and Daniel, p. 55.

10. Smith and Daniel, p. 62.

11. "Profiles of the American Cocker," a five-part series in *Grit and Steel*, October 1974: 27–28; November 1974: 32–32a; January 1975: 27–29; February 1975: 33d–33f; April 1975: 27–30. The noted item is from November 1974, p. 33.

12. *Grit and Steel*, November 1974: 32–33.

13. Crews, p. 8.

14. Crews, p. 8.

15. *Grit and Steel*, October 1974: 27.

16. *Grit and Steel*, November 1974: 32a.

17. Crews, p. 10.

18. Atyeo, p. 104.

19. Quoted in Smith and Daniel, p. 123.

20. Crews, p. 14.

21. *Grit and Steel*, January 1975: 27; April 1975: 28.

22. Atyeo, p. 104.

23. Smith and Daniel, p. 282, quoting Christian Adams, "Frank Perdue is Chicken," *Esquire*, April 1973.

24. Peter Singer, *Animal Liberation* (New York: Avon, 1977).

25. Smith and Daniel, pp. 122–123.

26. Smith and Daniel, p. 124.

CLIFFORD GEERTZ

Deep Play: Notes on the Balinese Cockfight

It is this essay by one of the world's leading anthropologists which, more than anything ever written on the cockfight, has brought this subject to the attention of intellectuals in many academic disciplines. Based upon fieldwork carried out in 1958, this essay by Clifford Geertz of the Institute for Advanced Study at Princeton was first presented at a conference in Paris in October of 1970. Published in 1972, Geertz's "Balinese Cockfight" is not only required reading for both undergraduates and graduate students in anthropology, but for students in a wide variety of fields, including folklore. The combination of engaging language plus a noteworthy attempt to practice what Geertz himself terms "interpretive anthropology" have made this paper a modern-day classic. All contemporary research on the cockfight and analogous cultural phenomena must begin with Geertz's pioneering analysis of the Balinese data.

Geertz is less interested in the cockfight per se than the cockfight as a metaphor providing ready access to the subtleties and nuances of Balinese culture. From his perspective, the cockfight "and especially the deep cockfight, is fundamentally a dramatization of status concerns." He prefers to "treat the cockfight as a text," rather than treating it as a rite or pastime. As a text, it can be read or interpreted. Indeed, the very function of the cockfight, according to Geertz, is interpretive. "It is a Balinese reading of Balinese experience; a story they tell themselves about themselves."

Not everyone agrees with Geertz as to what precisely the story is that the Balinese are telling about themselves in the cockfight. See, for example, William Roseberry, "Balinese Cockfights and the Seduction of Anthropology," Social Research *49 (1982): 1013–1028; Vincent Crapanzano, "Hermes' Dilemma: The Masking of Subversion in Ethnographic Description," in J. Clifford and G. E. Marcus, eds.* Writing Culture *(Berkeley: University of California Press, 1986), pp. 51–76; and David Jacobson,* Reading Ethnography *(Albany: State University of New York Press, 1991), pp. 49–54.*

For more of Geertz's stimulating discussions about the nature of anthropological research, see his The Interpretation of Cultures *(New York: Basic Books, 1973);* Local Knowledge: Further Essays in Interpretive Anthropology *(New York: Basic Books, 1983); and* Works and Lives: The Anthropologist as Author *(Stanford: Stanford University Press, 1988). For earlier discussions of the Balinese cock-*

Reprinted by permission of *Daedalus: Journal of the American Academy of Arts and Sciences,* from the issue entitled "Myth, Symbol, and Culture," (Winter 1972, vol. 101, no. 1), pp. 1–37.

fight, see R. Van Eck, "Schetsen uit het Volksleven in Nederlandsche Oost-Indië (I. Het Hanengevecht)," De Indische Gids *1 (1879): 102–118; and F. C. E. Knight, "Cockfighting in Bali,"* Discovery *2d series, 3.23 (1940): 77–81.*

The Raid

Early in April of 1958, my wife and I arrived, malarial and diffident, in a Balinese village we intended, as anthropologists, to study. A small place, about five hundred people, and relatively remote, it was its own world. We were intruders, professional ones, and the villagers dealt with us as Balinese seem always to deal with people not part of their life who yet press themselves upon them: as though we were not there. For them, and to a degree for ourselves, we were nonpersons, specters, invisible men.

We moved into an extended family compound (that had been arranged before through the provincial government) belonging to one of the four major factions in village life. But except for our landlord and the village chief, whose cousin and brother-in-law he was, everyone ignored us in a way only a Balinese can do. As we wandered around, uncertain, wistful, eager to please, people seemed to look right through us with a gaze focused several yards behind us on some actual stone or tree. Almost nobody greeted us; but nobody scowled or said anything unpleasant to us either, which would have been almost as satisfactory. If we ventured to approach someone (something one is powerfully inhibited from doing in such an atmosphere), he moved, negligently but definitively, away. If, seated or leaning against a wall, we had him trapped, he said nothing at all, or mumbled what for the Balinese is the ultimate nonword—"yes." The indifference, of course, was studied; the villagers were watching every move we made and they had an enormous amount of quite accurate information about who we were and what we were going to be doing. But they acted as if we simply did not exist, which, in fact, as this behavior was designed to inform us, we did not, or anyway not yet.

This is, as I say, general in Bali. Everywhere else I have been in Indonesia, and more latterly in Morocco, when I have gone into a new village people have poured out from all sides to take a very close look at me, and, often, an all-too-probing feel as well. In Balinese villages, at least those away from the tourist circuit, nothing happens at all. People go on pounding, chatting, making offerings, staring into space, carrying baskets about while one drifts around feeling vaguely disembodied. And the same thing is true on the individual level. When you first meet a Balinese, he seems virtually not to relate to you at all; he is, in the term Gregory Bateson and Margaret Mead made famous, "away."[1]

Then—in a day, a week, a month (with some people the magic moment never comes)—he decides, for reasons I have never been quite able to fathom, that you *are* real, and then he becomes a warm, gay, sensitive, sympathetic, though, being Balinese, always precisely controlled person. You have crossed, somehow, some moral or metaphysical shadow line. Though you are not exactly taken as Balinese (one has to be born to that), you are at least regarded as a human being rather than a cloud or a gust of wind. The whole complexion of your relationship dramatically changes to, in the majority of cases, a gentle, almost affectionate one—a low-keyed, rather playful, rather mannered, rather bemused geniality.

My wife and I were still very much in the gust of wind stage, a most frustrating, and even, as you soon begin to doubt whether you are really real after all, unnerving one, when, ten days or so after our arrival, a large cockfight was held in the public square to raise money for a new school.

Now, a few special occasions aside, cockfights are illegal in Bali under the Republic (as, for not altogether unrelated reasons, they were under the Dutch), largely as a result of the pretensions to puritanism radical nationalism tends to bring with it. The elite, which is not itself so very puritan, worries about the poor, ignorant peasant gambling all his money away, about what foreigners will think, about the waste of time better devoted to building up the country. It sees cockfighting as "primitive," "backward," "unprogressive," and generally unbecoming an ambitious nation. And, as with those other embarrassments—opium smoking, begging, or uncovered breasts—it seeks, rather unsystematically, to put a stop to it.

Of course, like drinking during prohibition or, today, smoking marihuana, cockfights, being a part of "The Balinese Way of Life," nonetheless go on happening, and with extraordinary frequency. And, like prohibition or marihuana, from time to time the police (who, in 1958 at least, were almost all not Balinese but Javanese) feel called upon to make a raid, confiscate the cocks and spurs, fine a few people, and even now and then expose some of them in the tropical sun for a day as object lessons which never, somehow, get learned, even though occasionally, quite occasionally, the object dies.

As a result, the fights are usually held in a secluded corner of a village in semisecrecy, a fact which tends to slow the action a little—not very much, but the Balinese do not care to have it slowed at all. In this case, however, perhaps because they were raising money for a school that the government was unable to give them, perhaps because raids had been few recently, perhaps, as I gathered from subsequent discussion, there was a notion that the necessary bribes had been paid, they thought they could take a chance on the central square and draw a larger and more enthusiastic crowd without attracting the attention of the law.

They were wrong. In the midst of the third match, with hundreds of people, including, still transparent, myself and my wife, fused into a single body around the ring, a superorganism in the literal sense, a truck full of policemen armed with machine guns roared up. Amid great screeching cries of "pulisi! pulisi!" from the crowd, the policemen jumped out, and, springing into the center of the ring, began to swing their guns around like gangsters in a motion picture, though not going so far as actually to fire them. The superorganism came instantly apart as its components scattered in all directions. People raced down the road, disappeared head first over walls, scrambled under platforms, folded themselves behind wicker screens, scuttled up coconut trees. Cocks armed with steel spurs sharp enough to cut off a finger or run a hole through a foot were running wildly around. Everything was dust and panic.

On the established anthropological principle, When in Rome, my wife and I decided, only slightly less instantaneously than everyone else, that the thing to do was run too. We ran down the main village street, northward, away from where we were living, for we were on that side of the ring. About half-way down another fugitive ducked suddenly into a compound—his own, it turned out—and we, seeing nothing ahead of us but rice fields, open country, and a very high volcano, followed him. As the three of us came tumbling into the courtyard, his wife, who had apparently been through this sort of thing before, whipped out a table, a tablecloth, three chairs, and three cups of tea, and we all, without any explicit communication whatsoever, sat down, commenced to sip tea, and sought to compose ourselves.

A few moments later, one of the policemen marched importantly into the yard, looking for the village chief. (The chief had not only been at the fight, he had arranged it. When the truck drove up he ran to the river, stripped off his sarong, and plunged in so he could say, when at length they found him sitting there pouring water over his head, that he had been away bathing when the whole affair had occurred and was ignorant of it. They did not believe him and fined him three hundred rupiah, which the village raised collectively.) Seeing my wife and me, "White Men," there in the yard, the policeman performed a classic double take. When he found his voice again he asked, approximately, what in the devil did we think we were doing there. Our host of five minutes leaped instantly to our defense, producing an impassioned description of who and what we were, so detailed and so accurate that it was my turn, having barely communicated with a living human save my landlord and the village chief for more than a week, to be astonished. We had a perfect right to be there, he said, looking the Javanese upstart in the eye. We were American professors; the government had cleared us; we were there to study culture; we were going to write a book to tell Americans about Bali. And we had all been there drinking tea and talking about cultural matters all afternoon and did not know anything about any cockfight. Moreover, we had not seen the village chief all day, he must have gone to town. The policeman retreated in rather total disarray. And, after a decent interval, bewildered but relieved to have survived and stayed out of jail, so did we.

The next morning the village was a completely different world for us. Not only were we no longer invisible, we were suddenly the center of all attention, the object of a great outpouring of warmth, interest, and, most especially, amusement. Everyone in the village knew we had fled like everyone else. They asked us about it again and again (I must have told the story, small detail by small detail, fifty times by the end of the day), gently, affectionately, but quite insistently teasing us: "Why didn't you just stand there and tell the police who you were?" "Why didn't you just say you were only watching and not betting?" "Were you really afraid of those little guns?" As always, kinesthetically minded and, even when fleeing for their lives (or, as happened eight years later, surrendering them), the world's most poised people, they gleefully mimicked, also over and over again, our graceless style of running and what they claimed were our panic-stricken facial expressions. But above all, everyone was extremely pleased and even more surprised that we had not simply "pulled out our papers" (they knew about those too) and asserted our Distinguished Visitor status, but had instead demonstrated our solidarity with what were now our covillagers. (What we had actually demonstrated was our cowardice, but there is fellowship in that too.) Even the Brahmana priest, an old, grave, half-way-to-Heaven type who because of its associations with the underworld would never be involved, even distantly, in a cockfight, and was difficult to approach even to other Balinese, had us called into his courtyard to ask us about what had happened, chuckling happily at the sheer extraordinariness of it all.

In Bali, to be teased is to be accepted. It was the turning point so far as our relationship to the community was concerned, and we were quite literally "in." The whole village opened up to us, probably more than it ever would have otherwise (I might actually never have gotten to that priest, and our accidental host became one of my best informants), and certainly very much faster. Getting caught, or almost caught, in a vice raid is perhaps not a very generalizable recipe for achieving that mysterious necessity of anthropological field work, rapport, but for me it worked very well. It led to a sudden and unusually complete acceptance into a society extremely difficult for outsiders to penetrate. It gave me the kind of immediate, inside-view grasp of an aspect of "peasant mentality" that anthropologists not fortunate enough to flee headlong with their subjects from armed authorities normally do not get. And, perhaps most important of all, for the other things might have come in other ways, it put me very quickly on to a combination emotional explosion, status war, and philosophical drama of central significance to the society whose inner nature I desired to understand. By the time I left I had spent about as much time looking into cockfights as into witchcraft, irrigation, caste, or marriage.

Of Cocks and Men

Bali, mainly because it is Bali, is a well-studied place. Its mythology, art, ritual, social organization, patterns of child rearing, forms of law, even styles of trance, have all been microscopically examined for traces of that elusive substance Jane Belo called "The Balinese Temper."[2] But, aside from a few passing remarks, the cockfight has barely been noticed, although as a popular obsession of consuming power it is at least as important a revelation of what being a Balinese "is really like" as these more celebrated phenomena.[3] As much of America surfaces in a ball park, on a golf links, at a race track, or around a poker table, much of Bali surfaces in a cock ring. For it is only apparently cocks that are fighting there. Actually, it is men.

To anyone who has been in Bali any length of time, the deep psychological identification of Balinese men with their cocks is unmistakable. The double entendre here is deliberate. It works in exactly the same way in Balinese as it does in English, even to producing the same tired jokes, strained puns, and uninventive obscenities. Bateson and Mead have even suggested that, in line with the Balinese conception of the body as a set of separately animated parts, cocks are viewed as detachable, self-operating penises, ambulant genitals with a life of their own.[4] And while I do not have the kind of unconscious material either to confirm or disconfirm this intriguing notion, the fact that they are masculine symbols *par excellence* is about as indubitable, and to the Balinese about as evident, as the fact that water runs downhill.

The language of everyday moralism is shot through, on the male side of it, with roosterish imagery. *Sabung,* the word for cock (and one which appears in inscriptions as early as A.D 922), is used metaphorically to mean "hero," "warrior," "champion," "man of parts," "political candidate," "bachelor," "dandy," "lady-killer," or "tough guy." A pompous man whose behavior presumes above his station is compared to a tailless cock who struts about as though he had a large, spectacular one. A desperate man who makes a last, irrational effort to extricate himself from an impossible situation is likened to a dying cock who makes one final lunge at his tormentor to drag him along to a common destruction. A stingy man, who promises much, gives little, and begrudges that is compared to a cock which, held by the tail, leaps at another without in fact engaging him. A marriageable young man still shy with the opposite sex or someone in a new job anxious to make a good impression is called "a fighting cock caged for the first time."[5] Court trials, wars, political contests, inheritance disputes, and street arguments are all compared to cock-fights.[6] Even the very island itself is perceived from its shape as a small, proud cock, poised, neck extended, back taut, tail raised, in eternal challenge to large, feckless, shapeless Java.[7]

But the intimacy of men with their cocks is more than metaphorical. Balinese men, or anyway a large majority of Balinese men, spend an enormous amount of time with their favorites, grooming them, feeding them, discussing them, trying them out against one another, or just gazing at them with a mixture of rapt admiration and dreamy self-absorption. Whenever you see a group of Balinese men squatting idly in the council shed or along the road in their hips down, shoulders forward, knees up fashion, half or more of them will have a rooster in his hands, holding it between his thighs, bouncing it gently up and down to strengthen its legs, ruffling its feathers with abstract sensuality, pushing it out against a neighbor's rooster to rouse its spirit, withdrawing it toward his loins to calm it again. Now and then, to get a feel for another bird, a man will fiddle this way with someone else's cock for a while, but usually by moving around to squat in place behind it, rather than just having it passed across to him as though it were merely an animal.

In the houseyard, the high-walled enclosures where the people live, fighting cocks are kept in wicker cages, moved frequently about so as to maintain the optimum balance of sun and shade. They are fed a special diet, which varies somewhat according to individual theories but which is mostly maize, sifted for impurities with far more care than it is when mere humans are going to eat it and offered to the animal kernel by kernel. Red pepper is stuffed down their beaks and up their anuses to give them spirit. They are bathed in the same ceremonial preparation of tepid water, medicinal herbs, flowers, and onions in which infants are bathed, and for a prize cock just about as often. Their combs are cropped, their plumage dressed, their spurs trimmed, their legs massaged, and they are inspected for flaws with the squinted concentration of a diamond merchant. A man who has a passion for cocks, an enthusiast in the literal sense of the term, can spend most of his life with them, and even those, the overwhelming majority, whose passion though intense has not entirely run away with them, can and do spend what seems not only to an outsider, but also to themselves, an inordinate amount of time with them. "I am cock crazy," my landlord, a quite ordinary *afficionado* by Balinese standards, used to moan as he went to move another cage, give another bath, or conduct another feeding. "We're all cock crazy."

The madness has some less visible dimensions, however, because although it is true that cocks are symbolic expressions or magnifications of their owner's self, the narcissistic male ego writ out in Aesopian terms, they are also expressions—and rather more immediate ones—of what the Balinese regard as the direct inversion, aesthetically, morally, and metaphysically, of human status: animality.

The Balinese revulsion against any behavior regarded as animal-like can hardly be overstressed. Babies are not allowed to crawl for that reason. Incest, though hardly approved, is a much less horrifying crime than bestiality. (The appropriate punishment for the second is death by drowning, for the first being forced to live like an animal.)[8] Most demons are represented—in sculpture, dance, ritual, myth—in some real or fantastic animal form. The main puberty rite consists in filing the child's teeth so they will not look like animal fangs. Not only defecation but eating is regarded as a disgusting, almost obscene activity, to be conducted hurriedly and privately, because of its association with animality. Even falling down or any form of clumsiness is considered to be bad for these reasons. Aside from cocks and a few domestic animals— oxen, ducks—of no emotional significance, the Balinese are aversive to animals and treat their large number of dogs not merely callously but with a phobic cruelty. In identifying with his cock, the Balinese man is identifying not just with his ideal self, or even his penis, but also, and at the same time, with what he most fears, hates, and ambivalence being what it is, is fascinated by— The Powers of Darkness.

The connection of cocks and cockfighting with such Powers, with the animalistic demons that threaten constantly to invade the small, cleared off space in which the Balinese have so carefully built their lives and devour its inhabitants, is quite explicit. A cockfight, any cockfight, is in the first instance a blood sacrifice offered, with the appropriate chants and oblations, to the demons in order to pacify their ravenous, cannibal hunger. No temple festival should be conducted until one is made. (If it is omitted someone will inevitably fall into a trance and command with the voice of an angered spirit that the oversight be immediately corrected.) Collective responses to natural evils—illness, crop failure, volcanic eruptions—almost always involve them. And that famous holiday in Bali, The Day of Silence (*Njepi*), when everyone sits silent and immobile all day long in order to avoid contact with a sudden influx of demons chased momentarily out of hell, is preceded the previous day by large-scale cockfights (in this case legal) in almost every village on the island.

In the cockfight, man and beast, good and evil, ego and id, the creative power of aroused masculinity and the destructive power of loosened animality fuse in a bloody drama of hatred, cruelty, violence, and death. It is little wonder that when, as is the invariable rule, the owner of the winning cock takes the carcass of the loser—often torn limb from limb by its enraged owner—home to eat, he does so with a mixture of social embarrassment, moral satisfaction, aesthetic disgust, and cannibal joy. Or that a man who has lost an important fight is sometimes driven to wreck his family shrines and curse the gods, an act of metaphysical (and social) suicide. Or that in seeking earthly analogues for heaven and hell the Balinese compare the former to the mood of a man whose cock has just won, the latter to that of a man whose cock has just lost.

The Fight

Cockfights (*tetadjen; sabungan*) are held in a ring about fifty feet square. Usually they begin toward late afternoon and run three or four hours until sunset. About nine or ten separate matches (*sehet*) comprise a program. Each match is precisely like the others in general pattern: there is no main match, no connection between individual matches, no variation in their format, and each is arranged on a completely ad hoc basis. After a fight has ended and the emotional debris is cleaned away—the bets paid, the curses cursed, the carcasses possessed—seven, eight, perhaps even a dozen men slip negligently into the ring with a cock and seek to find there a logical opponent for it. This process, which rarely takes less than ten minutes, and often a good deal longer, is conducted in a very subdued, oblique, even dissembling manner. Those not immediately involved give it at best but disguised, sidelong attention; those who, embarrassedly, are, attempt to pretend somehow that the whole thing is not really happening.

A match made, the other hopefuls retire with the same deliberate indifference, and the selected cocks have their spurs (*tadji*) affixed—razor sharp, pointed steel swords, four or five inches long. This is a delicate job which only a small proportion of men, a half-dozen or so in most villages, know how to do properly. The man who attaches the spurs also provides them, and if the rooster he assists wins its owner awards him the spur-leg of the victim. The spurs are affixed by winding a long length of string around the foot of the spur and the leg of the cock. For reasons I shall come to presently, it is done somewhat differently from case to case, and is an obsessively deliberate affair. The lore about spurs is extensive—they are sharpened only at eclipses and the dark of the moon, should be kept out of the sight of women, and so forth. And they are handled, both in use and out, with the same curious combination of fussiness and sensuality the Balinese direct toward ritual objects generally.

The spurs affixed, the two cocks are placed by their handlers (who may or may not be their owners) facing one another in the center of the ring.[9] A coconut pierced with a small hole is placed in a pail of water, in which it takes about twenty-one seconds to sink, a period known as a *tjeng* and marked at beginning and end by the beating of a slit gong. During these twenty-one seconds the handlers (*pengangkeb*) are not permitted to touch their roosters. If, as sometimes happens, the animals have not fought during this time, they are picked up, fluffed, pulled, prodded, and otherwise insulted, and put back in the center of the ring and the process begins again. Sometimes they refuse to fight at all, or one keeps running away, in which case they are imprisoned together under a wicker cage, which usually gets them engaged.

Most of the time, in any case, the cocks fly almost immediately at one another in a wing-beating, head-thrusting, leg-kicking explosion of animal fury so pure, so absolute, and in its own way so beautiful, as to be almost abstract, a Platonic concept of hate. Within moments one or the other drives home a solid blow with his spur. The handler whose cock has delivered the blow immediately picks it up so that it will not get a return blow, for if he does not the match is likely to end in a mutually mortal tie as the two birds wildly hack each other to pieces. This is particularly true if, as often happens, the spur sticks in its victim's body, for then the aggressor is at the mercy of his wounded foe.

With the birds again in the hands of their handlers, the coconut is now sunk three times after which the cock which has landed the blow must be set down to show that he is firm, a fact he demonstrates by wandering idly around the rink for a coconut sink. The coconut is then sunk twice more and the fight must recommence.

During this interval, slightly over two minutes, the handler of the wounded cock has been working frantically over it, like a trainer patching a mauled boxer between rounds, to get it in shape for a last, desperate try for victory. He blows in its mouth, putting the whole chicken head in his own mouth and sucking and blowing, fluffs it, stuffs its wounds with various sorts of medicines, and generally tries anything he can think of to arouse the last ounce of spirit which may be hidden somewhere within it. By the time he is forced to put it back down he is usually drenched in chicken blood, but, as in prize fighting, a good handler is worth his weight in gold. Some of them can virtually make the dead walk, at least long enough for the second and final round.

In the climactic battle (if there is one; sometimes the wounded cock simply expires in the handler's hands or immediately as it is placed down again), the cock who landed the first blow usually proceeds to finish off his weakened opponent. But this is far from an inevitable outcome, for if a cock can walk he can fight, and if he can fight, he can kill, and what counts is which cock expires first. If the wounded one can get a stab in and stagger on until the other drops, he is the official winner, even if he himself topples over an instant later.

Surrounding all this melodrama—which the crowd packed tight around the ring follows in near silence, moving their bodies in kinesthetic sympathy with the movement of the animals, cheering their champions on with wordless hand motions, shiftings of the shoulders, turnings of the head, falling back *en masse* as the cock with the murderous spurs careens toward one side of the ring (it is said that spectators sometimes lose eyes and fingers from being too attentive), surging forward again as they glance off toward another—is a vast body of extraordinarily elaborate and precisely detailed rules.

These rules, together with the developed lore of cocks and cockfighting which accompanies them, are written down in palm leaf manuscripts (*lontar; rontal*) passed on from generation to generation as part of the general legal and cultural tradition of the villages. At a fight, the umpire (*saja komong; djuru kembar*)—the man who manages the coconut—is in charge of their application and his authority is absolute. I have never seen an umpire's judgment questioned on any subject, even by the more despondent losers, nor have I ever heard, even in private, a charge of unfairness directed against one, or, for that matter, complaints about umpires in general. Only exceptionally well-trusted, solid, and, given the complexity of the code, knowledgeable citizens perform this job, and in fact men will bring their cocks only to fights presided over by such men. It is also the umpire to whom accusations of cheating, which, though rare in the extreme, occasionally arise, are referred; and it is he who in the not infrequent cases where the cocks expire virtually together decides which (if either, for, though the Balinese do not care for such an outcome, there can be ties) went first. Likened to a judge, a king, a priest, and a policeman, he is all of these, and under his assured direction the animal passion of the fight proceeds within the civic certainty of the law. In the dozens of cockfights I saw in Bali, I never once saw an altercation about rules. Indeed, I never saw an open altercation, other than those between cocks, at all.

This crosswise doubleness of an event which, taken as a fact of nature, is rage untrammeled and, taken as a fact of culture, is form perfected, defines the cockfight as a sociological entity. A cockfight is what, searching for a name for something not vertebrate enough to be called a group and not structureless enough to be called a crowd, Erving Goffman has called "focused gathering"—a set of persons engrossed in a common flow of activity and relating to one another in terms of that flow.[10] Such gatherings meet and disperse; the participants in them fluctuate; the activity that focuses them is discreet—a particulate process that reoccurs rather than a continuous one that endures. They take their form from the situation that evokes them, the floor on which they are placed, as Goffman puts it; but it is a form, and an articulate one, nonetheless. For the situation, the floor is itself created, in jury deliberations, surgical operations, block meetings, sit-ins, cockfights, by the cultural preoccupations—here, as we shall see, the celebration of status rivalry— which not only specify the focus but, assembling actors and arranging scenery, bring it actually into being.

In classical times (that is to say, prior to the Dutch invasion of 1908), when there were no bureaucrats around to improve popular morality, the staging of a cockfight was an explicitly societal matter. Bringing a cock to an important fight was, for an adult male, a compulsory duty of citizenship; taxation of fights, which were usually held on market day, was a major source of public revenue; patronage of the art was a stated responsibility of princes; and the cock ring, or *wantilan*, stood in the center of the village near those other monuments of Balinese civility—the council house, the origin temple, the marketplace, the signal tower, and the banyan tree. Today, a few special occasions aside, the newer rectitude makes so open a statement of the connection between the excitements of collective life and those of blood sport impossible, but, less directly expressed, the connection itself remains inanimate and intact. To expose it, however, it is necessary to turn to the aspect of cockfighting around which all the others pivot, and through which they exercise their force, an aspect I have thus far studiously ignored. I mean, of course, the gambling.

Odds and Even Money

The Balinese never do anything in a simple way that they can contrive to do in a complicated one, and to this generalization cockfight wagering is no exception.

In the first place, there are two sorts of bets, or *toh*.[11] There is the single axial bet in the center between the principals (*toh ketengah*), and there is the cloud of peripheral ones around the ring between members of the audience (*toh kesasi*). The first is typically large; the second typically small. The first is collective, involving coalitions of bettors clustering around the owner; the second is individual, man to man. The first is a matter of deliberate, very quiet, almost furtive arrangement by the coalition members and the umpire huddled like conspirators in the center of the ring; the second is a matter of impulsive shouting, public offers, and public acceptances by the excited throng around its edges. And most curiously, and as we shall see most revealingly, *where the first is always, without exception, even money, the second, equally without exception, is never such.* What is fair coin in the center is a biased one on the side.

The center bet is the official one, hedged in again with a webwork of rules, and is made between the two cock owners, with the umpire as overseer and public witness.[12] This bet, which, as I say, is always relatively and sometimes very large, is never raised simply by the owner in whose name it is made, but by him together with four or five, sometimes seven or eight, allies—kin, village mates, neighbors, close friends. He may, if he is not especially well-to-do, not even be the major contributor, though, if only to show that he is not involved in any chicanery, he must be a significant one.

Of the fifty-seven matches for which I have exact and reliable data on the center bet, the range is from fifteen ringgits to five hundred, with a mean at eighty-five and with the distribution being rather noticeably trimodal: small fights (15 ringgits either side of 35) accounting for about 45 per cent of the total number; medium ones (20 ringgits either side of 70) for about 25 per cent; and large (75 ringgits either side of 175) for about 20 per cent, with a few very small and very large ones out at the extremes. In a society where the normal daily wage of a manual laborer—a brickmaker, an ordinary farmworker, a market porter—was about three ringgits a day, and considering the fact that fights were held on the average about every two-and-a-half days in the immediate area I studied, this is clearly serious gambling, even if the bets are pooled rather than individual efforts.

The side bets are, however, something else altogether. Rather than the solemn, legalistic pactmaking of the center, wagering takes place rather in the fashion in which the stock exchange used to work when it was out on the curb. There is a fixed and known odds paradigm which runs in a continuous series from ten-to-nine at the short end and two-to-one at the long: 10–9, 9–8, 8–7, 7–6, 6–5, 5–4, 4–3, 3–2, 2–1. The man who wishes to back the *underdog cock* (leaving aside how favorites, *kebut*, and underdogs, *ngai*, are established for the moment) shouts the short-side number indicating the odds he wants *to be given*. That is, if he shouts *gasal*, "five," he wants the underdog at five-to-four (or, for him, four-to-five); if he shouts "four," he wants it at four-to-three (again he putting up the "three"), if "nine," at nine-to-eight, and so on. A man backing the favorite, and thus considering giving odds if he can get them short enough, indicates the fact by crying out the color-type of that cock—"brown," "speckled," or whatever.[13]

As odds-takers (backers of the underdog) and odds-givers (backers of the favorite) sweep through the crowd with their shouts, they begin to focus in on one another as potential betting pairs, often from far across the ring. The taker tries to shout the giver into longer odds, the giver to shout the taker into shorter ones.[14] The taker, who is the wooer in this situation, will signal how large a bet he wishes to make at the odds he is shouting by holding a number of fingers up in front of his face and vigorously waving them. If the giver, the wooed, replies in kind, the bet is made; if he does not, they unlock gazes and the search goes on.

The side betting, which takes place after the center bet has been made and its size announced, consists then in a rising crescendo of shouts as backers of the underdog offer their propositions to anyone who will accept them, while those who are backing the favorite but do not like the price being offered, shout equally frenetically the color of the cock to show they too are desperate to bet but want shorter odds.

Almost always odds-calling, which tends to be very consensual in that at any one time almost all callers are calling the same thing, starts off toward the long end of the range—five-to-four or four-to-three—and then moves, also consensually, toward the short end with greater or lesser speed and to a greater or lesser degree. Men crying "five" and finding themselves answered only with cries of "brown" start crying "six," either drawing the other callers fairly quickly with them or retiring from the scene as their too-generous offers are snapped up. If the change is made and partners are still scarce, the procedure is repeated in a move to "seven," and so on, only rarely, and in the very largest fights, reaching the ultimate "nine" or "ten" levels. Occasionally, if the cocks are clearly mismatched, there may be no upward movement at all, or even a movement down the scale to four-to-three, three-to-two, very, very rarely two-to-one, a shift which is accompanied by a declining number of bets as a shift upward is accompanied by an increasing number. But the general pattern is for the betting to move a shorter or longer distance up the scale toward the, for sidebets, nonexistent pole of even money, with the overwhelming majority of bets falling in the four-to-three to eight-to-seven range.[15]

As the moment for the release of the cocks by the handlers approaches, the screaming, at least in a match where the center bet is large, reaches almost frenzied proportions as the remaining unfulfilled bettors try desperately to find a last minute partner at a price they can live with. (Where the center bet is small, the opposite tends to occur: betting dies off, trailing into silence, as odds lengthen and people lose interest.) In a large-bet, well-made match—the kind of match the Balinese regard as "real cockfighting"—the mob scene quality, the sense that sheer chaos is about to break loose, with all those waving, shouting, pushing, clambering men is quite strong, an effect which is only heightened by the intense stillness that falls with instant suddenness, rather as if someone had turned off the current, when the slit gong sounds, the cocks are put down, and the battle begins.

When it ends, anywhere from fifteen seconds to five minutes later, *all bets are immediately paid.* There are absolutely no IOU's, at least to a betting opponent. One may, of course, borrow from a friend before offering or accepting a wager, but to offer or accept it you must have the money already in hand and, if you lose, you must pay it on the spot, before the next match begins. This is an iron rule, and as I have never heard of a disputed umpire's decision (though doubtless there must sometimes be some), I have also never heard of a welshed bet, perhaps because in a worked-up cockfight crowd the consequences might be, as they are reported to be sometimes for cheaters, drastic and immediate.

It is, in any case, this formal assymetry between balanced center bets and unbalanced side ones that poses the critical analytical problem for a theory which sees cockfight wagering as the link connecting the fight to the wider world of Balinese culture. It also suggests the way to go about solving it and demonstrating the link.

The first point that needs to be made in this connection is that the higher the center bet, the more likely the match will in actual fact be an even one. Simple considerations of rationality suggest that. If you are betting fifteen ringgits on a cock, you might be willing to go along with even money even if you feel your animal somewhat the less promising. But if you are betting five hundred you are very, very likely to be loathe to do so. Thus, in large-bet fights, which of course involve the better animals, tremendous care is taken to see that the cocks are about as evenly matched as to size, general condition, pugnacity, and so on as is humanly possible. The different ways of adjusting the spurs of the animals are often employed to secure this. If one cock seems stronger, an agreement will be made to position his spur at a slightly less advantageous angle—a kind of handicapping, at which spur affixers are, so it is said, extremely skilled. More care will be taken, too, to employ skillful handlers and to match them exactly as to abilities.

In short, in a large-bet fight the pressure to make the match a genuinely fifty-fifty proposition is enormous, and is consciously felt as such. For medium fights the pressure is somewhat less, and for small ones less yet, though there is always an effort to make things at least approximately equal, for even at fifteen ringgits (five days work) no one wants to make an even money bet in a clearly unfavorable situation. And, again, what statistics I have tend to bear this out. In my fifty-seven matches, the favorite won thirty-three times overall, the underdog twenty-four, a 1.4 to 1 ratio. But if one splits the figures at sixty ringgits center bets, the ratios turn out to be 1.1 to 1 (twelve favorites, eleven underdogs) for those above this line, and 1.6 to 1 (twenty-one and thirteen) for those below it. Or, if you take the extremes, for very large fights, those with center bets over a hundred ringgits the ratio is 1 to 1 (seven and seven); for very small fights, those under forty ringgits, it is 1.9 to 1 (nineteen and ten).[16]

Now, from this proposition—that the higher the center bet the more exactly a fifty-fifty proposition the cockfight is—two things more or less immediately follow: (1) the higher the center bet, the greater is the pull on the side betting toward the short-odds end of the wagering spectrum and vice versa; (2) the higher the center bet, the greater the volume of side betting and vice versa.

The logic is similar in both cases. The closer the fight is in fact to even money, the less attractive the long ends of the odds will appear and, therefore, the shorter it must be if there are to be takers. That this is the case is apparent from mere inspection, from the Balinese's own analysis of the matter, and from what more systematic observations I was able to collect. Given the difficulty of making precise and complete recordings of side betting, this argument is hard to cast in numerical form, but in all my cases the odds-giver, odds-taker consensual point, a quite pronounced mini-max saddle where the bulk (at a guess, two-thirds to three-quarters in most cases) of the bets are actually made, was three or four points further along the scale toward the shorter end for the large-center-bet fights than for the small ones, with medium ones generally in between. In detail, the fit is not, of course, exact, but the general pattern is quite consistent: the power of the center bet to pull the side bets toward its own even-money pattern is directly proportional to its size, because its size is directly proportional to the degree to which the cocks are in fact evenly matched. As for the volume question, total wagering is greater in large-center-bet fights because such fights are considered more "interesting," not only in the sense that they are less predictable, but, more crucially, that more is at stake in them—in terms of money, in terms of the quality of the cocks, and consequently, as we shall see, in terms of social prestige.[17]

The paradox of fair coin in the middle, biased coin on the outside is thus a merely apparent one. The two betting systems, though formally incongruent, are not really contradictory to one another, but part of a single larger system in which the center bet is, so to speak, the "center of gravity," drawing, the larger it is the more so, the outside bets toward the short-odds end of the scale. The center bet thus "makes the game," or perhaps better, defines it, signals what, following a notion of Jeremy Bentham's, I am going to call its "depth."

The Balinese attempt to create an interesting, if you will, "deep," match by making the center bet as large as possible so that the cocks matched will be as equal and as fine as possible, and the outcome, thus, as unpredictable as possible. They do not always succeed. Nearly half the matches are relatively trivial, relatively uninteresting—in my borrowed terminology, "shallow"—affairs. But that fact no more argues against my interpretation than the fact that most painters, poets, and playwrights are mediocre argues against the view that artistic effort is directed toward profundity and, with a certain frequency, approximates it. The image of artistic technique is indeed exact: the center bet is a means, a device, for creating "interesting," "deep" matches, *not* the reason, or at least not the main reason, *why* they are interesting, the source of their fascination, the substance of their depth. The question why such matches are interesting—indeed, for the Balinese, exquisitely absorbing—takes us out of the realm of formal concerns into more broadly sociological and social-psychological ones, and to a less purely economic idea of what "depth" in gaming amounts to.[18]

Playing with Fire

Bentham's concept of "deep play" is found in his *The Theory of Legislation*.[19] By it he means play in which the stakes are so high that it is, from his utilitarian standpoint, irrational for men to engage in it at all. If a man whose fortune is a thousand pounds (or ringgits) wages five hundred of it on an even bet, the marginal utility of the pound he stands to win is clearly less than the marginal disutility of the one he stands to lose. In genuine deep play, this is the case for both parties. They are both in over their heads. Having come together in search of pleasure they have entered into a relationship which will bring the participants, considered collectively, net pain rather than net pleasure. Bentham's conclusion was, therefore, that deep play was immoral from first principles and, a typical step for him, should be prevented legally.

But more interesting than the ethical problem, at least for our concerns here, is that despite the logical force of Bentham's analysis men do engage in such play, both passionately and often, and even in the face of law's revenge. For Bentham and those who think as he does (nowdays mainly lawyers, economists, and a few psychiatrists), the explanation is, as I have said, that such men are irrational—addicts, fetishists, children, fools, savages, who need only to be protected against themselves. But for the Balinese, though naturally they do not formulate it in so many words, the explanation lies in the fact that in such play money is less a measure of utility, had or expected, than it is a symbol of moral import, perceived or imposed.

It is, in fact, in shallow games, ones in which smaller amounts of money are involved, that increments and decrements of cash are more nearly synonyms for utility and disutility, in the ordinary, unexpanded sense—for pleasure and pain, happiness and unhappiness. In deep ones, where the amounts of money are great, much more is at stake than material gain: namely, esteem, honor, dignity, respect—in a word, though in Bali a profoundly freighted word, status.[20] It is at stake symbolically, for (a few cases of ruined addict gamblers aside) no one's status is actually altered by the outcome of a cockfight; it is only, and that momentarily, affirmed or insulted. But for the Balinese, for whom nothing is more pleasurable than an affront obliquely delivered or more painful than one obliquely received—particularly when mutual acquaintances, undeceived by surfaces, are watching—such appraisive drama is deep indeed.

This, I must stress immediately, is *not* to say that the money does not matter, or that the Balinese is no more concerned about losing five hundred ringgits than fifteen. Such a conclusion would be absurd. It is because money *does*, in this hardly unmaterialistic society, matter and matter very much that the more of it one risks the more of a lot of other things, such as one's pride, one's poise, one's dispassion, one's masculinity, one also risks, again only momentarily but again very publicly as well. In deep cockfights an owner and his collaborators, and, as we shall see, to a lesser but still quite real extent also their backers on the outside, put their money where their status is.

It is in large part *because* the marginal disutility of loss is so great at the higher levels of betting that to engage in such betting is to lay one's public self, allusively and metaphorically, through the medium of one's cock, on the line. And though to a Benthamite this might seem merely to increase the irrationality of the enterprise that much further, to the Balinese what it mainly increases is the meaningfulness of it all. And as (to follow Weber rather than Bentham) the imposition of meaning on life is the major end and primary condition of human existence, that access of significance more than compensates for the economic costs involved.[21] Actually, given the even-money quality of the larger matches, important changes in material fortune among those who regularly participate in them seem virtually nonexistent, because matters more or less even out over the long run. It is, actually, in the smaller, shallow fights, where one finds the handful of more pure, addict-type gamblers involved—those who *are* in it mainly for the money—that "real" changes in social position, largely downward, are affected. Men of this sort, plungers, are highly dispraised by "true cockfighters" as fools who do not understand what the sport is all about, vulgarians who simply miss the point of it all. They are, these addicts, regarded as fair game for the genuine enthusiasts, those who do understand, to take a little money away from, something that is easy enough to do by luring them, through the force of their greed, into irrational bets on mismatched cocks. Most of them do indeed manage to ruin themselves in a remarkably short time, but there always seems to be one or two of them around, pawning their land and selling their clothes in order to bet, at any particular time.[22]

This graduated correlation of "status gambling" with deeper fights and, inversely, "money gambling" with shallower ones is in fact quite general. Bettors themselves form a sociomoral hierarchy in these terms. As noted earlier, at most cockfights there are, around the very edges of the cockfight area, a large number of mindless, sheer-chance type gambling games (roulette, dice throw, coin-spin, pea-under-the-shell) operated by concessionaires. Only women, children, adolescents, and various other sorts of people who do not (or not yet) fight cocks—the extremely poor, the socially despised, the personally idiosyncratic—play at these games, at, of course, penny ante levels. Cockfighting men would be ashamed to go anywhere near them. Slightly above these people in standing are those who, though they do not themselves fight cocks, bet on the smaller matches around the edges. Next, there are those who fight cocks in small, or occasionally medium matches, but have not the status to join in the large ones, though they may bet from time to time on the side in those. And finally, there are those, the really substantial members of the community, the solid citizenry around whom local life revolves, who fight in the larger fights and bet on them around the side. The focusing element in these focused gatherings, these men generally dominate and define the sport as they dominate and define the society. When a Balinese male talks, in that almost venerative way, about "the true cockfighter," the *bebatoh* ("bettor") or *djuru kurung* ("cage keeper"), it is this sort of person, not those who bring the mentality of the pea-and-shell game into the quite different, inappropriate context of the cockfight, the driven gambler (*potét*, a word which has the secondary meaning of thief or reprobate), and the wistful hanger-on, that they mean. For such a man, what is really going on in a match is something rather closer to an *affaire d'honneur* (though, with the Balinese talent for practical fantasy, the blood that is spilled is only figuratively human) than to the stupid, mechanical crank of a slot machine.

What makes Balinese cockfighting deep is thus not money in itself, but what, the more of it that is involved the more so, money causes to happen: the migration of the Balinese status hierarchy into the body of the cockfight. Psychologically an Aesopian representation of the ideal/demonic, rather narcissistic, male self, sociologically it is an equally Aesopian representation of the complex fields of tension set up by the controlled, muted, ceremonial, but for all that deeply felt, interaction of those selves in the context of everyday life. The cocks may be surrogates for their owners' personalities, animal mirrors of psychic form, but the cockfight is—or more exactly, deliberately is made to be—a simulation of the social matrix, the involved system of crosscutting, overlapping, highly corporate groups—villages, kingroups, irrigation societies, temple congregations, "castes"—in which its devotees live.[23] And as prestige, the necessity to affirm it, defend it, celebrate it, justify it, and just plain bask in it (but not, give the strongly ascriptive character of Balinese stratification, to seek it), is perhaps the central driving force in the society, so also— ambulant penises, blood sacrifices, and monetary exchanges aside—is it of the cockfight. This apparent amusement and seeming sport is, to take another phrase from Erving Goffman, "a status bloodbath."[24]

The easiest way to make this clear, and at least to some degree to demonstrate it, is to invoke the village whose cockfighting activities I observed the closest—the one in which the raid occurred and from which my statistical data are taken.

As all Balinese villages, this one—Tihingan, in the Klungkung region of southeast Bali—is intricately organized, a labyrinth of alliances and oppositions. But, unlike many, two sorts of corporate groups, which are also status groups, particularly stand out, and we may concentrate on them, in a part-for-whole way, without undue distortion.

First, the village is dominated by four large, patrilineal, partly endogamous descent groups which are constantly vying with one another and form the major factions in the village. Sometimes they group two and two, or rather the two larger ones versus the two smaller ones plus all the unaffiliated people; sometimes they operate independently. There are also subfactions within them, subfactions within the subfactions, and so on to rather fine levels of distinction. And second, there is the village itself, almost entirely endogamous, which is opposed to all the other villages round about in its cockfight circuit (which, as explained, is the market region), but which also forms alliances with certain of these neighbors against certain others in various supra-village political and social contexts. The exact situation is thus, as everywhere in Bali, quite distinctive; but the general pattern of a tiered hierarchy of status rivalries between highly corporate but various based groupings (and, thus, between the members of them) is entirely general.

Consider, then, as support of the general thesis that the cockfight, and especially the deep cockfight, is fundamentally a dramatization of status concerns, the following facts, which to avoid extended ethnographic description I will simply pronounce to be facts—though the concrete evidence-examples, statements, and numbers that could be brought to bear in support of them is both extensive and unmistakable:

1. A man virtually never bets against a cock owned by a member of his own kingroup. Usually he will feel obligated to bet for it, the more so the closer the kin tie and the deeper the fight. If he is certain in his mind that it will not win, he may just not bet at all, particularly if it is only a second cousin's bird or if the fight is a shallow one. But as a rule he will feel he must support it and, in deep games, nearly always does. Thus the great majority of the people calling "five" or "speckled" so demonstratively are expressing their allegiance to their kinsman, not their evaluation of his bird, their understanding of probability theory, or even their hopes of unearned income.

2. This principle is extended logically. If your kingroup is not involved you will support an allied kingroup against an unallied one in the same way, and so on through the very involved networks of alliances which, as I say, make up this, as any other, Balinese village.

3. So, too, for the village as a whole. If an outsider cock is fighting any cock from your village you will tend to support the local one. If, what is a rarer circumstance but occurs every now and then, a cock from outside your cockfight circuit is fighting one inside it you will also tend to support the "home bird."

4. Cocks which come from any distance are almost always favorites, for the theory is the man would not have dared to bring it if it was not a good cock, the more so the further he has come. His followers are, of course, obliged to support him, and when the more grand-scale legal cockfights are held (on holidays, and so on) the people of the village take what they regard to be the best cocks in the village, regardless of ownership, and go off to support them, although they will almost certainly have to give odds on them and to make large bets to show that they are not a cheapskate village.

Actually, such "away games," though infrequent, tend to mend the ruptures between village members that the constantly occurring "home games," where village factions are opposed rather than united, exacerbate.

5. Almost all matches are sociologically relevant. You seldom get two outsider cocks fighting, or two cocks with no particular group backing, or with group backing which is mutually unrelated in any clear way. When you do get them, the game is very shallow, betting very slow, and the whole thing very dull, with no one save the immediate principals and an addict gambler or two at all interested.

6. By the same token, you rarely get two cocks from the same group, even more rarely from the same subfaction, and virtually never from the same sub-subfaction (which would be in most cases one extended family) fighting. Similarly, in outside village fights two members of the village will rarely fight against one another, even though, as bitter rivals, they would do so with enthusiasm on their home grounds.

7. On the individual level, people involved in an institutionalized hostility relationship, called *puik*, in which they do not speak or otherwise have anything to do with each other (the causes of this formal breaking of relations are many: wife-capture, inheritance arguments, political differences) will bet very heavily, sometimes almost maniacally, against one another in what is a frank and direct attack on the very masculinity, the ultimate ground of his status, of the opponent.

8. The center bet coalition is, in all but the shallowest games, *always* made up by structural allies—no "outside money" is involved. What is "outside" depends upon the context, of course, but given it, no outside money is mixed in with the main bet; if the principals cannot raise it, it is not made. The center bet, again especially in deeper games, is thus the most direct and open expression of social opposition, which is one of the reasons why both it and match making are surrounded by such an air of unease, furtiveness, embarrassment, and so on.

9. The rule about borrowing money—that you may borrow *for* a bet but not *in* one—stems (and the Balinese are quite conscious of this) from similar considerations: you are never at the *economic* mercy of your enemy that way. Gambling debts, which can get quite large on a rather short-term basis, are always to friends, never to enemies, structurally speaking.

10. When two cocks are structurally irrelevant or neutral so far as *you* are concerned (though, as mentioned, they almost never are to each other) you do not even ask a relative or a friend whom he is betting on, because if you know how he is betting and he knows you know, and you go the other way, it will lead to strain. This rule is explicit and rigid; fairly elaborate, even rather artificial precautions are taken to avoid breaking it. At the very

least you must pretend not to notice what he is doing, and he what you are doing.

11. There is a special word for betting against the grain, which is also the word for "pardon me" (*mpura*). It is considered a bad thing to do, though if the center bet is small it is sometimes all right as long as you do not do it too often. But the larger the bet and the more frequently you do it, the more the "pardon me" tack will lead to social disruption.

12. In fact, the institutionalized hostility relation, *puik,* is often formally initiated (though its causes always lie elsewhere) by such a "pardon me" bet in a deep fight, putting the symbolic fat in the fire. Similarly, the end of such a relationship and resumption of normal social intercourse is often signalized (but, again, not actually brought about) by one or the other of the enemies supporting the other's bird.

13. In sticky, cross-loyalty situations, of which in this extraordinarily complex social system there are of course many, where a man is caught between two more or less equally balanced loyalties, he tends to wander off for a cup of coffee or something to avoid having to bet, a form of behavior reminiscent of that of American voters in similar situations.[25]

14. The people involved in the center bet are, especially in deep fights, virtually always leading members of their group—kinship, village, or whatever. Further, those who bet on the side (including these people) are, as I have already remarked, the more established members of the village—the solid citizens. Cockfighting is for those who are involved in the everyday politics of prestige as well, not for youth, women, subordinates, and so forth.

15. So far as money is concerned, the explicitly expressed attitude toward it is that it is a secondary matter. It is not, as I have said, of no importance; Balinese are no happier to lose several weeks' income than anyone else. But they mainly look on the monetary aspects of the cockfight as self-balancing, a matter of just moving money around, circulating it among a fairly well-defined group of serious cockfighters. The really important wins and losses are seen mostly in other terms, and the general attitude toward wagering is not any hope of cleaning up, of making a killing (addict gamblers again excepted), but that of the horseplayer's prayer: "Oh, God, please let me break even." In prestige terms, however, you do not want to break even, but, in a momentary, punctuate sort of way, win utterly. The talk (which goes on all the time) is about fights against such-and-such a cock of So-and-So which your cock demolished, not on how much you won, a fact people, even for large bets, rarely remember for any length of time, though they will remember the day they did in Pan Loh's finest cock for years.

16. You must bet on cocks of your own group aside from mere loyalty consider-

ations, for if you do not people generally will say, "What! Is he too proud for the likes of us? Does he have to go to Java or Den Pasar [the capital town] to bet, he is such an important man?" Thus there is a general pressure to bet not only to show that you are important locally, but that you are not so important that you look down on everyone else as unfit even to be rivals. Similarly, home team people must bet against outside cocks or the outsiders will accuse it—a serious charge—of just collecting entry fees and not really being interested in cockfighting, as well as again being arrogant and insulting.

17. Finally, the Balinese peasants themselves are quite aware of all this and can and, at least to an ethnographer, do state most of it in approximately the same terms as I have. Fighting cocks, almost every Balinese I have ever discussed the subject with has said, is like playing with fire only not getting burned. You activate village and kingroup rivalries and hostilities, but in "play" form, coming dangerously and entrancingly close to the expression of open and direct interpersonal and intergroup aggression (something which, again, almost never happens in the normal course of ordinary life), but not quite, because, after all, it is "only a cockfight."

More observations of this sort could be advanced, but perhaps the general point is, if not made, at least well-delineated, and the whole argument thus far can be usefully summarized in a formal paradigm:

THE MORE A MATCH IS . . .

1. between near status equals (and/or personal enemies),
2. between high status individuals

THE DEEPER THE MATCH.

THE DEEPER THE MATCH . . .

1. The closer the identification of cock and man (or: more properly, the deeper the match the more the man will advance his best, most closely-identified-with cock).
2. The finer the cocks involved and the more exactly they will be matched.
3. The greater the emotion that will be involved and the more the general absorption in the match.
4. The higher the individual bets center and outside, the shorter the outside bet odds will tend to be, and the more betting there will be over-all.
5. The less an "economic" and the more a "status" view of gaming will be involved, and the "solider" the citizens who will be gaming.[26]

Inverse arguments hold for the shallower the fight, culminating, in a reversed-signs sense, in the coin-spinning and dice-throwing amusements. For deep fights there are no absolute upper limits, though there are of course practical ones, and there are a great many legend-like tales of great Duel-in-the-Sun combats between lords and princes in classical times (for cockfighting has always been as much an elite concern as a popular one), far deeper than anything anyone, even aristocrats, could produce today anywhere in Bali.

Indeed, one of the great culture heroes of Bali is a prince, called after his passion for the sport, "The Cockfighter," who happened to be away at a very deep cockfight with a neighboring prince when the whole of his family—father, brothers, wives, sisters—were assassinated by commoner usurpers. Thus spared, he returned to dispatch the upstarts, regain the throne, reconstitute the Balinese high tradition, and build its most powerful, glorious, and prosperous state. Along with everything else that the Balinese see in fighting cocks—themselves, their social order, abstract hatred, masculinity, demonic power—they also see the archetype of status virtue, the arrogant, resolute, honor-mad player with real fire, the ksatria prince.[27]

Feathers, Blood, Crowds, and Money

"Poetry makes nothing happen," Auden says in his elegy of Yeats, "it survives in the valley of its saying . . . a way of happening, a mouth." The cockfight too, in this colloquial sense, makes nothing happen. Men go on allegorically humiliating one another and being allegorically humiliated by one another, day after day, glorying quietly in the experience if they have triumphed, crushed only slightly more openly by it if they have not. *But no one's status really changes.* You cannot ascend the status ladder by winning cockfights; you cannot, as an individual, really ascend it at all. Nor can you descend it that way.[28] All you can do is enjoy and savor, or suffer and withstand, the concocted sensation of drastic and momentary movement along an aesthetic semblance of that ladder, a kind of behind-the-mirror status jump which has the look of mobility without its actuality.

As any art form—for that, finally, is what we are dealing with—the cockfight renders ordinary, everyday experience comprehensible by presenting it in terms of acts and objects which have had their practical consequences removed and been reduced (or, if you prefer, raised) to the level of sheer appearances, where their meaning can be more powerfully articulated and more exactly perceived. The cockfight is "really real" only to the cocks—it does not kill anyone, castrate anyone, reduce anyone to animal status, alter the hierarchical relations among people, nor refashion the hierarchy; it does not even redistribute income in any significant way. What it does is what, for other peoples with other temperaments and other conventions, *Lear* and *Crime and Punishment* do; it catches up these themes—death, masculinity, rage, pride, loss, beneficence, chance—and, ordering them into an encompassing structure, presents them in such a way as to throw into relief a particular view of their essential nature. It puts a construction on them, makes them, to those historically positioned to appreciate the construction, meaningful—visible, tangible, graspable—"real," in an ideational sense. An image, fiction, a model, a metaphor, the cockfight is a means of expression; its function is neither to assuage social passions nor to heighten them (though, in its play-with-fire way, it does a bit of both), but, in a medium of feathers, blood, crowds, and money, to display them.

The question of how it is that we perceive qualities in things—paintings, books, melodies, plays—that we do not feel we can assert literally to be there has come, in recent years, into the very center of aesthetic theory.[29] Neither the sentiments of the artist, which remain his, nor those of the audience, which remain theirs, can account for the agitation of one painting or the serenity of another. We attribute grandeur, wit, despair, exuberance to strings of sounds; lightness, energy, violence, fluidity to blocks of stone. Novels are said to have strength, buildings eloquence, plays momentum, ballets repose. In this realm of eccentric predicates, to say that the cockfight, in its perfected cases at least, is "disquietful" does not seem at all unnatural, merely, as I have just denied it practical consequence, somewhat puzzling.

The disquietfulness arises, "somehow," out of a conjunction of three attributes of the fight: its immediate dramatic shape; its metaphoric content; and its social context. A cultural figure against a social ground, the fight is at once a convulsive surge of animal hatred, a mock war of symbolical selves, and a formal simulation of status tensions, and its aesthetic power derives from its capacity to force together these diverse realities. The reason it is disquietful is not that it has material effects (it has some, but they are minor); the reason that it is disquietful is that, joining pride to selfhood, selfhood to cocks, and cocks to destruction, it brings to imaginative realization a dimension of Balinese experience normally well-obscured from view. The transfer of a sense of gravity into what is in itself a rather blank and unvarious spectacle, a commotion of beating wings and throbbing legs, is effected by interpreting it as expressive of something unsettling in the way its authors and audience live, or, even more ominously, what they are.

As a dramatic shape, the fight displays a characteristic that does not seem so remarkable until one realizes that it does not have to be there: a radically atomistical structure.[30] Each match is a world unto itself, a particulate burst of form. There is the match making, there is the betting, there is the fight, there is

118

the result—utter triumph and utter defeat—and there is the hurried, embarrassed passing of money. The loser is not consoled. People drift away from him, look through him, leave him to assimilate his momentary descent into nonbeing, reset his face, and return, scarless and intact, to the fray. Nor are winners congratulated, or events rehashed; once a match is ended the crowd's attention turns totally to the next, with no looking back. A shadow of the experience no doubt remains with the principals, perhaps even with some of the witnesses, of a deep fight, as it remains with us when we leave the theater after seeing a powerful play well-performed; but it quite soon fades to become at most a schematic memory—a diffuse glow or an abstract shudder—and usually not even that. Any expressive form lives only in its own present—the one it itself creates. But, here, that present is severed into a string of flashes, some more bright than others, but all of them disconnected, aesthetic quanta. Whatever the cockfight says, it says in spurts.

But, as I have argued lengthily elsewhere, the Balinese live in spurts.[31] Their life, as they arrange it and perceive it, is less a flow, a directional movement out of the past, through the present, toward the future than an on-off pulsation of meaning and vacuity, an arhythmic alternation of short periods when "something" (that is, something significant) is happening and equally short ones where "nothing" (that is, nothing much) is—between what they themselves call "full" and "empty" times, or, in another idiom, "junctures" and "holes." In focusing activity down to a burning-glass dot, the cockfight is merely being Balinese in the same way in which everything from the monadic encounters of everyday life, through the clanging pointillism of *gamelan* music, to the visiting-day-of-the-gods temple celebrations are. It is not an imitation of the punctuateness of Balinese social life, nor a depiction of it, nor even an expression of it; it is an example of it, carefully prepared.[32]

If one dimension of the cockfight's structure, its lack of temporal directionality, makes it seem a typical segment of the general social life, however, the other, its flat-out, head-to-head (or spur-to-spur) aggressiveness, makes it seem a contradiction, a reversal, even a subversion of it. In the normal course of things, the Balinese are shy to the point of obsessiveness of open conflict. Oblique, cautious, subdued, controlled, masters of indirection and dissimulation—what they call *alus,* "polished," "smooth,"—they rarely face what they can turn away from, rarely resist what they can evade. But here they portray themselves as wild and murderous, manic explosions of instinctual cruelty. A powerful rendering of life as the Balinese most deeply do not want it (to adapt a phrase Frye has used of Gloucester's blinding) is set in the context of a sample of it as they do in fact have it.[33] And, because the context suggests that the rendering, if less than a straightforward description is nonetheless more than an idle fancy, it is here that the disquietfulness—the dis-

119

quietfulness of the *fight*, not (or, anyway, not necessarily) its patrons, who seem in fact rather thoroughly to enjoy it—emerges. The slaughter in the cock ring is not a depiction of how things literally are among men, but, what is almost worse, of how, from a particular angle, they imaginatively are.[34]

The angle, of course, is stratificatory. What, as we have already seen, the cockfight talks most forcibly about is status relationships, and what it says about them is that they are matters of life and death. That prestige is a profoundly serious business is apparent everywhere one looks in Bali—in the village, the family, the economy, the state. A peculiar fusion of Polynesian title ranks and Hindu castes, the hierarchy of pride is the moral backbone of the society. But only in the cockfight are the sentiments upon which that hierarchy rests revealed in their natural colors. Enveloped elsewhere in a haze of etiquette, a thick cloud of euphemism and ceremony, gesture and allusion, they are here expressed in only the thinnest disguise of an animal mask, a mask which in fact demonstrates them far more effectively than it conceals them. Jealousy is as much a part of Bali as poise, envy as grace, brutality as charm; but without the cockfight the Balinese would have a much less certain understanding of them, which is, presumably, why they value it so highly.

Any expressive form works (when it works) by disarranging semantic contexts in such a way that properties conventionally ascribed to certain things are unconventionally ascribed to others, which are then seen actually to possess them. To call the wind a cripple, as Stevens does, to fix tone and manipulate timbre, as Schoenberg does, or, closer to our case, to picture an art critic as a dissolute bear, as Hogarth does, is to cross conceptual wires; the established conjunctions between objects and their qualities are altered and phenomena—fall weather, melodic shape, or cultural journalism—are clothed in signifiers which normally point to other referents.[35] Similarly, to connect—and connect, and connect—the collision of roosters with the devisiveness of status is to invite a transfer of perceptions from the former to the latter, a transfer which is at once a description and a judgment. (Logically, the transfer could, of course, as well go the other way; but, like most of the rest of us, the Balinese are a great deal more interested in understanding men than they are in understanding cocks.)

What sets the cockfight apart from the ordinary course of life, lifts it from the realm of everyday practical affairs, and surrounds it with an aura of enlarged importance is not, as functionalist sociology would have it, that it reinforces status discriminations (such reinforcement is hardly necessary in a society where every act proclaims them), but that it provides a metasocial commentary upon the whole matter of assorting human beings into fixed hierarchical ranks and then organizing the major part of collective experience around that assortment. Its function, if you want to call it that, is interpretive: it is a

Balinese reading of Balinese experience; a story they tell themselves about themselves.

Saying Something of Something

To put the matter this way is to engage in a bit of metaphorical refocusing of one's own, for it shifts the analysis of cultural forms from an endeavor in general parallel to dissecting an organism, diagnosing a symptom, deciphering a code, or ordering a system—the dominant analogies in contemporary anthropology—to one in general parallel with penetrating a literary text. If one takes the cockfight, or any other collectively sustained symbolic structure, as a means of "saying something of something" (to invoke a famous Aristotelian tag), then one is faced with a problem not in social mechanics but social semantics.[36] For the anthropologist, whose concern is with formulating sociological principles, not with promoting or appreciating cockfights, the question is, what does one learn about such principles from examining culture as an assemblage of texts?

Such an extension of the notion of a text beyond written material, and even beyond verbal, is, though metaphorical, not, of course, all that novel. The *interpretatio naturae* tradition of the middle ages, which, culminating in Spinoza, attempted to read nature as Scripture, the Nietzschean effort to treat value systems as glosses on the will to power (or the Marxian one to treat them as glosses on property relations), and the Freudian replacement of the enigmatic text of the manifest dream with the plain one of the latent, all offer precedents, if not equally recommendable ones.[37] But the idea remains theoretically undeveloped; and the more profound corollary, so far as anthropology is concerned, that cultural forms can be treated as texts, as imaginative works built out of social materials, has yet to be systematically exploited.[38]

In the case at hand, to treat the cockfight as a text is to bring out a feature of it (in my opinion, the central feature of it) that treating it as a rite or a pastime, the two most obvious alternatives, would tend to obscure: its use of emotion for cognitive ends. What the cockfight says it says in a vocabulary of sentiment— the thrill of risk, the despair of loss, the pleasure of triumph. Yet what it says is not merely that risk is exciting, loss depressing, or triumph gratifying, banal tautologies of affect, but that it is of these emotions, thus exampled, that society is built and individuals put together. Attending cockfights and participating in them is, for the Balinese, a kind of sentimental education. What he learns there is what his culture's ethos and his private sensibility (or, anyway, certain aspects of them) look like when spelled out externally in a collective text; that the two are near enough alike to be articulated in the symbolics of a single such text; and—the disquieting part—that the text in which this revelation is accomplished consists of a chicken hacking another mindlessly to bits.

Every people, the proverb has it, loves its own form of violence. The cockfight is the Balinese reflection on theirs: on its look, its uses, its force, its fascination. Drawing on almost every level of Balinese experience, it brings together themes—animal savagery, male narcissism, opponent gambling, status rivalry, mass excitement, blood sacrifice—whose main connection is their involvement with rage and the fear of rage, and, binding them into a set of rules which at once contains them and allows them play, builds a symbolic structure in which, over and over again, the reality of their inner affiliation can be intelligibly felt. If, to quote Northrop Frye again, we go to see *Macbeth* to learn what a man feels like after he has gained a kingdom and lost his soul, Balinese go to cockfights to find out what a man, usually composed, aloof, almost obsessively self-absorbed, a kind of moral autocosm, feels like when, attacked, tormented, challenged, insulted, and driven in result to the extremes of fury, he has totally triumphed or been brought totally low. The whole passage, as it takes us back to Aristotle (though to the *Poetics* rather than the *Hermeneutics*), is worth quotation:

> But the poet [as opposed to the historian], Aristotle says, never makes any real statements at all, certainly no particular or specific ones. The poet's job is not to tell you what happened, but what happens: not what did take place, but the kind of thing that always does take place. He gives you the typical, recurring, or what Aristotle calls universal event. You wouldn't go to *Macbeth* to learn about the history of Scotland—you go to it to learn what a man feels like after he's gained a kingdom and lost his soul. When you meet such a character as Micawber in Dickens, you don't feel that there must have been a man Dickens knew who was exactly like this: you feel that there's a bit of Micawber in almost everybody you know, including yourself. Our impressions of human life are picked up one by one, and remain for most of us loose and disorganized. But we constantly find things in literature that suddenly co-ordinate and bring into focus a great many such impressions, and this is part of what Aristotle means by the typical or universal human event.[39]

It is this kind of bringing of assorted experiences of everyday life to focus that the cockfight, set aside from that life as "only a game" and reconnected to it as "more than a game," accomplishes, and so creates what, better than typical or universal, could be called a paradigmatic human event—that is, one that tells us less what happens than the kind of thing that would happen if, as is not the case, life were art and could be as freely shaped by styles of feeling as *Macbeth* and *David Copperfield* are.

Enacted and reenacted, so far without end, the cockfight enables the Balinese, as, read and reread, *Macbeth* enables us, to see a dimension of his own subjectivity. As he watches fight after fight, with the active watching of an owner and a bettor (for cockfighting has no more interest as a pure spectator sport than croquet or dog racing do), he grows familiar with it and what it has to say to him, much as the attentive listener to string quartets or the absorbed viewer of still lifes grows slowly more familiar with them in a way which opens his subjectivity to himself.[40]

Yet, because—in another of those paradoxes, along with painted feelings and unconsequenced acts, which haunt aesthetics—that subjectivity does not properly exist until it is thus organized, art forms generate and regenerate the very subjectivity they pretend only to display. Quartets, still lifes, and cockfights are not merely reflections of a preexisting sensibility analogically represented; they are positive agents in the creation and maintenance of such a sensibility. If we see ourselves as a pack of Micawbers it is from reading too much Dickens (if we see ourselves as unillusioned realists, it is from reading too little); and similarly for Balinese, cocks, and cockfights. It is in such a way, coloring experience with the light they cast it in, rather than through whatever material effects they may have, that the arts play their role, as arts, in social life.[41]

In the cockfight, then, the Balinese forms and discovers his temperament and his society's temper at the same time. Or, more exactly, he forms and discovers a particular face of them. Not only are there a great many other cultural texts providing commentaries on status hierarchy and self-regard in Bali, but there are a great many other critical sectors of Balinese life besides the stratificatory and the agonistic that receive such commentary. The ceremony consecrating a Brahmana priest, a matter of breath control, postural immobility, and vacant concentration upon the depths of being, displays a radically different, but to the Balinese equally real, property of social hierarchy—its reach toward the numinous transcendent. Set not in the matrix of the kinetic emotionality of animals, but in that of the static passionlessness of divine mentality, it expresses tranquility not disquiet. The mass festivals at the village temples, which mobilize the whole local population in elaborate hostings of visiting gods—songs, dances, compliments, gifts—assert the spiritual unity of village mates against their status inequality and project a mood of amity and trust.[42] The cockfight is not the master key to Balinese life, any more than bullfighting is to Spanish. What it says about that life is not unqualified nor even unchallenged by what other equally eloquent cultural statements say about it. But there is nothing more surprising in this than in the fact that Racine and Molière were contemporaries, or that the same people who arrange chrysanthemums cast swords.[43]

The culture of a people is an ensemble of texts, themselves ensembles, which the anthropologist strains to read over the shoulders of those to whom they properly belong. There are enormous difficulties in such an enterprise, methodological pitfalls to make a Freudian quake, and some moral perplexities as well. Nor is it the only way that symbolic forms can be sociologically handled. Functionalism lives, and so does psychologism. But to regard such forms as "saying something of something," and saying it to somebody, is at least to open up the possibility of an analysis which attends to their substance rather than to reductive formulas professing to account for them.

As in more familiar exercises in close reading, one can start anywhere in a culture's repertoire of forms and end up anywhere else. One can stay, as I have here, within a single, more or less bounded form and circle steadily within it. One can move between forms in search of broader unities or informing contrasts. One can even compare forms from different cultures to define their character in reciprocal relief. But whatever the level at which one operates, and however intricately, the guiding principle is the same: societies, like lives, contain their own interpretations. One has only to learn how to gain access to them.

Notes

1. Gregory Bateson and Margaret Mead, *Balinese Character: A Photographic Analysis* (New York: New York Academy of Sciences, 1942), p. 68.

2. Jane Belo, "The Balinese Temper," in Jane Belo, ed., *Traditional Balinese Culture* (New York: Columbia University Press, 1970; originally published in 1935), pp. 85–110.

3. The best discussion of cockfighting is again Bateson and Mead's (*Balinese Character,* pp. 24–25, 140), but it, too, is general and abbreviated.

4. Bateson and Mead, *Balinese Character,* pp. 25–26. The cockfight is unusual within Balinese culture in being a single-sex public activity from which the other sex is totally and expressly excluded. Sexual differentiation is culturally extremely played down in Bali and most activities, formal and informal, involve the participation of men and women on equal ground, commonly linked as couples. From religion, to politics, to economics, to kinship, to dress, Bali is a rather "uni-sex" society, a fact both its customs and its symbolism clearly express. Even in contexts where women do not in fact play much of a role—music, painting, certain agricultural activities—their absence, which is only relative in any case, is more a mere matter of fact than socially enforced. To this general pattern, the cockfight, entirely of, by and for men (women—at least *Balinese* women—do not even watch), is the most striking exception.

5. Christiaan Hooykaas, *The Lay of the Jaya Prana* (London, 1958), p. 39. The lay has a stanza (no. 17) with the reluctant bridegroom use. Jaya Prana, the subject of a Balinese Uriah myth, responds to the lord who has offered him the loveliest of six hundred servant girls: "Godly King, my Lord and Master / I beg you, give me leave to

go / such things are not yet in my mind; / like a fighting cock encaged / indeed I am on my mettle / I am alone / as yet the flame has not been fanned."

6. For these, see V. E. Korn, *Het Adatrecht van Bali,* 2d ed. ('S-Gravenhage: G. Naeff, 1932), index under *toh.*

7. There is indeed a legend to the effect that the separation of Java and Bali is due to the action of a powerful Javanese religious figure who wished to protect himself against a Balinese culture hero (the ancestor of two Ksatria castes) who was a passionate cockfighting gambler. See Christiaan Hooykaas, *Agama Tirtha* (Amsterdam: Noord-Hollandsche, 1964), p. 184.

8. An incestuous couple is forced to wear pig yokes over their necks and crawl to a pig trough and eat with their mouths there. On this, see Jane Belo, "Customs Pertaining to Twins in Bali," in Belo, ed., *Traditional Balinese Culture,* p. 49; on the abhorrence of animality generally, see Bateson and Mead, *Balinese Character,* p. 22.

9. Except for unimportant, small-bet fights (on the question of fight "importance," see below), spur affixing is usually done by someone other than the owner. Whether the owner handles his own cock or not more or less depends on how skilled he is at it, a consideration whose importance is again relative to the importance of the fight. When spur affixers and cock handlers are someone other than the owner, they are almost always a quite close relative—a brother or cousin—or a very intimate friend of his. They are thus almost extensions of his personality, as the fact that all three will refer to the cock as "mine," say "I" fought So-and-So, and so on, demonstrates. Also, owner-handler-affixer triads tend to be fairly fixed, though individuals may participate in several and often exchange roles within a given one.

10. Erving Goffman, *Encounters: Two Studies in the Sociology of Interaction* (Indianapolis: Bobbs-Merrill, 1961), pp. 9–10.

11. This word, which literally means an indelible stain or mark, as in a birthmark or a vein in a stone, is used as well for a deposit in a court case, for a pawn, for security offered in a loan, for a stand-in for someone else in a legal or ceremonial context, for an earnest advanced in a business deal, for a sign placed in a field to indicate its ownership is in dispute, and for the status of an unfaithful wife from whose lover her husband must gain satisfaction or surrender her to him. See Korn, *Het Adatrecht van Bali;* Theodoor Pigeaud, *Javaans-Nederlands Handwoordenboek* (Groningen: Wolters, 1938); H. H. Juynboll, *Oudjavaansche-Nederlandsche Woordenlijst* (Leiden: Brill, 1923).

12. The center bet must be advanced in cash by both parties prior to the actual fight. The umpire holds the stakes until the decision is rendered and then awards them to the winner, avoiding, among other things, the intense embarrassment both winner and loser would feel if the latter had to pay off personally following his defeat. About ten percent of the winner's receipts are subtracted for the umpire's share and that of the fight sponsors.

13. Actually, the typing of cocks, which is extremely elaborate (I have collected more than twenty classes, certainly not a complete list), is not based on color alone, but on a series of independent, interacting, dimensions, which include, beside color, size, bone thickness, plumage, and temperament. (But *not* pedigree. The Balinese do not breed cocks to any significant extent, nor, so far as I have been able to discover, have they ever

done so. The *asil,* or jungle cock, which is the basic fighting strain everywhere the sport is found, is native to southern Asia, and one can buy a good example in the chicken section of almost any Balinese market for anywhere from four or five ringgits up to fifty or more.) The color element is merely the one normally used as the type name, except when the two cocks of different types—as on principle they must be—have the same color, in which case a secondary indication from one of the other dimensions ("large speckled" v. "small speckled," etc.) is added. The types are coordinated with various cosmological ideas which help shape the making of matches, so that, for example, you fight a small, headstrong, speckled brown-on-white cock with flat-lying feathers and thin legs from the east side of the ring on a certain day of the complex Balinese calendar, and a large, cautious, all-black cock with tufted feathers and stubby legs from the north side on another day, and so on. All this is again recorded in palm-leaf manuscripts and endlessly discussed by the Balinese (who do not all have identical systems), and full-scale componential-cum-symbolic analysis of cock classifications would be extremely valuable both as an adjunct to the description of the cockfight and in itself. But my data on the subject, though extensive and varied, do not seem to be complete and systematic enough to attempt such an analysis here. For Balinese cosmological ideas more generally see Belo, ed., *Traditional Balinese Culture,* and J. L. Swellengrebel ed., *Bali: Studies in Life, Thought, and Ritual* (The Hague: W. van Hoeve, 1960); for calendrical ones, Clifford Geertz, *Person, Time, and Conduct in Bali: An Essay in Cultural Analysis* (New Haven: Southeast Asia Studies, Yale University, 1966), pp. 45–53.

14. For purposes of ethnographic completeness, it should be noted that it is possible for the man backing the favorite—the odds-giver—to make a bet in which he wins if his cock wins or there is a tie, a slight shortening of the odds (I do not have enough cases to be exact, but ties seem to occur about once every fifteen or twenty matches). He indicates his wish to do this by shouting *sapih* ("tie") rather than the cock-type, but such bets are in fact infrequent.

15. The precise dynamics of the movement of the betting is one of the most intriguing, most complicated, and, given the hectic conditions under which it occurs, most difficult to study, aspects of the fight. Motion picture recording plus multiple observers would probably be necessary to deal with it effectively. Even impressionistically—the only approach open to a lone ethnographer caught in the middle of all this—it is clear that certain men lead both in determining the favorite (that is, making the opening cock-type calls which always initiate the process) and in directing the movement of the odds, these "opinion leaders" being the more accomplished cockfighters-cum-solid-citizens to be discussed below. If these men begin to change their calls, others follow; if they begin to make bets, so do others and—though there is always a large number of frustrated bettors crying for shorter or longer odds to the end—the movement more or less ceases. But a detailed understanding of the whole process awaits what, alas, it is not very likely ever to get: a decision theorist armed with precise observations of individual behavior.

16. Assuming only binomial variability, the departure from a fifty-fifty expectation in the sixty ringgits and below case is 1.38 standard deviations, or (in a one-direction test) an eight-in-one-hundred possibility by chance alone; for the below forty ringgits

case, it is 1.65 standard deviations, or about five in one hundred. The fact that these departures though real are not extreme merely indicates, again, that even in the smaller fights the tendency to match cocks at least reasonably evenly persists. It is a matter of relative relaxation of the pressures toward equalization, not their elimination. The tendency for high-bet contests to be coin-flip propositions is, of course, even more striking, and suggests the Balinese know quite well what they are about.

17. The reduction in wagering in smaller fights (which, of course, feeds on itself; one of the reasons people find small fights uninteresting is that there is less wagering in them, and contrariwise for large ones) takes place in three mutually reinforcing ways. First, there is a simple withdrawal of interest as people wander off to have a cup of coffee or chat with a friend. Second, the Balinese do not mathematically reduce odds, but bet directly in terms of stated odds as such. Thus, for a nine-to-eight bet, one man wagers nine ringgits, the other eight; for five-to-four, one wagers five, the other four. For any given currency unit, like the ringgit, therefore, 6.3 times as much money is involved in a ten-to-nine bet as in a two-to-one bet, for example, and, as noted, in small fights betting settles toward the longer end. Finally, the bets which are made tend to be one- rather than two-, three-, or in some of the very largest fights, four- or five-finger ones. (The fingers indicate the *multiples* of the stated bet odds at issue, not absolute figures. Two fingers in a six-to-five situation means a man wants to wager ten ringgits on the underdog against twelve, three in an eight-to-seven situation, twenty-one against twenty-four, and so on.)

18. Besides wagering there are other economic aspects of the cockfight, especially its very close connection with the local market system which, though secondary both to its motivation and to its function, are not without importance. Cockfights are open events to which anyone who wishes may come, sometimes from quite distant areas, but well over ninety per cent, probably over ninety-five, are very local affairs, and the locality concerned is defined not by the village, nor even by the administrative district, but by the rural market system. Bali has a three-day market week with the familiar "solar-system" type rotation. Though the markets themselves have never been very highly developed, small morning affairs in a village square, it is the micro-region such rotation rather generally marks out—ten or twenty square miles, seven or eight neighboring villages (which in contemporary Bali is usually going to mean anywhere from five to ten or eleven thousand people) from which the core of any cockfight audience, indeed virtually all of it, will come. Most of the fights are in fact organized and sponsored by small combines of petty rural merchants under the general premise, very strongly held by them and indeed by all Balinese, that cockfights are good for trade because "they get money out of the house, they make it circulate." Stalls selling various sorts of things as well as assorted sheer-chance gambling games (see below) are set up around the edge of the area so that this even takes on the quality of a small fair. This connection of cockfighting with markets and market sellers is very old, as, among other things, their conjunction in inscriptions (Roelof Goris, *Prasasti Bali,* 2 vols. [Bandung: N. V. Masa Baru, 1954]) indicates. Trade has followed the cock for centuries in rural Bali, and the sport has been one of the main agencies of the island's monetization.

19. The phrase is found in the Hildreth translation, International Library of Psy-

chology, 1931, note to p. 106; see L. L. Fuller, *The Morality of Law* (New Haven: Yale University Press, 1964), pp. 6ff.

20. Of course, even in Bentham, utility is not normally confined as a concept to monetary losses and gains, and my argument here might be more carefully put in terms of a denial that for the Balinese, as for any people, utility (pleasure, happiness . . .) is merely identifiable with wealth. But such terminological problems are in any case secondary to the essential point: the cockfight is not roulette.

21. Max Weber, *The Sociology of Religion* (Boston: Beacon Press, 1963). There is nothing specifically Balinese, of course, about deepening significance with money, as Whyte's description of corner boys in a working-class district of Boston demonstrates: "Gambling plays an important role in the lives of Cornerville people. Whatever game the corner boys play, they nearly always bet on the outcome. When there is nothing at stake, the game is not considered a real contest. This does not mean that the financial element is all-important. I have frequently heard men say that the honor of winning was much more important than the money at stake. The corner boys consider playing for money the real test of skill and, unless a man performs well when money is at stake, he is not considered a good competitor." W. F. Whyte, *Street Corner Society*, 2d ed. (Chicago: University of Chicago Press, 1955), p. 140.

22. The extremes to which this madness is conceived on occasion to go—and the fact that it is considered madness—is demonstrated by the Balinese folktale *I Tuhung Kuning*. A gambler becomes so deranged by his passion that, leaving on a trip, he orders his pregnant wife to take care of the prospective newborn if it is a boy but to feed it as meat to his fighting cocks if it is a girl. The mother gives birth to a girl, but rather than giving the child to the cocks she gives them a large rat and conceals the girl with her own mother. When the husband returns, the cocks, crowing a jingle, inform him of the deception and, furious, he sets out to kill the child. A goddess descends from heaven and takes the girl up to the skies with her. The cocks die from the food given them, the owner's sanity is restored, the goddess brings the girl back to the father, . . . reunit[ing] him with his wife. The story is given as "Geel Komkommertje" in Jacoba Hooykaas-van Leeuwen Boomkamp, *Sprookjes en Verhalen van Bali* ('S-Gravenhage: Van Hoeve, 1956), pp. 19–25.

23. For a fuller description of Balinese rural social structure, see Clifford Geertz, "Form and Variation in Balinese Village Structure," *American Anthropologist* 61 (1959): 94–108; "Tihingan, A Balinese Village," in R. M. Koentjaraningrat, *Villages in Indonesia* (Ithaca: Cornell University Press, 1967), pp. 210–243; and, though it is a bit off the norm as Balinese villages go, V. E. Korn, *De Dorpsrepubliek tnganan Pagringsingan* (Santpoort, Netherlands: C. A. Mees, 1933).

24. Goffman, *Encounters*, p. 78.

25. B. R. Berelson, P. F. Lazersfeld, and W. N. McPhee, *Voting: A Study of Opinion Formation in a Presidential Campaign* (Chicago: University of Chicago Press, 1954).

26. As this is a formal paradigm, it is intended to display the logical, not the causal, structure of cockfighting. Just which of these considerations leads to which, in what order, and by what mechanisms, is another matter—one I have attempted to shed some light on in the general discussion.

27. In another of Hooykaas-van Leeuwen Boomkamp's folk tales ("De Gast," *Sprookies en Verhalen van Bali,* pp. 172–180), a low caste *Sudra,* a generous, pious, and carefree man who is also an accomplished cockfighter, loses, despite his accomplishment, fight after fight until he is not only out of money but down to his last cock. He does not despair, however—"I bet," he says, "upon the Unseen World."

His wife, a good and hard-working woman, knowing how much he enjoys cockfighting, gives him her last "rainy day" money to go and bet. But, filled with misgivings due to his run of ill luck, he leaves his own cock at home and bets merely on the side. He soon loses all but a coin or two and repairs to a food stand for a snack, where he meets a decrepit, odorous, and generally unappetizing old beggar leaning on a staff. The old man asks for food, and the hero spends his last coins to buy him some. The old man then asks to pass the night with the hero, which the hero gladly invites him to do. As there is no food in the house, however, the hero tells his wife to kill the last cock for dinner. When the old man discovers this fact, he tells the hero he has three cocks in his own mountain hut and says the hero may have one of them for fighting. He also asks for the hero's son to accompany him as a servant, and, after the son agrees, this is done.

The old man turns out to be Siva and, thus, to live in a great palace in the sky, though the hero does not know this. In time, the hero decides to visit his son and collect the promised cock. Lifted up into Siva's presence, he is given the choice of three cocks. The first crows: "I have beaten fifteen opponents." The second crows, "I have beaten twenty-five opponents." The third crows, "I have beaten the King." "That one, the third, is my choice," says the hero, and returns with it to earth.

When he arrives at the cockfight, he is asked for an entry fee and replies, "I have no money; I will pay after my cock has won." As he is known never to win, he is let in because the king, who is there fighting, dislikes him and hopes to enslave him when he loses and cannot pay off. In order to insure that this happens, the king matches his finest cock against the hero's. When the cocks are placed down, the hero's flees, and the crowd, led by the arrogant king, hoots in laughter. The hero's cock then flies at the king himself, killing him with a spur stab in the throat. The hero flees. His house is encircled by the king's men. The cock changes into a Garuda, the great mythic bird of Indic legend, and carries the hero and his wife to safety in the heavens.

When the people see this, they make the hero king and his wife queen and they return as such to earth. Later their son, released by Siva, also returns and the hero-king announces his intention to enter a hermitage. ("I will fight no more cockfights. I have bet on the Unseen and won.") He enters the hermitage and his son becomes king.

28. Addict gamblers are really less declassed (for their status is, as everyone else's, inherited) than merely impoverished and personally disgraced. The most prominent addict gambler in my cockfight circuit was actually a very high caste *satria* who sold off most of his considerable lands to support his habit. Though everyone privately regarded him as a fool and worse (some, more charitable, regarded him as sick), he was publicly treated with the elaborate deference and politeness due his rank. On the independence of personal reputation and public status in Bali, see Geertz, *Person, Time, and Conduct,* pp. 28–35.

29. For four, somewhat variant, treatments, see Susanne Langer, *Feeling and Form*

(New York: Scribners, 1953); Richard Wollheim, *Art and Its Objects* (New York: Harper and Row, 1968); Nelson Goodman, *Languages of Art* (Indianapolis: Bobbs-Merrill, 1968); Maurice Merleau-Ponty, "The Eye and the Mind," in his *The Primacy of Perception* (Evanston: Northwestern University Press, 1964), pp. 159–190.

30. British cockfights (the sport was banned there in 1840) indeed seem to have lacked it, and to have generated, therefore, a quite different family of shapes. Most British fights were "mains," in which a preagreed number of cocks were aligned into two teams and fought serially. Score was kept and wagering took place both on the individual matches and on the main as a whole. There were also "battle Royales," both in England and on the Continent, in which a large number of cocks were let loose at once with the one left standing at the end the victor. And in Wales, the so-called "Welsh main" followed an elimination pattern, along the lines of a present-day tennis tournament, winners proceeding to the next round. As a genre, the cockfight has perhaps less compositional flexibility than, say, Latin comedy, but it is not entirely without any. On cockfighting more generally, see Arch Ruport, *The Art of Cockfighting* (New York: Devin-Adair, 1949); G. R. Scott, *History of Cockfighting* (1957); and Lawrence Fitz-Barnard, *Fighting Sports* (London: Odhams Press, 1921).

31. *Person, Time, and Conduct,* esp. pp. 42ff. I am, however, not the first person to have argued it: see G. Bateson, "Bali, the Value System of a Steady State," and "An Old Temple and a New Myth," in Belo, ed., *Traditional Balinese Culture,* pp. 384–402 and 111–136.

32. For the necessity of distinguishing among "description," "representation," "exemplification," and "expression" (and the irrelevance of "imitation" to all of them) as modes of symbolic reference, see Goodman, *Languages of Art,* pp. 6–10, 45–91, 225–241.

33. Northrop Frye, *The Educated Imagination* (Bloomington: Indiana University Press, 1964), p. 99.

34. There are two other Balinese values and disvalues which, connected with punctuate temporality on the one hand and unbridled aggressiveness on the other, reinforce the sense that the cockfight is at once continuous with ordinary social life and a direct negation of it: what the Balinese call *ramé,* and what they call *paling. Ramé* means crowded, noisy, and active, and is a highly sought after social state: crowded markets, mass festivals, busy streets are all *ramé,* as, of course, is, in the extreme, a cockfight. *Ramé* is what happens in the "full" times (its opposite, *sepi,* "quiet," is what happens in the "empty" ones). *Paling* is social vertigo, the dizzy, disoriented, lost, turned-around feeling one gets when one's place in the coordinates of social space is not clear, and it is a tremendously disfavored, immensely anxiety-producing state. Balinese regard the exact maintenance of spatial orientation ("not to know where north is" is to be crazy), balance, decorum, status relationships, and so forth, as fundamental to ordered life (*krama*) and *paling,* the sort of whirling confusion of position the scrambling cocks exemplify as its profoundest enemy and contradiction. On *ramé,* see Bateson and Mead, *Balinese Character,* pp. 3, 64; on *paling,* p. 11, and Belo, ed., *Traditional Balinese Culture,* pp. 90ff.

35. The Stevens reference is to his "The Motive for Metaphor," ("You like it under

the trees in autumn / Because everything is half dead. / The wind moves like a cripple among the leaves / And repeats words without meaning"); the Schoenberg reference is to the third of his *Five Orchestral Pieces* (Opus 16), and is borrowed from H. H. Drager, "The Concept of 'Tonal Body,' " in Susanne Langer, ed., *Reflections on Art* (New York: Oxford University Press, 1961), p. 174. On Hogarth and on this whole problem— there called "multiple matrix matching"—see E. H. Gombrich, "The Use of Art for the Study of Symbols," in James Hogg, ed., *Psychology and the Visual Arts* (Baltimore: Penguin Brooks, 1969), pp. 149–170. The more usual term for this sort of semantic alchemy is "metaphorical transfer," and good technical discussions of it can be found in M. Black, *Models and Metaphors* (Ithaca: Cornell University Press, 1962), pp. 25ff.; Goodman, *Languages of Art* pp. 44ff.; and W. Percy, "Metaphor as Mistake," *Sewanee Review* 66 (1958): 78–99.

36. The tag is from the second book of the *Organon, On Interpretation.* For a discussion of it, and for the whole argument for freeing "the notion of text . . . from the notion of scripture or writing," and constructing, thus, a general hermeneutics, see Paul Ricoeur, *Freud and Philosophy* (New Haven: Yale University Press, 1970), pp. 20ff.

37. Cf. Paul Ricoeur, *Freud and Philosophy.*

38. Lévi-Strauss's "structuralism" might seem an exception. But it is only an apparent one, for, rather than taking myths, totem rites, marriage rules, or whatever as texts to interpret, Lévi-Strauss takes them as ciphers to solve, which is very much not the same thing. He does not seek to understand the symbolic forms in terms of how they function in concrete situations to organize perceptions (meanings, emotions, concepts, attitudes); he seeks to understand them entirely in terms of their internal structure, *indépendent de tout sujet, de tout objet, et de toute contexte.* For my own view of this approach—that is suggestive and indefensible—see Clifford Geertz, "The Cerebral Savage: On the Work of Lévi-Strauss," *Encounter* 48 (1967): 25–32.

39. Frye, *The Educated Imagination,* pp. 63–64.

40. The use of the, to Europeans, "natural" visual idiom for perception—"see," "watches," and so forth—is more than usually misleading here, for the fact that, as mentioned earlier, Balinese follow the progress of the fight as much (perhaps, as fighting cocks are actually rather hard to see except as blurs of motion, more) with their bodies as with their eyes, moving their limbs, heads, and trunks in gestural mimicry of the cocks' maneuvers, means that much of the individual's experience of the fight is kinesthetic rather than visual. If ever there was an example of Kenneth Burke's definition of a symbolic act as "the dancing of an attitude" (*The Philosophy of Literary Form,* rev. ed. [New York: Vintage Books, 1957], p. 9), the cockfight is it. On the enormous role of kinesthetic perception in Balinese life, Bateson and Mean, *Balinese Character,* pp. 84–88; on the active nature of aesthetic perception in general, Goodman, *Languages of Art,* pp. 241–244.

41. All this coupling of the occidental great with the oriental lowly will doubtless disturb certain sorts of aestheticians as the earlier efforts of anthropologists to speak of Christianity and totemism in the same breath disturbed certain sorts of theologians. But as ontological questions are (or should be) bracketed in the sociology of religion, judgmental ones are (or should be) bracketed in the sociology of art. In any case, the

attempt to deprovincialize the concept of art is but part of the general anthropological conspiracy to deprovincialize all important social concepts—marriage, religion, law, rationality—and though this is a threat to aesthetic theories which regard certain works of art as beyond the reach of sociological analysis, it is no threat to the conviction, for which Robert Graves claims to have been reprimanded at his Cambridge tripos, that some poems are better than others.

42. For the consecration ceremony, see V. E. Korn, "The Consecration of the Priest," in Swellengrebel, ed., *Bali*, pp. 131–154; for (somewhat exaggerated) village communion, Roelof Goris, "The Religious Character of the Balinese Village," in Swellengrebel, ed., *Bali*, pp. 79–100.

43. That what the cockfight has to say about Bali is not altogether without perception and the disquiet it expresses about the general pattern of Balinese life is not wholly without reason is attested by the fact that in two weeks of December 1965, during the upheavals following the unsuccessful coup in Djakarta, between forty and eighty thousand Balinese (in a population of about two million) were killed, largely by one another—the worst outburst in the country. (John Hughes, *Indonesian Upheaval* [New York: McKay, 1967], pp. 173–183. Hughes's figures are, of course, rather casual estimates, but they are not the most extreme.) This is not to say, of course, that the killings were caused by the cockfight, could have been predicted on the basis of it, or were some sort of enlarged version of it with real people in the place of the cocks—all of which is nonsense. It is merely to say that if one looks at Bali not just through the medium of its dances, its shadowplays, its sculpture, and its girls, but—as the Balinese themselves do—also through the medium of its cockfight, the fact that the massacre occurred seems, if no less appalling, less like a contradiction to the laws of nature. As more than one real Gloucester has discovered, sometimes people actually get life precisely as they most deeply do not want it.

SCOTT GUGGENHEIM

Cock or Bull: Cockfighting, Social Structure, and Political Commentary in the Philippines

Directly inspired by Geertz's essay on the Balinese cockfight, anthropologist Scott Guggenheim undertook an in-depth study of the cockfight in the Philippines to test some of Geertz's hypotheses. Nowhere in the world is there more enthusiasm for cockfights than in the Philippines. Guggenheim had originally planned to write his doctoral dissertation on cockfighting in the Philippines, but his dissertation committee did not think the topic was "lofty enough" for such a purpose.

For earlier considerations of the Filipino cockfight, see Grace Helen Bailey, "The Cockpit and the Filipino," Overland Monthly 54 (1909): 253–256; Fitzhugh Lee, "Filipino's Favorite Sport," Overland Monthly 77 (1920): 20–22; Alejandro R. Roces, Of Cocks and Kites (Manila: Regal Publishing Co., 1959); and Angel J. Lansang, Cockfighting in the Philippines (Our Genuine National Sport) (Atlag, Malolos, Bulacan: Enrian Press, 1966).

Guggenheim, who works for the World Bank, is co-editor of Power and Protest in the Countryside: Studies of Rural Unrest in Asia, Europe, and Latin America *(Durham: Duke University Press, 1982).*

Few travellers to the Philippines fail to notice the large, ramshackle, silver-domed cockpits that stud the lowland landscape. Every Sunday morning, in thousands of villages throughout the Philippines, these rickety, trembling constructions fill to the rafters and beyond with anxious, eager men convinced that this is the day when they will pick only winners and return home rich.

Nor are cockpits confined to rural areas. Every city, if it is really a city, sports at least two cockpits, and innumerable *topadas*, illegal fights held in a cockpit hastily improvised from a bamboo pole and a quiet alley, where any man with the price of admission can drown the urban clatter in the thrills of total victory—or the shame of total defeat.

Despite the rather shamefaced efforts of Western-oriented progressives to

Reprinted from *Pilipinas: A Journal of Philippine Studies* 3.1 (June, 1982): 1–35. I am indebted to my colleague Professor Jim Anderson of the Department of Anthropology, University of California, Berkeley, for calling my attention to this important essay.

133

pretend that cockfighting is a rapidly dying sport, limited largely to illiterate peasants and the lazarus layer of the working class, cockfighting remains the premier pastime in the Philippines. Nearly every male adult, aspiring adult, adolescent, and schoolchild has his own pet theory to explain which breed of rooster produces the best fight, which chicken calisthenics are the most invigorating, and which diet is the most nourishing. In the countryside, copies of *Ang Sabugero,* the Filipino cockers magazine, are worth, if not quite as much as *Penthouse,* a great deal more than *National Geographic,* while in the cities its imported cousins, *Gamecock* and *Grit and Steel,* can readily fetch half a bottle of good Scotch. And even in the most remote corners of the country a little prodding extracts the most intricate, if not always the most accurate, details concerning the lives of the big-time cockers and their birds: Ricardo Silverio and his hired trainer from America, the Lacson's fabulous conditioning stalls, each of which has stereo music piped to an air-conditioned cage, the Enrile/de Guzman partnership which commandeered an Air Force plane to fly to Georgia in order to pick up three hundred thoroughbred roosters for the upcoming season, and the amazing adventures of the invincible, insatiable, Tony "the Terrible" Trebol.

Nevertheless, despite the inevitable fighting cock prominently staked outside of every small *sari-sari* store, left leg fastened to a lasso, right leg scratching through the sand for discarded grains of corn, despite the cock crow cacophony resounding through the villages at dawn, dusk, morning, noon and night, despite the hours and hours . . . and more hours of intricate argument pleasurably spent on cockpits, cockfights, and cocklore, despite the ubiquitousness of cockfighting themes in Philippine art, literature, and legend, careful studies of cockfighting are nowhere to be found in the anthropological literature concerned with lowland Philippine society.

Anthropologists working in other parts of the world have not been quite so remiss in their ethnographic duties. Most anthropologists who deal with cockfighting follow Clifford Geertz's (1972) pioneering study of Balinese cockfighting. While Geertz's analysis will be dealt with at greater length further on in this study, it is important to note here that Geertz argued for a purely interpretive approach to cockfights and by extension, to cultural analysis in general:

What sets the cockfight apart from the ordinary course of life, lifts it from the realm of everyday practical affairs, and surrounds it with an aura of enlarged importance is not, as functionalist sociology would have it, that it reinforces status discriminations (such reinforcement is hardly necessary in a society where every act proclaims them) but that it provides a metasocial commentary upon the whole matter of assorting human beings into fixed hierarchical ranking and then organizing the major part of collective existence around that assortment. Its function, if you want to call it that, is interpretive: it is a Balinese reading of Balinese experience, a history they tell themselves about themselves.[1]

Geertz's portrayal of cockfighting as a "cultural performance" bringing buried and partially buried cultural themes to center stage for public viewing has inspired many insightful and subtle studies of other cultural activities. Rosaldo's (1980) analysis of Ilongot headhunting, Logan's (1978) study of the Siennese *palio*, and Hunt's (1971) interpretation of Maya poetry are all heavily influenced by Geertz's analysis of Balinese cockfights.

Nevertheless, despite the compelling arguments Geertz puts forward in "Deep Play" for the relative autonomy of culture as well as the simple aesthetic beauty of the article, there are a number of problems with Geertz's discussions, especially with his theoretical inferences. Chief among these problems is Geertz's failure to specify which social relations cockfighting is silent about, as well as which ones it "comments" on; who understands the messages conveyed through cockfighting; or even how accurate a portrait of social relations is painted by the cockfight. These weaknesses ultimately derive from an inadequately developed theory of symbol formation and change.

If Philippine cockfighting provides any guide, and I shall show that there is a remarkable similarity in cockfight structure between Indonesia and the Philippines, not everybody "gets the point" of the cockfight. Some people do indeed see a metasocial commentary—a number of Filipino cockers who read "Deep Play" thought Geertz hit the nail right on the head. Some people see only a cockfight. Some people do not go to the cockpit and therefore see nothing at all.

Second, while Geertz presents Balinese cockfights as a more or less given symbolic structure, the history of Philippine cockfighting is marked by frequent (though not constant) efforts by different social groups to control the structure and organization of cockfighting. Similarly, there have been frequent attempts by powerful groups to control the meanings attached to cockfighting, as well as efforts to invert those meanings by the politically weak.

Finally, as Deborah Rubin[2] has argued, Geertz does not adequately bound the culture that cockfighting apparently comments on. While Geertz would confine the social referent of the metasocial commentary to Bali, the very act of participating in an activity banned in modern Indonesia makes a number of statements about ethnicity, nationalism and political subordination, as Geertz himself found out when he was very nearly arrested for watching the fights. But making references to these matters implies a social structure extending far beyond Balinese beaches. It also implies that cultural formation must be firmly rooted in sociopolitical process.

This paper is an attempt to deal with the above issues using data drawn from the Philippines. It is not intended as a critique of Geertz's original and stimulating analysis of Bali. While a comparison between the two cases is possible and desirable, my aim here is directed more towards adding to the ethnographic record of the Philippines. But just as Geertz was able to use cockfighting as a stepping-stone to a more general argument for an interpretive approach to symbolic structures, so can Philippine data be used to advocate a political economy of symbolism.[3]

The following essay is divided into four broad sections. I first present a brief history of Philippine cockfighting drawn primarily from archival sources and travellers' journals. The aim here is to indicate how some of the main social and political processes directing Philippine history have also, not surprisingly, played an integral role in structuring Philippine cockfighting. The second part describes contemporary cockfighting: what kinds of chickens fight, the different kinds of fights, the social organization of betting, and so on. If some readers find this part a bit tedious or gory, they will, I hope, indulge an excessively participant observer. Part Three moves from description to analysis. Using Bloch's argument[4] that the very structure of ritual limits the kinds of messages that can be conveyed, I suggest (following Geertz) that in effect hierarchy is built into Philippine cockfighting. It therefore does not lend itself to class-oriented confrontations as do other "secular rituals" such as *charivari, pasyon,* or baptism.[5] Nevertheless, cockfighting is not totally bound by rules and, given sufficiently selective evidence and judicious ignorance, it is possible to derive a range of alternative interpretations. A further, crucial variable is people's access to the ritual; in the case of cockfighting the ritual remains in the hands of elites. This makes cockfighting difficult to "re-interpret" in light of changing experience. I also examine cockfighting in a particular ethnographic context, the municipality of Piat in the northern Philippines. During the past decade Piat has experienced profound economic and political changes—although the structure of cockfighting remains the same. For many people, the political relationships described by cockfighting are even less plausible now than they were before the rapid and extensive proletarianization of the region. This section, therefore, explores some of the reasons why cockfighting remains meaningful to Piateños—and questions whether the meanings are indeed the same. The conclusion of the paper looks to the implications of this analysis for more general theories of symbolism.

History of Philippine Cockfighting

Contrary to popular belief in the Philippines, cockfighting was not introduced by the Spanish. One of the earliest explorers of the southern Philippines re-

136

ported seeing cockfights in Butuan, although he left no further information concerning how the fights were organized.[6] Antonio Pigafetta, who accompanied Magellan on his celebrated voyage around the world, wrote that on Palawan:

They have large and very tame cocks, which they do not eat because of a certain veneration they have for them. Sometimes they make them fight with one another and each one puts up a certain amount on his cock and the prize goes to him whose cock is the victor.[7]

One of the first moves of the Spanish in their new colony was to establish permanent, privately owned cockpits. This formed part of a more general effort to force dispersed, rural populations into permanent, nucleated settlements which could be guarded and taxed.[8]

In the early eighteenth century the Spanish, always eager to find ways to make their costly colony self-supporting, passed legislation to tax and regulate cockfighting. Licenses to operate cockpits were sold to the highest bidder; people operating cockpits without a legal concession could be arrested and fined. While these laws could only be enforced in Manila and in some of the larger provincial cities, cockfighting quickly began to send healthy profits to the Colonial coffers. At a time when the net profit for the tobacco monopoly, the single most profitable enterprise in the entire Colony, set a record of 620,000 pesos, the annual profit from the Manila cockpit alone was between 20,000 and 30,000 for the lucky fellow who won the franchise.[9] So popular was cockfighting, and so influential were cockpit operators, that priests stationed in the Philippines complained to the King of Spain that the Viceroy had been led by unscrupulous cockpit operators to spread the feast of Corpus Christi over three days instead of the normal one day simply in order to allow cockers more time to travel from cockpit to cockpit in pursuit of their sinful pleasure.[10]

In 1854 the government was able to collect some 80,000 Mexican silver dollars from the Tondo (Manila) cockpit and another 15–20,000 from each of the other provinces.[11] A new series of regulations passed in 1861 specified how the franchise auctions were to be conducted to ensure the maximum possible revenue for the government.[12]

It is not surprising that such large amounts of money were changing hands in the provincial cockpits, for this is the same period when the commercial economy was making a rapid expansion outwards.[13] For the remarkable mestizo landlords and shop owners who had taken over the rural economy, cockfighting provided both the symbols and the opportunity to display their rapidly improving social position. Few travellers to the Philippines in the second half of the nineteenth century failed to comment on the pervasiveness of cockfighting although it seems to have been a passion largely eschewed by the wealthiest Spanish who then, as now, preferred horse racing. Reports of bets by "Tagalogs and Chinese mestizos" that passed one thousand dollars per fight[14] are common, and few of the artists commissioned to pass to posterity the images of these new elites forgot to include their favorite roosters. Given the rigidity of Colonial society and the avidity of the rising elites to gain social recognition, Europeans frequently objected to cockfighting because it caused "the intermingling of grades of society" with a consequent "disruption of respect."[15]

Violation of caste barriers was not the only reason why the Spanish did not altogether approve of the sport. R. Ileto[16] (1979) has convincingly argued that another outcropping of folk culture, the *pasyon* (passion plays) provided Filipino insurgents with a vocabulary to voice their grievances against Spain in a language that appealed to large segments of the Filipino population normally left unmoved by more academic terminology. It would be surprising if the cockfight, an event built around life and death, victor and vanquished, pride and humiliation, etc., provided fewer metaphors useful to nineteenth-century revolutionaries. Furthermore, just as religious services gave revolutionaries the chance to hold public meetings where the Spanish could not easily interfere, so cockpits provided secure cover for rebels. Thus, Jose Rizal, the intellectual hero of the Philippine Revolution, set an entire chapter of his inspirational *Noli Me Tangere* in a cockpit. In the following passage, for example, two poor brothers are trying to decide if they should join a raid on the Spanish barracks:

> The referee, in accordance with official regulations, declared the red cock the winner. A savage roar greeted the verdict, a roar heard through the town, sustained and drawn out. Whoever heard it from afar would have understood that the favorite had lost. So it is among nations. The small nation that achieves a victory over a larger one tells and sings of it forever after.

> "Did you see that?" Bruno asked his brother sulkily, when the white cock, the favorite, had lost. "If you had believed me, we would have a hundred pesos by now. It's your fault we haven't a penny."[17]

Spanish ambivalence to cockfighting is reflected in the numerous and frequently changing regulations dealing with the sport. On the one hand they feared, as we have noted, large gatherings of people that were difficult to control: . . . as contemporary observers pointed out, stationing soldiers inside the cockpits was as likely to provoke a riot as to prevent one. On the other hand, cockpits were profitable businesses and their licensing provided cheap rewards to local functionaries.[18] In addition, some Spaniards thought that cock-fighting provided a useful safety valve which bled off social tensions. Although few thought that cockfighting was the ideal solution for social problems, many felt that there was nothing more convenient with which cockfighting could be replaced. Furthermore, the Spanish also felt that prohibiting cockfighting en-tirely would simply drive it underground rather than eliminate it, thereby re-moving the entire event from Spanish influence.

The Americans who replaced the Spanish at the turn of the century had fewer doubts about the worth of cockfighting. While a surprising number of American soldiers were themselves cockers, the official view was that the sport did nothing but encourage the natural indolence and vice of the Filipino. Hav-ing successfully concluded a campaign to ban cockfighting from the better part of the industrialized United States, and beset by armies of morally self-righteous and politically influential pressure groups, the new government made every effort to convince Filipinos to find a healthier form of entertain-ment. One of the earliest visitors to the Colony was happy to note in his mem-oirs that the newly introduced sport of baseball was so popular that it "emptied the cockpits to such an extent that their beneficiaries have attempted to secure legislation restricting the time it could be played."[19]

Apparently, baseball's success in keeping people out of the cockpit was quite shortlived, for in 1906 *The League of Moral Progress for Filipinos* called a meeting to discuss legal strategies that would keep Filipinos away from "this cruel sport." This meeting unleashed a typhoon of impassioned speeches, "letters to the editor," petitions and manifestos, ranging from one cocker who thought that cockfighting brings out the noblest side of an ignoble being, to a profound bit of reflection by Mr. Kinkaid, President of the League, who wondered, "How can a people who allow themselves to be known by the barbarous sport of cockfighting be allowed to govern themselves?"[20]

Not all Americans were so devoutly opposed to cockfighting. One admiring American traveller to the provinces north of Manila reported that:

Mr. Milloy, the son of a Canadian Presbyterian minister, has acquired the Tagalog language and has unusual success in reaching large crowds in the marketplace and at cockpits. He often holds his audience for hours as he reads and explains.[21]

One can easily imagine how entranced cockfighting *aficionados* must have been at having the fights delayed for several hours of Bible reading, a situation comparable, perhaps, to having Reverend Moon delay the Superbowl for a sermon on General MacArthur. One can also, therefore, imagine the nature of the colonial power structure that allowed itinerant ministers to singlehandedly cut short the fights.

Cockfighting has suffered the vicissitudes of political fashion since the Philippines gained independence from the United States in 1948. Clifford Geertz, writing on Balinese cockfights, suggests that cockfights were outlawed after Indonesia's independence:

> largely as a result of the pretensions to puritanism radical nationalism tends to bring with it. The elite, which is not itself so very puritan, worries about the poor, ignorant, peasant gambling all his money away, about the waste of time better devoted to building up the country. It sees cockfighting as "primitive" "backward" "unprogressive" and generally unbecoming to an ambitious nation.[22]

And it is quite true that in the Philippines, as in Indonesia, businessmen, professionals, and others of the "progressive elite" complain of peasants ruining themselves gambling, giving badly needed food to their birds instead of their children, and, more generally, degenerating into dissolute wretches struggling between Sundays the way alcoholics struggle between bottles of whiskey.

Unlike the Indonesian regime, however, the Philippine government has not banned cockfighting. Puritanical Philippine radical nationalists are not in power, nor is cockfighting confined to any one region as seems to be the case in Bali. Philippine nationalist thought, in fact, is somewhat divided on this issue. University intellectuals, rarely cockers themselves, recognize that most Americans and Europeans (at least those likely to visit the Philippines) do not approve of cockfighting and for that very reason denounce efforts to ban the sport as an infringement on national sovereignty. The government, perhaps recognizing that outlawing cockfighting would produce for the Philippines the same results as did Prohibition for the United States, has sought instead to regulate cockfighting by creating a Commission on Gamefowl. This commission not only controls the licensing of cockpits and permits for fights besides those held on the normal Sunday—village *fiestas*, for example, require a three day cockfight—but the Commission also issues breeders permits and import licenses. The Commission's power to regulate cock breeding is the result of lobbying by large breeders close to the Marcos administration; its effect is to place all large breeders on a short leash held by the government. While few people wealthy enough to import or extensively breed cocks depend on cockfighting for a living, dealing with the Commission requires complicated political negotiation; in a government preoccupied with political appearance, every little bit helps. More importantly, the proliferation of regulations increases the likelihood of a law being broken, thereby providing marvelous opportunities for selective enforcement.

A long section of the Civil Code of the Philippines carefully lays out regulations concerning cockpits.[23] All municipal officials—mayors, *barrio* captains (settlement heads—the lowest level in the executive branch of government), councilmen, and so on—are forbidden to have any managerial or proprietal role in a cockpit. The laws prohibiting official participation in cockpits are honored more in their breach than in their observance. Throughout the country, cockpits are effectively owned and managed by municipal mayors, although title is usually held by a trusted follower or in the name of a corporation.[24] These laws are designed to form part of the government's more general effort to prevent local officials from developing their own power bases. This is not unwarranted fear; one of the most powerful figures in Cagayan province built a great deal of his following by sponsoring extravagant cockfight derbies, following which he sponsored equally extravagant feasts. Currently being eased out of power by Manila, in 1980 this same official opened the annual gala cockfight of the provincial capitol with a long political invective against government agents "attempting to destroy him." His message, veiled, or course, in the language of the cockpit, was that he would not tolerate further efforts to undermine his position. The government, however responded by first ruining his cockpit's reputation and then by giving his license to someone else. This fellow, rumor has it, is moving to Connecticut. In the Philippines, where serious state-building has only begun in the past two decades, there are still quite a few powerholders at odds with the Manila government.

The future of cockfighting in the Philippines is not very clear. Many members of the Manila elite, whether from the universities, the offices of transnational corporations, or the mushrooming supply of government technocrats, are more likely to be found on the tennis courts than in the cockpits. This would suggest that on the one hand cockfighting in the Philippines is undergoing the same marginalization it suffered in Europe and America, where it is now a low-prestige sport limited mostly to rural workers and urban immigrants. On the other hand, many politicians and businessmen, especially those associated with the Marcos regime, are avid cockers. In the provinces, cockfighting is as popular as ever. Today, though cockfights are no longer broadcast on television, and international derbies featuring the most famous cockers in the world rate little more than a paragraph in the back of the *Bulletin Today,* cockfighting remains the most popular sport in the country.

This sketchy history of Philippine cockfighting suffices to show that the gross structure and at least some of the meanings of the cockfight make sense only when seen in historical perspective. During the early years of Spanish colonization, cockfighting went from being a relatively informal, impermanent activity to a taxed, regulated sport associated with the colonial government. Early in the nineteenth century, cockfighting became a central arena for cultural expression by a rising mestizo class despite, and perhaps because of, Spanish efforts to control the cockfight. Excluded from "high society" by the

141

Spanish, who naturally wished to preserve the trappings of power, the mestizos turned to other domains: fashions, literature, and cockfighting. Eventually the contradiction between an economically powerful indigenous entrepreneurial mestizo class and politically powerful colonizer produced the Philippine revolutionary movement. It is no surprise that during this period cockfighting increasingly acquired explicitly political connotations and cockpits became political as well as avian arenas.

Cockpits also figured in the American scheme to rebuild Philippine culture. Colonial power appeared in such crude scenes as the missionary imposing his solitary will on powerless Filipinos, and in more subtle efforts such as the American government's inclusion of morality lectures stressing the barbarity of Filipino customs such as cockfighting in the primary school curriculum.[25] Indeed, throughout this period the American government consistently opposed Filipino cockfighting, indolence, and intellectual inferiority to American ice-cream sodas, racial superiority, and higher mathematics. Not all myths think themselves through men; some get a little help.

Finally, the independent Philippine state has attempted to impose even greater control over the cockpits and cockfighting. Presidential decrees #449 and 1310, for example, regulate the location and frequency of cockfighting, while the newly created Gamefowl Commission demands an annual licensing fee and requires the employment of cockpit personnel registered with the Commission. The Philippine government also demands that each cockpit maintain at least one member of the integrated National Police force in the cockpit every time the doors are opened.

Not all changes in Philippine cockfighting have been so obvious, nor have they been limited to the broad structure of the event. The ongoing cultural impact of American colonialism continues to be refracted in the cockpit. Just as American colonial policy systematically favored the English-speaking, American-oriented elites that dominate the country to this day, the continued and growing prestige of cockers who adopt the American cocking styles, techniques, and even vocabulary derives from an "American-style" language of modernity. But before we can explore this further, it is necessary to say something about how cockfighting is actually carried out. Perhaps there is no better place to begin than with the birds.

The Cocks: Traditional and Modern Methods

Provided it is mature and reasonably well-nourished, almost any cock will fight other cocks, often to the death. However, just because all cocks will fight, it does not follow that they all fight equally well. Cocks, like people, have different fighting styles. Some are slow, strong, deliberate punchers, others uncork fusillades of fast but poorly aimed kicks, while still others weave from side to side to avoid body blows; some cocks fly high while others fight entirely on the ground, and so on.

Although feeding and training can improve the performance of a bird, most of the fighting style derives from the bird's breeding. All strains of fighting cock originated in South and Southeast Asia, but it was not until the European discovery of scientific breeding in the seventeenth and eighteenth centuries that families were inbred to weed out unfavorable traits. While themselves too heavily inbred to fight, (they become frail) inbred families can be combined like so many ingredients in a recipe to produce the fighting qualities desired by a breeder.

The indigenous Philippine roosters—*batangas, bolinaos,* and *palanans*— have not been inbred. Inbred roosters arrived in the Philippines in the 1930s when a group of Texas airmen stationed in Pampanga (near Manila) brought a strain of "Florida Typewriters" to the Anglo-Filipino pit in Mandaluyong. By Philippine standards, these "typewriters" were strikingly ugly, but they were strong, fast and, most importantly, they never gave up. They beat all challengers; local standards of beauty quickly changed. These were the first "Texas" cocks brought into the Philippines, and their success marked the beginning of scientific breeding for Philippine cockfighters.[26]

Like anything involving science in the Third World, scientific cock breeding is expensive. Brood stock, some of which has been inbred for more than a century, must be imported from the United States. Locally bred strains have only recently gained a modicum of popularity, and these are as expensive as imported seed fowl. Top quality brood stock starts at around four hundred dollars (U.S.) and can pass two thousand dollars for one cock and two hens.

Modern breeding in the Philippines is as advanced as breeding anywhere in the world today. Fighting crosses are computed on the basis of percentage of different gene groups. Discussions by breeders often sound like a foreign language. One successful blend, for example, is a 9/16 left-in lemon, 1/16 right marker blueface hatch, and a 3/8 out-and-out kelos. Needless to say, fluency in breeder's language is critical for social acceptance by the cockfighting *cognoscenti.*

The high cost of brood stock is not the only reason why breeding is so expensive. Professional breeders hatch their eggs in electric incubators and raise the chicks in heated, lit brooders. After two or three months the healthiest stags are turned loose (the sickly are either killed or given as "presents" to friends, relatives, or employees) on several hectares of rangeland where they spend the next few months developing strong bones and muscles as they scratch for bugs, spar, and learn to survive nature. When the young birds can seriously damage one another, they are caught, dubbed, banded, and tied (always by the left leg) to long cords beneath large, open-air teepees where they spend the next eighteen months maturing into strong, aggressive, fighting cocks.

Feeding and conditioning these birds is as elaborate as their breeding. By the time a cock enters a big-time cockpit, he has been heavily doped with steroids, hormones, vitamins, stimulants, and coagulants, conditioned on a carefully designed daily exercise program, and fed a diet containing exactly twenty-three per cent grain protein supplemented by eggs, liver, lettuce, carrots, tomatoes, buttermilk, and assorted secret ingredients.

Even a medium-sized breeder, one who raises two or three hundred birds every year, must have installations worth several hundred thousand pesos and maintain, year round, four or more full time employees to feed and care for the roosters. Large breeders' investments reach into the millions of pesos, and this is before the betting starts.[27]

Because modern breeding is so time-consuming and expensive, scientific breeding is controlled by a relatively small group of professional cock breeders and cockfighters. These people import the finest brood stock from the United States—a number of them actually fly to the United States simply to visit farms and buy roosters—and maintain sprawling, up-to-date farms. They by and large control all of the really big-time fights. There are two major breeding centers. One is in the central, sugar-producing islands of Negros, Iloilo, and Cebu; the other is in Manila and its immediate environs. The former group is made up primarily of old, established families connected to the sugar industry, while the latter, which is considerably younger in the cockbreeding business, is for the most part composed of people associated in one way or another with the Marcos regime.

While most of these breeders fight, many also sell their surplus cocks. There is no shortage of demand. Wealthy rural cockers, especially mayors who must provide quality entries during the annual derbies, exploit every possible connection, including paying exorbitant prices, to acquire choice cocks. Philippine cockfighting is big business.

Traditional Cocking

The scientific precision of modern cocking is not evident in the traditional methods of breeding, raising, and training cocks. To the extent that cocks are bred at all, it is by penning a proven winner together with an exceptionally pretty hen, regardless of gene types. Feed for the birds is mostly sifted corn plus whatever grubs and grain the cock can scratch up while on his tether, a far cry from the medically designed diets of the high-class roosters. Cocks are trained by what in Tagalog is called *kahig* ("tailing"), holding two roosters opposite one another and encouraging them to strike. Blowing smoke in their eyes, sticking chili up the anus, and caging them in dark boxes are all thought to increase their natural ferocity.

There are probably more folk beliefs concerning cockfighting than any other activity in Philippine culture. As might be expected in such a radically male sport, women and cocks do not get along. A ready-to-fight cock touched by a menstruating woman is sure to lose. Sex should be avoided before going to the cockpit; the man stupid enough to have sex before a match will be ignominiously humiliated when his bird runs away. On the other hand, exceptionally boastful cockers claim that sex before a fight improves their bird's performance. Sex is heartily recommended for after the fight when men no longer need to conserve their vital energies.

There are many different charms (*anting-anting*) that can help a cocker. The single most effective charm is the underwear of a virgin stolen on Good Friday and smuggled into Mass the following Sunday, during which it "receives Communion." Not so colorful but almost as effective is owning a three-legged cock (there are a few cocks that have a stub of a third leg; they are, so to speak, Golden Geese and are never fought). The three-legged cock is offered water from a special bowl. The bowl is then placed in front of all the cocks to be fought later that day. If the two-legged cocks drink the water, they will win; cocks that refuse to drink should be saved for a more auspicious day. (Curiously, scientific cockers argue that a properly conditioned bird will refuse to drink.)

Death is a theme prominent in cocking lore. Folk beliefs properly support the structural inversion of the good *anting-anting;* whereas the underwear of a young virgin guarantees good luck, contact with old widows brings disaster. Overtaking a funeral procession on the way to the cockpit is good luck, meeting one is bad. A peculiar form of bad luck is seeing a snake with toad legs sticking out of his mouth, a belief possibly related to cuckoldry.

Some beliefs are more systematized than others. The most elaborate belief system refers to *señal* divination, a type of avian palm reading premised on the belief that a cock's destiny can be uncovered through the arrangement of scales on his legs. A long groove running down the front of the leg (*baston*) is a good *señal* because it suggests that the cock will fight as if he had a real *baston* (club). A single scale surrounded by six smaller scales suggests that your cock will win but to avert future calamity in the cockpit you must use your winnings to buy beer and snacks for your friends. Other *señales* predict that your opponent will run away during the fight, what color opponent your cock should face, what time of the month to fight, and so on. *Señal* reading is an art best understood by old men and is taken quite seriously. Many cockers will shun what in sparring sessions was a spectacular fighter if a well-respected old man reveals an especially pernicious *señal* reading. There is a very rough correlation between age, social prominence and *señal* literacy, or rather, popular acceptance of *señal* readings.

Matching is another well-organized belief system. There are definite times in the day that favor certain colors. A *lasac* (spangled) should be fought after four in the afternoon, while a *talingaraw* (blue-dotted gray cock with white speckles) should be fought, if possible, in the morning. Colors are rated against one another. A *dalusapi* (black and red with yellow or white legs) is *pelo* (underdog) to a *talisayan* (yellow and black or white and black, with light legs) and will, all other things being equal, lose.

People can explain these beliefs in colors in a variety of ways. Some people are content with simply saying that this is what their parents taught them. Others claim that they built up their own system through observation; they believe in *señal* but not *pelo,* for example. Still others argue that since "Texas" cocks tend towards certain colors, these colors have a greater probability of containing a high percentage of Texas blood. Conversely, "off" colors should be fought in the morning because they have higher amounts of native blood and should be fought when they are less likely to encounter a high stake, "Texas" holdup. If pushed, many cockers will say that they first learned and accepted the belief and only subsequently tried to explain why they believed it. True hustlers confess that while they do not really believe in these things, they provide great opportunities for improving their matches.

The point of this exegesis of traditional versus modern methods (it could go on for pages) is not to show how advanced scientific cocking has become or how backward are old techniques. Very few people use either wholly traditional or wholly modern methods. In Piat, where I did my fieldwork, I met only one cocker who bred using genetic percentages, and it is only within the past few years that even the most prestigious cockers have begun to use fancy conditioning techniques. Indeed, for many people it is hard to argue that there are really two systems operating. For some people, the magic ingredient that makes for their success is the boiled duck embryo fed to the rooster the night before the fight; for others it is the little white pill pocketed from the local health clinic. For most people, the difference between traditional and modern cocking methods refers largely to the source of the knowledge rather than the substance. The truly valued cockfighting secrets are the formalized routines and diets gleaned from "big timers" who come from the city. Poor farmers may not know what twenty-three per cent grain protein is, but they can tell visiting cousins in the most solemn, scientific tones that the mayor feeds *eighteen* different ingredients to his roosters. And since the mayor is such a good fellow, he has graciously explained what they are, albeit, of course, only to his closest supporters. Thus, demonstrating yet again that a little knowledge is dangerous, cocks released in the pit occasionally collapse from overdoses of medicine, for if the little pill that a cousin got from the driver of a big-time Manila cocker worked well, then two must work better.

Most people likely to be called traditional now have many doubts about the old-fashioned methods of raising and training cocks, just as they have doubts about the old-fashioned methods of running a farm or a household. Today, only the poorest, oldest, most ignorant men, as the modern breed of chic cockers describe them, accept lopsided matches because they have an advantage in *señal, pelo,* or time of month. Even the poorest farmers recognize that feeding their cocks grain mixtures instead of corn produces a better performance from their roosters, and if more of them do not, it is partially because they have a hard enough time buying grain for their own families.

At the same time, those well-versed in the traditional methods continue to insist on their importance, although to an increasingly skeptical audience. Indeed, in Piat at least, a major subject of cockpit discussions was exactly how much to weight factors such as breeding versus *señal,* or chemical coagulants versus "blood thickening" foods. Not surprisingly, the people best able to take advantage of modern methods most enthusiastically embraced scientific breeding and conditioning. Denying the validity of old knowledge and monopolizing new sources is a time-honored technique for subverting the claims of traditional authority, even if that new knowledge consists of little more than knowing the generic name of a locally available drug.

We can conclude this discussion by noting that beneath the layers of customs, traditions, and conflicts, there really is a significant difference between cocks. In sheer physical terms, a well-bred, well-fed, and well-conditioned "Texas" rooster can deliver four times as many blows as his neglected native counterparts, not to mention differences in power, accuracy, and resistance. This is relevant because, as we have already mentioned, there is a very strong positive correlation between status and cock quality. Were cockfights randomly arranged, money would flow from poor to rich at a rate as terrifying as outside the cockpit. However, while cockfighting is most definitely not a redistributive ritual, neither is it run by reactionary Robin Hoods who pluck the poor to stuff the rich. Why people go to the cockfights—and a great deal more is involved than a massive fleecing of poorer cockers—and what takes place there require a short description of the actual event.

147

The Cockpit

Jose Rizal, writing at the close of the nineteenth century, described the contemporary cockpit:

> It had three main divisions. The entrance was a large rectangle approximately twenty meters by fourteen. There was a door in one of its sides, usually in the charge of a woman who collected the entrance fees. . . . In this first compartment of the cockpit might be found the pedlars of betel nut, cigars, sweetmeats, and other eatables. . . . This enclosure led to another slightly larger one, a kind of lobby where the public gathered before an actual cockfight. Here were to be found the majority of the fighting cocks, held to the ground by a cord fastened to a bone or a wooden nail; here were the gamblers, fanciers, and gaffers. Here bets were crossed, form studied, money borrowed amid oaths, promises and loud laughter. In one corner a sportsman handled his favorite cock, stroking its brilliant plumage; elsewhere another counted and studied the scales on a gamecock's legs; still others recounted the feats of past victors. . . . This place led to the pit proper, or ring, whose floor, surrounded by a bamboo fence, was higher than the other two compartments. In its upper part, almost reaching the roof, were stands for the spectators or, for they came to the same thing, the gamblers. During the fights these stands were filled with men and boys, shouting, cheering, sweating, quarrelling, swearing; fortunately there were almost never any women there. In the ring itself were the men of distinction, the wealthy, the famous gamblers, the concessionaire and the referee. The birds fought on the perfectly level ground, from which destiny distributed laughter or tears, plenty or want.[28]

Despite the use of more modern materials such as galvanized iron roofing rather than bamboo mats, electrical lighting, and, in the exceptionally luxurious cockpits, air-conditioning, sound systems and video instant-replay machinery, cockpits today look very much like the cockpits described by Rizal.

The Piat cock arena is typical of most rural cockpits. Built on the town mayor's enormous sugar plantation, the cockpit is well positioned to attract cockers from the five surrounding market towns that make up the Itawes district in the northern part of Luzon, as well as some cockers from the provincial capitol across the Cagayan river. The Piat cockpit was not always located where it is today. Prior to the election of the current mayor in 1966, the municipal cockpit was located in the center of town, near the house of the leader of the faction that subsequently lost the election. When Mayor Diaz took office, one of his first acts was to move the cockpit to his home barrio, in front of the house of his uncle who was, coincidentally, the leader of the WWII resistance and the most popular politician in the region. After the declaration of martial law in 1972, however, President Marcos passed a decree ordering all cockpits to be relocated at least one kilometer away from all municipal buildings, churches and schools. The mayor took advantage of this opportunity to move the cockpit to its current location on his plantation. Most cockpits in northern Luzon, apparently, have similar nomadic careers as political leadership changes hands.

Surrounding the cockpit are a number of makeshift stores offering food, beer, and the meat and fish that was not sold in the town market earlier in the morning. The cockpit management rents these stores for about 10 pesos per month. Because of the low rent and the well-heeled clientele, these stores are quite profitable and, since cockpit and ground are owned by the municipal mayor, they constitute a much desired pork-barrel handout.

The stores are staffed by women, as are the admission gates. On most Sundays, these stores boost sales by sponsoring poker games before the fights begin, but once the first cocks are matched all other gambling ceases until evening. In addition to offering refreshment and a place for post-fight analysis, these stores provide a convenient hideout for people who do not want to be seen in the cockpit, usually because they will be called upon to bet a bird that they do not really trust.[29]

Off to the side of the stores are some thirty-five bamboo cages where cocks can be left to rest while their owners are watching the fights. These are not very often used, however, as most owners are afraid of having their rooster poisoned while they are inside enjoying the fights. The majority of men bring their birds with them into the pit, arms shielding the body and hands covering the head so that nobody can slip a piece of insecticide-soaked corn into his beak. In a really big fight, cockers will bring their own holding pens and post guards around their birds to prevent meddling. Fixed fights and cheating have become an increasing problem in the Piat cockpit as a consortium of unscrupulous businessmen and army personnel have systematized what was formerly a sporadic and risky strategy.

Immediately outside the cockpit proper is a large, low, concrete rectangle. This is the *ulutan*. Men who wish to match their cocks sit on the *ulutan* to scan the field of prospective opponents. The *ulutan* is the place where cocks are incited to fight (*pag-uulot*) by placing them head-to-head with a possible opponent.

Periodically one of the straw-hatted men holding a cock will stop stroking the bird's neck and slowly carry the cock over to what may be a match. Gently setting his bird a few feet in front of the antagonist, the owner lightly taps his chicken's tailbones a few times to remind him that he is in a cockpit and to encourage him to show some proper spirit. The owner of the other either pushes his bird at the opponent—neither owner ever lets them actually make contact—or, to show that he is not interested in the match, simply picks up his

149

bird and moves to another part of the *ulutan.* Very little is actually said by the principals; most of the urging or dissuading is done by companions or by a cockpit matchmaker. During the height of the season, the *ulutan* quickly fills up with men and roosters and breaks up into small clusters of tightly-huddled men haggling over potential matches.

The Piat cock arena is a small, sandfilled square measuring some eight meters per side. It is completely surrounded by iron bars (fancier cockpits wall the bars with plexiglass) to prevent cowardly cocks from running out among the audience although occasionally a terrified, horribly undernourished bird manages to slip through the bars and escape, knife and all, into the audience.

Around the arena are a series of benches. This is the *preferencia,* the "reserved" section of the pit. Admission to the *preferencia* costs twenty pesos, as opposed to the usual two-peso entrance fee for the gallery, but the high price is really to keep undesirable people out. The people management wants in *preferencia* do not pay at all. Heavy bettors, high-status visitors, and foreigners are usually invited to sit in *preferencia*—indeed, a member of either of the first two groups would be highly insulted if he was not invited to *preferencia.* Cockpit managers constantly complain that every local *barrio captain* expects to be treated like visiting royalty.

Behind *preferencia* are layers of rough-hewn bleachers hanging from a confused network of struts, beams and supports. These are for the commoners. Admission here is part of the gate fee. Since the cockpit is invariably full to bursting, real enthusiasts will gingerly thread their way between the barbed wire to perch on the uppermost beams. These enthusiasts are not all young; one spry old Piateño of eighty-six regularly straddles the roof supports because, he says, it gives him the best view in the house.

During the height of the season, matching begins as early as nine in the morning and continues until seven at night. And Piat is considered a medium-sized barrio cockpit. Urban cockpits in Manila, for example, open their doors at seven in the morning and continue until two or three in the morning. Even this is trivial compared to some of the giant derbies which may have several hundred fights stretching over three or four days.

Matching

Matching cocks on an ordinary Sunday always follows the same course. Men carefully scan the *ulutan,* searching for a cock they think is a little smaller or lighter, or lower-blood, or badly trained, or *pelo,* or any one of the myriad variables that a good matchmaker must take into account when seeking an opponent. Very often someone has inside information on a cock; a resident of

Tuao tells his cousin from Piat that the handsome *talisayan* is fast but wild, or somebody saw the first win of the *dalusapi* and knows that it rushes; most probably his sidestepping *lasak* could outsmart it. Inside information is as good as gold; a cocker will very often give a weight advantage of one hundred grams or more, ensuring that the opponent will agree to the match, if he thinks that his own cock performs well against that particular style. Or again, it is important to know that the *hacendado* down the road buys first-class cocks from Manila for more than fifteen hundred pesos apiece, but his trainer steals their feed money and conditions the birds on yellow corn. A good matchmaker would rather fight the *hacendado* than the old Ilocano down the road who has three birds from his cousin in San Vicente—but who trains them with imported feeds and carefully regulated exercise.

Matchmaking is not an easy skill to acquire, and some people are known solely because of their matchmaking abilities. Cockers have all kinds of tricks to snare a good match. Holding the cock by the base of the tail makes him bend his knees so he looks shorter than he is. Some cockers, preferring an ugly but winning cock, clip the tail feathers, trim the comb high, and pull the little white feathers beneath the hackles, leaving a moth-eaten looking bird that seems to be a candidate for the stewpot rather than the coliseum. Still others try to match their cocks against smaller but "luckier" roosters; for example, birds whose color is favored at that particular time of day. Not only do cynics abound in cockfighting, but even believers disagree over how much weight should be given to *señal, regla,* or other beliefs.

Nevertheless, as we have noted, despite enormous differences in fighting prowess between birds, most of the time, approximately equal birds are fighting one another. "Holdup" matches (matches where there is a big difference in the size or quality of the birds) are hard to arrange. There are a number of mechanisms that militate against excessively unequal matches. Sportsmanship is not one of them. While some lip service is paid to the idea that, for example, it is shameful for a mayor to seek a fight with a farmer, given the right conditions most mayors would agree to such a match. Cockfighting, as one mayor told me, is a hustler's game, and it is not how you play the game that counts but whether you win or lose.

One reason equal cocks fight one another is the universally held belief in "blood." Cocks are ranked on a scale in which a one-hundred-percent pure imported "Texas" cock is the pinnacle and a one-hundred-percent native cock the pit. There are a number of features used to diagnose "blood." Cocks with small heads, thin legs, and long sickle feathers are high-blooded, while off-colors, large heads, and short wings suggest a strong infusion of native lines. As cocks are bred, the belief goes, their "blood" diminishes in quality. Two 100% imported birds will, if bred in the Philippines, produce a 90% or "island-born" cock; two crossed 90% birds yield an 80%, and then 75%, 60%, 40%, 30%, 15%, and native, or Tagalog cock. The system certainly has nothing to do with genetics; it is more akin to colonial caste ranking. It refers to the expected performance of the cock. In the majority of cases, a 90% cock is expected to make short work of a 15% cock, and for people to bet on a native against even a 15% "Texas" requires handicapping the "Texas." Even with the handicap, few cockers would want to own the low-blooded cock.

A second factor affecting matchmaking is the size of the *parada,* or center bet. In all fights, the total amount of money risked must be the same as that gained. While bets can usually be evened out by offering odds, there is a limit beyond which even the most attractive odds cannot draw bets on an obvious mismatch. Thus, for example, if a farmer were to approach a big-time with his small, ugly, mestizo (!) cock—perhaps he felt extraordinarily lucky that day— the big-timer might agree to the match. But more likely than not, the difference between the bets would be so great that the fight would be cancelled.

Cocks acquire reputations, either from people who have seen them fight before or through their owner. Because the overwhelming majority of fans attending the cockpit in Piat are from Piat and the three immediately neighboring municipalities, it is quite likely that any opponent of a Piat cock has a relative or friend in Piat who will pass him information about the Piat cocks. If the cock is already a winner, many people will have seen the fight (people's memories for fights are remarkable) and can judge if their own cock is comfortable facing that style. In addition, the reputation of an owner is crucial. Even a one-hundred-percent native cock is difficult to match if the owner is high-status. For the same reasons, a high-blooded cock is more easily matched if the owner is low-status and does not appear to be fronting for somebody else.

This raises an additional point concerning the bet and matchmaking. If a match is especially favorable, every acquaintance, friend, neighbor, and ally will try to enter as large a bet as possible with the owner. Refusing these bets is a socially risky thing to do, as we shall see further on. Hence, in a particularly lopsided match, the *parada* balloons beyond the ability of the cockpit to match all of the money regardless of the owner's own bet, and again the fight is cancelled.

Cockers relish the banter surrounding matchmaking. If the difference between birds is too great—if someone tries to match a pure "Texas" against another's mestizo—he is undoubtedly going to receive a sharp and nasty retort delivered with an ear-reaching grin: "Do you think that I have no eyes?" or "Berting wants to fight a cock that is already dead"—comments made all the more stinging because there is a highly appreciative audience ready to smirk at the man left without a snappy answer.

To continue though, normally men bunch around the principals and their

152

cocks, jostling for a view to make sure that their boy is not hustled or, should they think that they have an advantage in the match, provoking the opponent into making a hasty decision. Matchmaking can take quite some time since everyone is worried about being fooled into entering a bad match. Some match-makers, in fact, acquire such a reputation that for them simply to propose a match is sufficient reason for the opponent to refuse.

Once the match is agreed upon, the owners and their friends carry the roosters off to opposite sides of the cockpit to tie the *tari* (knives). The *tari* are privately owned—and expensive. A medium quality set of knives (they are made, appropriately enough, from American supplied armor piercing bullets . . . not quite a plowshare but certainly a step in the right direction) costs upwards of two hundred dollars (U.S.) per set. A *mananari* (knife tyer or, for those getting into the sport, "heeler") needs a minimum of eight.

Knife tying is exceedingly difficult. Most men do not know how to heel a cock correctly; a good *mananari* has been heeling since adolescence. The Piat cockpit maintains two *mananari* who will, for five or ten pesos if the cock wins, tie the *tari* for anyone who asks; however unless the cock belongs to the man-agement both of these heelers have the disconcerting habit of betting on the opponent. Most cockers bring a trusted *mananari* to the cockpit with them, and a cocker would not dream of going to a cockpit outside of his own municipality without an accompanying *mananari*. Cockers who enter the big-time derbies not only maintain a full time *mananari* equipped with several sets of custom-made *tari*, but, during the conditioning period, a number of them make video movies of their cocks so that the *mananari* can determine the exact striking angle.

The *tari* is almost always tied on the left foot. There is a commonly accepted system of handicapping used when the owners both like the match but there is a big difference between the cocks. Handicapping always involves the *tari*; a cock can be given a second *tari* if he is small, or the size of the larger bird can be offset by moving the *tari* to the right foot or further up the leg. Most of these systems depend more on disconcerting the *mananari* than actually incon-veniencing the bird: cocks are ambidextrous. An inexperienced *mananari*, how-ever, frequently makes mistakes when placing the *tari* in an unfamiliar posi-tion. And, as a popular saying has it, the *tari* is the life of the cock. In any case, handicapping occurs in less than ten percent of the matches and virtually never in a high-stake match.

While the *tari* is being tied, the owner and all of his supporters cluster around the cock except for one friend who is off spying on the opponent. The owner, or a very close friend, writes down what will become the *parada* (inside bet). If the owner is low-status, he will usually send a companion off to the relevant high-status people at the cockpit that day—his barrio captain, the

153

mayor, perhaps his employer, a judge who once did him a favor—to ask for their bets. This is important. If he fails to do this and the cock wins, the high-status people become quite indignant, complaining that they did not know that their "friend's" cock was being fought. Clearly, they say, the owner no longer "respects" his erstwhile benefactor. This can be a very serious accusation; some men will stay out of the cockpit for months and a few give up cockfighting entirely because they were publicly insulted by the mayor. This arrangement lends itself to face-saving theatrics by high-status cockers. Everybody knows whose cock is about to fight, and if they really wished to bet but had not been invited to join the *parada*, high-status men could easily send a messenger with their bet. Usually, if their bet does not enter the *parada* it is because they do not like the match or are annoyed with the owner. Acting the aggrieved party turns the tables, neatly handing fault of not making the proper loyalty bet (for, as we shall explain at greater length below, there is an obligation for patrons to bet on client's cocks as well as the reverse) to the owner.

The Fight: Preliminaries

Once the knife is tied, the real tension begins. The owner, making an unsuccessful effort to conceal his anxiety, lights a cigarette, downs a beer, and may even start to tremble with nervousness, all the while barraging his companions with questions: "Is it a good match?"; "Is the *tari* straight?"; "Do you think that we are taller?" and in general making a nuisance of himself. Many owners make it a practice not to enter the pit at all when their birds are fighting; they cannot stand the tension. Nervousness and excitement can reach quite a pitch. During my eighteen months stay two men died of heart attacks while their cocks were being fought (one of them had won).

The knives tied, bets taken, the cock given any last-minute pills, rubdowns, chilis or whatever, the owner, a backup man armed with the warm-up cock, and the huddle of supporters work their way through the crowd and into the arena. The cock is delicately dropped in his corner where he can crow, strut back and forth, and threaten his enemy on the other side of the cockpit. The owner, meanwhile, carefully scrutinizes the angle of the *tari*, checks his bird's droppings to make sure he has not been poisoned, and sizes up the enemy bird. Fights can be cancelled up until the moment when the birds are released, and should some last minute information arrive—for example, the enemy bird belongs not to the farmer who made the match but to the town mayor—men will invoke one of the many beliefs available for such contingencies (e.g., the bird pecked the sleeve of its handler) and back out of the match.

Once the birds are armed and brought into the pit, men who have been relaxing over a beer between fights drain their bottles and hurry back to their places. Inside, owners chat quietly with their seconds, flashing nervous smiles at friends and acquaintances outside the arena and writing down last-minute bets. People react differently to the strain. High-status cockers tend to play a devil-may-care role, smiling broadly, moving around the pit to chat with their friends, and making a few comments with the owner of the enemy bird. Low-status cockers are much grimmer; conversation with the enemy would be unthinkable unless it is to make nasty remarks.

Sooner or later the man holding the cock to be fought sidles up to the *kasedor* (head bookie) and quietly enters his bet. The *parada* is written down (it is legal evidence in case of subsequent quarrels), the handler returns to his cock's corner, and the handler of the second cock does the same thing. The *kasedor* directs the owner of the cock with the larger *parada* to the favorite's position, and the warmup begins. The noise gradually drops from a roar to relative silence; the betting has started.

Betting

Whatever the social, psychological, or political reasons why people attend cock-fights, any cocker will say the main reason he goes is to bet. And bet they do. The average total center bet for eighty-two fights in the Piat cockpit in May 1982, was 1,441 pesos with a maximum combined bet of 10,300 pesos. Piat is a *barrio* cockpit. In Tugeugarao, the capitol city of the region, bets occasionally pass 100,000 pesos per side, while in Manila bets regularly pass 500,000, and bets of 1,000,000 pesos, while not common, are not unknown either. Given that the supervisors of the largest estates in the Cagayan Valley make 15 pesos per day, cockfighting is clearly serious business; even the smallest bets are at least one week's wages for sugarcane cutters or, to put it another way, five to ten percent of the value of the rice harvest for farmers.

As in the Balinese cockfights studied by Geertz, there are two kinds of bet. The *parada* is a compound bet made up of the owner's bet together with the bets of his friends, neighbors, and allies and whatever additional amount is needed to equalize the two *paradas*. The inside bet is the official bet, backed by management and recorded by the *kasedor*. Should either side not be able to make good their loss, management will pay the winner (and arrest the loser). The cockpit management removes ten percent from the bet of all winners for cockpit fees.

Betting is tightly regulated by social conventions, a fact dramatically under-lined by the elaborate measures people take to avoid them. The most explicit of these concern political obligations, perhaps because political hierarchy is one

155

of the most explicit dimensions of rural hierarchy. If a mayor, for example, fights a cock, he can expect everyone in his municipality to bet on his cock if he is visiting another cockpit and at least everyone in his faction if he is fighting within the municipality. Similarly, a barrio captain can expect everyone in his barrio to support his cock. Thus, betting lines are pyramidical: councilmen support barrio captains, barrio captains support mayors, and mayors support governors. The converse is also true. The mayor will always support a barrio captain from his municipality against an opponent from another municipality; for him not to do so is a sure sign of political infighting. Mayors will actively discourage fights between barrio captains within their municipality; their effectiveness, as well as the lack of any horizontal solidarity, is shown by the frequency of fights between barrio captains of the same municipality when the mayor is away.

Kinship is another important variable. Close kinsmen always support one another's roosters. In theory, people should support any kinsmen, but in practice there seems to be little subjectively felt obligation beyond the second degree of collaterality. Of course, kin ties may be suddenly reactivated if it is desirable to bet with the *parada* rather than outside, and this is usually honored. Not supporting a close relative is a very serious offense.

Other factors taken into account are neighborhood, employment, or even ethnicity. Most coalitions, especially when the owners are high-status, are made up of men connected to the owner in a number of ways. When there are ties connecting men to both sides, they may, as Geertz reports for Bali, wander outside for a beer so that they do not have to pick. More likely, however, they will take advantage of the situation to bet on the cock of their choice rather than the owner.

Outside betting follows many of the same considerations of the inside bet, although to a much lesser extent; if the ties were all that binding on the outside bettors, they would have placed their bet in the *parada*. Still, most will try to carry out their moral obligation to villagemates, distant kinsmen, or whatever. Of course, for many outside bettors, especially when bets are low and socially unimportant people are fighting, there are no moral obligations.

It is extremely rare for both owners to produce the same sized *parada*. The difference may come from what is now the underdog who, suspecting that the opponent will enter a large bet, will often keep some money in reserve for just this purpose. Most cockers, however, do not like to be an underdog and hence bet all of their available money in the *parada*. Thus, the gap between the bets is usually too large for the underdog to make up by himself, and management must request contributions from the audience. If the cock in the "favorite" position appears smaller or weaker, the difference is made up practically instantly by bettors anxious to enter their bets on the underdog before they have to offer odds. More frequently, however, management must resort to *pago* (pay).

In *pago*, the *kasedor*, carrying his pen and notebook and accompanied by a cockpit *kristo* ("christ," or bookie), walks around the arena looking for well-known and well-heeled spectators. A short bit of *bola* (flattery) follows: "Mayor Hernandez, whose cock is as fatal in the henpit as it is in the cockpit . . . *PAGO ISANG LIBO!*" (pay one thousand pesos). . . . "Our beloved ex-mayor Panggulan who brought us all electricity and brownouts . . . *PAGO ISANG LIBO*," "Engineer Alfonso, our adopted Ibanag, *PAGO LIMANG DAAN*" (pay five hundred), "*DIFERENCIA TATLONG LIBO*" (three thousand remaining) . . . "*LARGA YA MANAGEMENT*" (Management makes up the rest). Needless to say, few men will refuse to pay after such a splendid announcement. A good *kasedor* can squeeze blood from a stone.

After all the stones have bled their last drops, the *kasedor* consults the owner of the favorite, inquiring whether he is satisfied with the even money. If the owner agrees, they can then offer odds to finish off the inside bet; if not the fight is cancelled and the next pair of birds brought into the arena. Usually the owners insist that at least their own bets and the bets of their closest allies be placed at even money, but if they are sure their bird will win even that is not essential. In any case, the owners of the cocks have ten minutes to cancel the fight, remove a portion of their bet, or cover the entire bet at various odds.

While the *paradas* are being evened, the only sounds in the cockpit are the *kristos* shouting odds or the *kasedor* making *pago*. Once the difference is made up from the audience, however, all hell breaks loose as the cockpit erupts into a frenzy of bets offered and bets taken. The initial outside odds are always the same as the last inside odds. They may stay there until the fight begins, but more frequently, the odds race up and down the betting scale as bettors offer the least favorable odds possible and still get a bet. Mistakes in judgment produce a small riot of bettors spinning the foolish fellow around by the shoulders, shaking fingers in his face to make sure that he understands their bets, and slapping his arms to make sure that their bet is the first to enter.

Odds in the Philippines follow a sliding scale that goes: even money, 10–9, 10–8, 9–8, 8–6, 10–7, 10–6, and 3–2 (the last two are prohibited in most cockpits because they encourage fixed fights). Bets are signalled with the fingers: fingers pointing down are the thousands of pesos, fingers horizontal the hundreds, and vertical fingers the tens. Tapping the head places the bet on the "favorite," while the reverse punch (*sahod*) bets on the underdog at 8–10. The hand signals are needed because bets are often made from opposite sides of the cockpit; the chances are good that the people standing near you are betting on the same cock you are (and for the same reasons).

The Fight

Once the sheaths are removed from the knives, the warm-up cocks passed over the bars to waiting hands in the audience, the times written down (fights lasting longer than ten minutes are automatic draws), and the ring cleared of all but the most important VIPs, the two handlers, the referee, and the cockpit owner, the fight is ready to begin. The referee wipes the *tari* with a small piece of cotton soaked in alcohol and beckons the releasers towards the center of the pit. The cocks are pointed at one another until their hackles rise. The handlers take a step backwards and release the cocks, making sure that the cock's left leg is dropped slightly behind the right to prevent the bird from laming himself as he runs towards his opponent.

All noise, whether betting, gossip, or chitchat, comes to an immediate halt as the crowd stretches to see the first blow. The enraged birds

> fly almost immediately at one another in a wing-beating, head-thrusting, leg-kicking explosion of animal fury so pure, so absolute, and in its own way so beautiful, as to be almost abstract, a Platonic concept of hate.[30]

Eventually, and in this case eventually can mean between twenty and thirty seconds, one of the birds is crippled or dying and unable to fight. The referee immediately picks up the two birds by their backs for the *sentencia* (decision). Facing one another, the birds peck. If neither, or both, peck, they are dropped to the floor. If a bird either pecks twice or kicks once, he is held beneath the head of his opponent to give him the chance to return the peck. If he fails to respond, he is dropped three times, first one meter away, then a half meter, and finally right underneath the nose of the soon-to-be-victor. Up until this time neither handler is allowed to touch the birds. But after the third *kareo* the loser is dropped in the dust while the winner is raised to the skies to the cheers of the crowd and the joy of his releaser who dances around the cockpit holding his victorious bird. The loser, meanwhile, retrieves his chicken—it is even worse if the bird ran—and, invariably alone, shuffles out of the arena to have the bird plucked, and to gather bets from his crestfallen friends.

As soon as the referee raises the winner, the cockpit is filled with a storm of crumpled money flying from one side of the pit to the other as the outside bets are paid off and the next pair of cocks is carried into the arena. If there is no fight immediately following, people pour out of the stands to congratulate the owner of the winner, inspect the bird's wounds and, in rare cases, console the loser. The loser, or one of his group, quickly pays the *parada* to the *kasedor*. A short while after, but never at the same time, the *kasedor* calls for the winner and pays off his bet minus the ten percent management fee.

Unfortunately, welshing on bets is not unknown. In rare cases, someone who bet on a "sure winner" without money attempts to slip out the door after the bird lost. If he is caught, his punishment is terrible. He is usually beaten, sometimes killed, and, what for many people is far worse, dragged into the arena where is he paraded around, insulted, kicked, and humiliated by policemen and fans before being hauled off to jail. Needless to say, this fate never awaits high-status welshers who can, in a pinch, write a check or ask the management to front the money. If they have enough supporters with them, they can simply manufacture an excuse and refuse to pay. In one well-known case, a particularly fierce mayor visiting a cockpit in the neighboring province pulled out his .45 and shot the about-to-be-victorious cock before the referee could finish the *sentencia*. He then claimed that because there was no final decision he should not have to pay. Since he was backed by three jeeploads of heavily-armed bodyguards, nobody pointed out the flaws in his argument.

Once outside of the cockpit, the owner of the winning bird pays off the members of his coalition. If the winner was the favorite and had to offer odds on the *parada,* the owner will give the best odds to his closest relatives and the politically important members of the group. Very often the others, who have just been given an unequivocal statement of where they stand with the owner, feel slighted, especially if they could have gotten better odds by betting outside rather than with the owner. Occasionally the owner, to assuage hurt feelings, will take the worst odds for himself. In fact, by the time the owner has figured out the bets, paid for the victory beers, bought meat for the family, and given *balato* ("tokens of appreciation") to well-wishers, friends who lost on other cocks, and smiling policemen, he often has almost nothing left for his efforts except a tired, stitched-up rooster.

The Interpretation of Cockfights

It is the betting that provides Geertz with an analytical scalpel with which he can dissect the Balinese cockfight. Noting that the heaviest bets and the most interesting matches are those between cocks belonging to community leaders, he suggests that what the Balinese see in the cockfight is a dramatization of social structure:

> The cocks may be surrogates for their owners' personalities, animal mirrors of psychic form, but the cockfight is—or more exactly, deliberately is made to be—a simulation of the social matrix, the involved system of cross-cutting, overlapping, highly corporate groups—villages, kingroups, irrigation societies, temple congregations, "castes"—in which its devotees live.[31]

Betting follows all of these intricate lines of affiliation. Men can never bet against a cock owned by a close relative. Closer relatives are supported against more distant relatives, and neighbors' cocks supported against cocks from further away. Because there is some variation in the principles of social organization in different parts of Bali, the exact betting rules will also vary, but the fundamental betting principle is that a man must always support the sociologically closer bird.

Geertz concludes that the main function of the cockfight is cognitive. The cockfight does not actually *do* anything; nobody's status changes, no new relationships are formed or old ones broken, social hierarchy is not affected, and the only participants who suffer any physical damage are the cocks. But by coupling personal identity, social organization, and hierarchy to a fatal fight between two chickens, the cockfight both lays the principles of social organization on the line, as it were, and shows just how necessary hierarchy is for social life:

> What, as we have already seen, the cockfight talks about most forcibly is status relationships, and what it says about them is that they are matters of life and death. That prestige is a profoundly serious business is apparent everywhere one looks in Bali—in the village, the family, the economy, the state. A peculiar fusion of Polynesian title ranks and Hindu castes, the hierarchy of pride is the moral backbone of the society. But only in the cockfight are the sentiments upon which that hierarchy rests revealed in their natural colors.[32]

At this point Geertz has shifted ground somewhat. Cockfighting, though providing a model of social structure, has another, more basic purpose: it offers a forum in which the Balinese display their most basic beliefs about man's nature. This accords well with Geertz's more general aim of reconstructing (or deconstructing) the models people use to make sense of the world: "societies, like lives, contain their own interpretations. One has only to learn how to gain access to them."[33] Cockfighting, in short, is a "metasocial commentary," a "story the Balinese tell themselves about themselves."

Geertz is not concerned with the "truthfulness" of the models conveyed by cockfighting. Indeed, he takes pains to point out that the cockfight does not say everything that can be said about Bali: analysis of other activities will show different sides of that complex culture:

> The cockfight is not the master key to Balinese life, any more than bullfighting is to Spanish. What it says about that life is not unqualified or even unchallenged by what other equally eloquent cultural statements say about it.[34]

160

The story that the Balinese tell themselves about themselves is remarkably similar to the story that the Filipinos tell themselves about themselves. The Philippine cockfight parallels Balinese cockfighting in a number of ways: the identification of self with cock, the "status bloodbath" that goes on in the pit, the requirement to follow lines of social affiliation in betting, and the omnipresence of hierarchy in virtually every aspect of the sport.

How reliable a guide to Philippine social structure does cockfighting provide? In the following section, I shall argue that far from illuminating the principles of Philippine social structure, cockfighting hides them. By using Bloch's and Kahn's[35] discussions of the nature of ideological formation, as well as case material from Piat, I shall also argue that the social theory contained in the cockfight legitmates elite power. Furthermore, there is a certain "phenomenological reality" to the theory; appearances often suggest that social structure is external to people. Nevertheless, changing material environments can also stimulate re-evaluations of the theory.

Another View of Piat

In a recent paper, I presented a preliminary analysis of changes in the economic and political organzation of Piat (1983). The argument can be summarized here to show that far from accurately depicting social structure, the model of Piat put forward in the cockfight obscures basic structural constituents.

There are roughly four main economic activities in Piat: small-scale farming (usually sharecropping), plantation work, sugar milling and refining, and assorted white-collar occupations. Most of the land in the town is controlled by two powerful families. Until recently, portions of these lands were sharecropped by tenants who grew a subsistence crop of corn or rice followed by a commercial crop of tobacco. Shortly after the nationwide declaration of martial law in 1972, a number of tenants received certificates of land transfer as part of the Agrarian Reform Program, and began making the obligatory cash amortization payments on their land. At about the same time, the government entered a partnership with seven of the most powerful figures in the country to open an enormous, heavily capitalized sugar mill and refinery. This complex began operations in 1978 and currently employs several hundred workers from Piat. To encourage sugarcane production, the government artificially ruined the tobacco market and began offering easy credit to landowners who wished to plant cane. Many did. Today, two sugar plantations dominate the easternmost portion of Piat. These plantations, each of which occupies more than two thousand hectares, are staffed by highly organized teams of wage laborers (mostly women) drawn from the nearby communities. During the four month milling season, the plantation work force is swelled by several hundred cane cutters brought by contractors from the Visayan speaking islands to the south.

All four activities are integrally dependent upon a capitalist market. This is obvious in the case of the sugar plantations, the refining mill, and the office occupations. Land reform beneficiaries are heavily dependent on capital inputs and market prices since they must meet their amortization payments by competing in a market where prices have been depressed by the success of the green Revolution in other parts of the country. Inadequate infrastructural support by the Ministry of Agrarian Reform, the small sizes of the parcels granted under the program, and the gradual subdivision of the land through inheritance are all working to drive farmers' production beneath the subsistence level, forcing them to seek work elsewhere. In fact, since most plantation workers live in farming households, one of the main effects of the land reform program in Piat has been to subsidize the sugar plantations by allowing plantation owners to pay less than the minimum daily wage needed for physical reproduction and still maintain a viable workforce.

In economic terms at least, there is no disjuncture between Piat and the national economy. Sugar production in Piat depends as much on an international division of labor that assigns sugar production to the Philippines and computer production to Japan as it does on any factors unique to Piat. Similarly, local production of high-yielding varieties of rice shows the tight connection between land reform beneficiaries in Piat and bioengineers in the International Rice Research Institute, not the gap between the "provincianos" and the urban intellectuals claimed by peasant and scientist.[36] Without focussing on the invisible yet pervasive commodity market, it would be impossible to make sense out of local economics.

A description of the local, regional, and national political structure would reveal the same processes at work. The increased centralization of the Philippine state has changed local politics in ways which cannot be explored here, only listed. First, the content and quality of local interactions with the national political machinery have intensified. Secondly, political resources have also changed. Whereas in the early part of the century political power grew out of the number of supporters a patron could mobilize, today many other factors are more immediately relevant, chief among them being support by the state apparatus. In other words, local power now flows from control of or relation to bureaucratic position, rather than the other way around. Third, local politicians now have little room for independent action, even at the local level. When Piat was a small, marginal, tobacco-growing community, Manila had very little interest in local politics. Now that the national sugar interests have invested in the region, and the region itself becomes a political battleground between at least two national factions, there is considerably less tolerance for local shenanigans. Real people are being killed.

This analysis, overly compacted though it is, has little to do with existing folk models of social structure and even less with the image of Piat conveyed in the cockfight. Any discussion of the economic dimension of local class structure, for instance, would place cane workers from Piat in the same category as cane workers from Faire, the neighboring municipality, and opposed to the plantation owners; precisely the opposite happens in the cockfight.

A look back at Geertz's work shows that a similar obfuscation of social structure is going on there as well. We find, for example, that:

> The cockfight is unusual within Balinese culture in being a single-sex public activity from which the other sex is totally and expressly excluded. Sexual differentiation is culturally extremely played down in Bali and most activities, formal and informal, involve the participation of men and women on equal ground, commonly as linked couples. . . . To this general pattern the cockfight, entirely of, by, and for men (women—at least *Balinese* women—do not even watch) is the most striking exception.[37] (emphasis in original)

Nor does the cockfight have very much to say about the social conflicts that led to the 1965 massacres which were, Geertz tells us in another footnote, the worst in Indonesia.

Cockfighting, Social Structure, and Traditional Authority

In an important pair of articles published in 1974 and 1977, Maurice Bloch has argued that there is a close connection between the social theory expressed in ritual and patterns of traditional authority. Bloch notes that the language used in ritual is markedly different from everyday language. Everyday language is flexible and creative. People can use everyday language for any number of tasks: ask for a drink, tell a joke, curse at the government, etc. Ritual language lacks this creative capacity. This is because ritual language is heavily formalized. People have little choice of form, style, words, or syntax.[38] Thus, it is impossible to use ritual language to refer to specific events. Furthermore, the syntactic rigidity of ritual language makes it impossible to use ritual to criticize existing social structure since ritual language has little or no referential content. To cite Bloch's example, it is impossible to argue with a song.[39] Thus, when ritual is fused with authority, it is impossible to criticize authority.

In short, merely by participating in the ritual one ends up supporting traditional authority:

> It is because the formalization of language is a way whereby one speaker can
> coerce the response of another that it can be seen as a form of social control. It is
> really a type of communication where rebellion is impossible and only revolution
> could be feasible.[40]

Cockfights certainly seem to fit many of Bloch's criteria for formalized
codes. The structure of each cockfight is exactly the same.[41] While it is possible to choose which of the two cocks to support, it is not possible to bet against
the social hierarchy itself. Furthermore, as we have already noted, the more
sociologically relevant the match, the less choice people have in betting. Symbolically at least, people will always be betting against their sociological peers
and supporting someone at a sociologically distinct level. Finally, the language
of the cockpit, like ritual language generally, sorts people out into the categories delimited by the folk theory of social structure.

Bloch's case is somewhat weaker when checked against the data from Piat.
When asked why the cheering is always louder when the underdog defeats the
favorite, a number of informants said (in so many words) that underdog victories showed that the poor farmer also has a chance. Even though in all of these
cases the owner of the underdog cock was anything but poor, people were able
to read variant meanings into the formal structure of the fight. It should also be
noted, however, that this particular interpretation *always* came from people
who had placed their bets outside and were therefore relatively distant from
the owners of the cocks. It would also be difficult to draw a hard and fast line
between challenging individual power holders and challenging the basic principles of stratification. In Piat, some people bet against the mayor because he
heads the opposing faction. Others, especially those heavily involved in land
reform, claimed they bet against him because he was the mayor. (Others bet
against him because they thought his bird would lose.) The point here is that
while Bloch is undoubtedly correct in suggesting that the formal structure of
the code may strongly influence what can be explicitly said in a ritual, popular
interpretations may vary for other reasons. Thus, in Piat illegal fights are sometimes held in some of the more remote settlements. Although they follow the
exact same rules as the legal fights, virtually every participant interviewed
claimed that they were held in part as a protest against the current autocratic
administration of the municipality. Given that these settlements are also sus-
pected of supporting the dissident New People's Army, at times, it seems,
cockfighting does not always support traditional authority. But it is important

to underline the fact that these cockfights are outside of elite control; merely participating in them is construed as an act of political protest. And in these settlements landlords, merchants, and political leaders hardly ever make an appearance at all, much less join a *topada* (illegal fight).[42]

In general, however, there is a certain rigidity both in the structure and context of cockfighting that makes it difficult to bring out non-hierarchical messages.[43] Philippine cockfighting is not illegal, only regulated. Hence, elites maintain control over the formal organization of the cockfight, and can also directly intervene in popular interpretations. Thus, local political leaders are incensed when supposed supporters do not bet on their cocks, and they are not very reticent about showing their displeasure. Similarly, two particularly radical reformers in Piat refuse to attend the cockpit at all because, they claim, no matter where they bet they had to support somebody they disliked.

A second, more important reason why cockfight ideology continues to make sense to people is that at the level of everyday experience the relationships described in the cockfight continue to be valid. The recent major changes in Piat—land reform, political consolidation by the state, and agro-industrial development—clearly derive from the role played by the Philippines in an international, class-structured economic system. Nevertheless, there are few indications that Piateños, other than the very wealthy, view social and economic relations in corresponding class terms. The development of the sugar industry, for example, seems to have benefitted the mayor and other estate individuals rather than a "capitalist class," despite the fact that the mayor became mayor and the estate owners possess valuable estates largely because of preexisting relationships to the means of production. As Joel Kahn has observed, while ideology does not adequately explain experience, neither does it contradict it.[44]

Nonetheless, folk models are changing. The recent political and economic developments are causing Piateños to seriously reevaluate dominant social patterns. Since the large landowners who controlled the political machinery no longer depend on electoral support, and sugar production has become vastly more appealing than tobacco or food-crop agriculture, landowners are rapidly withdrawing from any involvement in agricultural production. Land reform has shifted most agricultural risk and responsibility onto the cultivator, reducing landlord interest in sharecropper welfare still further; the few landlords who continue to plant corn and rice prefer to hire wage laborers to establishing patron-client relationships. As patron-clientage steadily becomes a shell of its former self, sharecroppers increasingly complain that they are being exploited—even though the actual share paid to the landlord has declined to nearly half the former amount. Landlords themselves complain that tenants are ungrateful—but practically always the favors that the tenants are ungrateful for refer to past generations, not current contributions, for there are very few of these.

Kinship is another area being reassessed. Kin connections are commonly used in Piat by plantation owners to secure full time members of the workforce, especially for managerial positions. Kin loyalties are one of the means commonly used to justify salaries considerably lower than those paid on nearby plantations owned by outside investors. But kinship is conveniently forgotten during layoffs, or when loans are needed, or for that matter, when someone commits a crime. A common complaint of Piateños is that their wealthy relatives seem to have forgotten the meaning of kinship.

Does the cockfight respond to these changes? The answer is by no means clear. The introduction of scientific breeding and conditioning mentioned in the second part of this paper is remembered by informants as dating only to the declaration of martial law in 1972. The astronomical betting, which has already removed cockfighting from the reach of the poorest Piateños, coincides with the tremendous cash influx caused by the introduction of sugarcane production.

None of these changes marks qualitatively new political structures. The vast authority of scientific breeding was easily appropriated by political leaders who not only learned English cocking language but were soon flying roosters and trainers to Piat from Manila. Attempts by Visayan engineers from the mill to enter collectively owned roosters work only if they do not cause conflicts with ranking politicians; for the moment, any conflict in betting is always resolved in favor of the politicians. As Bloch predicted, people dissatisfied with the social theory contained in cockfighting seem to have few options besides not going to the cockpit at all.

On the other hand, the content of the hierarchy portrayed in the cockfight has changed as plantations and sugarcane have replaced tenancy and tobacco. Just as there is no longer an economic fight between tobacco and sugar interests—the latter having decisively carried all fields—the most important matches are not between tobacco politicians and sugar barons, but between rich plantations owners and major political figures in the current administration. And throughout the province, the successful political consolidation by the martial law government has largely ended traditional political and cocking rivalries.

This shows up in the betting. Very, very few oppositionists can afford the stratospheric *paradas* of the modern, high-stake matches. In this sense, bet size is an increasingly accurate barometer of political power. Within the cockpit at least, elites able to participate in high-stake matching continue to benefit from the patronage system, while many of those recently tumbled from power find their *paradas* unable to keep pace with those of their erstwhile antagonists. Furthermore, while it is perhaps stretching a point, it is interesting to note that the really high-stake matches are relatively independent, in economic terms, of client support; during the town fiesta of Piat, for example, supporters' bets rarely approached ten percent of the total *parada*, whereas in normal, everyday fights between low-status people it usually constitutes at least half the total amount bet. This conforms very well to the changes in forms of social control discussed above.

Thus, despite the far-reaching changes over the past decade that have thrust a rather backwater, subsistence-oriented village to the center stage of a regional development program, few corresponding structural changes have appeared. Powerful individuals continue to dominate political and economic relationships. If asked, most Piateños would willingly agree that a patron-client model describes political relationships in Piat far better than does a model based on horizontal, class-oriented structures. Kahn's conclusion that patron-clientage is both a conscious model for behavior and

> a model of social structure built up on the observance of all interactions between superiors and inferiors whose differential access to wealth and power are defined by their place in the class structure[45]

is clearly relevant to Piat. For most Piateños, the social structure depicted in the cockfight rings unfortunately true to their perception of social reality.

Conclusions

This paper has argued that cockfighting reflects, reconstitutes, and distorts sociopolitical processes in the Philippines. Four points have been salient in the discussion.

First, the structuring of the symbols and activities that make up cockfighting are not a "given." Spanish and American colonialism, as well as post-Independence state-making, have not only provided a changing context for cockfighting, but have changed the sport itself. Some of these changes are obvious, such as the recent Presidential Decree ordering soldiers to be posted in the cockpits. Others are not so obvious, such as the grafting of "Texas" cocks, scientific breeding, and international cock derbies onto the already over-burdened symbolic structure of cockfighting. Others are positively obscure: the good luck charm made of blessed virginal underwear was obviously mean-ingless prior to the spread of Hispanic hymen hysteria to the Philippines. Symbols and meanings are constantly being added to and subtracted from the cockfight; this process is part of continuing social change.

The second point is related to the first. If cockfighting means different things in different circumstances, and can be used in varying ways by different people, it is nonetheless true that these uses are not infinite. Cockfighting is eminently suited for talking about hierarchy, and the overall message of the cockfight is that political hierarchy and political leadership are just and deserved. While the structure of cockfighting allows people to challenge particular occupants of leadership positions, it militates against challenging the system of hierarchy itself. This sets off the cockfight from those rituals where judicious emphasis on the "anti-structure"[46] can invert the existing structure. There is very little anti-structure in cockfighting.

I have further argued that the intractability of the cockfight towards nonhierarchical interpretations derives from both the structure of the ritual, as Bloch suggested, and the lack of access to the ritual structure of all people except the elites. There is no clear distinction between folk cockfighting and elite cockfighting that would allow the "folk" to change the event. For the moment, elites and commoners attend the same cockpits, and these are owned by the elites. Whatever change there is must come principally at the level of interpretation. In fact, structural flexibility is continuously diminished as the state standardizes cockpit rules and regulations.

Third, while I agree with Geertz that cockfighting is a "cultural performance," I disagree over the significance of that observation. Filipino cockfighting does provide an indigenous theory of Philippine society, just as Balinese cockfighting offers a "metasocial commentary" on Balinese society. Indeed, one can go even further, for not only does the Philippine cockpit provide the theory, but it is one of the very few places where men get together and work out the practice. It is primarily in the cockpit where men must untangle their many overlapping loyalties to different groups, all the more so now that local elections, formerly the other major context for this activity, have been abolished.

But the social theory expressed in cockfighting is of a very peculiar kind. As a theory, it is strikingly blind to social reality. There is, for example, no mention of women, despite women's prominent role not only in household management, but in marketing, agriculture, wage-earning labor, professional occupations, and politics. Nor does it say very much about what all those high-ranking people do to deserve their positions, besides buying expensive chickens. In short, the social theory expressed in the cockfight skews social reality. "Reading over the shoulder of our informants" the "story that . . . they tell themselves about themselves" is only the beginning. The anthropologist must also wonder why they tell that particular story, and how accurate a story is being told.[47]

The fourth and final point concerned the changing meanings ascribed to the cockfights. The major force behind these changes is found in changing social experiences in a rapidly differentiating society. This has affected the cockfight in two ways. First, within the event, new meanings, some latent within the structure, others simply tacked on, are brought to the fore while others lose importance. The recent entry of cock teams from the sugar factory adds a new dimension to social loyalties for many people—residence vs. place of work—never before faced by cockers. Secondly, as the relationships described by the cockfight become increasingly empty, the deeper meanings simply lose significance. Recent immigrants to the Cagayan Valley, for example, have no serious political, kinship, or residential connection to any of the important people in Piat. Few go to the cockpit, and those that do simply go to watch the cockfights, not the politics. People's understandings of cockfighting have changed because society changes.

Cockfighting provides important insights into Philippine society. Taken as a symbolic system, cockfighting successfully couples individual self-identity and self-esteem, social and political loyalties, and even aesthetic satisfaction to an elegant and exciting event. But while the ritual structure can set constraints on ritual interpretation, it cannot alone decide which particular interpretation will be dominant. The symbolic code is important, but people's life experiences outside of the ritual structure are also important. I have also argued that a third variable, access to the ritual, plays a central role in deciding ritual interpretations.

Notes

The author would like to thank Perla Makil, Laura Samson, Francis Parris, and the cockers of Piat, Cagayan, all of whom have commented on various portions of this paper.

1. In Clifford Geertz, ed., *The Interpretation of Cultures* (New York: Basic Books, 1973), p. 448, in which the essay was reprinted.

2. Deborah Rubin, "culture, Culture, and CULTURE: A Critique of Clifford Geertz." Manuscript, on file in the Anthropology Department, Johns Hopkins University.

3. The information for this study was gathered while I was completing a more general project on socio-economic development in the northern Philippines. While of the several hundred fights I attended the vast majority were in a single municipality, as I became more involved with the sport I visited cockpits throughout the Cagayan Valley and Ilocos, as well as a number in the provinces surrounding Manila. Unfortunately, my experiences in the really high-stake cockpits mentioned in the paper were limited to

those of spectator. However, sources of information for this paper range from imported American trainers to internationally known Manila cockers and to Atta, who has heard of cockfighting only through rumors.

4. Maurice Bloch, "Symbol, Song, and Dance; or is Religion an Extreme Form of Traditional Authority?" *European Journal of Sociology* 15 (1974): 55–81.

5. On *charivari, pasyon,* and baptism, see, respectively C. Tilly, "Charivaris, Repertoires, and Politics" (Ann Arbor: Center for Research on Social Organization, 1980 [working paper 214]); R. Ileto, *Pasyon and Revolution* (Quezon City: Ateneo de Manila University Press, 1979); and M. Taussig, "The Genesis of Capitalism Among a South American Peasantry: Devil's Labor and the Baptism of Money," *Comparative Studies in Society and History* 19.2 (1977): 130–155.

6. I am speaking of Father Urdaneta. See Carlos Seco, ed., *Obras de Don Martin Fernandez de Navarrete* (Madrid: Ediciones Atlas, 1975).

7. Antonio Pigafetta, *First Voyage around the World* (Manila: Manila Filipiniana Book Guild, 1969).

8. It is interesting to note that the contemporary Tagalog word for market, *palengke,* means "cockpit" in Spanish as well as, more generally, "stockade."

9. See E. DeJesus, *The Tobacco Monopoly in the Philippines: Bureaucratic Enterprise and Social Change: 1766–1890* (Manila: Ateneo de Manila Press, 1980), p. 140, and J. M. Zuñiga, *Status of the Philippines in 1800* (Manila: Filipiniana Book Guild, 1973), p. 238. Zuñiga, to be fair, adds that these astronomical profits were attained during wartimes.

10. Zuñiga, *Status of the Philippines,* pp. 238–240.

11. I. Gocharov, *A Journey to the Philippines.* Bound volume (Ateneo de Manila University: Filipiniana Collection, 1854).

12. C. B. Elliott, *The Philippines* (Indianapolis: Bobbs-Merrill, 1916), p. 263.

13. E. Wickberg, *The Chinese in Philippine Life* (New Haven: Yale University Press, 1966).

14. Gocharov, *A Journey,* p. 204.

15. Von Scherzer, *A Travel to the Philippines.* Bound volume (Ateneo de Manila University: Filipiniana Collection, 1896), p. 239.

16. R. Ileto, *Pasyon and Revolution* (Quezon City: Ateneo de Manila University Press, 1979).

17. Jose Rizal, *Noli Me Tangere* (Manila: Instituto Nacional de Historia, 1978), first published in N. Anima, *Stories of Philippine Cockfighting* (Manila: Omar Publications, 1973), p. 10.

18. See Elliott, *The Philippines,* p. 263

19. D. Worchester, *The Philippines, Past and Present* (New York: Macmillan, 1914), p. 414.

20. Anonymous, *Report of Meeting on Cockfighting* Unbound pamphlet (Ateneo de Manilla: Filipiniana Collection, 1907).

21. C. Devins, *An Observer in the Philippines* (New York: American Tract Society, 1905), p. 336.

22. Geertz, *Cultures,* p. 414.

23. Presidential Decree no. 449 ("The Cockfighting Law of 1974") and Presidential Decree 1310. Presidential Decree 1802 created the Philippine Gamefowl Commission.

24. This is common knowledge in the Philippines. However, to underline the point, at the first National Gamefowl Association Conference, which was held in Manila, there were separate registration forms for visitors, cockpit operators and promoters, and mayors. Informants also agreed that one of the first acts of any new mayor was to take over the cockpit.

At this same conference, cockpit owners were notified of their obligation to register with the Gamefowl Commission. One year later, 513 had complied. It is impossible to know how many cockpits there are in the Philippines; most people guessed over one thousand.

25. W. C. Forbes, *The Philippines Islands* (New York: Houghton Mifflin, 1928), p. 414.

26. This story is one of many. However, unlike the others, it was told to me by someone who claims to have been there, and it was subsequently repeated by other veteran cockers. In any case, all stories place the introduction of "Texas" cocks slightly before WWII. Interestingly, an old issue of *Grit and Steel* carried a reprinted story by an American veteran soldier describing his and his companions' adventures in Philippine cockpits during the American conquest at the turn of the century. He rather disingenuously adds that cockfighting more than anything else contributed towards American success in winning the hearts and minds of the Filipinos in the occupied territories.

27. In 1981, eight Philippine pesos were equal to approximately one U.S. dollar.

28. In Anima, *Stories*, pp. 7–8.

29. Cf. Geertz, *Cultures*, p. 439.

30. Geertz, *Cultures*, p. 422.

31. Geertz, *Cultures*, p. 436.

32. Geertz, *Cultures*, p. 447.

33. Geertz, *Cultures*, p. 453.

34. Geertz, *Cultures*, p. 452.

35. Bloch, "Symbol, Song, and Dance," and "The Past and the Present in the Present," *Man* (n.s.) 12.2 (1977): 278–292; J. Kahn, "Ideology and Social Structure in Indonesia," *Comparative Studies in Society and History* 20.1 (1978): 103–121.

36. Throughout this section I am drawing heavily on Kahn.

37. Geertz, *Cultures*, p. 418*n4*.

38. Bloch, "Symbol, Song, and Dance," p. 60.

39. Bloch, "Symbol, Song, and Dance," p. 70.

40. Bloch, "Symbol, Song, and Dance," p. 64.

41. The betting picture is actually slightly more complicated than what we have presented here. First, sociopolitical obligation in betting is felt much more keenly when a principal is fighting a cock than when he is merely supporting one. Thus, for example, while there is a general tendency to follow a mayor betting on one of his *barrio captain's* roosters, it carries nowhere near the same imperative as when he is fighting his own rooster, except, of course, for people from that *barrio*. Secondly, there is a tendency,

especially among elites, to form semi-institutionalized "no-fight" arrangements with people who are normally prime candidates for a match. Few plantation owners wish to fight each other, few engineers accept a match with each other, and few mayors willingly accept a match with each other within a region. As an anthropologist concerned with maintaining good relations with a wide range of people, I soon found myself without possible opponents except when visitors came to the cockpit. Since there are physically fewer possible opponents as one ascends the social hierarchy, this quickly creates situations where the people on top can actually fight only a handful of the hundreds of theoretically possible opponents. This trend is one of the driving forces behind "derbies" (cf. note 43).

42. I was able to attend only two of these. In both of them the fighting and betting was "red flag": all against all except for immediate kinship ties.

In fact, the argument connecting the cockfight to patron-clientage seems to work out too neatly. A cursory glance through the literature suggests that cockfighting is largely absent from most highland ethnic minorities, although since cockfighting is so rarely discussed even in lowland ethnographies it is difficult to tell whether this is an ethnographic construct. Urban workers, for whom patron-clientage is considerably less significant, do not follow the same complicated betting lines; in urban *topadas* and regular cockfights, matching and betting are "red flag." Finally, corporate technocrats, academics, and so on rarely go to the cockpit, except, as we mentioned earlier, those heavily tied into the national patronage structure. In any case, while the hypothesis would be nice to investigate further, the overall argument does not depend on it; changing interpretations of what is going are as relevant as actual attendance.

43. I do not deal here with derbies, another post-war import. In derby fighting, a cocker enters a team of cocks (anywhere from two to twelve). There is a minimum bet per cock, and a side bet for the entire team, winner take all. Cocks are matched anonymously, by weight. Derby fighting involves much higher stakes than does the ordinary "hackfight." The anonymity requirement creates all sorts of problems and is more often used as a face-saving excuse than as a way to avoid fights. Derbies generate a great deal of interest—they are always the centerpiece during a *barrio fiesta*—because only important people can afford to enter. In fact, during derbies people at the same status level often cooperate, combining roosters and bets. The betting, fight, and payment system are all the same as in ordinary fights. An extremely rare kind of fight is the *carambola*, in which many cocks are released into the pits at once, with the survivor (if there is one) collecting all of the bets and the dead roosters. Individual matches where two men enter a number of birds against each other ("mains"), which are common in the United States, are unknown in the Philippines except in theory; a shocked silence greeted my proposal to fight one with a local plantation owner who had attended fights in the U.S. While he agreed, everyone else thought this was a terrible idea (the news spread throughout the region within days) and it was allowed to die of neglect.

44. Kahn, "Ideology." Bloch puts this somewhat differently. He argues that in addition to the socially based (mystifying) ritual language, there is also a naturally based everyday language that supplies the concepts needed to criticize social structure: "The infrastructure has then its own cognitive system for the actors and its realization can be,

and is, used occasionally to challenge that other consciousness of an invisible system created by ritual: social structure. . . . In other words, people may be extensively mystified by the static and organic imaginary models of their society that gain a shadowy phenomenological reality in ritual communication; but they also have available to them another source of concepts, the use of which can lead to the realization of exploitation and its challenge" ("The Past and the Present," p. 287).

45. Kahn, "Ideology," p. 110.

46. V. Turner, *Dramas, Fields, and Metaphors: Symbolic Action in Human Society* (Ithaca: Cornell University Press, 1974).

47. S. Silverman, "On the Uses of History in Anthropology: The Palio of Siena," *American Ethnologist* 6.3 (1979): 412–436.

GARRY MARVIN

The Cockfight in Andalusia, Spain:
Images of the Truly Male

Anthropologist Garry Marvin originally went to Spain to study the bullfight for his doctoral dissertation at the University of Wales in 1982. During the course of his fieldwork in Andalusia, a Spanish friend remarked that a particular bullfighter they had just observed was "más valiente que un gallo ingles," which Marvin translates as "braver than a fighting cock." The comment piqued his interest enough to investigate the cockfight, which resulted in the following essay. The comparison of the cockfight with the bullfight with respect to Andalusian notions of masculinity makes this study especially valuable.

For Marvin's research on the bullfight, see Bullfight *(Oxford: Basil Blackwell, 1988). Marvin is also the co-author of* Zoo Culture *(London: Weidenfeld and Nicolson, 1987).*

Anthropologists who have worked in Andalusia have emphasized the vital importance, for both men and women, of the management of their sexual identities.[1] My particular interest in this area is that of masculinity, men's image of true maleness and the symbolic and expressive processes in celebratory or festive events which serve to emphasize that image. Men in this culture are preoccupied with behaving in a properly masculine way, and this is a theme which can be traced through many expressive cultural forms: in folklore genres, jokes, dance, religious processions, the bullfight, and, as will be argued in this article, in the cockfight.

This event has been chosen because, although it is a totally male-orientated event and based on masculine values, it is significant that these values are presented in terms of a competition between two male animals rather than two humans. The audience's appreciation and admiration of certain key qualities displayed by fighting cocks—for example, assertiveness, courage, tenacity, and refusal to submit in difficult circumstances—can be seen as extensions of ideal human male attributes. There are, however, other qualities displayed—

Reprinted from *Anthropological Quarterly* 57 (1984): 60–70.

physical aggression and competitiveness, for example—which are much more problematic in the human realm. It will be argued that for men to resort to physical violence is unacceptable behavior and yet there is obviously an interest in this display of male aggression and violence when it has been safely displaced from the human onto the animal realm.

One of the most significant points to emphasize about the cockfight as a total event is that not only do men gather to watch the birds, but it is important that when doing so they socialize in an exclusively male gathering; it is a time and environment totally devoted to maleness and masculinity. The fights themselves are obviously the focus of attention, but there is a bar attached to the arena and during the afternoon of the fights men spend a good deal of time there involved in the complex ritual process of male drinking and socialization (a process which has recently been analyzed in an article on this subject) Driessen 1983) with much of the conversation centering on opinions and judgment of what has been seen in the cockfight arena. The whole event, being an all-male gathering centered on a display or performance of maleness combined with peripheral activities of male sociability, thus serves to express and reinforce men's self-identity.

My attention was first drawn to the event when a Spanish friend of mine commented that a particular *torero* (bullfighter) we had just seen was "más valiente que un gallo ingles"[2] ("braver than a fighting cock"). At the time I was conducting fieldwork in Seville for a study of the *corrida de toros* (bullfight[3]) in Andalusian culture, and I was working towards an interpretation of the corrida as an important and significant cultural form based on a conflict between a dangerous wild animal and a human being: the dramatic presentation of certain male (both human and animal) qualities. I was naturally intrigued by the connection of images from the cockfight and the corrida in the comment quoted above. It explicitly compares the torero, traditionally regarded as the embodiment of the most highly-valued human male qualities, with an animal in terms of a particular quality—bravery. Although both the cockfight and the corrida are events celebrating male qualities, they are not completely analogous because in one, a male human being confronts a male animal, whereas in the cockfight two animals of the same species confront each other.

The cockfight is based on the fact that two cocks which are strangers to each other will fight if they come into close proximity. The fighting cock is perceived to be a creature which exhibits, in abundance, bravery, aggressiveness, and tenacity in difficult and painful situations, characteristics which Andalusian men in the main also value highly in men (there is an ambivalence about aggressiveness and this will be dealt with later). By creating a cultural event in which these qualities can be revealed before an audience, men who attend the cockfight are able to reflect on these qualities, and the importance of the qualities is reinforced. The event becomes like "a story they tell themselves about themselves" (Geertz 1971, 26). The analysis of the story reveals certain of men's views of what they are and how they ought to be.

The cockfight in Spain is not a prohibited event, held in secret, where those who attend risk prosecution if found, as is the case in many other countries. It is a legal event regulated by government decree (see *Boletín Oficial del Estado* 31 May 1979) and is controlled by the *Agrupación Sindical Nacional de Criadores y Exportadores de Gallos de Pelea y Aves Deportivas* (National Syndical Association of Breeders and Exporters of Fighting Cocks and Sporting Birds), which in turn is incorporated into the *Sindicato Nacional de Ganadería* (National Livestock Syndicate). The controlling body publishes a rulebook of some fifty articles dealing with the type of arena in which the event is to be held, the facilities which must be provided there, the functions of the officials, the people who may bring cocks to compete, the conditions of the birds, and their weighing and measuring. There are also rules covering the type of contests, the actual combat, and how many winners and losers shall be decided, and, finally, the rulebook also includes details of sanctions to be imposed on those who contravene any of the rules.

The cockfight is popular in many parts of Spain,[4] but my comments refer to the event as it takes place in Andalusia, the region with which I am best acquainted. The ethnographic details are drawn from the one hundred or so fights I witnessed and the conversations I had with the people associated with the event in a village just to the east of Seville.[5] The fights I attended took place on Sundays (the usual day for cockfights) from January until mid-summer when it becomes too hot for the birds to be able to fight. It is an indoor event and the fights take place in a specially constructed ring in part of an old wine warehouse (the bar at the front of the warehouse still functions) where a whole section, consisting of two main parts, a circular arena and a room, are walled off. The arena[6] measured about three meters in diameter and was surrounded by a wire fence, just under a meter high, to stop the birds from getting out. Around the walls of the room were individual boxes in which the birds were kept before their fight, and there was a balance for weighing the birds, as well as a sink with running water where they could be washed and tended after each fight.

The event usually begins around 12:30 or 1 o'clock in the afternoon, and during the hour or so before this time those men who have cocks to fight will bring them to the judge (who is appointed by the local syndicate) or his assistant to have them weighed and measured. The birds are weighed in pounds and ounces and their spurs are measured in millimeters. This last factor is of great significance and will be dealt with more fully later but it is important to note that in Spain the birds are not fitted with the razor-sharp metal spurs, spikes or blades which are used in other parts of the world; they use only their natural spurs. This means that a fight can last as long as thirty minutes (the maximum allowed); it does not simply depend, as most other cockfights do, on which bird is able to deal the first blow with its lethal metal spurs.

It is important to make one or two points about the birds themselves because they are rather special. It is difficult to place them in terms of general categories such as wild, game, tame, domestic, or pet. The fighting cock is not a wild bird in the sense that it is captured in the country and put in a cage; it is bred domestically. Some men have only a few birds and are intimately acquainted with their characteristics; they know them as individuals, but they are not treated as pets. Although it is bred domestically it is expected to show *bravura*[7] (wildness or ferocity); it must certainly not reveal meek or tame characteristics which would associate it with ordinary domestic poultry, characteristics which are despised in a fighting cock. It is significant that the controlling organization distinguishes between *gallos de pelea* (fighting cocks) and *aves deportivas* (literally "sporting birds" but could be translated as "game birds"). The latter, when bred by men, are released into the wild and should react as though they were "naturally" wild birds. The fighting cock is raised by man (although the process is somewhat different in that, unlike quails, pheasants, or partridges, the fighting cocks are known and treated as individuals, and the process of rearing is more complex) and is bred for a wildness perceived to be a natural or inherent characteristic of the creature. It is expected to reveal this wildness in an artificial, cultural setting rather than in the wild like game birds.

The fighting cock is very carefully prepared for its activities in the arena. It is given a special diet, it is regularly massaged, the feathers of the neck, back, belly, and tops of the legs are cut, it is shaved to the skin (so that it does not suffer from the heat), and its crest and cheek flaps are cut away when it is young, so that its opponent cannot gain an advantage by grabbing these with its beak during a fight. Each bird is kept in an individual cage, because two males kept together will fight to the death, and because males must be kept from females (because the breeder is producing pedigree birds and so does not want indiscriminate mating). The breeder keeps a very careful record of which male is mated with which female.

Each bird is "trained" by being put in a small arena to spar with another cock, but no damage is done because both birds have their spurs covered. The individual cages often have a swinging perch so that the cock develops strong leg muscles as it attempts to balance. Good leg development is also encouraged by having the bottoms of the cages criss-crossed with metal bars to force the cock to lift its legs and tread carefully. In these ways the breeders are developing the bird's physique in such a way as to help it in the arena; what they cannot influence is the essence of the fighting cock, the bravura, which is its driving force.

Once the birds are weighed and measured, each one is put into an individual box that is locked by the judge, who keeps the keys during the whole of the afternoon. Details of the name of the owner, the registration number of the bird, and its color, weight, and spur size are all recorded on a list which will later be copied into an official record book. One factor which is noted on this preliminary list is the price which each owner wishes to bet on his bird. This will not be recorded on the official lists which are sent to the provincial and national offices of the syndicate because it is illegal to bet at the cockfight. According to the regulations:

> en un sitio bien visible estará expuesto a los asistentes un letrero con letras de gran tamaño que diga: Se prohibe las apuestas . . . (Reglamento de Peleas 1973, article 15)

> in a place well visible to those attending, there will be a notice with large letters saying "Betting is prohibited. . . ."

At the ring I frequented there was no such notice; the betting was open (even the local police would call in to watch fights) and was certainly one of the most important features of the event for those attending.

When it seems that no more birds will arrive, the judge, assisted by the owners, attempts to make up pairs for the fights. Officially the only criteria for deciding the pairs should be those of weight and spur size; birds with equal weight and spur size should be put together, although it is officially allowed that the extra weight of one bird can be compensated for by extra spur size on the other; the ratio is one ounce of weight for one millimeter of spur (there are other allowances for cases such as half-blind birds, see *Reglamento de Peleas* 1973, article 17). What actually happens is that those deciding the pairings attempt to get birds of the same weight and spur size which also have the same amount of money placed on them by their owners. Sometimes it is impossible to find a suitable pairing for a bird, in which case it is returned to its owner and will not be fought on that afternoon.

By the end of the pairing, people have arrived to watch the fights. On a normal Sunday (that is to say, not one on which a competition is being held) there would be up to 150 people standing or sitting around the arena. The audience is mostly composed of men, although there are usually some children brought by their fathers, uncles, or grandfathers. Very few women attend (although they are not prohibited from doing so); on some afternoons I saw one or two who were the wives or girl friends of the younger men; I never saw middle-aged or older women. It is not an expensive event to attend: in 1979–1980, I paid fifty pesetas (the price of two coffees) for an unnumbered seat in the back row (there were only three rows) and the highest price was 150 pesetas for one of the numbered seats in the front row around the arena—seats which were usually taken by the breeders, cock owners and the regular betters. I am not able to comment on the composition of the audience in terms of social class because I was not familiar with the village, and the people I knew there were those I met during my membership in a bullfight club in a nearby village. My impression, though, is that the men were working-class and lower-middle class. This particular cockfight certainly did not attract the range of social classes which one would find at corridas in the nearby bullrings. Middle-class people I spoke to had a view of the cockfight as a rather low-class sport of working men. This is not to suggest that there are *no* middle-class aficionados of the cockfight, but they seemed to be rare.[8] The restricted appeal of the cockfight compared with that of the corrida is a topic I discuss briefly below.

When all is ready the judge takes his seat alongside the ring, and his assistant goes with the owners to collect the first birds. Although the birds have already been paired according to weight, they are both put into a balance hanging above the arena so that the audience can see that they are of equal weight. The owners hand the money they are betting on their birds to the judge, they place their birds in the arena, the gate into it is shut and the fight begins.

The fight may last up to thirty minutes, the maximum allowed, and the moment the birds are left together the assistant sets an alarm-clock (which is in public view) for twenty-eight minutes. If there is no winner when the clock rings, the judge announces, "He puesto el reloj" (I have set the clock) which means that he has set an hour-glass type timer which measures the two last minutes. The birds do not have to be persuaded to fight—they attack almost immediately. The fight tends to go in crescendos of activity; there is a frenzy when the birds first meet, the feathers on the neck are raised, the neck is stretched out towards the opponent and the first attack is launched. This frenzy then dies down as the birds move around each other, pecking at the head and chest and looking for an advantage, and it rises again as they begin to use their spurs. The main damage is done with the spurs; the bird leaps into the air, uses its wings for balance and slashes forward with its legs. The pecking at the head and chest contributes to the general attrition of the opponent. One can tell which bird is doing well by looking at the color of its spurs; if they are red, this is from the blood of the opponent and means that its attacks are successful.

In his analysis of the Balinese cockfight, Geertz comments that there is a close identification of men with their birds so that "it is only apparently cocks which are fighting there. Actually it is men" (Geertz 1971, 5). Unlike Bali, in Spain there is no identification of men as individuals with their cocks. Some men have a reputation as breeders and are admired for the quality of the birds they rear, but there does not seem to be any sense in which the cocks in the arena are projections or embodiments of their owners. Men are competing with each other, however, through the medium of what is going on in the arena. Men compete with each other by betting on the outcome of the fight. This competition is based on their knowledge of the behavior of fighting cocks and their ability to evaluate how the relationship between the two birds in the arena is developing. It is significant that bets are not made before the event, as in horse racing or greyhound racing, but during it. Bets can be made even up to the last few seconds of a fight. Luck (i.e., in making a successful bet) is of course a factor, but those who bet are able to observe how a fight develops and then make their assessment of which cock is most likely to win; an assessment backed by a willingness to stake money on it against someone else's assessment.

I have already mentioned the bet between the two owners made before the fight begins but apart from this dozens of bets are made during the course of a fight. All these bets are between individuals in the audience; there is no equivalent of a bookmaker nor does the judge play any part in it. The system is for individuals to call out offers for bets and for those who wish to accept the bet to call out an agreement. Bets are made at all stages of the fight although the greatest number are made at the beginning. The rise and fall of both the noise level in the calling of betting and the numbers of bets made indicates the changes of fortune in the fight itself.

There may not a be a winner to a contest; if, after thirty minutes one bird has not defeated the other in one of the ways described below, the judge calls ("*Tablas*") (a draw), the fight ends, and all bets are nullified. There are several ways for a cock to lose a fight,[9] the most obvious is for it to be killed by its opponent. In fact, because artificial spurs are not used, this rarely happens— in all the fights I attended I never saw it happen. The second way listed in the rulebook is called *canta la gallina* (literally "the hen sings") and refers to a bird which flees from its opponent whilst at the same time making a low clucking sound. What should be noted here is not only does the bird flee but it also makes what is perceived to be the sound of a hen, a female. This behavior is regarded as so reprehensible, for the cock is not acting as a true male, that special comment is made in the rulebook (something which does not occur under listings for other forms of losing) noting that such behavior is *un señal de cobardia* (a sign of cowardice). A bird which takes part in an initial series of blows and then flees without making a stroke against its opponent for two

180

minutes (but without "canta la gallina") also loses. If two birds totally refuse to fight, the contest will be declared null; if three pecks have been made the fight will be regarded as having started, and a bird which flees after that will be declared as having lost. The other definitions of losing a contest involve the cock voluntarily lowering its chest to the floor without its wings under it and without being forced to the floor by its opponent or by treading on its own wing. This is referred to *echada natural* (lying down naturally), and I take it to be regarded as a posture of submission or defeat. If the bird falls or is forced down and does not get up to make a stroke within one minute, it loses.

A distinction is drawn in the rules between fleeing and a refusal to fight, which are signs of cowardice and unacceptable behavior in a fighting cock, and being beaten as a result of a fight, which merely shows that although both birds have tried, one is better than the other. It is significant that one article states:

> A todo gallo huido se le cortaran, por el Juez o su Adjunto, las plumas de ambas alas y las de la cola a raiz de la carne y será descalificado (Reglamento de Peleas 1973, article 27).

> All birds which have "fled" will have the feathers of both wings and their tails cut down to the flesh by the judge or his assistant and will be disqualified.

Birds which flee are not acting as true fighting cocks; they are regarded as being cowardly because they refuse to engage in combat. They are no longer worthy of being regarded as fighting cocks and are thus physically marked as being unworthy of fighting again.

At the end of each fight the owners collect their birds from the arena, check them for injuries, wash and clean them with antiseptic, and, if necessary, carry out some preliminary curing treatment, such as suturing, before returning them to their boxes or travelling cases. While this is going on the next two birds are being taken into the arena.

Having outlined the structure of the event I now want to turn to the aspect which concerns me most in this article: masculinity. In all conversations concerning the cockfight, those involved with the event emphasized that is was *una cosa de hombres* (a man's thing). It is a totally male-oriented event: the audience is almost totally male, the birds which fight are male, and the virtues which are extolled are male virtues. In one sense, those qualities which aficionados look for in a fighting cock are extensions into the animal world of those qualities which Andalusian men generally look for in other men. The true man in this culture should be virile, courageous, assertive, in control of himself and his environment, and, if possible, in control of others as well. He should be able to accept misfortune, but rather than succumb to it, he should still struggle to

181

achieve his goals. An important part of men's self-image is expressed in sexual terms. Brandes writes:

> the locus of power and will, of emotions and strength, lies within the male geni- tals. Men speak as if they are impelled to act according to opinions and desires that originate in the testicles or penis. (Brandes 1980, 92)

In a similar way John Corbin comments:

> Manliness is thought to have a physiological basis—strength of character is equated with "having balls." (J. R. Corbin n.d., 4)

A true man should possess *cojones* (balls); it is this which allows him to act as a man ought to act; to have cojones allows men to act in difficult and dangerous circumstances. Sexual potency, courage, ability to assert oneself, and domina- tion are all intimately linked. Although, anatomically, all men have testicles (unless they are deformed or castrated), not all men are able to reveal, on a behavioral level, the quality of having cojones which is associated with, derived from or, projected onto testicles. Therefore, to say of a man "el tiene cojones" ("he has balls"), is not a reference to his anatomy but to the fact that he pos- sesses the quality valued in a "true" man.

The comment mentioned earlier, "Ese torero es más valiente que un gallo ingles" ("That torero is braver than a fighting cock"), which first drew my attention to the event, explicitly compares two items which are admired for their male qualities. The torero has traditionally been the epitome of masculin- ity for many in Spain (see Marvin 1982, 252 ff.), and the fighting cock is perceived to be a creature which, as natural characteristics, has the qualities of aggressiveness, courage, and tenacity. I was told on countless occasions that the essential prerequisite for a torero was that he have cojones, for without this quality he would not be able to overcome his fear and work close to the bull. Those who do not have this quality cannot impose their will on the bull; the imposition of the torero's will on the bull is the essence of the corrida. In a similar way I have heard men say of a particularly aggressive cock which is fighting with good style *"tiene los cojones de ganar bien"* (literally, "it has the balls to win well"), which means that because it possesses the essential attributes of a "true" male it will be able to impose its will on the other bird and win.

The cockfight is based on an observed fact of nature that two cocks in close proximity will fight, and out of this "natural fact" is created a cultural event. Although it is a "natural fact" that two cocks which are strangers will fight, the cockfight is artificial in that it forces two birds to stay in close proximity, whereas normally they would be able to avoid each other, or, if there was a confrontation, one would be able to flee. What provides the excitement and interest at the cockfight is being able to observe how the qualities of aggressiveness and tenacity are revealed when the two creatures are forced to confront each other with no chance of escape.

I suggested earlier that the cockfight could be interpreted as a story men tell themselves about themselves and that the analysis of the story reveals certain of men's views of what they are and how they ought to be. There is, however, an important sense in which the event is expressive of something men should not be and yet could be if they did not exercise control.

The issue here centers on physical aggressiveness. While aggressiveness is associated with the valued qualities of courageousness and assertiveness in men's behavior, there is an ambivalent attitude to it. It is certainly present in many of men's dealings with each other and in men's behavior in public in ways which communicate a potential for physical aggression (see Driessen 1983, 129), yet it is also held that such aggression should be controlled. Uncontrolled aggression, like uncontrolled sexuality, is unacceptable behavior. It indicates a loss of self-control, a defining quality of men (compared with animals) and one that is essential for a fully civilized man, and it moves him closer to the animal side of his nature: it brutalizes him. Street fighting, brawling, or any other form of physical aggression is unacceptable behavior and it is significant that in this culture there is very little interest in boxing, a celebration of male violence and courage. Even though boxing is controlled violence and subject to strict rules, the men with whom I spoke (they were aficionados of both the cockpit and the corrida) regarded boxing as unacceptable, brutish, and dishonoring. They could not understand how two men could willingly insult each other and demean themselves in such a public display of aggression.

Having said this about aggressiveness it ought to be emphasized that its opposite, timidness, meekness or withdrawal, is derided as a quality in men. The word to describe such a man is *manso,* a term which means tame or domesticated and, by extension, when referring to male animals, castrated. As mentioned above, the possession of cojones is an essential prerequisite for a true male in this culture. For a man to be labelled manso is to have his full masculinity denied.

Aggressiveness is something which is of concern to Andalusian men, but, because of its destructiveness, it cannot be allowed in the world of human affairs. The cockfight can be seen as an event which is explicitly concerned with violence and aggression. Creatures which are renowned for their aggressiveness, ferocity, and willingness to compete are allowed, or rather forced, to do battle without restriction. The important point is that they, unlike the men watching them, are supposed to, and encouraged to, give free expression to their animal nature; they should not exercise control. Indeed it is felt that one of the characteristics of animals is that they are unable to exercise control. The significant point is that the cockfight is not "real life"—it is a game or sport and the victims are animals. They are animals which are much admired for their particular qualities but they are animals nonetheless, and the consequences of that battle are therefore distanced from the men who watch. The display of physical aggression is admired and commented on, but it is displayed in an arena (both literally and metaphorically) where there is no danger to "the delicate web of human relationships."[10] Human social relationships are not affected as they would be in the case of aggression and violence between men. The theme of aggression and control will be taken up again when examining the concept of *aguantar* below.

Geertz has commented that cockfighting has no interest for the Balinese as a purely spectator sport (it is the betting which provides the real interest), but this is not so in Spain. I suspect that his comments might well apply in many parts of the world (and they are in the majority) where fighting cocks are fitted with artificial spurs and where a particular fight can only last a few minutes because the bird which has the luck or the skill to deliver the first blow is likely to be the winner. In Spain, where artificial spurs are not used and the battle is not so deadly, people attend much as people might attend a boxing match in this country, to watch the styles of the fighters and to see how these are used to defeat an opponent. As mentioned earlier, there is betting, and the betting does indeed create interest and excitement among those involved in it, but there are also very many people at any given cockfight who do not bet at all. I noted that generally, in an audience of between 100 and 120, there would be about twenty-five men betting on each fight. There might be a few more making small bets with their neighbors, but there were very many who attended week after week and did not bet at all. They were merely spectators who were interested in the whole process and development of the fights rather than just in the outcome.

The many aficionados I spoke to said that it was necessary to have a fight last a long time because that was the only way for the true quality of the birds to be revealed. An important exporter of fighting cocks to South America told me, "En America se juega el dinero, aqui se juegan los gallos" (literally, "In America it is money which plays, here it is the cocks"), meaning that the money involved in betting is the important factor in South America, whereas in Spain it is the fight which is in itself important. I was often told that in South America the fights were based on luck, whereas in Spain they were related to endurance and *casta*. This latter term refers to class or breeding and in this particular case refers to that inner quality which the bird has (or ought to have) because it is a fighting cock, a special bird rather than a mere farm-yard cockerel. Casta is a term which is also used of *toros de lidia* (bulls used in the corrida), which are perceived to be wild rather than domestic animals and are expected to reveal special qualities of courage and endurance in the difficult and painful circumstances of the arena. Many of my conversations with men who were aficionados of both the cockfight and the corrida had to do with whether bulls and cocks were animals *de la misma sangre* (of the same blood), that is to say, whether they were essentially the same sort of animals in terms of the characteristics which motivated them. Most agreed that they were, but debated whether it was the bull or the cock which was more courageous.

It was mentioned earlier that a man is expected to exercise self-control: to lose control, to allow an "other" (even if that "other" is his own passionate animal nature) to become the directing force in his life is to lose autonomy and the ability to exercise his will. Brandes makes an important general point about losing self-control in his examination of those jokes and pranks among Andalusian men which are based on attempts to undermine a man's confidence and provoke him into becoming upset and lose control of his temper. In many cases the intended victim in fact becomes the victor by not losing his temper and by going along with the joke, thus exercising control, whereas the person who becomes angry and thus loses control is regarded

> with contempt for his inability to maintain mastery over the situation and by extension, over his life in general. The incident becomes a demonstration of overall willpower. Men who disintegrate under the threat of aggression are scorned, while those who withstand it courageously are admired. (Brandes 1980, 123)

The refusal to disintegrate under pressure of whatever sort is a valued quality in this culture. The term used to express it is *aguantar* which, in the context of a difficult situation, means to resist or accept a situation without breaking down, to tolerate something disagreeable or to suffer patiently if one cannot do anything about it. One might be confronted by circumstances in which, although one cannot exercise one's will to change that situation, one can at least control oneself, withstand the pressure and refuse to collapse physically, mentally or emotionally: this is aguantar.

The term is used in the context of the cockfight and is extremely important for understanding the qualities expected of a good bird. Aguantar is used with regard to a bird which is obviously being extremely badly beaten, perhaps blinded and so severely injured that it hardly has the strength to stand up, let alone attempt a blow at its opponent, and yet it refuses to submit and put its chest to the ground. As one man commented admiringly to me, when explaining why a bird which was being particularly badly beaten refused to go down, "Es muerto ya pero es la raza que tiene" (literally, "It is dead now but it is the pedigree [or breeding] which it has"). By this he meant that the bird was as

185

good as dead but it was the particular quality it had by virtue of being a fighting cock which allowed it to remain standing and suffer even more blows. This is very much admired. It is such behavior which allows the fighting cock to be seen as a creature which embodies many male (and, when applied to men, masculine) qualities. It is valiant and fights ferociously to defeat its opponent, but even when it has no chance of winning it gives in only very reluctantly and often not at all.

Because the birds are not killed during the fight they may be used four or five times (good ones more than that) during the season, and thus each bird has the chance to learn how best to fight and to put that experience into practice in the next fight. Unlike the fighting bull which is expected merely to respond to its animal nature and attack, the fighting cock should both respond to its aggressive animal nature and be a skillful fighter as a result of its experience. Aficionados are therefore interested to know whether they are watching two unfought birds, two experienced birds or perhaps an experienced and an unexperienced bird.

Aficionados can explain quite readily what they look for in a good fight. There are styles of fighting which are aesthetically pleasing and regarded as honorable styles. Ideally, a bird should hold its head well up, attack forward with its beak and, when it is able to, with its spurs as well. Styles which are not regarded as pleasing are defensive styles. A bird which fights with its head well down and its chest covered so that the other bird cannot get a stroke in, or which gets itself under its opponent's wing so that it cannot be attacked while at the same time making slashing, under-cutting strokes, or which uses the technique of fleeing so that its pursuer follows and then suddenly turns on it with its spurs is not admired. It is admitted that these styles often win fights, but they are referred to as *feo* which means "ugly" and also "inappropriate," "unseemly," and, by implication, "shameful." Deceitfulness or trickery, even though they may be successful means to an end, are not admired in the cockfight nor generally in human affairs.

It was mentioned earlier that the cockfight does not appeal to as wide an audience as that of the corrida. The cockfight is both less elaborate and less elaborated in terms of performance compared with the corrida. Although men talk about "styles" of fighting cocks, there is a very limited repertoire and there is no attempt to structure this; the cocks are not performing. Although one cannot claim that the bull "performs" (except in the sense that it, like the fighting cock, unwittingly performs a role defined for it by man) in the corrida, the man certainly performs with it.[11] He consciously performs in the aesthetic sense—his relationship with the bull is developed as a performance. Even though the cockfight and the corrida rest on similar cultural values, the corrida is more of a spectacle than the cockfight. In the corrida, there is pageantry, costumes, and music; its basic element, the contest between two males, is wrapped in ceremony. The contest in the cockfight, however, is naked, basic, and unrelieved; the display of physical aggression is at a premium and for many it is too crude. Those who are primarily aficionados of the cockfight are usually aficionados of the corrida whereas those who are primarily aficionados of the corrida, even though they admit that *toreo* (the art of "bullfighting") is an art based on something bloody and unpleasant, are often unable to make the step down to the cockfight. The cockfight does not have the ceremonial elements of the corrida, nor does it have the celebratory value of the latter. The corrida is both a celebration in itself, internally, of masculinity, of the triumph of man over beast, and of culture over nature, and it is also used as an event to celebrate important occasions (see Marvin 1982, 124 ff.). The corrida is a richer, more complex event and carries more cultural weight than the cockfight.

The cockfight, though, is a celebration in that it is an event which extols certain aspects of masculinity. Although "masculinity" is a term which refers to a set of values associated with human males in a particular cultural context and we are here dealing with nonhuman animals, the values on which the event is based, or those incorporated within it, are those associated with human males. There is a movement backwards and forwards between the observation and interpretation of animal behavior and the images of masculinity in this context. Certain characteristics of cocks are observed by men (they are noticed in the first place because they relate to characteristics valued in men); this image of the birds' behavior is incorporated into men's self-imagery, the imagery is read back onto the birds' behavior as an evaluation of it, and then, through the cockfight (a cultural construct build around the cocks' natural characteristics), the imagery is read back once more by men. What the aficionado experiences is, to quote from Geertz once more,

> a kind of sentimental education. What he learns there is what his culture's ethos
> and his private sensibility (or, anyway, certain aspects of them) look like when
> spelled out externally in a collective text. (Geertz 1971, 27)

The cockfight, although it is an event which catches up the theme of what it means to be truly masculine in this culture, involves a displacement from the human onto the animal world. Human beings are thus protected from the direct articulation of powerful emotional forces which are potentially threatening for human relations if openly expressed by men. The aficionado is responsive to this demonstration of male qualities; he shares these values, that is why he is an aficionado of this event which puts a particular construction on certain values. Like Brandes' interpretation of Andalusian folklore genres, my suggestion is that the cockfight is an expressive cultural form which "reflect(s) shared

187

assumptions about masculinity and give(s) these assumptions a concrete reality" (Brandes 1980, 7). The aficionado's response to it forms part of the process of the establishment and affirmation of his masculine identity.

Notes

I am most grateful to Margaret Kenna and Henk Driessen for reading and commenting on earlier drafts of this article and to the anonymous reviewers whose detailed constructive comments helped me remove some foolish errors and rethink parts of the argument.

1. See for examples Brandes (1980; 1981), Ms J.R. Corbin; Ms. M. Corbin; Driessen (1983); Gilmore and Gilmore (1979); Gilmore (1980); Pitt-Rivers (1971); and Press (1980).

2. Some of those with whom I spoke referred to the bird as *el gallo ingles* (the English cock) and they suggested that originally the bird came from England. Others said that the name was incorrect and that its true name was *el gallo combativo espanol* (literally, the Spanish cock of fighting spirit) thus emphasizing its essential Spanishness. The rule book refers to it as *el gallo de pelea* (the fighting cock) or *el gallo de combate* (the "combat" cock).

3. The Spanish term *corrida de toros* (literally, "running of bulls") is normally translated into English as "bullfight." This term is a misleading translation because it gives an immediate false impression of the character of the event. Men do not "fight" bulls in the arena (see Marvin 1982, 349h). As there is no adequate English term, *corrida* is left in the original. There is no corresponding problem in translating the Spanish term for cockfight, *pelea de gallos* may be translated as cockfight (*pelear*=to fight in a physical sense) without creating any misunderstanding as to the nature of the event.

4. For example, the 1979 Spanish National Competition (the most recent for which I have information) brought together birds from the provinces of Valencia, Ciudad Real, Toledo, Madrid, Cordoba, Jaen, Castellon, Malaga, Seville, and Guadalajara.

5. Although the cockfight is legal, betting, as will be mentioned, is not. Betting does take place, however, so in order to protect the identity of those involved and because the remarks I make in the article do not depend on knowing the exact location of the village, I do not name it here.

6. The name of the arena is a *reñidero*, a word which derives from the verb *reñir* meaning to quarrel, to battle or come to blows, although in general usage it means to scold. Etymologically the word derives from the Latin *ringi* which, according to the *Breve Diccionario Etimológico de la Lengua Castellana*, means "to snarl showing teeth" when describing a dog, but also "to be choleric, angry or upset." This certainly gives a sense of the sort of atmosphere to be expected in the arena.

7. *Bravura*, when describing a fighting bull or a fighting cock refers to wildness or ferocity. For example, Dr. Zumel (President of the Taurine Federation), when asked

what was the basic and most essential quality of a fighting bull, replied, ". . . bravura no gobernable" (uncontrolled wildness). When used with reference to a man it usually means courage and stamina, qualities which are also associated with *bravura* when it is used to describe the animal.

8. I recognize that being unable to supply data on the composition of the audience in terms of social class is a weakness in that it would appear that the masculine self-image, the concern with that image, and the rituals involved in the recreation of the image do vary according to social class (see for example Driessen 1983, 131, and Gilmore and Gilmore 1979, 286–294). I hope to be able to deal with this issue in a wider study of the topic which is now in preparation.

9. Only the main ways are listed here; there are rules for more complex situations: for example, what happens if one bird is on the ground, being counted out, and the other falls, or if the clock has been set because the birds have separated and one then lowers its chest to the ground. All of these can be found under article 27 (a–h).

10. This quotation has been taken from a comment made by the reviewer of the article.

11. An important point here is that although there is a contest between the man and the bull the corrida is not perceived as an event in which physical aggressiveness plays anything but a minimal part. Although the torero commits a violent act in killing the bull with a sword (and before this violence is involved, with the inflicting of wounds by the *picador* and later the placing of *bandilleras*) the relationship between the torero and the bull is never seen as one involving aggression or violence.

References

Brandes, Stanley. 1980. *Metaphors of masculinity: Sex and status in Andalusian folklore.* Philadelphia: University of Pennsylvania Press.

Brandes, Stanley. 1981. "Wounded stags: Male sexual ideology in an Andalusian town." In Sherry B. Ortner and Harriet Whitehead, eds., *Sexual Meanings: The Cultural Construction of Gender and Sexuality,* pp. 216–240. Cambridge: Cambridge University Press.

Corbin, John. N.D. "Funerals, Bullfights and the 'Terrors' of 1936: Some Dialectics of Death in Southern Spain." Files of author, School of Economic and Social Studies, University of East Anglia, Norwich NR4 7TJ. U.K.

Corbin, Marie. N.D. "Male and Female in Andalusia." Files of author, School of Economic and Social Studies, University of East Anglia, Norwich NR4 7TJ, U.K.

Driessen, Henk. 1983. "Male Sociability and Rituals of Masculinity in Rural Andalusia." *Anthropological Quarterly* 56.3: 125–131.

Geertz, Clifford. 1971. "Deep play: Notes on the Balinese Cockfight." In Clifford Geertz, ed., *Myth, Symbol and Culture,* pp. 1–37. New York: Norton.

Gilmore, Margaret, and David D. Gilmore. 1979. " 'Machismo': A Psychodynamic Approach (Spain)." *Journal of Psychological Anthropology* 2.3: 281–299.

Gilmore, David D. 1980. *The People of the Plain: Class and Community in Lower Andalusia.* New York: Columbia University Press.

Marvin, Garry R. 1982. "La Corrida de Toros: An Anthropological Study of Animal and Human Nature in Andalucia." Doctoral dissertation, University of Wales, U.K.

Pitt-Rivers, Julian A. 1971. *People of the Sierra.* Chicago: University of Chicago Press.

Press, Irwin. 1980. *The City as Context: Urbanism and Behavioural Constraints in Seville.* Urbana: University of Illinois Press.

Sindicato Nacional de Ganaderia. 1973. *Agrupación sindical nacional de criadores y exportadores de gallos de pelea y aves deportivas.* Torrijos, Spain: Moreira.

FRANCIS AFFERGAN

Zooanthropology of the Cockfight in Martinique

The cockfight thrives throughout the Caribbean, especially in the islands influenced by French and Spanish traditions. Cuba and Puerto Rico, for example, have long cock-fighting histories; so also do Haiti and Martinique. Most of the accounts of cockfights in the Caribbean tend to be descriptive in nature rather than analytic. One of the notable exceptions is the following essay by anthropologist Francis Affergan, author of Anthropologie à la Martinique *(Paris: Presses de la fondation nationale des sciences politiques, 1983).*

In this essay, we find not only rich and welcome ethnographic detail, but a distinc-tively French anthropological approach to the data, namely, that of Lévi-Straussian structuralism. According to Claude Lévi-Strauss, perhaps the world's best known anthropologist, myth and other cultural products reflect a form of binary opposition and by articulating such opposition help to mediate it or suggest some kind of resolution albeit a temporary or illusory one. A standard example of Lévi-Straussian oppositions is that between "nature" and "culture," an opposition utilized by Affergan in his analysis of the cockfight on Martinique. However, Affergan's ingenious analysis of native categories, including cock classification systems and cocks' names leads him to propose a strikingly original symbolic and political interpretation of the cockfight in Martinique.

Affergan is nearly unique insofar as he fails to cite Geertz's 1972 essay on the Balinese cockfight. The great majority of his references is to the oeuvre of Lévi-Strauss, which, given his theoretical bias, is understandable. Still, one might argue that the failure to refer to Geertz and other earlier considerations of the cockfight does suggest a somewhat parochial form of scholarship. For a more conventional account of cockfights in Martinique, see André Champagnac, Coqs de Combat et Combats de Coqs á la Martinique *(Alfort: Maisons-Alfort, 1970),*

For a helpful introduction to Lévi-Strauss, see David Pace, Claude Lévi-Strauss: The Bearer of Ashes *(London: Routledge, Kegan Paul, 1983); for a sample of the voluminous scholarship by and about Lévi-Strauss, see Francois H. Lapointe and Claire C. Lapointe,* Claude Lévi-Strauss and His Critics: An International Bib-liography of Criticism (1950–1976) *New York: Garland, 1977). For Affergan's view of anthropology in general, see his* Exotisme et alterité: essai sur les

Reprinted from *Cahiers internationaux de sociologie* 80 (1986): 109–126. This essay was trans-lated from the French by Antonella Bertoli Johnston and Alan Dundes.

fondements d'une critique de l'anthropologie *(Paris: Presses universitaires de France, 1987).*

> I owe a cock to Asclepios, Crito.
> Pay him without fail, don't forget him.
> Plato, *Phaedo,* 118a

How is it that the last words of the first and greatest Greek philosopher, Socrates, were devoted to a reference to a cock? And how is it that no one, as far as we know, has been aware of this peculiar and final reference? Did this species previously play the role which, much later in the imaginary and symbolic system of the human intellect and language, western anthropology assigned to it? It is here our intent to try to answer this question through the study of men's and cocks' behavior, their emotional relationships, and their language ties in Martinique, based exclusively on the practice of cockfights there.

It is true that cocks fight amongst themselves, but before, during, and after, it is men who through the preparation, training, caring and naming of the cocks are the ones who weave (based on the model of their relationships to the cocks) their nominal and imaginary ties to society. Thus, we will be able to illustrate, validate, or invalidate the hypothesis expressed by Lévi-Strauss in *Le totémisme aujourd'hui,* and in *La pensée sauvage,* according to which hypothesis, on the one hand, "natural species would be selected because they are good to think about"[1] and, on the other hand, each species within the animal kingdom would constitute in miniature "a model of human society."[2] But let us first describe the zooethnological universe which we are considering.

It is probable that the taste for and the practice of cockfighting date from the introduction by Spaniards of the first domestic fowl to the Antilles of the North and Northwest, i.e., to Puerto Rico, Haiti, and Santo Domingo and Cuba. Numerous crossbreeds developed and we are able today to determine several types of fighting cocks which correspond to well-defined esthetic and combative criteria.

Let us eliminate immediately the ones which are not relevant: the common farmyard rooster which is a "street" rooster often called Creole, which is without pedigree and which lives only in chicken coops or derives from low extraction or as the result of great promiscuity. The second generic category, in opposition to the first one, is called *djem,* a term which designates *all* the fighting cocks: this category is further subdivided into two large classes which have no semantic relationship to each other:

192

1. *The origin or the geographical provenance.* This is a class which can be said to consist of five branches:
   - *gay* cocks: raised in Martinique and of a lesser quality than the others;
   - cocks from *Peru*, whose resemblance to eagles is notorious;
   - cocks from *Cuba,* which in general have a very pure pedigree;
   - cocks from *Trinidad,* the importation of which used to be prohibited but is now once again allowed;
   - cocks of mixed origin, the results from the *crossbreeding* of all of the above-mentioned categories, whose esthetic and fighting qualities can vary.
2. *The double structural criteria.* The esthetic qualities/fighting qualities:
   - esthetic qualities: we find in this subgroup three types of cocks, which can be distinguished by naming their combinations of colors:
     a) *bakivas* or *gros-sirop* cocks, whose plumage is red and black;
     b) *paille* cocks, whose plumage is silver-white;
     c) *caleguay* cocks, which have spots spread in speckled areas.
   - fighting qualities: These can be divided into two subgroups:
     a) cocks called *flyers,* which attack or flee by flying. They have a narrow stomach, thin thighs and long tails called "rudder tails";
     b) cocks called *walkers* or "Indian"; they attack or flee by walking; their stomach is large, their thighs are strong, and their tail is short and therefore cannot be used as a "chopper."

Now it is crucial to notice that when we compare the two typologies of qualities, namely esthetic and fighting, we find only one relevant connection: the *bakivas-gros-sirop* are also *flyers.* Thus for a Martiniquan breeder or trainer or simply a cockfight fan, the best cock is undeniably the *bakiva-gros-sirop-flyer.* In other words, the red and black plumage is culturally associated with the most agile, aggressive, and efficient combative attacks.

In order to keep in mind all these analytic classifications which are so essential for the understanding and explanation of how man names nature and humanity and why he thinks about them in that way, it is indispensable to have a synoptic table as an aid to getting a picture of all the factors involved (See figure below.)

. . .

A fighting cock is expensive; between five and ten thousand French francs, if it has already proven itself. A cock isn't ready to fight before three months of age at the minimum. Note that an order in 1962–1963 had permanently forbidden the practice of cockfights all over the territory of metropolitan France except in overseas territories and departments and in the Northern provinces. Today, only the DOM and TOM [generic term for French colonies] still enjoy this privilege that many people perceive as cruel.

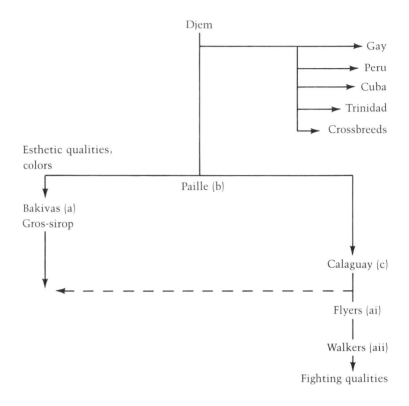

Fighting cock classifications

The issue of pedigree is a major one. It is sometimes written and sometimes oral. In the latter case, trust is total because it is the result of one's sacred word. In that way precisely, the spoken word is respected more than the written word. The proof of such confidence is provided *a contrario*, or if one prefers, by means of a negative hypothesis: (1) if there is a lie, it is the liar himself who will pay (whereas the written pedigree is often anonymous); (2) but, above all, the oral pedigree refers to a cock already well-known, and the latter will undoubtedly be recognized as such by the buyer, and the same goes for its ancestry. The need to certify in written words the pedigree of a famous cock therefore becomes useless. In addition, in order to avoid pitfalls and deceptions about the cock's qualities, the latter is first put into the presence of another cock, face to face, and the cock is then studied to see how he behaves, to learn if he has enough character and to see if his spurs are well centered and mobile. Afterwards, the cock is held to receive blows from the other cock which is being provoked. If it is an honorable cock, it must never run away. Finally, its health record is checked to see if the cock has received the official number of required injections and vaccinations.

The training and preparation of the cock for the fight follow a rigorous set of regulations which no breeder, in principle, would disregard for fear of losing or, even worse, being accused of cheating. The fighting cocks are raised and trained together in a community of cocks, the number of which can vary from ten to about fifty. Each cock enjoys its own home: a cage exposed to daylight and with a sliding board on the top part of it. The board protects the animal against a too intense sun or a heavy tropical rain. Food is put in the cage by gently sliding the same board. At night, a linen sheet covers the entire cage to keep the cock from being disturbed by the morning light or by numerous artifical lights which might shine into the yard (car headlights, street lights, lights from houses, etc.). The cock is also protected from the various dangerous creatures which can be found in the yard: crabs, centipedes, mongooses, snakes, spiders, and so forth.

Cocks seldom crow in the evening (between 7 and 9 p.m.); but they are active with a vengeance during siesta time (2 to 4 p.m.) and especially between 4 and 8 a.m. They compete then with one another, answering each other across bluffs and ravines.

The day of a fighting cock starts at about 7 in the morning. As soon as the caretaker arrives, he washes the cock. He then takes a mouthful of water and sprays it all over the cock's body. Note that the manager (or caretaker or trainer) can either carry out his duties while living at the owner's home or board the cock in his own yard.

The caretaker than starts the training, strictly speaking. First, he places the cock on a swing to strengthen its musculature. Then a mixture is prepared containing ninety-proof rum, cloves, salt, and various, carefully selected leaves, and the mixture is then vigorously rubbed on the cock's legs up to its stomach. The skin is forced to redden. At this time, in order to avoid sunstroke and burns, the animal must stay in the shade.

As for the food, the portions are prepared and distributed according to a very strict regime; corn, tomatoes, liver, bananas, honey, twice a day if the date of the fight is still far off, only once a day when the date is close at hand. Let us note that on the day of the fight the cock does not eat. Often, in order to strengthen and stimulate the cock, vitamin C is administered once or twice a day either by injection or by mixing it in its food.

The cutting of the plumage is performed at a determined time called the trimming period, the end of October, so that by the beginning of the season, in July, the feathers have grown back enough. The length of the feathers is planned in such a way that they reach the shoulders, allowing the cock to protect itself from the enemy by bristling them up in front of its face like armor. The feathers of the legs and back are trimmed up to the crop. The wings, most of the time, remain as they are. The feathers of the tail are trimmed in an aerodynamic fashion so as to facilitate the take-off.

Every morning, a dummy cock (or puppet) is set up in front of the fighting cock to make it run towards this and train for the fight. Sometimes an ordinary cock is presented, with its spurs covered up, to avoid injury, but also to measure the intelligence and intuitive sense of the fighting cock. As for the spurs, if the cock is well equipped, it will keep the ones it was born with. These are then cut, polished, and sharpened. If the spurs aren't strong enough, the cock will be provided with artificial ones made of steel, but this is done only at the last moment in order to avoid accidents.

The beak will also play a crucial role in the selection made by the trainer among all his fighting cocks, for it is essential that the animal be able to hold its adversary firmly and for a long enough time to be able to simultaneously hit it with its spurs.

Sexual abstinence during training is strictly enforced. In the cockfighting community, it is often said that the female dictates the behavior of males and therefore one must beware of the female. The hen, since it doesn't fight, can spend time seducing, annoying, and teasing; the cock's behavior at this time is worth noticing: far from bristling up the feathers of its neck, as it will do during a fight, it now swings its body to one side, straining its muscles to the extreme, and letting a wing fall with which it sweeps the ground. In Creole language, it is said *Coqla ka karé douven poul la.* However, in general hens aren't usually allowed even to come near the cage the night before or the same day of the fight for fear of dissipating the cock's energy.

Maybe we should specify here that the cock finds itself isolated in a cage as early as one week of age; because even while under the mother's wing the little male chicks will fight with one another, being *aware* of their destiny, often fighting to the death.

On a technical level, the training proceeds in the following manner: the animal is held by the tail and forced to run in place, the purpose being to measure its capacity for speed and fighting. Then, in an arena, in an attempt to have the rooster get a feel for what the real conditions of the fight will be, the cock is forced to run around for a long time in order to take the fat off its heart and to measure the duration of its breath.

Around 5 or 6 p.m., the cock is brought back to its evening cage, upon which a sheet is dropped.

Notice finally, before we move on to the study of the fight itself, that the trimming of the tail and wings is meant to insure the cock's survival even apart from the fight. Indeed, in the pelting rain, when it comes down sideways, the cock folds its head into its neck so that the water drips down the length of its body and is directly drained off at its tail, without collecting and stagnating on the wings and back. In some ways, the cock's body becomes aerodynamic, functioning in the same way as an umbrella. The selection of a good cock also depends upon the criterion of height. If the cock is too high (i.e., too tall), the risk is that it could be hit in the liver by a smaller adversary. Therefore, it is cocks of medium height which are selected.

. . .

Early on the morning of the day of the fight, the cock is taken to the *pill* (a kind of wooden arena, covered by a roof made of corrugated iron, usually found in open country) where it is taken in charge, watched and controlled by a caretaker especially designated for this task. Then the grooming takes place: the cock is sniffed, rubbed, and closely examined. In particular, it is necessary to verify that there is no poison hidden in any part of its body and that there are no traces of grease on its skin: in brief, to ensure that there is no cheating. Then the caretaker sucks the spurs "to prove" that they are clean. In addition, the cock must drink the water in which it is bathed for the same reason.

Then comes the crucial time of weighing, crucial because only cocks of equivalent stature and weight can be matched. Weight is measured in pounds and ounces. Generally, a cock weights between two and three pounds. A cock whose weight is slightly more or less than that of his opponent could eventually be accepted by giving away or taking off ounces if the owners agree. Then the platform of the scale is shaken to remove the dust. It is noteworthy that the concern for cleanliness sometimes borders on manic obsession.

Each preparatory phase leading to the fight is marked by the sound of a bell. This holds for the spurring phase, in the course of which the natural spur of the cock is sharpened and an artificial spur is retrieved from another cock killed during a previous fight. The false spur is attached to the natural one to strengthen it. If the latter is broken, a metal prosthesis is attached, and to protect the cock's leg, it is first wrapped in a plaster cast.

Then the "tableau de mariage" ("marriage list") is presented, which consists of giving a name to each cock opposite the name of the cock's owner. We will return to the critical issue of naming, but we can already mention some of the names proposed: "Shoot," "War," "Paterson," "Pompidou," "Electric," "Pitiless."

Then the "marriage" takes place where the cocks are paired off for the fight: such and such cock against such and such other cock. Then something is attached to the lower part of the legs, i.e., the spurs are tied to the ankles, with special care given for the angle of attack. The cocks are "held across" each other to verify the size and shape of their respective beaks; the neck is checked—it must never be greasy (this is a matter of eliminating any possibility of "glissement," "slippage," because honest combat requires taking hold of one's adversary.) Ninety proof alcohol is rubbed over the whole body of the animal and lemon on its spurs. Right before the opening of hostilities, each owner holds his cock in front of him, inciting it to fight by means of passes involving three or four blows of the head and beak with its designated opponent.

There are two types of bets: the ones that are called "on the list" and the ones called "behind." The first one takes place before the fight and consists of establishing a list on which the owner and his backers (in other words, all the people who have chosen his cock) figure out the amount of money they have bet. An owner can bet against his own cock. It often happens that the judge, who is also the collector of money, holds in his hands a bundle of several millions of old French franc bills, yet without having written down at any time which sum of money belongs to whom. When the moment comes, he will be able to identify all the faces and will know without ever making a mistake who the owner of every single 100-franc note is. Let us note for now that this extraordinary memory is obviously based on a very complex set of relationships which govern the naming reference system and the configural/spatial system on the steps of the *pill*. In this context, let us add that the owners are often identified by their cocks. It even happens that a cock can be so famous that the name of its owner is ignored by the gallery such that the owner will therefore be called by the name of his cock.

The second type of bet, called "behind," takes place once the fight has started and stays open until the last minute of the hostilities. Men shout at each other, stand up, yell out numbers, without using the help of the collector. A bettor can, for example, propose a wager of "20 to 13" to the whole gallery. He who accepts makes a sign with his hand meaning "OK." One's given word is sacred. In a society strangely aggressive and violent in a self-destructive way,[3] fair play is the rule. With this type of bet, nothing is written down, but since everyone has been a witness, no one would dare to cheat or deceive. It is crucial to differentiate the behavior of soccer fans on the steps of a stadium, very often violent, from that of cockfight fans, who are certainly excited, but never vindictive. In addition, the commitment to the cocks evolves with the fight, but bets must absolutely stop when the white light is switched off.

While the fight proper unfolds, a whole set of lights and bells signal the time and mark the various episodes and numerous stages of the fight. The green light "signifies" the beginning of hostilities. A referee makes sure that everything goes along smoothly and he stays on duty for the entire day, a day which

198

can consist of up to half a dozen fights in the same *pill*. When a cock begins to weaken, a white light starts to flicker. It will turn red if the cocks remain on their feet and alive, in other words, if the fight ends in a draw. The fight is won when one of the two cocks is standing and pinning its adversary's shoulders to the ground, but without killing it. If during the time the white light is on, the fight resumes normally, the judge switches to the green light without waiting to see whether the fight is between cocks equally able to fight or between incapacitated cocks.

The blows given are diverse. Generally, the cock uses his beak and his spurs, with which he hits the neck, eyes, or stomach of his opponent. He can also use his fan-shaped tail. The duration of a fight varies from five to twenty minutes when the cocks are of identical strength. Either of the two owners can request to have the combat come to an end if he fears for the death of his animal or if he is concerned about its serious or incurable wounds.

Many cocks become blind in one or both eyes. It is well known that a cock which is blind in one eye can fight with even more relentlessness and cruelty. If the eyes have been wounded, the cock must remain in total darkness for several days after the fight.

In the arena, the cock walks around with a proud, "throw out its chest" gesture, shows off a lot, and tries to impress its adversary by moving and behaving in a swaggering manner. It is interesting to note that man, when dominated and crushed by uncontrollable forces, very often behaves in a way similar to the natural behavior of the cock. The excessive, outward appearance is similar. By the same token, one can observe similarities between the hopeless violence of the cock in the *pill* and the internalized yet redundant aggression of the man who is oppressed by another culture on his *own* island. Has automatic mimesis taken place or is this the conformity of a culture with respect to the stable and repetitive nature of an animal species?[4] This is one of the questions we will raise in our conclusion.

Also, men communicate with their cocks during the combat: "pull, attack there, go that way. . . ." The owner or the fan who has bet behaves like the manager of a boxer who would advise or encourage his fighter according to the situation. In any case, a man after having directed commands, recommended feints, or shouted warning signals to his protége will often exit the *pill* without having any voice left.

When a cock is severely wounded, it is kept alive for reproductive purposes—if it has comported itself well. On the other hand, if it has been cowardly or weak, and if in addition it was killed during or as a result of the fight, it will be hung up by a rope until beasts of prey (birds or mongooses) come to dismember it. It is never taken down. If it is still alive after the fight, one *can* cut off its head and consume it.

. . .

It is now understood that natural species aren't selected because they are "good to eat" but because they are "good to think about."

Claude Lévi-Strauss[5]

It is now our intention to evaluate the relevance of this quotation through the study of the function attached to, on the one hand, the cocks, and, on the other hand, the cockfights, within the context of the social organization, the symbolic behavior, and the emotional and imaginary values of the people of Martinique.

Logically and epistemologically, two questions have to be answered. The first one consists of asking whether cocks as a natural species can be separated from the practice of cockfighting: in other words, whether the fight is part of the conceptual essence of the cock, or, to return to the same issue, whether the fight belongs, analytically speaking, to the cock. The second, more complex question relates to knowing whether there is any incompatibility between a natural species "good to eat" and a natural species (the same one) "good to think about." Is the relationship one of inclusion or exclusion? However, in order to answer these two questions, we must first gather information about the function of naming (or of designating) attached to the practices and to the totality of the world surrounding cocks. When a Martiniquan names or calls his cock in a certain way, or when he names or calls someone else by making an explicit or implicit reference to the names of cocks, or to names given to certain war-like figures of fighting cocks, what is he doing? Is he rediscovering the primitive function of any language, namely the function of symbolization? Is he structuring his cultural world by embracing a natural universe? What is he signifying? Proverbs and names are two symbolic markers of the utmost importance because, in addition to their function of denotation, they always signify something else (a figure, a trope) other than their single literal meaning.

Thus *Kavalíe vol a dam* means: (1) That a cock must always have an adversary; (2) that a good cock never hesitates to fly towards its adversary (rather than walking towards its opponent); (3) that the winner is associated with maleness (with a strong emphasis on virility) and the loser with femaleness (*dam*), with a strong derogatory connotation because it is better to be a true woman than a false man. Similarly, *Tou bon coq ka joind' bon coq* means that the combat will be interesting only if it is fair, the latter condition is fulfilled only when the two cocks facing one another have equal weapons; it implies that a cock known for a certain degree of valor would agree to fight only with another cock known for a similar degree of valor. Otherwise, the first one would lose its honor as well as the critical necessity for recognition.

200

Finally, the expression "*Kourir rond*" designates a tricky strategy of feint which consists of slipping away by going around the *pill* to better confuse the adversary and then, by brutally turning around, to attack the adversary when the latter gets out of breath. It is well known in Martinique that similar gestures (flexing, waddling, gesticulating, stiffening . . .) to those employed by fighting cocks are found in human combats whose techniques stem from the period of slavery and which appear to be halfway between dance and wrestling (*ladja, calenda, damié* . . .). Who then is miming whom? It is very difficult to answer this question because it implies knowing whether the war-like posturings of the cock are innate or whether they have been taught by the trainer. The aggressive impulse is genetic; the perfectability of the body is gained thanks to the efforts of the manager. The behavior in the arena, albeit esthetic, is still instinctual and to that extent is not perfectible. Can we then say that the natural species of fighting fowl represent for man a model to follow?

It is obvious that the fighting cock during its exercises or in the arena appears so handsome and proud that men do not hesitate to compare it precisely to "a handsome and proud man." The man of the Antilles, assimilated and deprived of real power, "compares" himself (in other words, throws out his chest and shows off) according to the image of the fighting cock strutting in the *pill*. On the other hand, the cock is a real object of loving passion for his master, who caresses, fondles, embraces it, and addresses it with words of love. By doing this, man intends to make the cock feel supported and therefore motivated to win. The owner remains convinced that if he takes too little care of his cock, the latter will not be a "winner." But isn't that an excuse *a posteriori*, and, by invoking a goal of interest, does he not want to mask an apparent disinterest in an authentic passion of love which is not admissible because it is now acknowledged? Doesn't the solid, stable, and natural character of love for the cock compensate for the emotional and political deficiencies from which the Martiniquan certainly suffers as soon as one recognizes his ambivalent position, which leads to self-destruction? The natural species is not so much good to think about because it is constitutive of a cultural structure; it would be good to resort to and finally good to think about because it fills up the historic gap created by the double process of cultural detachment and pretense. The lack of mastery over oneself in its frenetic race towards an eternally displaced identity[6] thus finds a resting-place, a stage of renewal and recognition in the passion of love for the warrior cocks.

This is demonstrated by the numerous modes by which naming and designations vary (to name and to call by a name belong to a linguistic class open to symbol and figurative speech; to designate is like denotation, which would be closer to the literal meaning).

The question would be to know, when one designates or calls a cock by a name (or anything from a cock to an image of a cock), whether one names, signifies, or classifies, or whether one uses the three operations at the same time; and finally, one needs to ask, do these distinctions have any relevance to Martinique?

What are the names given to fighting cocks? We have chosen to mention and comment upon the following examples: "Rocket," "Electric," "Pompidou," "Pierre Messmer," "Galvao," "War," "Reflex," and "Stainless Steel." The first level of semantic interpretation that comes to mind is that of denotation. If a particular cock has been given the name "Pompidou," it is obviously to honor a presidential trip to the French Antilles; "Rocket" designates an animal which has acquired a reputation for hitting fast and hard, and for moving with lightning speed from one place to another within the arena. Or furthermore, if another cock has been named "War," it is to pay homage to its formidable fighting qualities and to its inveterate taste for conflict. This type of explanation does not take into account the symbolic function of language, but even if we knew whether a word connoted a further nuance or a meaning more figurative than the reverse side of a reality which has only two sides, we would not understand, if we remained at this level, why certain cocks' names don't conform to this "double-side" rule, i.e., why certain sequences of reality that we want to report remain concealed; and, finally, we would miss the esthetic and emotional function peculiar to this as to any chain of signifiers. Briefly then, how can one confirm that all language is initially ambiguous?

Lévi-Strauss writes that as far as proper names are concerned, one can only "identify the other by assigning it to a class" or "by pretending to give the other a name, identifying oneself through it." In other words, either one classifies the other, or "one classifies oneself," and the author immediately adds, "most often one does both at the same time."[7]

It is not at all certain that when, for example, a Martiniquan calls his cock "Stainless Steel," he is operating within the nowadays famous categorization of the "three domains," that is, to name it as "member of a class," "as member of the subclass of available names within the class, and finally as member of the class formed by my personal intentions and preferences."[8]

The first reason is that "Stainless Steel" doesn't belong to the subclass of available names within the class. Moreover, "Stainless Steel" can just as well designate a dog or even a human being who had demonstrated exceptional physical or moral qualities. Not only is this name carried by only one sinngle fighting cock at a time, but also, and this obviously is a contradiction, other individuals, human or animal, can be given the same nickname.

If we follow the text of Lévi-Strauss, there remains one solution: "Stainless Steel" is a "made-up" name which designates the class of the one who does the naming. In other words, the owner would designate himself as being a member of that group of men who have physical and moral qualities similar to unmalleable steel. But what about "Galvao" which, in contrast to "Stainless Steel," doesn't belong to the word classes of the language? If "Stainless Steel" still means something, "Galvao" means nothing at all. The latter would then be a unique and indelible mark of identity.

By that we mean not only, using the hypothesis of Russell and Frege, that "Galvao" isn't a class which belongs to any other class, but that this name isn't a class at all, since it doesn't contain any member. Thus "Galvao," we can at least presume, designates and signifies that only one single cock can be called in that fashion, and that, above all, there is only one man on earth who has given such a name to his cock. This is the reason why, as we mentioned above, "Galvao" can just as well designate the owner of the animal. In naming that which he loves the most and by so doing naming himself, the Martiniquan is enabled to conform to the only practice of identification possible, the symbolic and unrestricted invention of names. And far from being used for any classification, such a name points to uniqueness, to, in other words, escaping from belonging to any class, even as a unique member. Since the formation of identity doesn't function normally in Martinique due to a short-circuit in the reciprocal relationship with the Other—in other words, since the Martiniquan doesn't have access to either the proposition "I am a Martiniquan," or the proposition "I am a Frenchman"—self-identification through animals is the only course open to him. The cock is indeed the only element of nature which by its war-like qualities could substitue for the real historic struggle between ex-slave and ex-master that could not take place. This discovery is then to be found within a relationship free from human disturbance. However, let us note that it is not direct self-attribution since it is expressed indirectly via the cock.

Thus, if the natural species of fighting fowl constitutes "a model in miniature of human society,"[9] it is by inversion or asymmetry.

The behavior and fighting of cocks draw the portrait, in counterpoint, of an ideal society which does not exist. In the filigree of this model, a society is formed which suffers from the impossibility of naming others. The difference between self and Other is no longer conceivable because the Martiniquan has himself become his own Other. Since the process of differentiation has failed, every designation will reveal declassification rather than classification, and will mark the absence of a recognizable Other. The attainment of individuation takes place thus without the context of belonging. Naming indicates then an empty space.

We could not complete our initial diagram by the designation of semantic and linguistic connections which tie together the natural species of "fighting cocks" and the human society of Martinique; what we could observe was that only the act of fighting counts. Indeed, everything happens as if the cock were only the attribute or predicate of the class of fighters, the fighter becoming the subject.

Three Categories of Naming

In the figure above, *b* and *c* are named entirely with respect to esthetic qualities, the color (therefore space) refers to a close proximity (horizontally) where
only the relation of position counts. At this level, *b* and *c* can't be the best
models since society doesn't function horizontally in a way that would be satisfactory for the formation of identity: the color and the social function of the
Martiniquan are devaluated. At this level also, the relation to language is
metonymical: the cocks' names will generally be borrowed from the chain of
first and last names which are "already" human (e.g., "Pierre Messmer" or
"Pompidou"). Finally, from the point of view of meaning, the relationship of
such naming is only syntagmatic or syntactic. In other words, it only borrows
epithets or color terms from the chain of a previously constituted language:
aii, with regard to qualities which are above all warlike
- the relationship of naming, which designates strictly human qualities, in
  depth (e.g., endurance or running),
- the relationship animal/man is vertical, entailing, in other words, semantic
  similarity (e.g., man walks like a marching-cock),
- the relationship to language is metaphorical, as in "Rocket," "Electric," "Reflex," "Stainless Steel,"
- the relationship between naming and thinking is paradigmatic, with the task
  of reflection consisting of selection and substitution;
a and *ai together* (in other words, at the same time and together)
- esthetic *and* war-like qualities,
- perfect combination between the two,
- the cock must be handsome *and* know how to "fly,"
- the linguistic example can be provided by "Galvao,"
- thought invents names of evasion in order to achieve individualization and to
  flee from the bonds of assimilation and from the blocking of the process of
  identity-formation.

. . .

But man isn't content just to give a name to his cock; he also names certain
other men in reference to this animal that will thus attain an authentically
mythical dimension.

The expression *Ti coq* designates the young man who has begun his love life and who begins to be involved in relationships with girls. However, since birth, the boy is praised and rewarded (for being a male) by means of this expression. Not only is he a "little cock," but he must prove it to those around him and so live up to this appellation. The synonymous expression is *Ti mal* (little male). There is no doubt that the model which is here being imitated is the natural one of the fighting cock. Thus the species becomes discriminatory and has the function of creating categories among men and between men and women.

In addition, the male anatomical sex organ is often designated by the word "coq," especially in cases where it is a matter of recounting a sexual or erotic experience.

It seems evident that masculine sexuality is thought about and experienced in accordance with the triple category of brutality, combat, and speed in imitation of the fighting cock. But exactly why is it the cock's sexuality and not that of some other animals? Let us immediately set aside the hypothesis according to which the cock would be a good model by reason of the exclusion of another function, namely to serve as food. The species of fighting fowl would not be a pertinent category in this case since some cocks are, under certain circumstances, consumed after the fight. And even if it were the case, we would then have only binary relationships of inclusion/exclusion, which couldn't take account of the richness of ties of symbolic similarity, resemblance, and difference that unite man and his cock that we have sought to elucidate above.

In other words, the question becomes: why are fighting cocks able to furnish "a natural model of differentiation to create differences between men"?[10]

We can still follow Lévi-Strauss's text regarding the generic hypothesis of the animal species "in and of itself" as a model of diversity as the means for considering "the diversity of human functions,"[11] but the specific choice of fighting cocks is still not explained. This is because the fighting cock is not merely a subcategory of the totality constituted by all animal species. The fighting cock is thought about and experienced as a separate category, different from other animals and itself differentiating other animal species. To that extent, it is outside of any class. The fighting cock is an item of recognition and an agent of discrimination between a symbolic "nobility" and the people. The differentiation of social functions is blurred by the process of assimilation which creates confusing values: the real social struggle can therefore hardly conceal its historical efficacy. There remains the division by means of fighting cocks which thus take the place of conflicts of recognition. Thus one differentiates oneself by affirming oneself as (a) a real male, (b) a real "Don Juan" with women," (c) of light color or at least of "ascending" color (from black to less black), (d) a man who doesn't hesitate to "engage in fights" at the least sign of disrespect. It can be said of these phenomena that they are "compensatory" or "vicarious" insofar as the behaviors which they imply require only a symbolic power of facade or parade, the authentic power remaining inaccessible and far removed.

Indeed, "the animal appears like a conceptual tool possessing numerous possibilities of deconstructing or reconstructing any domain whatsoever, situated in synchrony or diachrony, concrete or abstract, nature or culture."[12] However, if we were to depend solely upon this structural aspect, we would fail to explain why it is, first of all, a fighting species whose warlike performances are the product of a long cultural effort (cultural because it is basically human). Moreover, we would act as if the repressive situation particular to assimilated cultures leading to unmade protests and demands for *quid pro quo* did not exist. However, it seems to us, and this will be our final hypothesis, that the essential factor which allows us to understand why the fighting cock has been chosen as the animal emblematic of struggle consists of one single level, where for the moment in any case the struggle can be conducted: the symbolic and esthetic level.

That we believe in the thesis according to which the fighting cock delineates in his disputatious behavior and in filigree the extremely painful reality of psychosocial relationships of an entire society permits us to insist all the more on the crucial fact that, indeed, this animal is not sacred and the rituals connected with training and the fight itself only symbolize the incapacity to secure any real power. There is no underlying meaning to reveal. The ritual is political, in its original sense. In other words, it is profane, playing on physical and manipulatable forces and energies (muscles, feints, parades, etc.). From this arises the conception of human sexuality. Finally, this is the reason why the fighting cock can simultaneously serve as a model of thought and as something to be consumed. And if the origin of the symbolic is situated at the level of the transition from nature (empirical reality and function of the cock) to Culture (diversion, power struggle, playful use of the cock, etc.), one can without fear of contradiction affirm that there isn't any incompatibility in eating an object which is used for thinking—quite the contrary, since one eats only what is homologous to oneself, or, rather, what can be assimilated. The consumption does not involve any ritual or sacred aspect. The sole modalities of the life and death of the cock are symbolic (one must die with honor and in proving one's courage). This is the reason why eating and thinking about a cock are always considered together, the two actions being inseparably linked. And if any taboo exists, it applies only to the cowardly or weak animal, and, therefore, to a form of behavior and not to the process of dying itself, which is natural. In addition, there isn't any obligation attached to consumption. One eats the cock if one wishes. There isn't any prohibition impinging on its consumption, since, just as what is conceivable and what entitles me to think about the world becomes mine after absorption by my thought; likewise I eat only what I think can be equated to me. To consume constitutes, therefore, an act of double recognition of myself and of the world which thus becomes mine and with which I can finally identify myself. By its triple function (it is conceivable, it makes things conceivable, and it is consumable), the fighting cock facilitates the process of identification and of self-identification, otherwise blocked, by opening a way to attain the double recognition of self by the Other and of the Other by the self.

Notes

1. Claude Lévi-Strauss, *Le totémisme aujourd'hui* (Paris: PUF, 1980), p. 132
2. Claude Lévi-Strauss, *La pensée sauvage* (Paris: Plon, 1962), p. 271.
3. We would like to refer you to our book: *Anthropologie à la Martinique,* Paris: Presses de la fondation des sciences politiques, 1983.
4. It can even happen on the steps of the arena that men mime the fighting of cocks to such an extent that they imitate the gestures, the blows, and the evasive dodges by making faces which make human the bestial and natural confrontation.
5. Lévi-Strauss, *La pensée sauvage,* p. 271.
6. See our article "Je est-il un autre? ou l'identité deplacée," *Les Temps modernes* (1983): 441–442.
7. Lévi-Strauss, *La pensée sauvage,* p. 240.
8. Lévi-Strauss, *La pensée sauvage,* p. 242.
9. Lévi-Strauss, *La pensée sauvage,* p. 271.
10. Lévi-Strauss, *La pensée sauvage,* p. 143.
11. Lévi-Strauss, *La pensée sauvage,* p. 164.
12. Lévi-Strauss, *La pensée sauvage,* p. 196.

ONDINA FACHEL LEAL

The Gaucho Cockfight
in Porto Alegre, Brazil

Thus far we have presented essays treating the cockfight in Asia, Southeast Asia, the South Pacific, Europe, North America, and the Caribbean. Yet one of the areas of the world where the cockfight flourishes most is Latin America. No survey of cockfighting scholarship can be complete without some coverage of the active traditions found in Colombia, Mexico, Venezuela and the other countries in Central and South America. The following study of the Gaucho traditional cockfight which takes place in the border area between Brazil and Argentina was part of a doctoral dissertation in anthropology at the University of California, Berkeley, in 1989. What makes this splendid reportage so remarkable is the fact that the author is not only a native of Brazil, but a female anthropologist. The cockfight, as has been amply demonstrated, is typically a male preserve, making it all the more difficult for a woman to carry out extensive fieldwork on this subject. The extraordinary ethnographic detail Dr. Ondina Leal was able to elicit is a testament to her fieldwork expertise. Dr. Leal is Professora Titular at the Programa Pós Graduação em Antropologia Social at the Universidade Federal do Rio Grande do Sul. in Porto Alegre, Brazil.

Not only does Leal present one of the most complete descriptions of cockfighting in a particular cultural context to date, but she also offers some imaginative interpretive remarks as a result of combining Lévi-Straussian binary oppositional theory with center-and-periphery theory. (For a consideration of this latter theory, see Edward A. Shils, Center and Periphery: Essays in Macrosociology *[Chicago: University of Chicago Press, 1975].)*

What do the two bleeding cocks fighting to their deaths mean to the breathless gauchos watching them? What understandings and emotions regarding what is at stake in each fight do these watchers share? In this essay I will search for an answer to these questions through an analysis of the cockfighting activities in Rio Grande do Sul, Brazil. Cockfighting is one among various discourses—an

Reprinted from Ondina Fachel Leal, "The Gauchos: Male Culture and Identity in the Pampas," unpublished doctoral dissertation in anthropology, University of California, Berkeley, 1989, pp. 210–247.

208

especially dramatic one—which celebrate gaucho identity and express the content of the gender-demarcated gaucho culture. All such discourses on gaucho identity use animal metaphors and involve conflict and notions of honor, but perhaps none of them possesses the enunciatory power of cockfights. Cockfighting is a celebration of masculinity where men, through their cocks, dispute, win, lose, and reinforce certain attributes selected as male essence. In the fighting, that which is assumed to be animal nature—courage, fierceness, strength, and pride—becomes human nature, or, more precisely, men's nature: the animal's attributes are symbolically transferred to the men who possess the cocks.

Cockfighting is not just a localized cultural survival,[1] nor is it an activity restricted to rural gauchos. In southern Brazil, it is an urban event which draws together cocks and men from different places. Wherever cockfights take place, the involvement of the audience and the intensity of feelings aroused by these performances are so striking that I believe this subject deserves further anthropological attention and analysis.

Quantitatively considered, cockfighting is perhaps not very representative of gauchos. Not all gauchos, nor even the majority of them, are *cockers* (*galistas*, i.e., cock breeders, trainers, or cockfighting addicts).[2] Nevertheless, the symbols, meanings, and feelings that surround cockfighting can be taken as those most representative of gaucho ethos. The gauchos themselves (*gauchos* here in its restricted sense of *estância* workers) consider the breeding of fighting cocks and cockfighting as a practice peculiar to the gaucho.[3]

Cockfighting is an ancient and worldwide sport with historical and geographical differences, and with statuses that vary from illegal, illegal but tolerated, to legal or even royal, according to national laws and circumstances. Regardless of its variations, cockfighting is always a male activity. In this essay, I will introduce cultural data from cockers' own specialized literature on cocking, when relevant, to support possible generalizations.

Cockfighting originated in the Orient and was introduced into Europe in the fifth century B.C. It was popular in Greece, and the Romans spread it throughout their empire. It was a national tradition in early England, and Spaniards carried cockfighting to the Americas.[4]

Argentina was colonized by Spain and, later, strongly dependent economically, politically, and culturally on England. In both Spain and England, cockfighting has been a strong cultural tradition, and we find references to cockfighting as early as the 1700s among Argentinean gauchos. For this reason, the Argentinean gauchos are usually identified as the source of cockfighting among gauchos. Brazilian society in general considers cockfighting to be Spanish or Gaucho, rather than Portuguese or Brazilian. Nowadays, however, cockfights are more popular, better-organized, and institutionalized in Brazil than in Argentina or Uruguay. In contrast to Argentina and Uruguay, cockfighting is not forbidden in Brazil, although there, too, it is a very discreet, an almost invisible activity. Its legality may be a good reason, albeit not a sufficient one, for its larger popularity in Brazilian territory. I shall return to this point later.

During my fieldwork I never witnessed cockfighting in Uruguay—which does not mean it does not exist there—but the region where I conducted my research is on the frontier of Brazil, and cockfights in that region are usually held in the cities on the Brazilian side. Certainly the cockfights that I observed, in Uruguaiana (a Brazilian city on the border with Argentina), for example, have a definite Argentinean audience. This sort of *play* with the national frontier establishing new boundaries occurs with other types of gambling, with the flow of goods and pricing, with political ideas, legislation, and even cultural rules. In general, people living on the border manipulate regulations and meanings to their best advantage; the tendency is that the less strict will rule.

The data presented in this chapter is drawn mainly from my observations in a *rinhadeiro* (cockfighting house) in Porto Alegre. Given the nature of the subject—cockfighting is relatively infrequent, conducted in a self-proclaimed male space and in semi-secrecy—continuous and long-term research was required to penetrate this closed universe. In Porto Alegre, the city where I live, I was able to carry out systematic observations for a period of over two years. The data on Porto Alegre reveals how folk practices are interwoven with modern ones; how the traditional is sufficiently dynamic to be redefined and reinvented, and to present itself in new forms or new contexts.[5]

Cocks and Their Ownership

Walking in a suburban area of any city in Rio Grande do Sul, someone with an intruding anthropologist lens can occasionally find game cocks in their cages or a cockfighting training session going on in a house courtyard. But cockfighting is a serious business as well as a popular tradition; it involves a considerable amount of money, and one will not find fighting cocks out in the streets with other common fowl. Cockfights happen only at special places, with special cocks and at proper times.

Cockfighting tournaments are the only occasion in which cocks actually fight, and many cocks from different owners are necessary for a tournament. A man will never pit his own cocks against each other except for training purposes, in which case the cocks wear protective leather muffles over their spurs and beaks. The whole point of cockfighting is that a man competes with another man, using his cock as a mediator.

The *possession* of a cock can either be real, through actual ownership, or symbolic. Betting, emotional involvement with a cock, the activity of training a cock, or the specialized knowledge of cocking and the mastery of a particular cock's life history and kinship records are effective alternative ways of *having a cock*. In fact, symbolic ownership is the most important way of establishing links both with cocks and among men in every cockfighting performance. The link among men, the man-cock-man bond, the rivalry of one man betting *against* another is provisional, lasting only as long as the match; it is redefined according to the cock one bets on in each new cockfight. The link man-cock lasts longer. As the cockers put it: "If you believe in a cock, when his bruises have healed, and he fights again in another tournament, you are expected to be loyal and bet on him again." Cockfighting always tends to be a big event because, as they say: "There is no fun in playing always against the same cocks because then the result of the matches doesn't bring surprises."

People will not get together only to watch a few matches. Each game cock breeder will bring those of his cocks which are ready (*prontos*) to be matched. If ten breeders with an average of two cocks each participate, this will mean long hours of cockfighting, since the matches may not have a time limit: the cocks fight to their exhaustion, which sometimes means their death. Regular tournaments happen once every two weeks, depending on the season.[6] A tournament takes at least an entire day, beginning early in the day. Usually it takes the whole weekend, and on holidays, it may last three or four continuous days. The audience of cockers (*galistas* or *aficcionados*) seems to be able to watch with the same intense enthusiasm no matter how many there are, as long the cocks in question are "fine cocks." A well known cock which has won on many other occasions, one strong enough to survive a good adversary, or a cock with an impressive genealogy, the son or grandson of a champion, will have a larger audience and attract higher bets.

For betting purposes and as part of general representation of the cockfighting public, the cock is only identified by its male line. An ideal of a self-generated male species certainly is part of the men's imagery about cocks. Although some breeders caution that is incorrect to perceive the cock only by its *male line*, saying that a cock inherits *fighting spirit* and *aggressiveness* from the father's line but *gameness* from the hen, others insist that a cock that comes from a line of fighters as a rule will produce only fighters. In the heat of a battle in the pit it is not uncommon to hear comments about "the mother's blood is showing" referring to the cock which is losing.

The notion that fighting cocks are rare, expensive, and very special is constantly stressed. In the cockfights that I observed, the majority of the cocks were *bankiva* cocks, also called "English." Their colors are a mixture of black

211

and red with a red-brown tone. The cock has long legs and thighs, a broad chest, and stands in an upright position. This body posture and attitude in fighting is identified as "dignidade" ("dignity").

Usually cocks start to fight only when they are two to three years old. A bankiva cock may live (if it survives the fights) up to six or seven years. Another game cock breed, the bantam, also called "the Malay," is considered of poor quality. "Race" (*raça*) is a concept used to define cocks. A cock is not only *of* bankiva or bantam race, but it also *has race,* meaning an eagerness to fight, vim and vigor, and dignity. Ethnic stereotypes overlap the cock breeds' actual origins. In a fight between a Malay (bantam) and an English (bankiva) cock, the first, which is heavier, is considered a "ground" combattant while the latter is a flyer, which flies to hit its adversary with its spurs and beak. Fights between cocks of different breeds are unusual, as "ground" and "flying" usually refer to fighting strategies and style.[7] During a fight, every movement of the cock is followed by the crowd's cheers of "go ahead!" "mount him!" (*monta nele! trepa nele!*). As "to mount" or "to climb" (*trepar*) are also expressions commonly used to refer to sexual intercourse, usually implying the man's position in the sexual act, the crowd's cheers are not only metaphorical. The fight is a succession of alternate bows, gestures, and movements on the part of each cock as they use subordinate and dominant body positions to achieve victory. The men, through these dialectical moves of their cocks, gain or lose masculinity in every round. On the *estâncias* away from the atmosphere of cockfighting, I collected a folk stanza, in which the erotic association between "mounting" and ."fighting" is clear:[8]

Quien tuviera la suerte	Who would have the luck
que tiene el gallo,	that the cock has,
que en medio de la juria	that in the middle of the fight
monta a caballo.	mounts on horse.[9]

"Dignity" refers to the cock's body posture while standing, striking, or even while being beaten, as well as the cock's attitude and its way of looking at men and other cocks. Dignity is a sort of arrogance. Those qualities associated with cocks are usually immaterial items (where even objective characteristics, such as breed, becomes "race," a subjective category). Although subjective, the cocks are prized by such characteristics, and a man will acquire these qualities by buying the cock, betting on it, or even just cheering for it. Different ways of owning the cock (such as actual ownership, being the cock's handler, or betting on a cock) will entitle a man to different degrees of ownership over it. What is really being *sold* are those abstract attributes, which are taken as *natural:* "vim,

212

vigor and victory," as an old English cocker's advertisement put it.[10] Nature itself is a cultural category here.

Interesting enough, in my data, "dignity" to a certain extent replaces the idea of "victory" in the British cocker's ad. Consistent with an ethos of "el sentimento tragico de la vida" (*"the tragic feeling of life"*) characteristic of gaucho culture, "dignity" is connected with the ability to endure suffering stoically, heroically. To win is an important, but not the most important, part of cockfighting. Every sequence of blows is significant by itself, and each is long enough to offer some winning recompenses even if the cock does not win in the end.

We can see the cockfight as a play of images where ultimately what is at stake is masculinity, not cocks, and not even "ambulant penises" as Bateson, Mead, or Geertz have suggested. Bateson and Mead (1942) and Geertz (1973) were dealing with another social context, Bali, where this interpretation may be applied. I wonder if the equation cocks = penises is not an oversimplification specific to English-speaking people.[11] Even if in Bali this semantic identification exists (this is not the case in gaucho culture or the Portuguese and Spanish languages), to take "cock" for "penis" may be to reduce a symbol to its signifier, not to its meaning. In my understanding, phallus itself is a sign invested with the meaning of manliness and power: androcentric cultures ascribe power to the ones who have penises. In contrast to Bateson and Mead, Geertz does not limit his analyses to the cock as a phallic symbol, as masculinity and status concern are his main points.

For the men crushed together watching the cockfights, individual cocks are being sacrificed to a greater cause, an ideal of manliness. Necessarily one of the cocks will win, so men and manliness will always win. The logic here is that of the sacrifice: the men *own* the victim, and the victim is different from the sacrificer. As in any sacrifice ritual, there is an act of abnegation, since the sacrificer deprives himself and gives up something.[12] In this profane worship of manliness, the men's sense of abnegation, their sense of *necessary sacrifice*, finds compensation in the cock's "dignity": he suffers but he is not a loser, his honor is saved if he (the man and the cock) knows how to suffer and thus preserve his masculinity.

If a cock fights to the death, never running from the pit, or never "crying like a chicken" (*cacarejando feito galinha*); and if, even when badly wounded, he keeps fighting back, his honor and the man's honor is not at risk: A man may lose money, but not his honor. Actually, when the cock is badly hurt, perhaps suffering some sort of neurological trauma, he may "start to cry like a chicken." This is considered the ultimate insult to its owner and its supporters: symbolically at that moment, the cock and the men become females. This is associated with the other meanings of the word *chicken* in common usage: "loose woman" and coward.

To better understand male and female gender attributions in the representation of the men involved with cockfighting, it is worth quoting a cockers' manual:

> Females are strongly sexual and henceforth impulsive. Their actions are instinctively generated by feelings and they need the presence of a male. They are amorous, though they do not show it. Just as most female beings [*sic*]. Nature made them so and provided that their actions be governed by their sexual impulses. Males are cooler in disposition and have developed a different brain. They act according to logic and brains are stimulated by external impressions. Females act impulsively and their nerve centers are stimulated by internal impressions. They are closed related to nature and can by this fact not go over certain limits. (Finsterbusch 1929, 166)

A cocker may breed many cocks, but few will be fine cocks. A fine cock is a bankiva cock, with a certified genealogy, but it is also a cock with other subjective attributes such as "race" and "dignity," one that is a real warrior and fearless conqueror in the pit, bringing honor to his owner, to his handler, and to those who expect him to win.

Breeding game cocks is an expensive activity. The cocks need heated rooms in the winter, air-conditioning in the summer, warm food, and a special diet. Cocks also receive constant training and intensive care while recuperating from fights, and they may need one or more handlers or trainers. The cocks' genealogy and fighting curriculum, common conversation topics at cockfights, imply a good deal of grooming, manipulation, and intervention, as well as capital investment. The cock's expenses include occasional air fare and hotel accommodations for the owner, the handler, and the cocks.[13]

Cock owners are usually people from a rural area; even those who live in the cities usually have rural origins. The breeding of game cocks is a secondary activity for most, and they can afford to hire people to take care of their cocks. They run other businesses, or they may be veterinarians, cattle breeders, or landlords. Cocking is considered a sport, a hobby, "an activity one engages in for love, not for money." Although it can become a very profitable investment, men will insist that in other investments there are fewer risks, and that they are engaged in this sort of activity just for pleasure. The sale price of a bankiva cock may go up to $2000 (US), mainly if they are sold to cockfighting adherents outside of Brazil. There is a generalized idea among gauchos that the best cocks are the gaucho cocks, that is, cocks from this region of Brazil where the bankiva is bred. Here bankiva is equated with gaucho.

214

Breeding for export at high prices in the international market is a recent business. People call it, with irony, "The Bolivian Connection." Most of the exported cocks go to Bolivia: "You know, Bolivia has their cocaine's *nouveau riche*, they are crazy about cocks and gambling, but they don't have any tradition in breeding bankiva cocks." Someone else adds: "They buy a cock just for one fight, because they use Bolivian spurs (sharp metal needle-like spurs) and no cock survives it. It's stupid, because even the winner won't survive the fight in condition to have another fight." Cocks are also exported to the United States (to Filipinos in the United States, it is said). These cocks, too, get into the United States through the Bolivian circuit: that is, cocks and cocaine go together through the same illegal channels.[14] Many cockers, the ones who do not own cocks, are very critical of this kind of business. They say cocking will end up becoming a big business. In fact, since cocks have became more valuable, bets are higher, cocker societies more organized and bureaucratized. Nowadays, in large cities, cockfighting has a solid middle-class audience.

Gauchos, the workers on extensive cattle farms, the specific group with whom I worked, will be at a rinhadeiro cheering for a cock only on special occasions, since organized tournaments tend to take place only in cities and betting is relatively expensive. More important than their presence at cockfights is the place of fighting cocks in gaucho imagery, in tales, metaphors, and poetry. Reciprocally, the gaucho image is a part of the cockers' societies, helping legitimize cockfighting under the rubric of "traditional folk culture." In cockfighting events, it is considered appropriate to dress as a gaucho, to drink *chimarrão* (mate), to barbecue beef, and to speak using the gaucho vocabulary and accent.

The metamorphosis of the gaucho into a cock and, vice versa, of the cock into a gaucho, is explicit in the gauchos' representations of themselves, and it is present in gaucho lore (Hernandez 1967 [1872], 337):

Vos sos pollo, [. . .]	You are only a young chicken [. . .]
En las rinas he aprendido	I've learned my lesson from cockfights
a no peliar sin puyones.	never to fight without spurs.

The well known verses of a popular poet from the region where my field work took place provide an exemplary illustration of the conjunction man/cock.[15]

Valente galo de briga,	Brave fighting cock,
Gasca vestido em penas	*Gasca*[16] dressed in feathers!
Quando arrastas a chilenas[17]	When dragging your spurs
No tambor de um rinhadeiro	In a rinhadeiro pit

215

No teu ímpeto guerreiro
Vejo um gaúcho avançando
Ensaguentado, peleando
No calor do entrevero!

Pois assim como tu lutas,
Frente a frente, peito nu
Lutou tambem o chirú
Na conquista deste chão.
E como tu—sem paixão
Em silêncio, ferro a ferro
Caía sem dar um berro
De lança firme na mão!

Evoco neste teu sangue
Que brota rubro e selvagem,
Respingando na serragem,
Do teu peito descoberto,
O *guasca* no campo aberto,
De poncho feito em frangalhos
Quando riscava os atalhos
Do nosso destino incerto.

Deus te deu, como ao gaúcho
Que jamais dobra o penacho,
Essa altivez de índio macho
Que ostentas já quando pinto;
E a diferença que sinto:
E que o *guasca,* bem ou mal
Só luta por um ideal
E tu brigas por instinto!

Por isto é que em uma rinha
Eu contigo sofro junto,
Ao te ver quase defunto,
De arrasto, quebrado e cego
Como quem diz: "Não me entrego
Sou galo; morro e não grito

Cumprindo o fato maldito
Que desde a casca eu carrego."

E ao te ver morrer peleando
No teu destino cruel,
Sem dar nem pedir quartel

With your warrior grit
I see a gaucho advancing
Bloody, fighting
In the heat of the pit!

Just as you fight,
Face to face, bare breast. So too
Long ago, fought the *chirú*[18]
Conquering this soil.
As you routinely toil
In silence, in combat to the death,
Fallen without a scream or breath
Holding the lance tight!

Evoking in your blood
Which spurts savage, maroon,
Haphazardly to dust strewn,
From your heart, revealed,
Guasca on a open field,
From a poncho[19] tattered,
To the winds you scattered,
Of our fate, unsealed.

God gave you, as to the Gaucho,
A crown you never hide,
This male Indian pride,
That since chick you've shown;
It's the difference that I have known:
While the *guasca,* for good or for ill
Only fights for an ideal,
You fight on instinct alone!

That's why in a fight,[20]
I feel your pain,
When I see you about to be slain,
blind, broken, dragging yourself
As saying: "I won't surrender myself
I'm a cock; I face death without a cry
        or shout,

This cursed fate I must carry out
Since my hatching such is the path that
        I wend."

When I see you dying and fighting
Your cruel destiny your only cause,
No time for rest, no time to pause,

Rude gaúcho emplumado	Rude feathered gaucho, fate you defy,
Meio triste, encabulado,	A part of you sad, a part of you shy,
Mil vezes me perguntei:	A thousand times I cry:
Por que e que não boliei	I hesitated. Why
Pra morrer no teu costado.	Didn't I, alongside you, die?
Porque na rinha da vida	Because in the *rinha* of life
Já me bastava um empate!	Just to tie is all I seek,
Pois cheguei no arremate	Though twisted and beaten, without beak
Batido, sem bico e torto	At the end of the fight I did arrive,
E só me resta um conforto	There is one comfort I can derive,
Como a ti, galo de rinha,	Fighting cock, as you showed me
Que se alguem dobrar-me a espinha	If ever a time that someone should fold me
Há de ser depois de morto!	It will never be while I'm alive!

Without a doubt, cockfighting is a dramatization of male identity. The verses are typical of gaucho aesthetics, emotions, and metaphors. First, the analogy man/cock refers not just to any kind of man, but means gaucho/cock. As is constant in this culture, ethnic identity overlaps gender identity and excludes females. A second aspect is the saga of the gaucho as an historically oppressed social group. Third, the analogy concludes with the notion of the refusal to submit, and of pride, not in winning, but in fighting. The metaphor here equates fighting with the gaucho's struggle to maintain his values, his identity, his "dignity." In the concluding statement, we see the gaucho's intimacy with death. Death is always an honorable life solution.

Pits and Fights

In order for those gifted cocks, whose supreme desire seems to be to fight each other, to be together, men also have to get together. Men will come from different cities, break their everyday routine, and create a well-delimited space to praise their cocks, and the male condition of the men and their cocks. Since cocks fight continuously, men will be continuously together. They will eat and spend day and night together, creating an extraordinary situation out of their ordinary lives, a situation imposed upon the men by their cocks.

The rinhadeiro is a large enclosed building, a sort of sport gymnasium where the cockfights take place. From the outside we do not see any sign indicating that this is a cockfighting place or a cockers' society. Sometimes it is built behind store or a restaurant, and except for a sudden influx of people on weekends, nothing calls our attention to this place. This gym is a large space with no full interior dividing walls; in the different points of the building many different activities go on at the same time. What is most striking upon entering a rinhadeiro is the contrast between the cocks and the enormous space around them, and the immediate realization that one has penetrated into a totally male domain.

A rinhadeiro has two or more pits. The main pit, called *tambor*, is about five meters in diameter. It is surrounded by an upholstered wall less than sixty centimeters high. Auxiliary pits, called *rebolo*, are smaller in diameter (about three meters) and are also enclosed by low walls. All the pits have carpeted floors. Each pit is surrounded by many rows of chairs, with the first row of chairs contiguous to the pit and at the same level with it. The next row is farther and higher from the pit and every ring of seats larger than the preceding one. The seats in the first row of the main ring are upholstered with the same material that covers the ring wall around the cocks. Each of the chairs in the first row has a man's last name printed in a small metal plaque fixed to the chairs. These chairs are the permanent seats of well known cockers who run the society and have paid for those seats. Even when they are absent, nobody sits in these privileged spots close to the fighting cocks. The center of each pit is highly illuminated either by a skylight or, at night, by artificial light. There is a circular heater hanging over the pit which is used during the winter.

The magnificence of the space, the arrangement of the chairs and illumi-nated spots give the impression of a Greek theatre or, perhaps, a coliseum, since stage and seats are entire circles. The posted rules, padded seats, the cleanliness of the place, the attention of the audience, every detail to the drama of the pit conveys the understanding that we are watching a play.[21] The figure below shows the space arrangement of the rinhadeiro.

At one corner of the rinhadeiro is a table with scales, where the cocks are weighed by a referee just before a fight. The cocks are matched by their weight. At tournaments, the main matches are prearranged. The name of the cock's owner with the cock's weight at its side is written on a blackboard posted above the pits. Most of the cocks do not have names of their own, but are referred to by their owners' names, although while fighting, they are given nicknames to distinguish them from their opponents: "the red," "little black," "the bald," "the little." Owners' names and the terms specifying cocks are totally confounded in the cheers of the men during the fights.

The difference of weight between two cocks who are going to fight each other cannot be greater than fifty grams. On the table where the cocks are weighed, sharp metal spurs and metal beaks are fixed to the cocks by their handlers. The spurs' and beaks' sharpness is measured by the referee. Only one kind of spur is allowed. "Bolivian heels," steel needle-shaped spurs, are

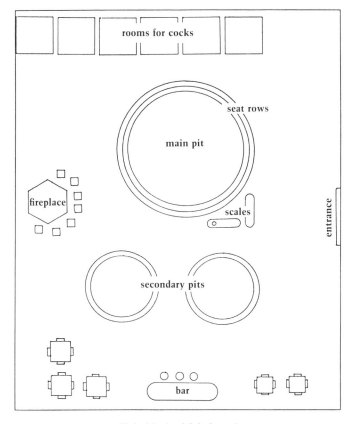

Rinhadeiro (cockfight house)

forbidden. During the fight, each cock owner or handler can reset fallen spurs only once on each of the cock's legs.

Fighting rules change from city to city, from rinhadeiro to rinhadeiro. The rules are posted on one of the walls and the referee's word is always final. Cockfighting in big tournaments usually has a time limit of one and a half or two hours for each match, with rounds of fifteen or twenty minutes and a break of two or five minutes each. The break is called *refresco* ("refreshment"), and it is the time during which the handler or the owner will take intensive care of his cock's wounds. To start or restart a fight, the handlers *encostam* the cocks, i.e., they try to make the cocks engage each other. This is repeated three times. If

219

the cocks refuse to fight, the fight is cancelled and the owners of the cocks are shamed.

Rinhadeiros usually have a bar or a restaurant, where they serve coffee, beer, and soft drinks on a counter. *Churrasco,* barbecued beef, is prepared in the traditional gaucho way either in a ground fire in the yard, where the meat is roasted on spits, or on a special grill. Joking about "we are eating your cock" goes on, but I never observed any barbecue other than beef during cockfights. Somehow it seems totally inappropriate to eat chicken there.

Cockfighting brings together breeders from diverse cities, regions and countries. During every cockfighting event, the betting and cheering for different cocks is extremely dynamic and there is no regularity in the alliances among men in the audience. On the contrary, as I mentioned earlier, there is a sort of fidelity between men and cocks; when the same cock fights again the same men are expected to bet on the same cocks. Although important bonds among men are not established through betting, there are pre-existing links among them, and their constant attendance at the rinhadeiro reinforces those links. During cockfights, groups of friends cluster together, and class and ethnic origin plays a role in the pattern of the affinities. More than once during my interviews, a particular complaint appeared which was told in a gossipping intonation:

> The Jews come here just because they are crazy about money and love gambling, but they do not have any tradition in cockfighting and don't know nothing about cocks.

To which is immediately added: "But they know how to maintain a contract and to keep the word." Meaning by that, that only men who share the gaucho code of honor participate in cockfighting; the comment was addressed to group of men identified as Jews.[22]

The general atmosphere in a cockfighting house is that of camaraderie. There is a rivalry and competition among men that seems to take the form of joking. In one of the rinhadeiros, a sign in large letters painted on the pit wall reads: "While the cocks fight, the men fraternize" ("Enquanto os galos brigam os homens confraternizam").[23] In fact every time there is a public polemic on the subject, part of the cockers' argument in defense of cockfighting is that violence is natural to man and that they need to channel it through ritual means. Their own perception of it is very close to that of sacrifice: cockfighting is a response to imperative needs, from a power above themselves—nature, which demands that violence and death must be played out.

Cockfights are not forbidden in Brazil, but occasionally organizations such as societies for the protection of animals or neighborhood associations initiate a debate in the mass media against it. It is unlikely that cockfights will ever be forbidden there, or that its actual prohibition would restrict the practices of such a culturally legitimated activity.[24] Nevertheless, it is enveloped in secrecy, in order to avoid public polemic, to preclude female presence, and to maintain a selected audience of men initiated in this practice. The seclusion of cockfighting is a way of controlling the betting, to keep cockfighting a private affair among "men of honor" who know its code. The climate of secrecy cultivated around cockfighting also gives it a desirable aura of exclusivity and complicity that reinforces male identity and links among men and their group.

There are two kind of bets: the *Central* betting with a pre-established price which is done only between the owners of the two cocks that are fighting. It is also "central" in the sense that it is "centralized" by "the house" (the rinhadeiro), with the rules of the cockers' association defining prices. "Lateral" betting is done between any two individuals in the audience, without any sort of bureaucratic intermediation. Any man in the audience may shout out his odds: "Two against one on the *Pintado*" (bettors use either a nickname for the cock or the cock's owner's name). As in an auction, someone else will indicate with a discreet gesture that he is willing to take the bet. The bids are numerous, continuous, and ever changing in each cockfight. The amounts are usually lower than the central betting, but probably the total amount of money wagered in peripheral bets is higher then in the central one. The bets are relatively high, and a clear class distinction exists between those who can afford to bet and those who just watch the fights. This parallels the place where men sit in the rinhadeiro: the farther they are from the pit, the farther they are from the higher bets, or even from the possibility of betting.

The bets, as with many things in gaucho culture, rely on oral contract, on a man's word enforced by group cohesion and a shared sense of honor. Sometimes no word is even spoken; two men look at each other and a contract is made. It is unthinkable that bets not be paid.

Every rinhadeiro has posted rules on moral conduct, but no explicit rule about the obligation to pay bets. This concerns only the men who are engaged in the betting. Regulations include items such as "it is forbidden to fight inside this place" (referring to fights among men, I suppose); or "it is forbidden to be drunk"; and even "animal abuse inside this society will be severely punished."[25]

All fights start at the main pit, and cocks will fight there at least the first half hour, depending on the total number of fights scheduled for the event. After the second or third break, the cocks will be transferred and will continue to fight in one of the other pits. The walls of the pit, padded with a synthetic material, become blood soaked. At some intervals, the janitor carefully washes the pit walls with a sponge and water or alcohol.

By the time the cocks are switched to secondary pits, the fight is already defined; that is, the audience knows who the winner will be, and there is less interest in it. Most of the public will remain in the main pit for the next fight. A few men, a sort of close-cock escort, will follow the cocks. The escort of the losing cock will be quiet, almost solemn, sharing solidarity and "dignity" with the cock and among themselves. Unless one of the cocks runs away, "cries like a chicken," or if the losing cock makes an unexpected movement, the crowd in the secondary pit will follow the cock's fate in silence. If the cock is being struck or if it is dying with "dignity," no one will make jokes. The obligation to follow one's own losing cock is a rule of honor. However, the men whose cock is winning (with exception of his handler), may choose not to go to the next pit, even when the cock seems to be as badly injured and bloody as the other. Sometimes a cock may react unexpectedly, changing the result of the fight. In such a case, men scream, some cheering, others in despair, and most of the people from the main pit run to the other pit. The bets are promptly paid in cash, but only at the moment the referee decides the fight is over.

At one end of the gymnasium are some small closed individual rooms which are used by the handlers to take care of and exercise the cocks before the fight. Preparing the cock to enter into the scene is a private matter and is done behind closed doors. In those small rooms, men massage their cocks with heated almond oil and warm them up with exercise. They will give some liquid to the cocks that first was warmed up in the man's mouth. They will feed the cocks through their own mouth, in a mouth to mouth operation. Dope is forbidden by the rules, but it seems impossible to verify if a cock is actually doped or not. Talk about doping is always going on, and endless discussions are held as to what is natural and can be given to the cocks. In fact, every handler acts as if he had a magic potion, a special gesture, or a spell to treat the cock.

During each of the cockfight's three-minute breaks, when the judge rings the bell, the man in charge of the cock will run into the pit, hold his cock, wrapping it immediately in a towel. The man warms up some alcohol in his mouth, and then throws it over the cock, with the man's mouth so close to the cock that he actually licks the cock and sucks the cock's bruises. At each fight interval, he feeds the cock with a few drops of water or saliva and brandy, the secretion that the man warms first in his mouth, in this mouth-to-mouth resuscitation. When the cock is badly injured, apparently dead, and the bell rings, the man will massage the cock with quick movements and will put the cock's entire head inside his mouth in a desperate attempt to revive the cock for the coming round.[26]

Fighting cocks have trimmed combs, because combs are easy targets for the adversary. They also have shaved legs and thighs. An infusion of oil and boiled herbs is constantly massaged on the cock's skin. It is believed that the oil and a regular sun tan on the cock's legs will make his skin less sensitive to pain and he will be able to fight longer.

Cocks are also placed on a rigorous diet and not permitted sexual intercourse for long periods before fighting. Their diet is based on heated moistened bread and cooked grains, boiled milk, and ground cooked meat. The cocks are kept in individual cages apart from the hens. The cock's sexual activity is rigorously controlled: the cock will have contact with only one chicken for reproduction purposes. It is believed that sexual abstinence will give it the strength and will to fight, and that decreased sexual activity will create better quality semen. The underlying assumption is that sexual intercourse or even the contact with a female turns the male into a weaker being. "Fighting spirit" is understood to be a direct consequence of sexuality and virility.

To train a game cock also means to tame him, as the cock is supposed to be wild otherwise. To achieve this, he has to be trained to tolerate men and to stay in the pit without being distracted by the public. This taming is done basically by handling the cock and by segregating it from other cocks. Man's intimacy with the cock is intense; caring for a cock implies affection and the exchanges of bodily fluids from man to cock and cock to man. An old English cocker's manual has a detailed description of how to care for a cock:

> and then with your spit moistening his head all over, turn him into the pit to prove his fortune. When the battle is ended the first thing you do, you shall search his wounds, and as many as you can find, you shall with your mouth suck the blood out of them, then warm them very well with warm urine, to keep them from ranckling, and then presently give him a roule or two of your best scouring, and so stove him up as hot as you can, both with sweet straw and blanketing in a close blanket for all night, . . . you shall suck his wounds again, and bathe with warm urine . . . , and give the cock a good handful of bread to eat out of warm urine. . . . (Markham 1649, 116)

The procedure I observed in caring for cocks was similar to the one described here; the same basic actions are performed, but to lesser extremes. It is important to note that British pre-Victorian game cock breeders' manuals are part of breeders' literature in Brazil. When a good quality cock leaves the pit badly hurt, there is a general commotion and his owner or handler carefully examines his wounds. As soon as the cock is better, the handler checks the cock's sexual organs to see if they have been affected: with the cock supine the man gently rubs behind the cock's leg in the direction of its testicles. If the cock ejaculates and the sperm contains blood, it is considered that the cock is seriously hurt and will not be able to fight again. Special prescriptions and methods on how to take care of cocks are always kept secret.

Nature and Culture: The Wild and the Tamed

Cocks are masculine symbols, but my point here is to show how these symbols of masculinity spring from the context of the gaucho culture. The association men/cocks, which seems to be self-evident in cultures that have the word *cock* as a signifier for penis, is not an obvious one in gaucho culture. I am not denying the semantical association man/cock; rather I am suggesting that in cockfighting situations, the meaning of cock imagery cannot be reduced to the notion of male genitals, for the reason that masculinity is not reducible to natural anatomical attributions. In gaucho culture, maleness has to be constantly achieved and proved among the male peer group. That is to say, it is not enough to have a penis to be a man. The penis is only a distinctive mark; a man acquires masculinity if he is invested with a set of values such as honor, dignity, braveness, righteousness. If he is able to perform the tasks and rites which assure masculinity, he becomes a "man," he acquires the "phallus," which means he gains prestige and power. Regarding cocks, breeders' manuals indicate that:

> The male comes into the world with natural prerogatives, but must fight and play his life to put these into play. (Finsterbusch 1929, 172)

"To be a cock" in gaucho dialect (and this is true of Brazil in general) means to be a man, which entails *having power.* In male slang, "Quem e o galo aqui?" ("Who is the cock here?"), is best translated as "who is the boss here?" *Galo* is not just man, but necessarily the boss or the most skilled or prestigious man. *Galeza* ("cockness") is a neologism used by teenager boys in Brazil to impute cocks' attributes to man.

Cocks and cockfighting carry a sexual content. The cockers say of their fighting cocks that if a cock is with a hen, the cock is extremely pugnacious and jealous of men. It is said also that hens confined without cocks assume the copulation position when a man enters in the chicken house and tries to pick them up, and that they do not behave so with women.[27] My data on sexual attraction magic also indicates the connection between cocks and virility: a tea of cock's spurs is recommended for sexual potency; a paste of fresh chicken excrement is prescribed so that the beards of male teenagers will grow faster.

Therapeutic and reinvigorating powers are assigned to game-cock's comb (cf. Finsterbusch 1929). Jokes are made about "mounting" (*trepar*) or "eating" (*comer*) "someone's cock" (that is to say, the cock's owner) in the cockfight situation. Both words, *trepar* and *comer*, in Brazilian Portuguese are used for coitus, while *cock* can stand for man, although not for man's genitals. It is important to note that the meaning of laughter here has special cultural references. The men play with their sexuality as much as they play with their cocks to settle and to reassure themselves what manliness is all about. Yet regarding sexual intimacy between cock and man, the fact that chickens are, at the level of imagery and actual experience, one of the animals with which boys engage in sexual practices cannot be put aside.[28]

My intention here is not to demonstrate the connection between cocks and maleness, but to indicate *how* in a specific situation—in cockfighting—a referent, *cock*, assumes a given meaning, "manliness," and becomes a symbol. Particular symbols are parts of larger ones and refer ultimately to a whole into which they are inserted. The issue here is how symbolic representations are constructed or, in other words, how an encoding process is established in a given reality.

In reviewing the data presented, first in reference to the space of the cockfighting and, second, concerning the care and manipulation of the cocks, there are some elements which can be seen as recurrent.

In relation to the spatial organization of a rinhadeiro, we have two main elements: the center and the periphery. During a cockfight, cocks are in the center of the ring, men around its border; cocks are inside, men are outside (see diagram on p. 219). This coincides with the low/high dichotomy in relation to the position of the seats and male hierarchy. The low/high or near/far binary opposition is also homologous to hot/cold of the actual illumination and heating in the rinhadeiro.

Except for the judge (who is neutral by definition), no man will step inside the pit. The pit is a *clean* space with carpeted floor and washed walls. Blood is part of this cleanliness. Blood is thought of as hot, savage, and pure. The blood is washed away after each fight when the combatants are changed, but during the fight, the blood is left on the walls, and carries the connotations of the purity of sacrificial blood. The public space is noisy, dirty, and polluted. Clear rules determine that smoking, eating, and alcoholic drinking have to be done away from the pit. The traditional *chimarrão*, the gaucho hot tea, is the only drink allowed close to the pit.

In regard to betting, there is an inversion in terms of high/low, center/periphery dynamics: the higher betting is *central* (in their words) while the *lateral* bets cost less and are more numerous.

Choosing "center" and "periphery" as the terms for an organizing principle around which we can order recurrent circumstances and attributes, we may construct the following diagram:

	Center	Periphery
	cock	**man**
position	low near inside	high far outside
situation	light clean hot	dark dirty cold
bets	expensive few	cheap numerous

In regard to the relationship between cocks and the men who care for them, we may take as signifying elements the terms "wild" and "tamed," which at another level of abstraction may be defined as "nature" and "culture." Regarding this, we have information on food, on the manipulation of cocks, and on the bodily fluids of man and cock:

Nature	Culture
cock	man
wild	tamed
semen	saliva
blood	urine
receives	sucks
hot	cold
cold	hot
cooked	raw
clean	dirty

In the dynamic of caring for the cocks, we have first, the man as a giver of heat, warm food, and the man's own body fluids to the cock, and the cock as a receiver. At another level, we can think of these interactions as an exchange,

226

since man sucks and licks the cock, in which situation the man is the receiver and the cock a giver. The cock's blood in the middle of the pit can be seen as the cock's sacrificial offering to the man. Traditionally, societies encircle what is defined as culture. Man and a given culture is central, and everything outside this core will be understood as part of the "other," as the "wild:" as "nature.[29] But here what we have is a reorganization of the wild, and its space—the game cock space—becomes the central spot. Indeed, the ring, or the pit, works here at both levels, at a metonymical and at a metaphorical level: the center of the ring has the heat (and the heater), it is the cleanest spot (constantly warmed alcohol bath of the cock), and it is also the most illuminated. It is through the inversion of the classical attributions of the dichotomy, "nature" and "culture," that the man here redefines these domains. This is, to a certain extent, a strategy, one which permits him to own the wild and to own nature. In cockfighting, nature is, *par exellence,* the place of strength and power.

The bloody drama is a gratifying scene that functions as a strong signifier which encompasses all the maleness signified. The cock has been carefully nurtured by man, even with man's own products, his body fluids, for a long period. Metaphorically the cock is full of semen and holds man's fluids. Man's fluids (food, saliva, urine) become cock's fluids (semen and blood). When, in battle, cocks are ripped and their insides come out in the form of blood, men symbolically *obtain* the cock's fluids, which thus become their own and reach their plenitude. The cock's inside, i.e., the cock's fluids, encode male values.

The narcissistic component of this game of manliness is clear: men think of themselves as strong, brave, and handsome individuals. The sexual energy of these individuals is carefully cultivated to be driven toward each other in the fight, a moment where sexuality, aggressiveness, and masculinity become one. The definition of cockfighting as a male space, the mechanisms of continuous exchange through betting, the experience of an extraordinary time during the tournaments (when the fights go on without stopping for the night), the shared feeling of secrecy in engaging in this activity together, and men's notion of sacrifice, of a worship of masculinity—all these are elements that effectively reinforce the male group solidarity and consensus about what should constitute male roles in society. Perhaps man's narcissistic process of identification as male, which is inseparable from its homosexual component, might find in the choreography of the two bloody cocks fighting a vicarious satisfaction of homosexual drives.

We can return now to the question posed at the beginning of this essay: The intimacy cock/man, which is basically an exchange of attributes, is essential to the construction of maleness. Man acquires ownership over what he elects as animal nature, basically strength and power, and makes them part of human nature. This process of "naturalizing" certain attributes relies on previous and well-demarcated categories of what is nature and what is culture. Power in gaucho classification is part of nature; one way to obtain power is to have dominion over nature.

Men's profound psychological involvement with their cocks exists because this underlying symbolic coherence is present. Conversely, men who share this symbolic universe find these practices highly gratifying and absorbing. Cockfighting has enormous symbolic efficacy, embodying practices which validate a given symbolic universe.

Notes

1. Among the very few anthropological works on cockfighting, are Geertz's insightful essay "Notes on the Balinese Cockfight" (Geertz 1973), and the brief comments of Bateson and Mead (1942).

2. I will be using the English terms "cocker" for *galista* and "cocking" for *fazer rinha*, to breed cocks and to participate in cockfighting. In English, as in Portuguese and Spanish, these words are part of a specialized vocabulary of the people involved with this activity. For reference to these terms in English see for example W. Sketchley (1814) and Gilbey (1912). As classical British cocker's manuals for cock breeding are part of Gaucho cocker culture, this material is specially pertinent here.

3. For a description of cockfighting among gauchos see Ebelot (1978 [1889]), Laytano (1984), Mantegazza (1916 [1876]), Seitenfus (1967), and Teixeira (1986).

4. For a historical account of cockfighting, see Boulenger (1912), Finsterbusch (1980), Llanes (1981), and Sarabia (1972).

5. Porto Alegre is the capital city of the state of Rio Grande do Sul. It is a modern and industrial city with a population of 1 million. The best example of this articulation between the traditional and the modern is that a cockfight was the opening scene of one of the soap operas (*O Outro*) from the main national television network, in which one of the actors portrayed a stereotyped gaucho.

6. The regulation of one main cockers' society sets a time limit of one and one half hour per match; other organizations or less structured cockfights do not have a time limit. The cockfighting season extends from May or June to December or January. The rest of the year the cocks are molting.

7. It should also be pointed out that the classification of cocks into *ground* and *flyer* parallels the contrast between *ground* worker ("peão de chão" or "peão caseiro") and mounted worker ("peão campeiro") in the gauchos' life on the *estância*. The first is identified as passive, feminine, and tied to the ground; the second is identified with mobility, freedom, and dominance.

8. Gonzáles (1943) also makes reference to this poem as of Argentinean origin.

9. In Spanish or in Portuguese "cock" rhymes with "horse" (*gallo/caballo; galo/cavalo*) strengthening the semantic association between them.

10. A nineteenth-century English advertisement selling game cocks says: "Old En-

glish Game fowls / To all parts of the inhabited world / These birds are full of / *Vim, Vigour and Victory*" (Sketchley, 1814).

11. English speaker reaction to the title of this chapter indicated to me how much the meaning of *cock* is confined to "penis." The homonym does not occur in gaucho speech, Portuguese or Spanish.

12. On the rationale of the sacrifice, Hubert and Mauss state: "For the sacrifice to be truly justified, two conditions are necessary. First of all, there must exist outside the sacrificer things which cause him to go outside himself, and to which he owes what he sacrifices. Next, these things must be close to him so that he can enter into relationship with them, find in them the strength and assurance he needs, and obtain from contact with them the benefits that he expects from his rites" (1964:101).

13. In Santa Rosa, a Brazilian city on the Argentina border, a fancy hotel advertises, together with its apartments, special rooms with air-conditioning for cocks.

14. The *San Francisco Chronicle* of 24 November 1988 published a news item from San Jose, California under the title "Cockfight Surprise in Drug Raid." The narcotics unit searching a home during a drug raid found thirty caged fighting cocks and more than two hundred cockfighting spurs in a home. The suspects were charged for sale and possession of cocaine and possession of cockfighting equipment.

15. Jaime Caetano Braum, *Potreiro de Guachos* (1979), translated by David Lampert. This poem was also cited by Teixeira (1986) in his work on cockfighting.

16 *Gasca* originally meant an old and hard piece of leather. According to the context it can mean "penis," "man," "Gaucho," or "hard and strong man," or even, as in this case, the word may be a condensation of all those meanings.

17. *Chilenas* ("Chileans") are the kind of spurs used by gauchos. Spurs for cocks are called "Bolivians" when long and sharp, or are just called "spurs" (*esporas*).

18. *Chirú:* gaucho of Indian origin.

19. The *poncho* is typical of gaucho clothing.

20. The original refers to *rinha,* the cockfight. The word is also employed (without losing its cockfight connotations) to a fight or dispute between men.

21. Mantegazza (1916 [1876]) in early anthropological work in this region describes the cockfighting setting in Argentina as a *theatre.* Geertz' 1973 article also stresses this point: Balinese cockfighting is a *play* about their society.

22. This information was collected in a rinhadeiro in Porto Alegre, a city that has a large Jewish community.

23. Cf. Teixeira (1986).

24. My assumption that it is unlikely that cockfighting would be forbidden relies on the Brazilian population's cultural tolerance for practices that are usually forbidden in other countries. Moreover, black cocks (not game cocks) and goats are ritually sacrificed in the African-Brazilian religions widespread in Brazil. Political organizations that depend on popular support would never openly take the initiative against popular customs. The general attitude is that there are more important things than cockfighting to worry about, such as infant mortality, inflation, and economic dependence. On the contrary, these cultural practices tend to be incorporated by government agencies as folklore and symbols of identity. Interestingly, cockfighting was forbidden for a short

period in Brazil by a presidential decree in May 1961, which caused strong popular reaction and was cancelled in July 1962. It seems that the main motive for this prohibition was that the father of the president responsible for the decree (Janio Quadros) killed himself because he had lost a considerable amount of money betting on cockfighting. The personal motive of the legislation against cockfighting made the law itself totally ridiculous.

25. In the original, article 18: "Será severamente punido pela diretoria o frequentador que, no recinto da sociedade, infrinja mal tratos aos animais ou os sacrificar, bem como aquele que se portar de maneira incoviniente." (*Sociedade Avicola Bankivia* at Porto Alegre).

26. Boulenger (1912, 353) presents a poem of Victor Breda on cockfighting which describes well the man's attempt to revive the cock at the fight breaks: "Lui caresse la tête et de sa main pressant / Le col qui s'engorgeait, en fait sortir le sang. / Le coq, grâce à ce soin, ressuscite à la vie / et reprend sur-le-champ sa première énergie."

27. Finsterbusch (1929, 189) also refers to this sexual behavior and to this attraction between cocks and men.

28. The chickens used in bestiality are not this species of fowl; they are not game hens.

29. For a classical structuralist approach to nature and culture, see Lévi-Strauss (1964).

References

Bateson, Gregory, and Margaret Mead. 1942. *The Balinese Character: A Photographic Analysis.* New York: New York Academy of Sciences.

Boulenger, Jacques. 1912. *Animaux de Sport.* Paris: Pierre Lafitte.

Dingwall, Alexander. 1928. *The Handling and the Nursing of the Game Cocks.* Chicago: Dingwall and Paton.

Ebelot, Alfredo. 1978. Riñas de Gallos (1889). In Horacio Jorge Becco, ed., *El Gaucho: Documentacion-Iconografia.* Buenos Aires: Editorial Plus Ultra.

Finsterbusch, C. A. 1980. *Cockfighting All Over the World.* Hindhead, U.K.: Saiga.

Geertz, Clifford. 1973. "Deep Play: Notes on the Balinese Cockfight." In Clifford Geertz, ed., *The Interpretation of the Cultures: Selected Essays.* New York: Basic Books.

Gilbey, Walter. 1912. *Sport in Olden Time.* London: Vinton.

Gonzáles, Manuel. 1943. *Trayectoria del Gaucho y su Cultura.* Havana: Ucar, Garcia e Cia.

Hernandez, José. 1967 [1872]. *The Gaucho Martin Fierro.* Albany: State University of New York Press.

Hubert, H. and Marcel Mauss. 1964 [1898]. *Sacrifice: Its Nature and Function.* Chicago: University of Chicago Press.

Laytano, Dante. 1984. *Folclore do Rio Grande do Sul: Costumes e Tradições Gauchas.* Porto Alegre: EDUCS/Martin Livreiro.

Lévi-Strauss, Claude. 1964. *Le Cru et le Cruit.* Paris: Plon.

Llanes, Ricardos. 1981. *Canjas de Pelotas e Renideros de Antano.* Buenos Aires: Cadernos de Buenos Aires, n. 58.

Mantegazza, Pablo. 1916 [1876]. *Viajes por el Rio de la Plata y el Interior de la Confederation Argentina.* Buenos Aires: Coni Hermanos.

Markham, Gervase. 1649. *The Husbandmans Recreations.* London: William Wilson, St. Pauls Churchyard.

Proud, P. 1903. *The Game Fowl: Old and Modern.* London: The Feathered World.

Sarabia Viejo, Maria. 1972. *El Juego de Gallos en Nueva Espanha.* Seville: Escuela de Estudios Hispanoamericanos de Sevilla.

Seitenfus, Walter. 1967. *Rinha de Galo.* Porto Alegre: Comissão Gaucha de Folclore.

Sketchley, W. 1814. *The Cocker.* London: Croft.

Teixeira, Sergio. 1986. "Rinha de Galo: Legitimação e Identificação." Paper presented at the 12th meeting of ANPOCS. Campos de Jordão.

Cockfighting on the Venezuelan Island of Margarita: A Ritualized Form of Male Aggression

Approximately twenty miles off the coast of eastern Venezuela lies Isla de Margarita. From September 1987 through May 1988, H. B. Kimberley Cook carried out extensive ethnographic fieldwork on that island on the subject of aggression. This fieldwork plus three earlier visits, the first of which occurred in 1979, included an investigation of the local cockfighting tradition on the island. It was not easy to do so because women were not welcome at cockfights.

In her 1991 UCLA doctoral dissertation (pp. 18–19), H.B. Kimberley Cook describes her difficulties: "The fact that I am a woman ethnographer made it difficult to study cock fighting but also led to some interesting insights. Cock fighting is a strictly male activity and my informants initially insisted that I drop this from my study. After three months of my incessant nagging, they graciously consented to allow me to attend the cock fights at the gallera on Sundays. I attended several cock fights and supplemented my data with the help of three male informants who I met with individually. My presence at the gallera, however, was an act of deviance which gave me a painful yet firsthand experience on how social control operates in the community. I eventually stopped collecting data on cock fighting because of the trouble it was causing. . . ."

As was the case in Leal's preceding account of the Gaucho cockfight, the present female ethnographer's description and analysis of the cockfight in Venezuela are exceptionally insightful. Indeed, it may be fair to say that the two essays on the cockfight by women contain more valuable data leading to a psychologically illuminating picture of this male-centered event than anything hitherto written by men.

For other accounts of cockfighting in Venezuela, see J. A. de Armas Chitty, "Les Riñas de Gallos en el Oriente del Guárico," Archivos Venezolanos de Folklore *2–3 (1953–1954): 149–158; M. Acosta Saignes, "Introducción al estudio de la gallina en al folklore de Venezuela,"* Tradición *6 (1954): 29–46; L. G. Marquez,* Reglamento del Club Gallistico de Caracas *(Caracas: Tip. Londres, 1954); and*

Reprinted from H. B. Kimberley Cook, "Small Town, Big Hell: An Ethnographic Study of Aggression in a Margariteño Community," unpublished doctoral dissertation in anthropology, University of California, Los Angeles, 1991, pp. 79–94. The dissertation is in *Antropológica* 4 (1993) published by the Instituto Caribe de Antropología y Sociología in Caracas.

G. A. Pérez, La Pelea de Gallos en Venezuela: Léxico, Historia y Literatura *(Caracas: Ediciones Espada Rota, 1984).*

Cockfighting is central to the lives of the residents of San Fernando. One fishermen stated that: "You can die of hunger but there will always be a *gallera* (cockfighting rink)." Others claim that there is one in every town: "You may not be able to get food but there will be a gallera. There is one everywhere. If there is one house built, there will be a gallera."

Cockfighting is a strictly male event that involves ritualistic and real aggression. Women are not welcome. In San Fernando, the rink is located on the outside of town so as not to disrupt the course of daily life. Nevertheless, cockfighting is an on-going preoccupation that affects the lives of everyone.

My aim in studying cockfighting was not to gain a true understanding of the sport itself. For detailed information on the sport of cockfighting in Venezuela, see Pérez, *La Pelea de Gallos en Venezuela.* For the purposes of this study, I view cockfighting as a context from which cultural values and behaviors could be elicited and observed. In this essay, I will discuss some common themes which underlie cultural patterns of hostility, and discuss processes used in the expression and mediation of aggression during cockfighting. Before doing so, I will describe the nature and scope of data I collected on cockfighting activities.

My information on cockfighting is taken mainly from interviews and observations made in the town of San Fernando. I relied on three sources of information, which include observations of daily activities related to cockfighting, my attendance at the gallera on Sundays, and interviews with informants.

Daily activities include the care and handling of cocks that aim at maintaining the animal's health and stimulating its fighting, aggressive spirit. Care first of all involves attention to the animal's diet. According to one informant: "Some people don't know how to take care of cocks. They just throw the corn kernels on the ground, in the dirt. You should take care of a cock just like yourself, like a person. The food should be kept clean, and one should measure out the same amount of kernels each day (exactly forty). Cocks should be fed each day at the same time, in the morning, so that they can work it off. If you feed a cock after twelve a.m., it becomes fat and lazy." In addition to their regular food, cocks are also given lemon and sugar which, according to their owners, insures that they will be healthy and stimulated. Care also involves the use of human remedies, which include vitamin pills, creams used for cuts to prevent infections, and eye drops purchased at the local pharmacy. Although cockfighters have different regimes, all of my informants agree that cocks should be exercised "just like a person." Exercise strengthens the cock and insures that it will not become *echado* (exhausted) during the fight.

In Margarita, cockfighters handle their roosters in the same fashion as reported by Geertz in his description of Balinese cockfighters.[1] They are held in one hand and stroked by the other from the neck to the end of the tail. They are held close to the ground and bounced between the loins of their owners. Their feathers are trimmed and they are bathed with alcohol. They are endowed with human-like attributes of loyalty, valor and, most of all, virility. When I asked one *gallero* (cockfighter) how to choose a cock, he looked at me and smiled and responded: "The same way you choose a man."

Cockfighting is a male event, and my attendance at the gallera on Sundays was, needless to say, unwelcome. Women know a considerable amount about cockfighting and in previous years did attend cockfights in San Fernando when the rink was smaller and located within the community. When I arrived to do fieldwork in May of 1987, I expressed my interest in cockfighting but was told that it is no longer a place for women to go. "Nowadays," they said, "the island is filled with lots of strangers from *Tierra Firme* and from other countries. It's not that there is violence at the gallera, it's just that there are a lot of strangers who are *sinvergüenzas* (disrespectful). They wouldn't understand that you are a student, and they might say insulting things to you."

After three months of persisting, and because of the kindness of my informants, it was finally agreed that I could attend if I went with one of the fishermen from the community. First, I was afraid that the women in town would object, but instead they asked me how my study was going and gave me suggestions, such as: "Don't take your notebook, take a little, tiny piece of paper. Hide it in your pocket, make your notes when nobody is looking." At first I felt this to be dishonest, but later realized that "cheating," as long as one gets away with it, is part of the game.

On the first Sunday that I attended, I arrived at the rink in the early morning and found that the fights were already under way. Several vehicles had arrived with galleros (cockfighters) from other parts of the island and from outside of Margarita.

Cockfighting in San Fernando is carried out with typical native Margariteño informality. The rink, which is roughly ten feet in diameter, is bordered by a wooden bench with numbers for seats which in theory should be purchased by the participants for the duration of the fights. The owner of the rink does not sell tickets but rather makes his profits from a small stand located near the rink from which he sells beer. A large wooden box with a chamber for each of the two animals is suspended on a rope and lowered to the floor. At the beginning of each fight, the cocks are placed in each side. The trap doors to each cham-

ber are simultaneously lifted and the fight begins. Most of the time this procedure is followed for a few fights, after which it is ignored and the cocks are
impatiently let go into the rink.

Cockfighting can be conducted with a judge whose responsibility it is to
weigh the animals before the game, to insure that they are *en oro* ("equal"). He
checks for signs of cheating and determines the outcome of the fight. For his
services he usually takes a percentage of the winner's profits. The locals in San
Fernando prefer to fight *a la guerra*, which dispenses with this formality and
leaves the outcome to the general consensus of the participants.

Cockfighting is a game of skill. In San Fernando, its informal nature does
not detract from the game but rather provides a structure in which various
skills and techniques can be used to increase one's chances of winning. In
addition to the selection, care, and handling of the cocks before the game, a
tremendous amount of skill is required in the process of betting that evolves
throughout the fight. Native Margariteños say that in order to bet well you
have to have a brain like a computer.

Essential to betting is the ability to evaluate the condition of the cocks during
the fight.[2] According to some informants, it is important not only to evaluate
the amount of injury (blood on the animal) of the cock you are betting on, but
also to determine which cocks actually have blood on their *espuelas* (spurs)
which is an indication that they are successfully attacking their opponents.
Cocks that spend too much time being chased around the rink are determined
to be cowards, hence a source of amusement, and usually end up a victim of "el
gallo negro" ("the frying pan").

Subversive activities, which in other societies might be regarded as
unsportsman-like, are normal and expected practices that can affect the outcome of matches. The informal style of cockfighting which is preferred in San
Fernando Abajo leaves open the possibility that such activities can be successfully implemented. For example, in San Fernando a judge is not necessarily
required to clean the fighting spurs of each cock before a fight. Some cock
fighters take advantage of this by applying poison to their cock's spurs before
the fight, which is an effective method of eliminating the opponent's cock early
on in the game. Several homemade poisons are concocted. The most commonly mentioned ones are substances drawn from venomous fish such as *bagre*
and *raya*. The poisons are covertly applied to the single fighting spur on each
leg of the cock immediately before the event. If applied too early, there is the
danger that the cock might accidentally scratch and poison itself before the
fight.

Another method used is to apply a noxious, unpleasant smelling substance
underneath the wings of your own cock. When the fight begins and the cocks

started to lift and flap their wings, the odor reportedly sends the opponent's cock running in the opposite direction, and gives the illusion that it is afraid to fight. Thus one wins by default.

A far riskier method is to actually do physical damage to your opponent's fighting cock immediately before the fight. As one informant puts it: "While your opponent is drinking, you wait until he is looking the other way. You pinch a small bone on the back of his rooster. This doesn't kill it but it makes the cock hurt. It makes it sore so that it is hard for it to lift its legs in the fight. This way your cock has a better chance of striking first." One way of avoiding this being practiced on your own animal is to transport it to the rink in a bag which is designed to protect it from such subversive activities. It also has the advantage of concealing your fighting cock from the scrutinizing eye of competitors who attempt to evaluate its fighting ability before the match.

There is an agreed-upon code of ethics that accompanies the above-mentioned techniques for winning. First, if you are caught using one of them before the fight starts, you are not allowed to play. Your opponent, angered, will withdraw from the competition, or the cheater's cock will be eliminated. If a cheater gets away with it undetected, it is considered to be fair. If a cock wins, and it is discovered after the fact that an illegitimate technique was used, the outcome of the fight is unaffected. In this respect, cheating is considered to be part of the game.

The informal nature of cockfighting in San Fernando also provides fertile ground for the expression of aggressive behaviors which are not normally allowed in other social contexts. Traditional values of being *tranquillo, sano,* and showing *respeto,* are suspended at the gallera. Although I was initially assured that there was no problem with fist-fighting or violence at the cockfights, and although I never witnessed it personally, incidents of physical aggression occurred and were reported to me in the course of my fieldwork. And, in fact, stories of fighting that occurred before my field work in 1987–1988 began to surface in the memory of my informants.

The atmosphere at the gallera is always tense and filled with excitement. Most human interchanges consist of verbal yelling, or running across the center of the rink in the middle of a fight to "up" a bet or to argue over one. Occasional insults and fist-waving occur and frequently lead to outbreaks of physical aggression which consist of pushing and shoving, and an exchange of blows. In San Fernando Abajo, fist-fighting is not taken lightly. When it breaks out at the gallera, the crowd jumps in and separates the fighters and leads them away from the scene until things cool down. I have a well-substantiated incident of an outsider who drew a weapon and was immediately jumped upon by the crowd and asked to leave. No one was injured in this incident, which was considered a rare and horrifying event to my native informants, and not acceptable behavior, even at the gallera.

What is interesting is not that physical aggression occurs, but rather the way in which similar cases are interpreted differently. When a fight occurs at the gallera the story immediately circulates around the town. If outsiders are involved, their behavior is usually interpreted as bad. They are accused of being *mala gente* (bad people), who are *sin vergüenza* (shameless). Insiders are evaluated by a more elaborate set of criteria which usually has to do with the amount of resources they have. Individuals who are economically responsible to their families, have a large number of kin, or compadres, and are generous with other townsmen, are most likely to be given the benefit of the doubt. In these cases, their acts of physical aggression are often interpreted as *repugnancia*, which refers to childish roughhousing. A few fishermen have reputations as fighters but are simultaneously hard-working and responsible in other areas of life. Their aggression is often looked at as a form of entertainment for townsmen, who exclaim laughingly: "Oh look, X is at it again."

As a female ethnographer, my participation at the gallera was of course severely restricted. On the first Sunday I showed up at the rink, the local townsmen rationalized my presence there by exclaiming: "Well, why not, the gallera is for everyone, it's for fun, it's a business." But as was originally predicted by my informants, after a few Sundays at the gallera, rumors started to circulate. One male informant told me that some of the men were insulting me by saying that I was only there to "*meterse entre los hombres*" (get close to men). It was clear that a woman had no place there, and my role soon became one of an unwelcome but tolerated observer.

During the course of my fieldwork, I met individually with three close male informants who answered my questions about practices I observed in the rink. Some of our discussions dealt with the sexual symbolism of cockfighting. For example, when I asked why my presence at the rink was unwelcome, one informant said: "It's not that you are unwelcome; the problem is that when you try to participate it just does not work. For example, when a cockfighter wants to increase the amount of a previously made bet, he will provoke his opponent into doing so by yelling: 'abre las piernas' ("spread your legs"). But you see, if they yell that at you, it doesn't come out the same. It's embarrassing and awkward and doesn't mean the same thing." When I asked my informant what it means when a man yells this expression to a betting partner, he said: "It just means, 'come on, bet higher.' " I was also curious as to why women don't *pelear gallos* (fight cocks). I was told: "When men and women *pelear gallos*, and the woman loses, she ends up pregnant." The proper expression is to "echar una pelea," which with its more neutral terms means simply to cockfight.

A few of my informants mentioned a belief that the behavior of fighting cocks is affected by the moon. During a certain time of the month they are supposedly "weaker" than in the rest of the month. Although my informants did not elaborate on this point, I suggest that a clear association can be made between a perceived cycle of aggression in fighting cock behavior and the human female menstrual cycle.

Themes Underlying Cultural Patterns of Hostility

Cockfighting is, in part, a ritualistic form of aggression which serves as a format or context in which culturally derived patterns of hostility can be expressed, negotiated, and temporarily resolved. The symbolism underlying cockfighting in San Fernando suggests two spheres of conflict. Cockfighting first and foremost represents a fight between a man and himself. It is a medium in which culturally patterned contradictions concerning male sexuality are brought forth and exorcised. Second, the cockfight is a competition between individual men who vie for public recognition of their superior virility among each other and within the community.

There are two competing and contradictory themes in the male self-concept which surface in activities relating to cockfighting. The first of these is a cross-sex identification which is evident in the belief that cocks, like women, have a monthly cycle.[3] As was mentioned above, it is believed that cocks are weaker, less aggressive during certain periods of the month. The expression "abre las piernas," which is yelled at a betting partner during a fight, is provocative because of the underlying insinuation that if one does not have the courage to up a bet, he is weaker and unable to compete, like a woman. Similarly, the expression "pelar gallos" evokes a similar concern with a cross-sex identification. As I stated earlier, it refers to the act of copulation between men and women, and, further, that when women lose, they end up pregnant. I initially believed that this simply indicated misogynist attitudes on the part of men. But what is interesting about this expression is that men and women do not "pelar gallos" or, literally, "fight cocks." I suggest that this expression has implications on both the personal, psychological level as well as the interpersonal one. On the personal, psychological level it implies that when a man fights cocks and loses, he personally loses his identification with the virile, masculine part of himself. On the interpersonal level, it implies that when two individual men fight cocks and one loses, the loser assumes a feminine role.

The threat of a feminine identification helps to explain the extreme importance placed on the concept of virility, or *machismo*, which is a defense against inner feminine identifications. The emphasis on virility is especially evident in the association that men have with their individual fighting roosters. It is no mistake that cocks were chosen for this sport. As my informants point out: "If you put two cocks together, they have to fight to the death, or until one gives up and runs away." The nature of care that cocks receive aims at embellishing this biological predisposition for uncontrollable aggression. The pride and personal association that owners feel with their virile charges is evident in symbolic masturbation, such as the careful cleaning, stroking, bouncing, and constant handling that fighting cocks receive from their owners.

This cross-sex identity complex in males is not entirely confined to the rink but spills over into the sexually antagonistic attitudes that both men and women exhibit in this society. The location of the rink on the outside of town does little to isolate the raucous, rowdy, and drunken behavior of cockfighting enthusiasts from the rest of the community. While carrying out their domestic activities on Sundays, women make frequent reference to the "childish" and "useless" behavior of their men through insulting comments and gestures.

The Expression and Mediation of Aggression

In San Fernando, cockfighting is an activity which is geographically, temporally, and socially separated from the community at large. Cultural values of moral authority are temporarily set aside and aggressive behaviors such as pushing, shoving, and fist-fighting are included as possible and somewhat expected behaviors. The gallera is an interesting context for observing aggression, because it is the only place where women do not participate in the control and mediation of aggression. Under normal circumstances, women in San Fernando play a major role in the mediation and control of aggression. Several of my female informants say: "The gallera is the only place where we can not "parar el macho" ("control male aggression"). Nonetheless, the way in which aggression is mediated and controlled at the gallera is very similar to the way it is controlled elsewhere; the style and processes are the same.

As suggested above, the processes used in the mediation of aggression at the gallera depend upon an individual's membership in the social structure. Cockfighters who are not Venezuelans, who are from the mainland, or who are not kinsmen or *compadres* of one of the local townsmen are considered to be strangers or outsiders. Their aggressive behavior is treated differently from that of men who are tied to the community through kinship, economic, or friendship obligations.

The yelling, shoving, and pushing that goes on at the gallera is considered to be a regular and frequent occurrence at the fights. When an outsider engages in physical aggression such as fist-fighting, it is viewed more harshly than

239

when a townsman engages in similar activities. They are treated with suspicion and labeled as "*sin vergüenza*," "*mala gente*" (shameful, bad people). In contrast, the same shoving, pushing, or occasional fist-fighting by an insider is treated less severely and is judged as being "*repugnancia*," which translates as roughhousing, or playing around, as being, in other words, part of the fun. Oftentimes the aggressive behavior of townsmen is rationalized by some item in their personal history: "X is upset because his father has recently died." When an act of physical aggression occurs, it is dealt with by the group, which descends upon the combatants and separates them until they cool off. Undesirable individuals can be effectively excluded from further participation simply by the fact that no one will bet with them. According to my informants, in serious cases the police are called, although I have never heard of a case where this was done. The fact that outsiders' aggression, although similar to that of townsmen, is viewed as being more serious is related to the lack of control that locals feel they have over them. Unlike townsmen, when the fight is over the outsider simply can leave the gallera. His "bad" behavior cannot impinge on other economic and social areas of his life.

In contrast, the aggressive behavior of townsmen is interpreted and judged by a wider range of criteria related to the amount of personal resources he holds. These resources include the number of kin that one has in his own and other communities, the amount of economic responsibility that one shows towards his family, the amount of money one has, one's generosity with kin, *compadres*, and townsmen, and one's ability and willingness to work hard. The more resources that a person has, the more likely his aggression will be interpreted as simple *repugnancia*, or enthusiasm.

Notes

1. Clifford Geertz. "Deep Play: Notes on the Balinese Cockfight," in Geertz, ed., *The Interpretation of Cultures* (New York: Basic Books, 1973), pp. 418–419.
2. For detailed information on betting procedures, see Omar Alberto Pérez, *La pelea de gallos en Venezuela: Lexico, Historia y Literatura* (Caracas: Ediciones Espada Rota, 1984), 103–105.
3. While in the field, I initially believed that the behavior of men at the gallera represented misogynist attitudes of men. The idea that they represent an underlying cross-sex identity complex was suggested to me in 1988 by my Venezuelan colleague, Dr. Jorge Armand.

ALAN DUNDES

Gallus as Phallus: A Psychoanalytic Cross-Cultural Consideration of the Cockfight as Fowl Play

My own interest in the cockfight began with my reading of Clifford Geertz's 1972 essay on the Balinese cockfight. It so impressed me that I assigned it regularly in my annual graduate seminar on folklore theory. Over the years, as I listened to graduate students report on Geertz's essay, I became more and more convinced that there was more to be said on the subject. Finally, in 1991, I set about to find out what else had been written on the cockfight, believing as I do in the academic credo that all new research should begin where other researchers have ended theirs—this to avoid the time-wasting and futile effort involved in reinventing the wheel. The very best of the essays I found are included in this casebook. Drawing upon the rich ethnographic detail contained in the books and articles devoted to the cockfight, I attempted to find a symbolic structure which might illuminate the cockfight not just in one particular culture, but possibly to some extent in all those cultures in which the cockfight is found. (It is for the reader to decide whether the symbolic interpretation of the cockfight I propose is convincing or not.)

My students warned me that if members of the fraternity of cockfighters were to read this casebook—and my essay in particular, they might not like my analysis. They might even be offended by it. My response is that scholarship is not a popularity contest. The important question is not whether any one individual does or does not "like" my interpretation, but whether my interpretation has any validity. If it does, does it represent any advance in our understanding of the cockfight?

Since my analysis of the cockfight presumes the existence of an unconscious *element in the participation and enjoyment of cockfighting, I would hardly expect most cock-fighters to be consciously aware of this element. Moreover, I would not expect them necessarily to accept my explanation of the cockfight. The whole point of folklore in general, and the cockfight as an instance of folklore, is to allow individuals to do or say things they could not otherwise do or say. If people actually knew what they were doing, e.g., in telling a joke, they could not participate in that activity, e.g., tell that joke. It is in the final analysis precisely the* unconscious *content of folklore (as fantasy) which*

Reprinted from L. B. Boyer and R. Boyer, eds., *The Psychoanalytic Study of Society*, 18, pp. 23–65, by permission of the publisher. Copyright © 1993 by The Analytic Press.

allows it to function as it does, that is, as a socially sanctioned outlet for the expression of taboo thoughts and acts. That is why making the unconscious content conscious is always intellectually dangerous and why it inevitably encounters powerful resistance.

The cockfight is one of the oldest, most documented and most widely distributed traditional sports known to man.* It has been reported in ancient India (Sarma 1964; Bhide 1967; Chattopadhyay 1973), ancient China (Cutter 1989a, b), ancient Iran (Modi 1911), and ancient Greece (Witte 1868). From Greece, cockfighting moved to Rome, as mosaics attest (Magaldi 1929). The earliest recorded cockfight in China dates from 517 B.C. (Cutter 1989a, p. 632; 1989b, p. 10), which would make cockfighting at least 2500 years old. (See also Danaë 1989, p. 34, who suggests that cockfighting existed before 2000 B.C.) The antiquity of cockfighting in India is attested by a specific reference in the *Kama Sutra* (3d century A.D.), Chapter 2 of Part I, where young women are advised to study some sixty-four arts, of which number 41 includes "The rules of cockfighting," the clear implication being that a woman would be more pleasing to men who are vitally interested in such activities (Vatsyayana 1963, p. 14).

There is some consensus that the cock itself (and perhaps the cockfight) may have originated in southeast Asia (Peters 1913, p. 395; Tudela 1959, p. 14), where it diffused to China, India, and eventually Iran and on to classical Greece and Rome before moving to Western Europe and thence to the Caribbean. The cock may have come to the New World as early as the second voyage of Christopher Columbus in 1493 (Tudela 1959, p. 15). From Asia, the cockfight spread eventually nearly throughout the Americas. The cockfight, however, is by no means universal, as it seems never to have spread to any great extent to native North and South America or to sub-Saharan Africa.

Once popular in much of western Europe, including England (Pegge 1773; Egan 1832; Boulton 1901), Scotland (Beattie 1937); Ireland (Beacey 1945; O'Gormon 1983), and Wales (Peate 1970), cockfighting is still to be found in the north of France (Demulder 1934; Cegarra, 1987, 1988, 1989), in Belgium (Desrousseaux 1886, 1889, pp. 115–124; Delannoy 1948; Remouchamps and Remacle 1949), and in Spain (Justo 1969; Marvin 1984). Nowhere is

*I am indebted to Rafaela Castro Belcher and Margot Winer for their bibliographical surveys of cockfighting compiled in my folklore theory seminars in 1976 and 1986 respectively. For additional references, I am grateful to Jim Anderson, Caroline McCullagh, Judy McCulloh, Dan Melia, and Herb Phillips. I thank folklore archivist Almudena Ortiz for her assistance in translating several Spanish idioms, and my student Mariella Jurg for translating several passages from Dutch to English.

cockfighting enjoyed more than in southeast Asia, as is confirmed by reports from Borneo (Barclay 1980), Celebes (Kaudern 1929, pp. 337–348), and Java (Serière, 1873, pp. 92–10; Kreemer 1893; Soeroto 1916–1917), Malaysia (Wilkinson 1925), the Philippines (Bailey 1909; Lee 1921; Lansang 1966; Guggenheim 1982), Sarawak (Sandin 1959), Sumatra (Scheltema 1919), and, of course, Bali (Eck 1879; Knight 1940; Bateson and Mead 1942; Geertz 1972; Picard 1983). Cockfighting is equally popular in the Caribbean (Challes 1972), for example, in Martinique (Champagnac 1970; Affergan 1986); in Haiti (Paul 1952; Marcelin 1955a, b); in Cuba (Wurdemann 1844, pp. 87–93; Hazard 1871, pp. 191–195), and in Puerto Rico (Alonso 1849, pp. 77–93; Dinwiddie 1899; Cadilla de Martinez 1941; Calderin 1970; Feijoo 1990). There are cockfight enthusiasts throughout Latin America, for example, in Argentina (Mantegazza 1916, pp. 69–71; Saubidet 1952, pp. 345–356); Brazil (Leal 1989); Colombia (Léon Rey 1953); Mexico (Mendoza 1943); and Venezuela (Armas Chitty 1953–1954; Acosta Saignes 1954; Marquez 1954; Perez 1984; Cook 1991, pp. 79–94).

In the United States, cockfighting is technically banned in most states. Nevertheless, we have published accounts of cockfights from California (Beagle 1968); Connecticut (Liebling 1950); Florida (Vogeler 1942); Georgia (Hawley 1987); Louisiana (Del Sesto 1975; Hawley 1982; Donlon 1991); New York (Hyman 1950); North Carolina (Roberts 1965; Herzog 1985); Tennessee (Cobb 1978; Gunter 1978), Texas (Braddy 1961; Tippette 1978); Utah (Walker 1986); Vermont (Mosher 1989, pp. 96–102); and Virginia (Anderson 1933; Carson 1965, pp. 151–164), among others.

Some of the abundant literature devoted to cockfighting includes detailed discussions of the various "rules" that prevail in different locales (cf. Eck 1879; Nugent 1929; Saubidet 1952, pp. 354–356; Marquez 1954; Champagnac 1970, pp. 58–65; Herzog 1985; Harris 1987). Other writings are concerned with the elaborate intricacies of breeding and caring for fighting cocks—one source noted 253 different names of breeds and cross-breeds, and this list included only English-language designations (Nugent 1929, p. 79; see also Jull, 1927; Finsterbusch 1980). A number of how-to manuals are incredibly specific and include the minutiae of recommended regimen right down to the details of diet (see, e.g., Phillott 1910; Feijoo 1990).

The cockfight has been a source of inspiration for a host of poems and short stories (Fraser 1981; Cutter 1989b) as well as paintings (Tegetmeier 1896; Bryden 1931; Gilbey 1957; Marçal 1967, pp. 350–351; Cadet 1971, pp. 159–165). There is, for example, an entire Irish novel based on cockfighting (O'Gormon 1983; for an American novel, see Willeford 1972). Cockfighting has its own folk speech, which has led to the compilation of cockfight slang glossaries (Jaquemotte and Lejeune 1904; Mendoza 1943; Saubidet 1952, pp. 345–354; León Rey 1953; Marcelin 1955b; Perez 1984, pp. 17–78). In English, too, the cockfight has provided a rich set of metaphors for everyday life. The phrases "to turn tail," "to raise one's hackle(s)," and "to show the white feather" are some of the most familiar (Scott 1957, pp. 118–119). Similarly, to be "cocky" or "cocksure," or to be "cock of the walk" (Gilbey 1957, p. 24), and perhaps "to pit" (someone against another) presumably derive ultimately from the lexicon of cockfighting. There is one etymology, possibly a folk etymology, for the word "cocktail," that supposedly comes from "cock ale" or a liquid concoction designed to serve as a tonic to strengthen fighting cocks (Nugent 1929, p. 80). It is also tempting to ponder the possible metaphorical associations of the "cock" found in guns (as in "Don't go off half-cocked") or in pipes where cocks regulate the flow of liquids (or gases). Among the more esoteric cockfighting traditions that have been studied are the names of fighting cocks in Brazil (Teixeira 1992) and the folk art motifs used to decorate the carrying boxes used in northern Utah (Walker 1986, pp. 39–41).

Most considerations of cockfighting invariably cite the classical instance of Themistocles, who was leading his Athenian army against the Persians in the fifth century B.C. when he chanced to see some cocks fighting. His alleged, but oft-quoted, remarks were: "These animals fight not for the gods of their country, nor for the monuments of their ancestors, nor for glory, nor for freedom, nor for their children, but for the sake of victory, and that one may not yield to the other" (Pegge 1773, p. 137). This impromptu speech supposedly inspired and rallied the troops of Themistocles. (The standard source is Aelian, *Varia Historia* 2: 28; cf. Bruneau 1965, p. 107.)

Particular techniques are found in specific local cockfighting traditions. Some of these seem to be quite ancient. For example, there is an arcane system of cockfighting lore in the Philippines that suggests that there are definite times of the day that favor cocks of a particular color (Guggenheim 1982, p. 11). This set of associations of calendar and cock color is almost certainly related to a complex "cock almanac" reported in south India (Saltore 1926–1927, pp. 319–324).

The most common form of cockfight involves a one-on-one confrontation between two equally matched cocks, a battle that may be interspersed with standard periods of respite. Yet there is considerable variation within the one-to-one scenario. For example, a nineteenth-century account of cockfighting in Cuba summarizes some of the alternatives:

There are various modes of fighting: *Al cotejo*—that is, in measuring, at sight, the size or spurs of both chickens. *Al peso*—or by weight, and seeing if the spurs are equal. *Tapados*—where they settle the match without seeing the chickens, or, in fact, "go it blind." *De cuchilla*—when they put on the artificial spurs, in order to make the fight sharper, quicker, and more fatal. *Al pico*—when they fight without any spurs. (Hazard 1871, pp. 192–193)

There were other, more elaborate forms of cockfighting. These include the battle royal and the Welsh main, once popular in England. We may cite an eighteenth-century description of these special forms of cockfighting:

What aggravates the reproach and the disgrace upon us Englishmen, is those species of fighting which are called the Battle-royal, and the Welsh-main, known nowhere in the world, as I think, but here; neither in China, nor in Persia, nor in Malacca, nor amongst the savage tribes of America. These are scenes so bloody as almost to be too shocking to relate; and yet, as many may not be acquainted with the horrible nature of them, it may be proper, for the excitement of our aversion and detestation, to describe them in a few words. In the former an unlimited number of fowls are pitted; and when they have slaughtered one another for the diversion, dii boni! of the otherwise generous and humane Englishman, the single surviving bird is to be esteemed the victor, and carries away the prize. The Welsh-main consists, we will suppose, of sixteen pair of cocks; of these the sixteen conquerors are pitted a second time; the eight conquerors of these are pitted a third time; so that, incredible barbarity! thirty one cocks are sure to be most inhumanly murdered for the sport and pleasure, the noise and nonsense, nay, I must say, the profane cursing and swearing, of those who have the effrontery to call themselves, with all these bloody doings, and with all this impiety about them, *Christians.* (Pegge 1773, pp. 148–149; see also Boulton 1901, pp. 189–190)

As the unmistakable tone of the preceding passage reminds us, a large part of the mass of writings devoted to the cockfight concerns the question of whether the sport should be banned on the grounds of excessive cruelty to animals. According to one source (Powel 1937, p. 191), the Society for the Prevention of Cruelty to Animals insists that the cockfight "is a blot on civilization's fair escutcheon." The typical strategy of the humane protest against cockfighting consists of simply describing cockfights in gory detail:

In almost every fight at least one cock is seriously multilated or killed. In about half of the fights, more or less, *both* birds are maimed beyond further use if not killed. Eyes are gouged out, abdomens slit and slashed until the birds are anguished monstrosities, legs and wings are broken. But so long as a bird can and will keep facing towards the opposing cock he is left in the pit and cheered for his "courage." (Anon. 1952, p. 11; cf. Hawley 1989)

Of course, the cockfighting community has fought back. One of their common arguments is that cockfighting is much less cruel than other sports, less cruel, for example, than boxing, in which men may be maimed or even killed. In England, cockfighting, which is illegal, is compared to foxhunting, which is legal, by one cocker as follows: "Cockfighting isn't as unfair as foxhunting, you see. One of my cocks has a 50–50 chance of winning. What chance has a fox got when there are fifty hounds chasing him? A million to one shot of getting away" (Penrose 1976, p. 236). Another standard argument is that cocks are naturally inclined to fight, and that man is only facilitating or expanding on what occurs by itself in nature. Even the use of gaffs or blades is defended on the grounds that they are "used solely to end a fight quickly, and the winner will then return to his harem to propagate his species whilst the loser will die the death he has chosen" (Jarvis 1939, p. 378). Incidentally, there are many different types of gaffs, for instance "brike special, skeleton, split socket, bayonet, jagger, regulation, and hoisters" (Jones 1980, p. 144; cf. Worden and Darden 1992).

Another argument put forth by cockfighters is "that it is impossible to make a cock fight an adversary if the bird does not wish to fight. . . . If at the particular moment the joy of battle is not in him, neither skill by the 'setter' nor insult by the adversary will make him fight. The game-cock is never an unwilling gladiator" (James 1928, p. 140). Yet another popular argument is that people raise chickens to be slaughtered for food—think of all the fried chicken franchises in the United States alone. Is that more cruel to the species than cockfighting? Cockfighters are wont to point out that chickens raised for market may be slaughtered when they are anywhere from eight to ten weeks of age. In contrast, a gamecock

> will not even be fought before he's one year old and during that one year, he will receive excellent care. . . . Many are retired to stud after only three or four wins. The question seems to be whether it is less cruel for the cock to be killed by a man rather than by another cock. (Tippette 1978, p. 274; see also Allred and Carver 1979, p. 59)

Despite continuing efforts to ban the cockfight, there are places where cockfighting is legalized. In the north of France near the Belgian border, there are thirty-two authorized "gallodromes" (Cegarra 1989, p. 671). In Puerto Rico, there are reportedly six hundred cockpits with 100,000 fights annually, attended by two million spectators. Promoted by the island's official Department of Recreation, cockfights are even broadcast on television (Bryant 1991, p. 20). Even in places where cockfighting is officially illegal, it thrives.

While the vast majority of the written reports of cockfighting tends to be purely descriptive and not the least bit analytic, there is a small body of literature that seeks to interpret the cockfight. Of these, unquestionably the most famous is Clifford Geertz's (1972) "Deep Play: Notes on the Balinese Cock-fight." This essay marks a turning point in the history of cockfight scholarship. All modern writing on the subject is directly or indirectly derived from Geertz's discussion of the Balinese material. Geertz argued in his interpretation of the cockfight "the general thesis is that the cockfight, and especially the deep cockfight, is fundamentally a dramatization of status concerns" (p. 18). According to Geertz,

> What sets the cockfight apart from the ordinary course of life . . . [is] that it provides a metasocial commentary upon the whole matter of assorting human beings into fixed hierarchical ranks and then organizing the major part of collective existence around that assortment. (p. 26)

Geertz thus interpreted the cockfight exclusively in terms of Balinese social organization or social structure.

Geertz's reading of the Balinese cockfight has attained the status of a modern classic in anthropology (Watson 1989) although it has received some criticism (Roseberry 1982; Parker 1985; Schneider 1987). Anthropologist James A. Boon (1977), an expert on Balinese ethnography who is understandably reluctant to criticize one of his former mentors, remarked that "Geertz does not survey the range of Balinese cockfights; rather he telescopes repeated observations into an ideal-typical description of a choice elaboration of the form in one village area" (p. 33). More severe is Vincent Crapanzano (1986), who, although very admiring of Geertz's "interpretive virtuosity" (pp. 53, 75), contends that Geertz offered his own subjective interpretation of the Balinese cockfight. Moreover, Crapanzano argues, Geertz presented little or no empirical evidence in support of his interpretation (pp. 72–75). Crapanzano concludes there is "no understanding of the native from the native's point of view. There is only the constructed understanding of the constructed native's constructed point of view," and Geertz's "interpretation is simply not convincing" (p. 74; cf. Fine 1992, p. 248).

Crapanzano's critique is echoed by Jacobson (1991), who maintains that Geertz made assertions unsupported by ethnographic data.

> Yet no evidence presented warrants conclusions about how Balinese think or feel about themselves or their society. Whereas the language and rules of the cockfight are described in detail, perceptions are simply attributed to Balinese. In short, Geertz develops his interpretation of the interpretive function of the Balinese cockfight by stating and restating his claims without providing data that substantiate them. He presents no evidence for accepting his reading of the "text." (pp. 52–53)

Unlike Crapanzano and Jacobson, anthropologist Scott Guggenheim (1982) has himself made an ethnographic study of a cockfight, in this case in the Philippines. Guggenheim agrees with Geertz that cockfighting is a "cultural performance" (p. 29), but he disagrees that the cockfight provides an indigenous or native model of social structure or status hierarchy. In some ways, Guggenheim argues, the cockfight in the Philippines is "strikingly blind to social reality" and the cockfight as folk model "skews social reality" (p. 29). In this context,

> There is, for example, no mention of women, despite women's prominent role not only in household management, but in marketing agriculture, wage-earning labor, professional occupations, and politics. Nor does it say very much about what all those high ranking people do to deserve their positions, besides buying expensive chickens. (p. 29)

The theoretical issue here, with respect to the role and function of folklore in culture—and the cockfight is an example of folklore: it is a traditional game or sport—is that the old-fashioned Boasian notion of "folklore as culture reflector," which wrongly assumed a one-to-one relationship between folklore and culture, is inadequate. Folklore, to be sure, does articulate and sometimes enforces the norms of a culture, but it also, often at the same time, offers a socially sanctioned *escape* from those norms. This is what Bascom (1954) called the paradoxical double function of folklore (p. 349). To the extent that folklore involves fantasy, and I believe that it does to a very great extent, the literal one-to-one relationship posited between folklore and culture automatically assumed by a majority of anthropologists and folklorists is doomed to failure as a methodological principle designed to illuminate the content of folkloristic phenomena. Just as anthropologists inevitably assume that myths provide a "charter" for belief in social organization, á la Malinowski's literal, anti-symbolic theory of myth, so Geertz and others wrongly interpret the cockfight as a charter or articulation of social structure, status hierarchy in particular. Guggenheim (1982) is on the right track in pointing out that the cockfight in the Philippines hardly qualifies as a model of normal Filipino social structure—why are women left out of the cockfight, he asks? But like other anthropologists who have considered the cockfight, he fails to appreciate its obvious and overt symbolism.

Although Guggenheim pays the usual social anthropological lip service to symbolism, his conclusions show that he too has missed the basic underlying significance of the cockfight: "Taken as a symbolic system, cockfighting successfully couples individual self-identity and self-esteem, social and political loyalties, and even aesthetic satisfaction to an elegant and exciting event" (p.

30). How do Geertz's and Guggenheim's interpretations of the cockfight compare with other anthropological analyses of the same event? Del Sesto (1980) sees the cockfight as "a symbolic representation of man's continual struggle for survival, as displays of courage and bravado in the face of adversity, and as attempts to understand the meaning and suffering of death" (p. 275). Parker (1986) claims that "the cockfight can be seen as a contest that is totally concerned with violence, competition, and aggression" (p. 26). Several ethnographers have sensed the importance of the masculine elements inherent in the cockfight. Marvin (1984), in his study of the Andalusian cockfight, sees it as a confirmation of male values:

> In all conversations concerning the cockfight those involved with the event emphasized that it was *una cosa de hombres* (a men's thing). It is a totally male-oriented event, the audience is almost totally male, the birds which fight are male and the virtues which are extolled are male virtues [p. 64].

Marvin concludes, "The cockfight, though, is a celebration in that it is an event which extols certain aspects of masculinity" (p. 68).

This view is echoed by Leal (1989), one of the few women to analyze the cockfight. In a superb ethnographic account, she also suggests that "cockfighting is a celebration of masculinity where men, through their cocks, dispute, win, lose, and reinforce certain attributes chosen as male essence" (p. 210). This report from Brazil reaches conclusions similar to those of another female ethnographer who investigated cockfighting in northern France near the Belgian border. The latter confirms the masculinity aspect: "cockfights represent only one exclusive part of human society, that of the virile element" (Cegarra 1988, p. 55). Similarly, Danaë, in his magisterial survey of cockfighting worldwide, concludes with a discussion of cockfighters as an esoteric masculine society (1989, pp. 227–247). Affergan, in his study of cockfighting in Martinique, claims it is an outlet for male identity and aggression by male members of an oppressed group (1986, p. 120), while Kimberley Cook, in her analysis of cockfighting in Venezuela, sees it as a "ritualistic form of aggression" where men vie to gain public recognition of their virility (1991, pp. 89–90).

All these interpretations of the cockfight, in my opinion, are flawed to some extent. Perhaps the most obvious methodological weakness is the failure to employ a comparative, cross-cultural perspective. The quintessential anthropological credo of cultural relativism notwithstanding, it is always a mistake to study data from one particular culture as if it were peculiar to that culture if comparable, if not cognate, data exist in other cultures. The cockfight is found outside of Bali, the Philippines, Louisiana, Tennessee, Brazil, northern France, Martinique, and Venezuela. Hence any would-be interpretation of the cockfight based on data from just one of these locations is bound to be inadequate. Let us assume, strictly for the sake of argument, that Geertz's interpretation of the Balinese cockfight as a "native" representation of Balinese status concerns is correct. If so, what, if anything, does this tell us about about the possible significance of the cockfight in all of the other many cultures in which the cockfight occurs? Balinese social structure is not to be found in Puerto Rico or Belgium. The point is that if an item of folklore has cross-cultural distribution, it must be studied from a cross-cultural perspective, especially if one is interested in possible symbolic aspects. This does not mean that the cockfight necessarily means the same thing in all of its cultural contexts—although this cannot be ruled out a priori. The study of a cross-cultural phenomenon in just one cultural context is clearly a limited, partial one. In that sense, all previous studies of the cockfight have been limited and partial.

Along with the plea for a larger comparative perspective to view the cockfight, I suggest that the cockfight itself cannot be understood without being seen as an exemplar of a more comprehensive paradigm involving male gladiatorial combat. There are many forms of male battle, running the gamut from simple children's games to all-out war. It is my contention that the cockfight can best be analyzed as part and parcel of that paradigm.

Accordingly, let us begin our consideration of the cockfight as an instance of the broad category of male competitive games and sports. I believe one can discern a common underlying symbolic structure shared by most if not all such activities. It might be useful to distinguish three basic variants with respect to the nature of the participants. The first would be human male versus human male. This category includes fencing, boxing, wrestling, tennis, badminton, ping-pong, and such board games as chess and checkers. By extension, it could also subsume male team sports such as football, soccer, hockey, lacrosse, basketball, and so on. The second category would be human male versus male animal. Perhaps the classic illustration of this category is the bullfight. The third category would be male animal versus male animal. Here the obvious example is the cockfight.

It is my contention that all of those games and sports are essentially variations on one theme. The theme involves an all-male preserve in which one male demonstrates his virility, his masculinity, *at the expense of a male opponent.* One proves one's maleness by feminizing one's opponent. Typically, the victory entails (no pun intended!) penetration. In American football, the winning group of males get into their opponents' "end zones" more times than their opponents get into their end zones (see Dundes 1987, pp. 178–194). In the bullfight, the battle of man against bull is to determine whether the matador penetrates the bull or whether the bull's horns penetrate the matador. The penetrator comes away triumphant and with his masculinity intact; the one *penetrated* loses his masculinity. In the case of the bullfight, the expertise and skill of the matador can be rewarded with different degrees of symbolic castration of the bull. The bull, if penetrated cleanly and dextrously, may have his hooves, ears, or tail cut off to be "presented" to the successful matador.

The cockfight, despite its great antiquity and it continued popularity into the twentieth century, has never been properly understood as male phallic combat. Despite an enormous literature devoted to the cockfight ranging from vivid descriptions to purported analyses, there is to my knowledge no single discussion that takes adequate account of the symbolic nature of the contest. I should like to test my hypothesis that the cockfight is a thinly disguised symbolic homoerotic masturbatory phallic duel, with the winner emasculating the loser through castration or feminization. I believe that the evidence for this interpretation is overwhelmingly abundant and cross-cultural in nature. Nevertheless, it seems to me that the symbolic meaning of the cockfight is not consciously recognized either by those who participate in the event or those who have written about it. The sole exception occurs in Cook's chapter on cockfighting on the island of Margarita off the coast of Venezuela in her 1991 doctoral dissertation, when she remarks "that when two individual men fight cocks and one loses, the loser assumes a feminine role" (1991, p. 98; see also Affergan 1986, p. 119). Baird (1981–1982, p. 83) claims that among the ancient Greeks the cockfight symbolized homosexual rape.

Let us first consider the gallus as phallus. In all of the many essays and monographs devoted to cockfighting, only a few actually comment on the phallic nature of the cocks. Scott (1941) in a paragraph in his survey volume *Phallic Worship* does mention the phallic significance of the cock (p. 262), but in his full-length history of cockfighting (Scott 1957), he drew no inferences from this. In Geertz's (1972) essay, which was first presented at a conference held in Paris in October of 1970, we are told:

> To anyone who has been in Bali any length of time, the deep psychological identification of Balinese men with their cocks is unmistakable. The double entendre here is deliberate. It works in exactly the same way in Balinese as it does in English, even to producing the same hired jokes, strained puns, and uninventive obscenities. (p. 5)

It is a pity that Geertz was not a bit more ethnographically specific here, inasmuch as he failed to give even a single example of the "tired jokes" and "uninventive obscenities." Tired jokes and uninventive obscenities constitute valuable folkloristic data that any journeyman folklorist fluent in the language would have almost certainly recorded. Geertz (1972) does cite Bateson and Mead's (1942) contention that the Balinese conception of the body "as a set of

251

separately animated parts" allows them to view cocks as "detachable, self-operating penises, ambulant genitals with a life of their own" (p. 5), but then claims that he does "not have the kind of unconscious material either to confirm or disconfirm this intriguing notion." Again, one regrets his failure to collect the jokes, puns, and obscenities available to him. So, although Geertz did nominally acknowledge that cocks "are masculine symbols *par excellence*" among the Balinese, this fact did not play a major part in his interpretation of the cockfight as a whole.

The English word "cock," meaning both rooster and phallus, is the subject of wit among cockfighters in the United States. According to Hawley (1982), "One Florida informant was heard to say 'My cock may not be the biggest, but it's the best in this county.'" Apparently such double meanings were so common as to make older cockers use the term "rooster" in mixed company (p. 105; see also Baird 1981).

Among the various surveys of the folklore of cocks (e.g., Gittée 1891; Fehrle 1912; Rasch 1930; and Coluccio 1970), only a few bother to mention the cock as a symbol of virility (Castillo de Lucas 1970, pp. 363–364; Cadet 1971, p. 109). The phallic associations of the rooster, even apart from its apparent potential for magical resuscitation in cockfighting, explains why the cock was a logical, if not psychologically obvious, choice as a symbol for resurrection (Modi 1911, p. 112). Resurrection, if understood as reerection, or even in the narrow Christian sense of rising miraculously from the dead, is perfectly understandable in cockfight terms. There are numerous reports in the cockfight literature of a cock, apparently totally vanquished and lying motionless, somehow managing to recover sufficiently to arise and earn a victory over its opponent. This phallic symbolism would help explain why the cock is so often found atop penile Christian architectural constructions such as church towers, often in the form of weather-vanes which pointedly mark wind direction (see Callisen 1939; Kretzenbacher 1958; Cadet 1971, pp. 166–168, 199–204; see also Forsyth 1978 and Baird, 1981–1982). The same rationale would illuminate the occurrence of a cockfight motif on sarcophagi and other funerary monuments (Bruneau 1965, p. 115; Forsyth 1978, pp. 262–264). It would also elucidate the frequent occurrence of the "Coq gaulois" as an emblem mounted on the prows of French warships (Vichot 1970).

Occasional comments indicate that cockfighting is analogous to sexuality. In a Filipino cockfighting manual we are told, "An ideal cock must be able to top a hen several times before letting her get up, because sex and gameness complement each other. . . . Indeed, no other sport has as much connection with sex as cockfighting" (Lansang 1966, pp. 41, 59, 139). The explicit anthropomorphic projection upon roosters and chickens in the Philippines is such that a strict double standard is maintained. Cocks are expected to indulge themselves, but hens are considered to be "sexually promiscuous" (p. 151), and breeders must keep watch over hens in the barnyard "because the hen is a natural whore" (p. 140).

Similar male chauvinism is found in other descriptions of chickens and roosters:

> Females are strongly sexual and thus impulsive. Their actions are instinctively generated by feelings, and they need the presence of a male. They are amorous. Nature made them so and provided that their actions be governed by their sexual impulses. Males are cooler in disposition and have developed a different brain. They act according to logic. Females act impulsively. (Finsterbusch 1980, p. 166)

Hard to believe that these are descriptions of chickens and roosters, and not humans!

It is likely that the symbolic equation of cock and human phallus exists regardless of whether or not the term for "rooster" in a given culture refers explicitly to the male organ. In Spanish and Portuguese, for example, we are told that this verbal equation does not exist. However, in Brazil, a "tea of cock's spurs is recommended for sexual potency" (Leal 1989, p. 241). In an Arabic tract from the thirteenth century we learn, "If you take a cock's blood and mix it with honey, and place it on the fire, and apply the mixture to the penis of a man, it will increase his virile power as well as his sexual enjoyment" (Phillott 1910, p. 91). Moreover, if a woman ate a cock's testicles after intercourse, she greatly increased her chances of becoming pregnant (Smith and Daniel 1975, p. 54; Hawley 1982, p. 106). In other words, customs and belief systems make the connection between rooster and phallus perfectly clear. There are also numerous winged phallic amulets in the shape of cocks (Baird 1981–1982, p. 84).

The sexual component is alluded to only en passant by most writers on cockfights, if it is mentioned at all. In an essay in *Esquire*, Crews (1977) remarked that when a man's cock quits in the pit, he suffers profound humiliation. *When a man's cock quits!* Yes, that's part of the ritual, too. Perhaps the biggest part. A capon—a rooster that has been castrated to improve the taste of the meat—seldom crows, never notices hens, and will hit nothing with spur or beak. But a game fowl is the ultimate blend of balls and skill, all of which is inextricably bound up with the man who bred it and fed it and handles it in the pit (p. 8). Attributing "balls" to cocks is not all that unusual. In Andalusia, for example, according to Marvin (1984, p. 66), men may say admiringly of an especially aggressive cock "tienes los cojones de ganar bien" ("it has the balls to win well") (p. 65). The same idiom is found in Nathanael West's account of a cockfight in *The Day of the Locust*, when the Mexican cocker Miguel praises a red rooster: "That's a bird with lots of cojones" (West 1950, p. 123). One difficulty in "proving" the sexual component of the cockfight lies in the fact that such a component is largely unconscious. Consequently, it is not easy to obtain informant confirmation of the symbolism through interviews. Wollan (1980) phrased the problem as follows:

> How much of this symbolism is present in modern cockfighting, and how much of it would be understood by cockers themselves, is difficult to say. How to research the topic is equally puzzling. Conversation promises to yield little information about cockfighting as a symbol, and certainly nothing about its sexual dimensions. Hence, interpretation of a sort not commonly done, certainly not in fashion in the social sciences, would seem indispensable. (p. 28)

Hawley, whose 1982 Florida State doctoral dissertation in criminology sought to define cockfighters as a deviant subculture, claimed that in his field experience "sexual entendre was encountered infrequently. . . . However, the implicit sexual nature of the activity was omnipresent" (p. 104). Still, he admitted, "Sexual animism was definitely the most difficult cultural theme to study in any fashion systematically or haphazardly . . . [and] a ticklish subject to study in the field under the best of conditions" (pp. 107, 147). Hawley himself does not doubt "the significance of the cock as a symbol of aggressive, male-oriented sexual behavior." In his words, "The cock is, to all appearances, a walking unselfconscious set of eager genitals . . . the cock represents male sexuality raised (or lowered) to the most primitive extremity." But, Hawley remarks, "the obvious sexual significance of the cock is characteristically ignored by the cocking fraternity in all but the most casual and relaxed settings" (p. 121). Hawley might have added the anthropological and folkloristic fraternities as well. A far too typical comment contained in one of several essays devoted to a twenty-year retrospective view of Geertz's 1972 essay exemplifies the "meaningless" school of interpretation. One of the co-authors, a Louisiana native who wrote his Master's thesis on Louisiana cockfights, claimed he "found many, if not most, of the same metaphors in cockfights in southern Louisiana that Geertz observed in Bali," but his "reading was that cockfights there had no deep meaning but were just for fun" (Chick and Donlon 1992, p. 239).

Yet the sexual symbolic significance of the "cock" is attested by countless bawdy jokes. One exemplar can stand for many: Q. What is the difference between a rooster and Marilyn Monroe? A. A rooster says "Cock-a-doodle-do." Marilyn Monroe says "Any cock'll do." It may or may not be relevant that St. Augustine in his interesting fourth-century discussion of cockfights discusses them in a paragraph that begins with a consideration of the sexual organs of animals which one cannot bear to look at (Russell 1942, p. 95).

If we accept the premise that the gallus can symbolically be a phallus, and if we provisionally accept the possibility that there is an underlying sexual component in the cockfight, we must next emphasize that the cockfight is an all-male event. Women do not usually attend cockfights. An early eighteenth-century account of cockfighting in England specifically remarks that "ladies never assist at these sports" (Saussure 1902, p. 282). Geertz (1972) even bothers to comment that "the cockfight is unusual within Balinese culture in being a single-sex public activity from which the other sex is totally and expressly excluded" (p. 30*n*). Even in those cultures where women are permitted to observe cockfights, they are not active participants and do not handle the cocks. Some women resent their virtual exclusion from the world of cockfighting, and they resent as well the extraordinary amount of time their male companions devote to that world. From northern France we have a report of a female reproach that carries an overt sexual connotation: "He holds his cocks more often than he holds me" (Cegarra 1988, p. 58). Also from northern France, we find a distinction between women who may kill chickens as part of preparing food and men who are involved in cockfights. The fighting cock is a wild animal whose death, necessarily violent, is symbolic. The arming of cocks for battle is an affair of men, not women, and should not be confused with the domestic household requirement of killing chickens for food (p. 59).

The separation from women in cockfights is also signaled by the fact that the roosters themselves are not permitted access to hens during the period immediately preceding a cockfight. This form of quarantine is surely analogous to the modern-day football coach's forbidding his players to spend the night before a game with their wives or girlfriends, or to a bullfighter's sexual abstinence the night before a bullfight. Here is an account of the training of roosters in the Texas-Mexico area:

> The most important experience of the young stag commences when his trainer moves him from his solitary cage and places him in a hennery. There he bosses his harem of hens, living and learning the meaning of his cockhood. Later, when the trainer takes him away from the pullets, the cockerel turns into a bird of Mars. Now he has a lust to fight, his lust arising from his strong sex drive. (Braddy 1961, p. 103)

In another account from Texas, we are informed, "They have had no food this morning, and for two weeks have been penned up and deprived of female company" (Gard, 1936, p. 66).

In the Philippines, "it is a mistake to release your stag in a place where too many hens are kept, for so many hens make him tread often, and much treading greatly debilitates a bird and makes him feeble when he comes to fight" (Lansang 1966, p. 61). We learn that in Martinique sexual abstinence during the cocks' training is strict and that one makes a concerted effort to keep hens away from the cages in which the cocks are contained the evening before or the day of the cockfight for fear the cocks will dissipate their energies (Affergan 1986, p. 114). In the north of France, too, keeping the cock in isolation away from females is suppose to increase his aggressivity tenfold (Cegarra 1989, p. 673).

In Brazil, cocks

> are not permitted sexual intercourse for long periods before fighting. . . . It is believed that sexual abstinence will give [them] the strength and will to fight, and that decreased sexual activity will create better quality semen. The underlying assumption is that sexual intercourse or even contact with a female will turn the male into a weaker being. (Leal 1989, p. 238)

In some traditions, the handler as well as the cock must abstain from heterosexual intercourse. In the Philippines, "sex should be avoided before going to the cockpit; the man stupid enough to have sex before a match will be ignominiously humiliated when his bird runs away." However, "Sex is heartily recommended for after the fight, when men no longer need conserve their vital energies" (Guggenheim 1982, p. 10).

The renunciation of heterosexuality in conjunction with the cockfight seems to support the idea that the cockfight is an all-male, or homosexual, affair. Thus, if the gallus is a phallus and if there is a sexual component to the cockfight, it is a matter played out between two sets of males: roosters and men. In this sexual battle, one begins with *two* males, but ends with *one* male and *one* female. Is there any evidence to support this contention? In Malaysia, the term used for matching two roosters for a forthcoming fight may be relevant. "The stakes are all deposited with a stake-holder (who receives a percentage for his good services); and the cocks are plighted or 'betrothed' to one another by the simple ceremony of allowing each bird one single peck at its rival" (Wilkinson 1925, p. 65). The curious idiomatic usage of the word "betrothal"—the author does not provide the Malay native term—for the matching of two male cocks is significant. They are mates, analogous to heterosexual humans, but the fight is to determine which one will be the male and which the "female." In Bali, according to Bateson and Mead (1942), "In speaking of real courtship, the Balinese liken the behavior of boy and girl to that of two cocks straining toward each other with their heads down and their hackle feathers up" (p. 172). That the Malay term and Balinese image are not flukes

256

is corroborated by a parallel custom in Martinique in which the two cocks to be paired in combat are said to be joined in "marriage" (Champagnac 1970, p. 72; Affergan 1986, p. 115). Of possible relevance to the matrimonial metaphor is the Anglo-American usage of the term "flirt" to refer to the initial contact of the two cocks (Egan 1832, p. 152; Worden and Darden 1992, p. 277).

In one of the finest ethnographic accounts of the cockfight to date, Leal (1989) describes the crowd's cheers during a typical Brazilian bout.

> During a fight every movement of the cock is followed by the crowd's cheers of "go ahead! Mount him! (*monta nele! trepa nele!*)." Inasmuch as "to mount" or "to climb" (*trepar*) are also expressions commonly used to refer to sexual intercourse, usually implying the man's position in the sexual act, the crowd's cheers are not only metaphorical [pp. 217–218].

Here is certainly incontrovertible evidence supporting the equation of "gallus as phallus." Leal even recorded a folk poem that confirms the already explicit erotic significance of "mounting":

Quien tuviera la suerte	Who would have the luck
que tiene el gallo	that the cock has,
que en medio de la juria	that in the middle of the fight
monta a caballo.	to be mounted on a horse. (p. 218)

The allusions to courtship, marriage, and mounting do underscore the sexual nuances of the cockfight, but what evidence is there to support the proposition that the loser in a cockfight is deemed a female?

In a cockfight, sometimes a cock will freeze in the face of a feared opponent. This so-called tonic immobility (Herzog 1978) might simply be a desperate defense mechanism, that is, playing dead to prevent the dominant cock from attacking further. More commonly, a cock that loses its nerve may choose to flee. In an account from Texas, we are told:

> When a beaten gamebird decides to withdraw from the battle, he lifts his hackle, showing to the spectators the white feathers underlying his ruff. This act gave rise to the famous expression "showing the white feather," which symbolizes coward-ice. (Braddy 1961, pp. 103–104)

In the north of France, a cock that flees, crying, is immediately declared to have lost if his opponent is standing (Demulder 1934, p. 13). Such flight and such crying are deemed cowardly acts. In Belgium, too, a cock that starts crying is declared vanquished (Jaquemotte and Lejeune 1904, p. 226). In the mid-nineteenth century, the pioneering Italian anthropologist and sexologist

Paolo Mantegazza, perhaps best known for his Frazerian survey, *The Sexual Relations of Mankind* (1916), visited Argentina, where he described a cockfight. He remarked on the different ways the fight could end. One way involved an exit from the arena "siempre abierta para los cobardes" (always open for cowards) in which a bloody and beaten rooster might sing, calling for aid from the hens of his harem (p. 69).

There is even better evidence that winning in a cockfight is associated with masculinity, whereas losing is considered to belong to the realm of the feminine. In Venezuela, one may hear a spectator yell, "Vamos, como tu padre!" ("Let's go, like your father!") to exhort a cock to do better (Marquez 1954, p. 45); in Brazil, during a cockfight, one may hear comments referring to the losing cock along the lines of "the mother's blood is showing" (Leal 1989, p. 216).

In Colombia, a cock that runs away is thought to cry like a chicken (León Rey 1953, p. 93). In Mexico, to be a "gallo-gallina," a rooster-hen, is to be a coward or homosexual (Mendoza 1943, p. 123). In Venezuela, there is a general folk belief that a rooster who "clucks" like a chicken is a sure sign of an imminent disgrace (Acosta Saignes 1954, p. 39). In Andalusia, too, a cock may lose a fight by fleeing from its opponent while making a low clucking sound. This is called "canta la gallina," which may be translated as "the hen sings" (Marvin 1984). Anthropologist Marvin astutely observes, "What should be noted here is not only does the bird flee but it also makes what is perceived to be the sound of a hen, a female. This behavior is regarded as reprehensible, for the cock is not acting as a true male" (p. 64). Here is prima facie evidence that the loser in the Andalusian cockfight is considered to be a chicken rather than a rooster, a female rather than a male. In Borneo, we find a possible parallel; we are told that "occasionally the bird was "chicken," and ran after the first scuffle (Barclay 1980, p. 18), although it is not altogether certain whether "chicken" is a native-language term in Borneo or not. The placing of it in single quotes suggests, however, that it might be. Of course, in American folk speech, to be "chicken" is to be cowardly, especially among a group of male peers.

The feminization of the loser in a cockfight cannot really be disputed. In Martinique, there is a proverb "Kavalie vol a dam," which presumably has a literal meaning of "a cavalier flies to a lady [dame]." The proverb refers to the fact that there must always be an adversary for a cock, but, more important in the present context, that a good cock never hesitates to fly toward his opponent (as does a man toward a woman). The winning cock affirms his maleness, his virility, while the loser is forced to take the female role with a strongly negative connotation. It is clearly preferable to be a true female than a false (effeminate) male (Affergan 1986, p. 119). Also in Martinique we find the idiom "faire la poule" (to be chicken) applied to a cock who cowers in front of an opponent, refusing to fight (Champagnac 1970, p. 35). Leal (1989) reports that in Brazil, if a losing rooster attempts to run from the pit "crying like a chicken" (cacarejando feito galinha), this would constitute the worst kind of dishonor to the cock's owner and supporters since "symbolically at that moment the cock and the men become females." "Chicken" is a slang term for both "loose woman" and coward (p. 211). Such data support our contention that the losing cock in a cockfight becomes feminized, becomes a chicken.

Other details of the cockfight take on new significance in the light of the argument here proposed. These details include specific techniques designed to stimulate or revive a wounded cock. Prefight preparation sometimes involved inserting stimulants in prescribed orifices. For example, in Bali, according to Geertz (1972), red pepper might be stuffed down a cock's beak or up its anus to give it spirit (p. 6). Guggenheim (1982) reported that in the Philippines "sticking chili up the anus" (p. 10) was thought to increase the cock's "natural ferocity." In Belgium, just before a fight a cock might be given a piece of sugar soaked in cognac (Remouchamps and Remacle 1949, p. 65).

Another prefight ritual is reported from Haiti. There, in order to convince the judge that no poison has been placed on a particular cock's spurs—poison that would unfairly eliminate the opposing cock if it entered its bloodstream—the cock's handler will suck the spurs of his cock and perhaps also the beak and neck of his bird as well (Marcelin 1955b, p. 59). For the same practice in the Philippines, see Roces (1959, pp. 65–66); for Martinique, see Affergan (1986, p. 115). There also the cock is forced to drink the water in which he is bathed. This is similar to a technique in southern Louisiana where an official uses a wet cotton ball to wipe the metal gaffs after which he squeezes water drops into the cock's mouth (Donlon 1990, 282; 1991, p. 106). In Venezuela, Cook (1991, p. 92) notes the poison is applied at the last minute, right before the fight starts because otherwise the cock with the poisoned spur might accidentally scratch itself.

This practice is reasonable enough, but a similar one used to resuscitate wounded cocks during a fight requires a different rationale. In Bali, during breaks in the fight, handlers are permitted to touch their birds to revive them. The handler "blows in its mouth, putting the whole chicken head in his own mouth and sucking and blowing, fluffs it, stuffs its wounds with various sorts of medicines, and generally tries anything he can think of to arouse the last ounce of spirit which may be hidden somewhere within it" (Geertz 1972, p. 9). An earlier account of cockfighting in Bali confirms that the handlers try to revive their cocks' "ardour by petting, massage or by blowing into their beaks" (Knight 1940, p. 81), This means of "sucking the wounds of an injured cock is one of the oldest prescriptions for healing a bird" (Smith and Daniel 1975, p.

86). A physician traveling in Cuba in the mid-nineteenth century confirmed the practice as he reported seeing owners "sucking the whole bleeding head repeatedly" (Wurdemann 1844, p. 92). The technique continues to be popular and is reported from Tennessee (Gunter 1978, p. 166; Cobb 1978, p. 92) and Texas (Braddy 1961, p. 105) among other places. Literary critic Stanley Edgar Hyman (1950), describing a cockfight he attended in Saratoga Springs, New York, in the summer of 1949, noted the following:

> For centuries, it has been the custom for the handler during the breaks in the fighting, to wipe the blood out of his chicken's eyes on his mouth—a procedure that undoubtedly goes back to the ancient ritualistic origins of the sport, which are to be found in cock sacrifice and blood-drinking. (p. 101)

Hyman, of course, presented not one shred of documentary evidence for his hypothetical ritual origin of the practice. He was well known for his ardent advocacy of "myth-ritual" theory, according to which all folklore was supposedly a survival from an original ritual of some kind (see Bascom 1957). In some versions of the practice, the handlers blow water on the wounded cock, but some cockfighters preferred the licking system "because of the supposed healing power of human saliva" (Cobb 1978, p. 92). An informant at a New York state cockfight claimed that cold water is dangerous for the birds' systems but that "human saliva not only is just the right temperature but is well known to have effective germicidal properties (Hyman 1950, p. 101).

After a fight is over, a handler may attempt to apply a more conventional disinfectant to the cock's wounds such as tincture of iodine, but one old tradition (in Belgium and in England) insists that it is preferable to urinate on the wounds immediately after the combat on the grounds that urine is the best of disinfectants (Remouchamps and Remacle 1949, pp. 75–76; Scott 1957, p. 49). There are also reports that a cock should be fed urine. Scott (1957) remarked, "I well remember a famous exhibitor telling me some thirty years ago that the secret of getting birds into perfect show condition was to feed them on wheat which had been steeped in urine" (p. 42). In Brazil a handler "will put the cock's entire head inside his mouth in a desperate attempt to revive the cock for the coming round" (Leal 1989, pp. 237–238). Leal has offered an ingenious interpretation of the exchange of bodily fluids between man and cock (p. 244). The man gives his body fluids saliva and urine to the cock while the cock gives his blood to the man: "Man's fluids (food, saliva, urine) become cock's fluids (semen and blood)" (p. 246). Still, the act of sucking the cock's whole head seems to require further explanation. In Venezuela, for instance, the practice is called "mamar el gallo" (Olivares Figeroa 1949, p. 186), which might be translated as "sucking the cock"—"mamar" being the same word used for babies' nursing; mamar as in mammary gland, and ultimately the term "mama."

Hawley (1987), in his description of cockfights in the southern United States writes, "The handlers try to revive the weakened birds by various seemingly bizarre methods: taking the bleeding bird's head into his mouth to warm it and drain blood from its lungs" (pp. 22–23). Hawley (1982) mused about this practice in his unpublished doctoral dissertation, not in print.

> Occasionally the seemingly bizarre resuscitative behavior in which handlers indulge during cockfighting has been observed to be the source of some coarse, jocular, and sometimes disapproving commentary from spectators and informants. As one might expect, when a handler puts a wounded cock's head in his mouth to suck out the blood, he is indeed engaging in behavior that some would find highly fraught with sexual implications. Since, according to informants, this maneuver is highly efficacious in reviving fatigued birds, perhaps the sexual *entendre* is unwarranted. It is, nonetheless, a disconcerting sight for the uninitiated to behold. (p. 106)

There is another curious technique sometimes employed to revive a wounded cock. A Georgia informant, for example, after remarking, "I've seen guys put a whole chicken's head in their mouth," went on to describe another practice, "And one trick I've seen . . . they will blow that chicken in his vent, you know, if he's about dead or about cut down or something. They'll blow him back there to try to help him get a little air and get him cooled off" (Anon. 1984, p. 483). A striking parallel to this practice is reported from south India. Among the people of Tuluva, we learn that

> sometimes, the beaten cock will again be encouraged to fight, by its owner, who, after taking it to a place near by, will pour cold water over its head or will air it through the anus. . . . The method of airing through the anus is a very curious one, and they say cocks, once beaten, if they survive this process of resuscitation, generally strike down cock after cock in the combat, much to the pride of their owners. (Saltore 1926–1927, p. 326)

According to anthropologist Peter Claus (1992, personal communication), who has carried out extensive fieldwork among the Tulu, the Tulu handlers still engage in this technique of reviving an injured or fatigued cock. In fact, blowing in the cock's anus is even used jokingly as a metaphor in everyday life. For example, if a student were tired and nervous about a forthcoming examination, a friend might facetiously volunteer to blow in his anus to inspire him to put forth greater effort in studying for the exam. There is apparently an analogous procedure employed with cattle in India. Gandhi (1929) in his autobiography spoke against "the wicked processes . . . adopted to extract the last drop of milk from . . . cows and buffaloes" and even went so far as to claim that it was this very process of "phooka" ("blowing") that had led him to give up drinking milk altogether (pp. 245, 474).

In our attempt to demonstrate that the cockfight is a homoerotic male battle with masturbatory nuances, another important facet of the event must be considered. As Guggenheim (1982) put it, "Whatever the social, psychological, or political reasons why people attend cockfights, any cocker will say the main reason he goes is to bet" (p. 19). In the Celebes, "Cock-fights are always connected with betting" (Kaudern 1929, p. 340). Geertz (1972), after an initial overview of the generic Balinese cockfight, gave considerable detail of the intricate betting system employed by the participants and observers of the cockfight. Geertz failed to note that betting accompanies cockfights in almost all parts of the world where cockfighting occurs. This omission is one consequence of his failure to consult other ethnographic reports of the cockfight, even those concerned with the phenomenon in Bali (Eck 1879; Knight 1940) or nearby Java (Kreemer 1893; Soeroto 1916–1917), another area studied by Geertz. Usually the betting is one-to-one, that is, one person will call out a bet and another person will accept it (Parker 1986, p. 24). In this way, the betting scenario mirrors the one-on-one action of the fighting cocks. A cocker turned academic describes betting in his thesis as follows: "Betting at cockfights is an overt expression of machismo. The larger the bet the bigger the man. . . . In a cockfight the betting opponents are in a face-to-face confrontation, a man-against-man contest so to speak" (Walker 1986, p. 49).

While one may well applaud Geertz's (1972) poetic insight that the cockfight's "function, if you want to call it that, is interpretive: It is a Balinese reading of Balinese experience; a story they tell themselves about themselves" (p. 26), one may not agree with Geertz about what that story is. Is the Balinese cockfight simply an extended metaphor for the Balinese social status hierarchy? And what is the connection between the gambling behavior of the Balinese (and others) and the cockfight proper? Had Geertz or other anthropologists been at all familiar with the psychoanalytic theory of gambling, he might have been better able to relate the two sections of his essay: the cockfight and the betting on the cockfight.

Ever since Freud's brilliant (1928) paper on "Dostoevsky and Parricide," the psychoanalytic community has been aware of the possibility that gambling is a symbolic substitute for masturbation. "The passion for play is an equivalent of the old compulsion to masturbate; 'playing' is the actual word used in the nursery to describe the activity of the hands upon the genitals" (p. 193). Actually, Ernst Simmel (1920) had previously suggested that "the passion for gambling thus serves auto-erotic gratification, whereby the playing is fore-pleasure, the gaining orgasm, and the loss ejaculation, defecation and castration" (p. 353). Lindner (1953) discussed the gambling-masturbation equation with clarity:

> Now gambling and masturbation present a wide variety of parallels—Both are repetitive acts, both are compulsively driven, and the nervous and mental states accompanying the crucial stages in the performance of each are almost impossible to differentiate. (p. 212)

A characteristic of gambling that is perhaps most reminiscent of masturbatory activity is the "inability of the gambler to stop" (Fuller 1977, p. 28), even when winning. Here we cannot help but be reminded of the Filipino manual on cockfighting that warns against "holding-handling" the cock in public, as "handling is habit-forming and once acquired, it is hard to get rid of" (pp. 97–98). As we shall seek to demonstrate, both the cockfight itself and the gambling that accompanies it are symbolic expressions of masturbatory behavior.

It should be noted that not all psychiatrists agree with the Freudian hypothesis of a masturbatory underpinning to compulsive gambling. However, for every psychiatrist who says, "In my experience with compulsive gamblers I find no support for Freud's formulation that compulsive gambling is a replacement for compulsive masturbation" there is one who reports, "What I had found, in my one patient (a gambler), to be the core of the psychopathology—the struggle against masturbation the content of his unconscious masturbation fantasies" (Niederland et al. 1967, pp. 180, 182). Fuller (1977), in the most extensive survey of the psychoanalytic study of gambling to date, concurs that masturbation may underlie it, but he argues that there is an anal component as well (to the extent that gamblers play with money—a fecal symbolic substitute).

The somewhat eccentric Wilhelm Stekel (1924) regarded sexuality as the most important component of gambling, and he used a bit of folkloristic evidence, a proverb, to support his contention. The proverb "Glück in Spiel, Unglück in der Liebe" (p. 240; see also Greenson 1947, p. 74), unquestionably a cognate of the English proverb "Lucky at cards, unlucky in love," does suggest a kind of limited good. There is only so much luck (= sexual energy). If one uses it up in gambling, for example, playing cards, then there will be insufficient for heterosexual lovemaking. There is some clinical evidence to support this conclusion. It involves a compulsive gambler who fell in love. "He had abandoned gambling during the 18 months of his involvement, and resumed it when "the love" was discarded (Galdston 1960, p. 555). This view that there is a finite amount of sexual capacity, or perhaps of sexual fluid, is reminiscent of old-fashioned views of masturbation. The idea was that all the ejaculations resulting from masturbation decreased the amount of sexual fluids available for heterosexual acts. The connotations of the German word "Spiel" in the proverb, analogous to the English word "play," do include explicit allusions to masturbation (see Borneman 1971). The proverb might then be rendered, "Lucky in masturbation, unlucky in (heterosexual) love." (This discussion of the proverb is mine, not Stekel's.) The proverbial equation might also be relevant to the alleged connection between gambling and impotence. The argument is essentially that the "excitement of gambling and the symbolic equivalents for sexual release built into many games serve as a substitute for sexual relationships" (Olmsted 1962, pp. 104–105, 120).

According to Bolen and Boyd (1968), "Latent homosexual manifestations are present in the antifeminine aspect of the gambling hall where there is relative exclusion of women and 'antifeminine vocabulary' (i.e., queens [in card games] are referred to as 'whores')" (p. 622; see also Greenson 1947, pp. 64–65). Greenson (1947) had this to say about the homosexual component of gambling:

> The fellow gamblers are cohorts in homosexual activities. Gambling with other men was equivalent, in the unconscious, to comparing penises with other men; winning meant having the largest penis or being the most potent. Excitement together often represented masturbation. (p. 74)

Greenson was speaking in general about gambling and not with reference to the cockfight, but his comments do seem applicable to the cockfight. The allusion to penis comparison cannot help but remind us of the care with which cocks are weighed—in the United States, the cocks are matched on the basis of weight down to ounce distinctions. Bateson and Mead (1942) note that in Bali "before the fight each man holds the other man's cock so that he can feel the enemy cock's strength and make sure that it is not much stronger than his own (p. 140). In this context, the cockfight might be construed as a metaphorical performance of a phallic brag session: "My cock is stronger than yours" or "My cock can outlast yours." This view is confirmed by a statement made by a cocker who wrote a thesis on cockfighting in Utah: "As a man's own penis or cock is the staff of his manhood so by extension is his fighting cock an extension of himself. The man whose cock lasts the longest and thus wins the fight is judged the better man. A man's own sexual prowess is largely judged by how long he can maintain an erection. The obverse helps prove this statement. A man who is plagued with premature ejaculation is someone to be pitied and given professional counseling. Thus by association a man who has a battle cock with staying power [and] pride and [which] fights to the end is macho indeed" (Walker 1986, pp. 59–60).

Bergler (1957), expanding on Freud's analysis of gambling, argued that "the unconscious wish to lose becomes . . . an integral part of the gambler's inner motivation" (p. 24; see also 1943, pp. 379, 381; Fuller 1977, p. 88). The logic, in part, is that if gambling is really symbolic masturbation, then the participant should feel guilt for this act and should expect to be punished by a parent or parental surrogate. Bergler (1943) even goes so far as to speak of the gambler as a "naughty" child who expects punishment after performing his forbidden act (p. 386). According to this logic, the gambler is obliged to play until he loses because losing constitutes a form of punishment by an external authority, that is, fate.

The question is: to what extent, if any, is it legitimate to interpret the cock-fight (and the gambling that accompanies it) as a symbolic form of male mastur-bation? Here we may turn to the relevant ethnography to find an answer to this question. Time and time again, we read reports of how much time a cock handler devoted to grooming and stroking his bird. In the Philippines, we learn, "the cock is handled and petted daily by his master" (Lansang 1966, p. 140). Bailey (1909) described a cock tied on a wagon in the Philippines as being "unremittingly fondled" (p. 253). Again from the Philippines, a how-to primer for cock handlers warns against excessive handling or stroking of the cock, especially in public. "You can do the holding-handling at home as much as you desire." But the prospective cock handler is told in no uncertain terms that "handling" is habit-forming and, once acquired, hard to get rid of (Lansang 1966, pp. 97–98). The grooming behavior found in the Philippines is by no means unique. In Martinique, "the cock is the object of a veritable loving passion on the part of its master, who caresses, fondles, kisses it and tells it sweet words" (Affergan 1986, p. 119).

What about Bali? Knight (1940) reported, "You may be sure to find any |male| member of the village community from the age of fifteen up to eighty using any leisure moments toying with and fondling their birds" (p. 77). Bate-son and Mead (1942) described Balinese behavior in similar detail:

> The average Balinese man can find no pleasanter way to pass the time than to walk about with a cock, testing it out against the cocks of other men whom he meets on the road. . . . Ruffling it up, smoothing it down, ruffling it up again, sitting among other men who are engaged in similar toying with their cocks—this passes many hours of the long hot afternoons. (pp. 24–25)

Long before Geertz (1972) described the Balinese cockfight, Bateson and Mead (1942) had remarked, "The evidence for regarding the fighting cock as a genital symbol comes from the postures of men holding cocks, the sex slang and sex jingles, and from Balinese carvings of men with fighting cocks" (p.

140). Yet, despite this insight and such commentaries accompanying photographs as "Many men spend hours sitting, playing with their cocks" (p. 140), Bateson and Mead stop short of calling the cockfight itself a form of mutual symbolic masturbation. On the other hand, according to Olmsted (1962), "Bateson and Mead have remarked on the fact that in Bali, cocks are first taken to, and held and petted and fondled at just about the time that masturbation must be given up as 'babyish' . . ." (p. 181). This observation (which unfortunately is not documented by Olmsted) clearly suggests that cock grooming is a direct substitute for masturbation (see figure below). In a fascinating gestural comparison, Bateson and Mead (1942) claim that a mother "may ruffle the penis [of a baby] upward with repeated little flicks, using almost the exact gesture that a man uses when he ruffles up the hackle feathers of his fighting cock to make it angry" (p. 131).

Even Geertz (1972) could hardly avoid the overt behavior of the Balinese:

> Whenever you see a group of Balinese men squatting idly in the council shed or along the road in their hips down, shoulders forward, knees up fashion, half or more of them will have a rooster in his hands, holding it between his thighs, bouncing it gently up and down to strengthen its legs, ruffling its feathers with abstract sensuality, pushing it out against a neighbor's rooster to rouse its spirit, withdrawing it towards his loins to calm it again. (p. 6)

Geertz never once mentioned the word "masturbation," nor do any of the other post-Geertzian analysts of the cockfight except for Cook, in her 1991 doctoral dissertation, who calls "the careful cleaning, stroking, bouncing and constant handling that fighting cocks receive from their owners" a form of "symbolic masturbation" (1991, p. 98).

For those skeptics who may not be able to see the possible symbolic meaning of a handler's massaging the neck of his cock, I call their attention to the fact that in American slang "to choke the chicken" is a standard euphemism for masturbation and that a "chicken-choker" is a male masturbator (Spears 1990, p. 33).

Once the masturbatory underpinnings of the cockfight are recognized, many of the details of the cockfight can be much better understood. For example, there is a common rule that the handler can touch his own bird, but should at no time touch the opponent bird. In Tennessee, for example, "when a cock hangs a gaff in its opponent, the informant stated 'never touch another guy's bird' " (Cobb 1978, p. 93). Ostensibly the rule is to prevent someone unethical from harming the opponent bird, but symbolically it suggests that one is expected to handle only one's own phallus. The same rule is reported in the Philippines. When cocks are being matched, we are told, "don't let anyone

This sequence of images of a group of Balinese men sitting with their prize cocks shows clearly how (and *where*) the cock is held, as well as the typical, arguably autoerotic hand grooming movements. I thank Professor Herb Phillips for sharing this "home movie" footage and Gene Prince for transferring the images.

267

hold your cock to avoid regrets later" (Lansang 1966, pp. 96, 179). Filipinos in California adhered to the same code: "You never do that, touch someone else's bird" (Beagle 1968, p. 29).

Typically, cocks are kept in covered baskets right up until the time they are scheduled to enter the pit. The cock is *exposed* at the last minute for everyone to admire (and to encourage betting). After the exposure, the opposing cocks are juxtaposed so that they are in striking or pecking distance of one another (so as to stimulate them to want to fight). We can now more fully appreciate the possibly symbolic significance of the particular means handlers use to resuscitate flaccid cocks. By taking the cock's head into their mouths and sucking on it and blowing on it, we would seemingly have an obvious case of fellatio. Normally, it is considered demeaning for a male to indulge in such behavior—at least in public. It is worth recalling that the term of choice in Anglo-American slang for someone who performs such an act is "cock sucker." (The reference to "blowing" may carry a similar symbolic association. It is interesting that an Irish description refers to a handler who "put his bird's head into his own mouth to revive it. It used to work all right but whether he was sucking or blowing, I could not decide" (Crannlaighe 1945, p. 512). Also relevant may be the gambler's custom of "blowing" on dice before throwing them.)

Additional ethnographic evidence alludes to oral-genital acts. In Brazil, the cockpit may have a bar or restaurant adjacent where drinks and barbecued beef are available. Leal (1989) reports that men may joke along the lines of "We are eating your cock," even though chicken is not served there (p. 232). Such specifics of joking behavior (of the sort Geertz, 1972, mentioned but failed to record) is absolutely critical for a full understanding of the symbolic significance of the cockfight. According to Leal (1989), "Jokes are made about 'mounting' (*trepar*) or 'eating' (*comer*) 'someone's cock' (that is to say, the cock's owner) in the cockfight situation. Both words, *trepar* and *comer*, in Brazilian Portuguese are used for coitus while *cock* can stand for man, although not for a man's genitals" (p. 241).

Another piece of ethnographic data from Brazil bears on the connection between cockfighting and masturbation.

> When a good quality cock leaves the pit badly hurt there is a general commotion and his owner or handler carefully examines his wounds. As soon as the cock is better, the handler checks the cock's sexual organs to see if they have been affected: with the cock supine the man gently rubs behind the cock's leg in the direction of its testicles. If the cock ejaculates and the sperm contains blood, it is considered that the cock is seriously hurt and will not be able to fight again. (Leal 1989, pp. 239–240; see also Finsterbusch 1980, p. 245)

In a novelistic account of a cockfight set in northern Florida, massaging a cock's testicles is deemed a foul disqualifying that cock. The explanation: "You rub a cock's balls and you take every speck of fight right out of him. It's a deliberate way of throwing a fight" (Willeford 1972, pp. 180–181).

Usually, the masturbatory aspects of the cockfight are not quite so overt. An 1832 account of a cockfight in England describes one individual attending a cockfight:

> He was trying to look demure and unmoved . . . but I was told that he was a clergyman, and that he would be "quite up in the stirrups" when the cocks were brought in. He forced himself to be at ease; but I saw his small, hungry, hazel eyes quite in a fever—and his hot, thin, vein-embossed hand, rubbing the unconscious nob of his umbrella in a way to awaken it from the dead—and yet all the time he was affecting the uninterested, incurious man! (Egan 1832, p. 151)

Fuller (1977) remarked that sometimes, especially in fictional accounts of gambling, "the masturbatory element erupts through its defenses" (p. 101), which seems to apply to the abstemious clergyman attending a cockfight and rubbing the nob of his umbrella.

The present argument also illuminates the fact that cockfights are illegal in many countries. No doubt being outside the law makes cockfights more exciting for those participating. In other words, it is illegal to play with cocks in public; hence, one must do it *sub rosa*, in secret. That authorities ban cockfighting but then allow it to take place in secret locations seems to confirm its symbolic value. Masturbation is typically proscribed by parents, but masturbation occurs nonetheless. We can now better appreciate Geertz's description of a Balinese cockfight. "This process . . . is conducted in a very subdued, oblique, and even dissembling manner. Those not immediately involved give it at best but disguised, sidelong attention; those who, *embarrassedly*, are involved, attempt to pretend somehow that the whole thing is not really happening (Geertz 1972, p. 8, my emphasis).

Other symbolic inferences can be drawn from the notion that the cockfight may be a sublimated form of public masturbation. Harris (1964, p. 515) quoted earlier psychoanalysts who suggested that orgasm and death might be symbolically equivalent. We know that even in Shakespeare's day not only did "cock" mean "penis" (Partridge, 1960, p. 88), but "to die" meant to experience orgasm (p. 101). So, metaphorically speaking, if one's cock dies, one achieves orgasm. In the cockfight, if one's cock dies and the opponent's does not, one loses money as well; that is, one is punished for reaching orgasm in an all-male environment in a mutual-masturbation duel. The bleeding of the losing cock

269

further strengthens the image insofar as there is a visually empirical loss of fluid for all the world to see. Of course, the winning cock may bleed as well. Presumably both masturbators lose fluid at the end of the cockfight, the difference being that the winner is not punished, but rather is rewarded for outlasting his opponent, the loser. He has masturbated but remains alive perhaps to masturbate on another occasion. That a particularly strong cock may fight again and again demonstrates the "repetition compulsion" aspect of cockfighting (and masturbation).

If the cockfight does represent symbolic masturbation with grown men playing with their cocks in public, all the details from the grooming behavior to the gambling make sense. The grooming, involving the heavy use of the *hands* is analogous to shaking dice, shuffling cards, or pulling the handles on slot machines (one-armed bandits). Although Geertz (1972) made passing reference to "a large number of mindless, sheer-chance type gambling games (roulette, dice throw, coin-spin, pea-under-the-shell)" (p. 17), it was actually Bateson and Mead (1942) who reminded us that the dice thrown at a cockfight are "spun with the hand" (p. 143). The cockfight involves not only the risk of injury to or the loss of one's cock, but also the loss of money wagered on the fight. Losing would constitute "punishment" for indulging in symbolic masturbation while winning would permit great elation as having masturbated and gotten away with it. The Balinese say "Fighting cocks . . . is like playing with fire only not getting burned" (Geertz, 1972, p. 21). As Lindner (1953) put it, winning confirms the gambler-masturbator's feelings of omnipotence (p. 216). To be rewarded for masturbating is surely flying in the face of convention. In most cockfights, however, there are more losers than winners.

If a gambler's losing is a form of symbolic castration, as Freudians suggest (Fuller 1977, p. 102), then betting in a cockfight would exactly parallel the symbolic infrastructure of the cockfight itself. If one's cock loses by being put out of commission or by being killed, this would be a symbolic instance of castration. (One reminded of Cicero's quip in *Pro Murena* when, in trying to ridicule Zeno's Stoic teachings such as the idea that all misdeeds are equal, he remarked "The casual killing of a cock is no less a crime than strangling one's father" [Cicero 1977, p. 263].) If one had bet on one's cock and lost, the castration would be corroborated and confirmed. If, on the other hand, one's cock prevails, one avoids the immediate threat of castration, and if one wins the bet on one's cock, one does the same thing symbolically speaking.

From the foregoing analysis, one can see that the link between the cockfight and the betting associated with it is much less obscure. *Both* the cockfight *and* the betting are related to male masturbation. We can, then, also better understand why women are not welcome at cockfights. Geertz (1972) noted that the cockfight was unusual in Balinese culture "in being a single-sex public activity from which the other sex is totally and expressly excluded" (p. 30n). But he offered no explanation whatsoever for this. If men are competing in public with their cocks, one can easily appreciate why they prefer to do so without women present. In terms of the thesis of this essay, the whole point of the phallic competition is to "feminize" one's opponent. This symbolic feminization becomes less meaningful in the presence of actual women.

We may now have insight into some of the first reports of cockfighting in England and western Europe. According to most histories of cockfighting, the sport seems to have emerged among adolescent schoolboys, a custom that goes back to the middle ages (Anon. 1888, p. 812; Demulder 1934, p. 13; Vandereuse 1951). This schoolboy tradition of cockfighting continued into the early twentieth century (Cegarra 1988, p. 56). Often there would be a series of elimination bouts, with the schoolboy owner of the winning cock called "Roi du Coq" ("King of the Cocks") (Vandereuse 1951, p. 183). There were related customs in which a rooster was beheaded (Vandereuse 1951, p. 197; see also Coluccio 1970, pp. 75–76) or a group of boys threw sticks at a rooster suspended between two trees. The boy whose stick delivered the death blow was proclaimed king (Vandereuse 1951, p. 199). Given the symbolic analysis of the cockfight proposed here, it seems perfectly reasonable for it to be popular in all-male secondary schools.

One more element in the totality of cockfighting is, I believe, worthy of mention. It concerns the breeding of roosters. Many of the treatises on cockfighting offer advice about how best to produce a "game" cock. One old Georgia informant reported:

> Those chickens were raised—most of 'em came from one hen and one rooster. They single mated 'em. They'd take the offspring from that and test 'em in the pit to see whether they suited them or not. If they did, then they'd take six full sisters and the sisters' father or grandfather and they'd breed all those hens. That's what they call inbreeding and line breeding. (Allred and Carver, 1979, p. 52)

In one of the many books devoted to cockfighting, we find an alternative term: "Full blood" mating. " 'Full blood' mating was approved; father with daughter, mother with son, brother with sister" (Gilbey 1912, p. 89). The oedipal implications of such breeding practices are obvious enough. "You can only try your hens single breeding them and keeping exact records of their sons' performances, and when you come across a true-blooded hen, do not hesitate to breed the choicest son back to his mother" (Finsterbusch 1980, p. 165). According to this same source, "when fowls are bred in, it can be done in two forms: (1) in a vertical sense, i.e., from parents to offspring and grandparents to grandchildren; or (2) in a horizontal sense, i.e., from sister to brother or inter-cousins" (p. 140).

In a cockfighting novel, we are told that a cock bred from a father and a daughter "usually runs every time," whereas "those bred from mother and son have the biggest heart for fighting to the death" (Willeford 1972, p. 39). Breeders may well argue for the genetic efficacy of such inbreeding, but from a psychoanalytic perspective—in which breeders might be said to identify with their cocks (and their behavior), such breeding might constitute wishful thinking as well as fantastic acting out. The point is that such fantasies would not be at all inconsistent with masturbation.

With all of the rich ethnographic detail available in print concerning the cockfight, it is surprising to read what anthropologists have written about it. The refusal to acknowledge the existence of clear-cut symbolic data can only be attributed to what might generally be characterized as an anti-symbolic stance among social and cultural anthropologists. So-called symbolic anthropologists are among the chief examples of those espousing what I would term an anti-symbolic stance. Symbolic anthropologists unfortunately define symbolism very narrowly, typically limiting it to matters of social structure.

Although some authors (e.g., Hawley 1989) have observed a "sexual subtext" in the cockfight, they are quick to say that "sometimes a cockfight is just a cockfight or a gaming opportunity, and not an implicit homoerotic struggle" (p. 131). Hawley, for example, differs with "animal rights activists, who see cockfighters (and hunters and gun owners) as 'insecure about their masculinity' " (p. 131). (For attempts to disprove the negative stereotypes of cockfighters see Bryant [1991]; and Bryant and Li [1991].) A cocker who temporarily turned academic to write a thesis about cockfighting in northern Utah remarked: "Most leave a cockfight as emotionally and physically spent as if they had engaged in extreme sexual activity. I am not saying the release is sexual, but the physical and emotional release is very similar" (Walker 1986, p. 28). Geertz (1972), after dutifully noting phallic elements, totally ignored them in his analysis of the Balinese cockfight as being a metaphor for concerns about status and hierarchy.

Leal (1989), notwithstanding her splendid ethnographic documentation of the phallic nature of the Brazilian cockfight, declines to interpret it along such lines. Says Leal:

> We can see the cockfight as a play of images where ultimately what is at stake is masculinity, not cocks, not even "ambulant penises" as Bateson, Mead or Geertz suggested. . . . I wonder if the equation cocks = penises is not an oversimplification, specific to English-speaking people. . . . In my understanding, phallus itself

272

is a sign invested with the meaning of manliness and power: androcentric cultures ascribe power to the ones who have penises. In contrast to Bateson and Mead, Geertz does not limit his analysis to the cock as a phallic symbol; masculinity and status concern are his main points. (p. 220)

Thus Leal falls back to a nonphallic reading when she says, "Without doubt cockfighting is a dramatization of male identity" (p. 227). Her position is stated clearly enough:

> The association men/cocks, which seems to be self-evident in cultures that have the word *cock* as a signifier for penis, is not an obvious one in gaucho culture. I am not denying the semantical association man/cock; rather I am suggesting that in cockfighting situations, the meaning of cock imagery cannot be reduced to the notion of male genitals. . . . (p. 240)

For Leal, if a man is able to "perform the tasks and rites which assure masculinity he becomes a *man;* he acquires the *phallus,* which means he gains prestige and power" (p. 240). It should be noted that in northeast Brazil—far from where Leal carried out her fieldwork—little boys' genitals can be called "pintinho" ("little chick"), in contrast to adult men's, which are often called "galo" ("rooster") (Linda-Anne Rebhun 1992, personal communication). Still, Leal's view is echoed by Marvin (1984), who in his ethnographic account of cockfights in Andalusia noted, "Unlike Bali, in Spain there is no identification of men as individuals with their cocks" (p. 63). Certainly the data from English is more explicit. One thinks of the slang term "pecker" for penis, for example. In a cockfight where both cocks are wounded, it is the one who is still able to "peck" his opponent who is declared the winner. The pecker wins!

My own view is that it is not an oversimplification found exclusively among English-speaking people to equate cocks and penises, especially in view of the ample evidence of that equation available wherever cockfighting exists. The data from Bali and from Brazil are exceptionally explicit, even though both Geertz (1972) and Leal (1989) tend to dismiss the obvious phallic implications of their data in favor of interpretations that favor emphases on "status" and "prestige and power." Indeed, it is my opinion that it is an oversimplification of the cockfight to claim that it is only about status hierarchy and prestige.

The predictable tendency of social anthropologists to interpret virtually all aspects of culture solely in terms of social structure and social organization is easily discernible in previous readings of the cockfight. The combination of the bias toward social structure and the bias against psychoanalytic symbolic interpretation has prevented anthropologists from understanding the explicit implications of their own ethnographic data. It is ironic and paradoxical that social anthropologists—as well as conventional folklorists—invariably condemn Freudian interpretations as *reductionistic*, whereas in fact it is social anthropologists who are reductionists. They reduce all folkloristic phenomena (such as myths and cockfights) to reflections of social structure.

Geertz (1972) and those anthropologists who have followed his basic approach to the cockfight have erred in not being comparative in perspective, in failing to see the cockfight as a form of mutual masturbation or a phallic brag duel, in not offering a plausible explanation as to why women are unwelcome at cockfights, and, above all, in misreading the overall symbolic import of the cockfight with its paradigmatic aim of feminizing a male opponent either through the threat of castration (via the gaff or spur) or by making the losing cock turn tail to be labeled a female "chicken."

Psychoanalysts, to my knowledge, have not considered the cockfight. Ferenczi (1913) did discuss the case of a five-year-old boy who very much identified with roosters (to the extent of crowing and cackling) but who was also at the same time very much afraid of roosters. Ferenczi suggested that the boy's morbid dread of cocks "was ultimately to be traced to the threat of castration for onanism" (p. 212).

Is there any evidence of symbolic castration in the traditional cockfight? I argue that all those versions of the cockfight which involve the attachment of sharp metal spurs (also called "heels" or "slashers") to the cock's feet add a castrative element to the sport. Some cultures forbid the use of such armor, in which case the natural spurs of the rooster may serve a similar purpose. Placing spurs on one's cock essentially entails arming a phallus. It is, in my view, symbolically equivalent to competitive kite-fighting in southeast Asia and elsewhere, where a young man will attach pieces of broken glass to his kite string. He does so with the hope that his kite-string will sever that of his opponent. In kite-fighting, the initial action is get one's kite up (a symbolic erection), but this is quickly followed by the battle to cut one's opponent's kite off. Bateson and Mead (1942, p. 135) noted that kite-fighting is a form of "vicarious conflict" analogous to cockfighting, but did not explicitly mention castration. In cockfighting, one puts sharp blades on one's cocks to cut down one's opponents' cocks. If the gallus is a phallus, then cutting a cock could properly be construed as symbolic castration. There is an anecdote about a Javanese official who was employed by the Dutch government which lends credence to this interpretation. When asked by the Dutch authorities to take action against illegal cockfights, he did not want to betray his own people and refused to do so. Instead, he proposed to castrate the cocks so that they would not wish to fight. No one paid any attention to the new rule because the men felt that if they castrated their cocks, they themselves would be castrated as well (Serière 1873, p. 101).

If my analysis of the cockfight as a symbolic, public masturbatory, phallic duel is sound, one should be able to understand why participants might be reluctant or unable to articulate consciously this symbolic structure. In effect, the cockfight is like most folklore fantasy: its content is largely unconscious. If the participants consciously realized what they were doing, they would in all probability not be willing to participate. It is precisely the symbolic façade that makes it possible for people to participate in an activity without consciously understanding the significance of that participation.

Less forgivable and understandable is the utter failure of anthropologists and folklorists to decipher the symbolic significance of the cockfight. Anthropologists can presumptuously label their superficial ethnographic descriptions of the cockfight as "deep," but calling "shallow" deep does not make it so. Perhaps psychoanalytic anthropologists and folklorists should not really complain. If conventional anthropologists and folklorists actually understood the unconscious symbolic dimensions of human behavior—such as that consistently demonstrated in the cockfight—there would be far fewer challenges for psychoanalytic anthropologists and folklorists to take up.

Bibliography

Acosta Saignes, M. 1954. "Introduction al estudio de la gallina en el folklore de Venezuela." *Tradición* 6.15: 29–46.

Affergan, F. 1986. "Zooanthropologie du combat de coqs à la Martinique." *Cahiers Internationaux de Sociologie* 80: 109–126.

Allred, K. & Carver, J. 1979. "Cockfighting." *Foxfire* 13:50–61, 151–172.

Alonso, M. A. 1849. *El Gibaro: cuadro de costumbres de la Isla de Puerto-Rico.* Barcelona: D. Juan Oliveres.

Anderson, R. L. 1933. "Chicken-fight." *Amer. Mercury* 30: 111–115.

Anon. 1888. "Fighting-cocks in Schools." *Chamber's J.*, 65:812–814.

Anon. 1952. "Your Taxes Support Cockfights." *National Humane Rev.*, 40.11: 10–11, 25.

Anon. 1984. "Cockfighting." *Foxfire;* 8: 385–487.

Armas Chitty, J. A. De 1953–1954. "Las rinas de gallos en el Oriente del Guárico. *Archivos Venezolanos de Folklore,* 2–3: 149–158.

Axon, W. E. A. 1899. "Cock-fighting in the Eighteenth Century." *Notes & Queries,* 9th Series, 4: 62–64.

Bailey, G. H. 1909. "The Cockpit and the Filipino." *Overland Monthly* 54: 253–256.

Baird, L. Y. 1981. "O.E.D. Cock 20: The Limits of Lexicography of Slang." *Maledicta* 5: 213–225.

Baird, L. Y. 1981–1982. "Priapus gallinaceus: The Role of the Cock in Fertility and Eroticism in Classical Antiquity and the Middle Ages." *Stud. Iconogr.* 7–8: 81–111.

Barclay, J. 1980. *A Stroll Through Borneo*. London: Hodder & Soughton.

Bascom, W. R. 1954. "Four Functions of Folklore." *J. Amer. Folklore* 67: 333–349.

Bascom, W. R. 1957. "The Myth-ritual Theory." *J. Amer. Folklore* 70: 103–114.

Bateson, G. & Mead, M. 1942. *Balinese Character: A Photographic Analysis*. New York: New York Academy of Sciences.

Beacey, P. 1945. "Prelude to a cockfight." *The Bell* 11: 574–576.

Beagle, P. S. 1968. "Cockfight." *Saturday Evening Post* 241.17: 28–29, 76–77.

Beattie, G. 1937. "The Scottish Miner and his Game-cock." *The Scots Magazine* 14:213–217.

Bergler, E. 1943. "The Gambler: A Misunderstood Neurotic." *J. Criminal Psychopathol.* 4: 379–393.

Bergler, E. 1957. *The Psychology of Gambling*. New York: Hill & Wang.

Bhide, V. V. 1967. "Cock in Vedic Literature." *Bharatiya Vidya* 27: 1–6.

Bolen, D. W. & Boyd, W. H. 1968. "Gambling and the Gambler: A Review and Preliminary Findings." *Arch. Gen Psychiat.* 18: 617–630.

Boon, J. A. 1977. *The Anthropological Romance of Bali 1597–1972*. Cambridge: Cambridge University Press.

Borneman, E. 1971. *Sex im Volksmund*. Reinbek bei Hamburg: Rowohlt Verlag.

Boulton, W. B. 1901. *The Amusements of Old London*, vol. 1. London: John C. Nimmo.

Braddy, H. 1961. "Feathered Duelists." In M. C. Boatright, W. M. Hudson and A. Maxwell, eds., *Singers and Storytellers*, pp. 98–106. Dallas: Southern Methodist University Press.

Bruneau, P. 1965. "Le motif des coqs affrontés dans l'imagerie antique." *Bulletin de correspondance hellénique* 89: 90–121.

Bryant, C. D. 1991. "Deviant Leisure and Clandestine Lifestyle: Cockfighting as a Socially Disvalued Sport." *World Leisure and Recreation* 33: 17–21.

Bryant, C. D., and L. Li. 1991. "A Statistical value profile of cockfighters." *Sociology and Social Research* 75: 199–209.

Bryden, H. A. 1931. "Cock-fighting and its Illustrations." *The Print Collector's Quart.* 18: 351–373.

Cadet, A. 1971. "Le Coq." *Société d'Etudes Folkloriques du Centre-Ouest: Revue de recherches ethnographiques* 5: 99–112; 144–168, 199–210, 292–308.

Cadilla De Martinez, M. 1941. "De los gallos y sus peleas." In *Raices de la Tierra*, pp. 145–166. Arecibo, PR: Tipografia Hernandez.

Calderin, G. G. 1970. "El gallo de pelea." *Isla Literaria* 10–11: 16–18.

Callisen, S. A. 1939. "The Iconography of the Cock on the Column." *Art Bull.* 21: 160–178.

Carson, J. 1965. *Colonial Virginians at Play*. Williamsburg: University Press of Virginia.

Castillo De Lucas, A. 1970. "El gallo: Simbolismo refraneado de su preferente figura en la alfareria popular." *Revista de Etnografia* 14: 361–367.

Cegarra, M. 1987. *Le Cercle, le plume, le sang: étude anthropologique des combats de coqs dans le Norde de la France*. Paris: Mission du Patrimonie ethnologique.

Cegarra, M. 1988. "Les coqs combattants." *Terrain* 10: 51–62.

Cegarra, M. 1989. "Les combats de coqs dans le nord de la France." In M. Segalen, ed., *Anthropologie Sociale et Ethnologie de la France*, pp. 671–676. Bibliothèque des Cahiers de l'Institut de Linguistique de Louvain 44, vol. 2. Louvain-La Neuve: Peeters.

Challes, M. De 1972. "Cockfighting in the 19th Century Caribbean." *Caribbean Rev.* 4.4: 12–14.

Champagnac, A. 1970. *Coqs de combat et combats de coqs à la Martinique.* Alfort: Maisons-Alfort.

Chattopadhyay, A. 1973. "Cocks in Ancient Indian Life." *J. Oriental Instit.* 23: 197–201.

Chick, G., and Donlon, J. 1992. "Going out on a Limn: Geertz's 'Deep Play: Notes on the Balinese Cockfight' and the Anthropological Study of Play." *Play & Culture* 5: 233–245.

Cicero, 1977, "Pro Murena." In *Cicero in Twenty-Eight Volumes*, vol. 10, pp. 167–299. Cambridge: Harvard University Press.

Cobb, J. E. 1978. "Cockfighting in East Tennessee." In C. H. Faulkner and C. K. Buckles, ed., *Glimpses of Southern Appalachian Folk Culture*, misc. paper no. 3, pp. 175–196. Tennessee Anthropological Association.

Coluccio, M. I. 1970. "El gallo." *Revista de Ethnografía* 14: 59–81.

Cook, H. B. K. 1991. "Small Town, Big Hell: An Ethnographic Study of Aggression in A Margariteno Community." Ph.D. dissertation, University of California, Los Angeles.

Crannlaighe, P. O. 1945. "Cock Fighting." *The Bell*, 19: 510–513.

Crapanzano, V. 1986. "Hermes' Dilemma: The Masking of Subversion in Ethnographic Description." In J. Clifford and G. E. Marcus, ed., *Writing Culture*, pp. 51–76 Berkeley: University of California Press.

Crews, H. 1977. "Cockfighting: An Unfashionable View." *Esquire* 87.3: 8, 12, 14.

Cutter, R. J. 1989a. "Brocade and Blood: The Cockfight in Chinese and English Poetry." *Tamkang Rev.*, 19: 631–661.

Cutter, R. J. 1989b. *The Brush and the Spur: Chinese Culture and the Cockfight.* Hong Kong: Chinese University Press.

Danaë O. 1989. *Combats de coqs: Histoire et actualité de l'oiseau guerrier.* Paris: Editions L'Harmattan.

Del Sesto, S. L. 1975. "Roles, Rules, and Organization: A Descriptive Account of Cockfighting in Rural Louisiana." *Southern Folklore Quart.* 39: 1–14.

Del Sesto, S. L. 1980. "Dancing and Cockfighting at Jay's Lounge and Cockpit: The Preservation of Folk Practices in Cajun Louisiana." In R. B. Browne, ed., *Rituals and Ceremonies in Popular Culture*, pp. 270–281. Bowling Green, OH: Bowling Green University Popular Press.

Delannoy, R. 1948. *Coqs de combat et combats de coqs dans le nord le Pas-de-Calais.* Paris: R. Foulon.

Demulder, R. 1934. "Coqueleux et combats de coqs dans le nord de la France." *Revue de Folklore Français* 5: 8–14.

Desrousseaux, A. 1886. "Les combats de coqs en Flandre." *Revue des Traditions Populaires* 1: 338–339.

Desrousseaux, A. 1889. *Moeurs Populaires de la Flandre Française,* vol. 2. Lille: L. Quarre.

Dinwiddie, W. 1899. *Puerto Rico: Its Conditions and Possibilities.* New York: Harper & Brothers.

Donlon, J. 1990. "Fighting Cocks, Feathered Warriors, and Little Heroes." *Play & Culture* 3: 273–285.

Donlon, J. G. 1991. "Leisure Most Fowl: Cock Fighting in a Cultural and Historic Milieu." Master's thesis, University of Illinois.

Dundes, A. 1987. *Parsing Through Customs: Essays by a Freudian Folklorist.* Madison: University of Wisconsin Press.

Eck, R. V. 1879. "Schetsen uit het Volksleven (I. Hanengevecht)." *De Indische Gids,* 1: 102–118.

Egan, P. 1832. *Book of Sports and Mirror of Life.* London: T. T. & J. Tegg.

Fehrle, E. 1912. "Der Hahn im Aberglauben." *Schweizerisches Archiv für Volkskunde,* 16: 65–75.

Feijoo, L. J. R. 1990. *Apuntes sobre el arte de castar gallos de pelea.* Puerto Rico: Taller Gráfico Gongolí.

Ferenczi, S. 1913. "A Little Chanticleer." In *First Contributions to Psycho-Analysis,* pp. 204–213. London: Karnac Books, 1980.

Fine, G. A. 1992. "The Depths of Deep Play: The Rhetoric and Resources of Morally Controversial Leisure." *Play & Culture* 5: 246–251.

Finsterbusch, C. A. 1980. *Cock Fighting All Over the World.* Hindhead, U.K.: Saiga.

Forsyth, I. H. 1978. The Theme of Cockfighting in Burgundian Romanesque Architecture. *Speculum* 53: 252–282.

Fraser, H. M. 1981. "The Cockfight Motif in Spanish American Literature." *Inter-Amer. Rev. Bibliog.* 31: 514–523.

Freud, S. 1928. "Dostoevsky and Parricide." *Standard Edition* 21: 173–194. London: Hogarth Press, 1961.

Fuller, P. 1977, "Introduction." In J. Halliday & P. Fuller, ed., *The Psychology of Gambling,* pp. 1–114. New York: Penguin.

Galdston, I. 1951. "The Psychodynamics of the Triad, Alcoholism, Gambling and Superstition." *Mental Hyg.* 35: 589–598.

Galdston, I. 1960. "The Gambler and his Love." *Amer. J. Psychiat.* 117: 553–555.

Gandhi, M. K. 1929. *The Story of My Experiments with Truth,* 2 vols. Ahmedabad: Navajivan Press.

Gard, W. 1936. "Rooster Fight." *Southwest Rev.* 22: 65–70.

Geertz, C. 1972. "Deep Play: Notes on the Balinese Cockfight." *Daedalus* 101.1 1–37.

Gilbey, J. 1957. "Cockfighting in Art." *Apollo* 65: 22–24.

Gilbey, W. 1912. *Sport in the Olden Time:* London: Vinton.

Gittée, A. 1891. "De Haan in de Volksverbeelding." *Volkskunde* 4: 154–166.

Greenson, R. R. 1947. "On Gambling." *Amer. Imago* 4.2: 61–77.

Guggenheim, S. 1982. "Cock or Bull: Cockfighting, Social Structure, and Political Commentary in the Philippines." *Pilipinas* 3.1: 1–35.

Gunter, C. R., Jr. 1978. "Cockfighting in East Tennessee and Western North Carolina." *Tennessee Folklore Soc. Bull.* 44: 160–169.

Harris, H. I. 1964. "Gambling Addiction in an Adolescent Male." *Psychoanal. Quart.* 33: 513–525.

Harris, J. 1987. "The Rules of Cockfighting." In F. E. Abernethy, ed. *Hoein' The Short Rows*, pp. 101–111. Dallas: Southern Methodist University Press.

Hawley, F. F. 1982. "Organized Cockfighting: A Deviant Recreational Subculture." Ph.D. dissertation, Florida State University.

Hawley, F. F. 1987. "Cockfighting in the Pine Woods: Gameness in the New South." *Sport Place* 1.2: 18–26.

Hawley, F. F. 1989. "Cockfight in the Cotton: A Moral Crusade in Microcosm." *Contemp. Crises* 13: 129–144.

Hazard, S. 1871. *Cuba with Pen and Pencil.* Hartford, CT: Hartford Publishing Company.

Herzog, H. A., Jr. 1978. "Immobility in Intraspecific Encounters: Cockfights and the Evolution of "Animal Hypnosis." *Psycholog. Record* 28: 543–548.

Herzog, H. A., Jr. 1985. "Hackfights and Derbies." *Appalachian J.* 12: 114–126.

Herzog, H. A., Jr. & Cheek, P. B. 1979. "Grit and Steel: The Anatomy of Cockfighting." *Southern Exposure* 7.2: 36–40.

Hyman, S. E. 1950. "Department of Amplification." *The New Yorker* 26.11: 100–101.

Jacobson, D. 1991. *Reading Ethnography.* Albany: State University of New York Press.

James, L. 1928. "The Ancient Sport of 'Cocking.' " *Natl. Rev.* 92: 138–143.

Jaquemotte, E., and Lejeune, J. 1904. "Vocabulaire du coqueli." *Bull. Société liegeoise de littérature wallonne* 45: 225–230.

Jarvis, C. S. 1939. "Blood-sports and Hypocrisy." *Cornhill Mag.* 159: 368–378.

Jones, R. 1980. "Chicken Fighting is a Hobby." *Foxfire* 14: 143–150.

Jull, M. A. 1927. "The Races of Domestic Fowl." *Nat. Geogr. Mag.* 51: 379–452.

Justo, E. 1969. "Las peleas de gallos." *Revista de Dialectologia y Tradiciones Populares* 25: 317–323.

Kaudern, W. 1929. *Ethnographical Studies in Celebes,* vol. 4. The Hague: Martinus Nijhoff.

Knight, F. C. E. 1940. "Cockfighting in Bali." *Discovery,* 2d series. 3.23: 77–81.

Kreemer, J. 1893. "De Javaan en zijne hoenders." *Mededeelingen van wege het Nederlandsche Zendelinggenootschap* 37: 213–225.

Kretzenbacher, L. 1958. "Der Hahn auf dem Kirchturm." *Rheinisches Jahrbuch für Volkskunde* 9: 194–206.

Lansang, A. J. 1966. *Cockfighting in the Philippines (Our Genuine National Sport).* Atlag, Malolos, Bulacan: Enrian Press.

Leal, O. F. 1989. "The Gauchos: Male Culture and Identity in the Pampas." Ph.D. dissertation, University of California, Berkeley.

Lee, F. 1921. "Filipinos' favorite Sport." *Overland Monthly* 77: 20–22.

Leon Rey, J. A. 1953. "Rinas de gallos y vocabulario de gallistica." *Revista Colombiana de Folklore* 2: 79–96.

Liebling, A. J. 1950. "Dead Game." *The New Yorker* 26.6: 35–45.
Lindner, R. 1953. "The Psychodynamics of Gambling." In R. Lindner, ed., *Explorations in Psychoanalysis*, pp. 197–217. New York: Julian Press.
Magaldi, E. 1929. "I 'Ludi Gallinarii' a Pompei." *Historia* 3: 471–485.
Mantegazza, P. 1916. *Viajes por el Río de la Plata.* Buenos Aires: Universidad de Tucumán.
Mantegazza, P. 1935. *The Sexual Relations of Mankind.* New York: Eugenics Pub.
Marçal, H. 1967. "O Galo na Tradição Popular." *Revista de Etnografia* 9: 345–408.
Marcelin, M. 1955a. "Jeu de coqs." *Optique* 13: 35–41.
Marcelin, M. 1955b. "Termes de gagaire ou de combat de coqs." *Optique* 20: 51–59.
Marquez, L. G. 1954. *Reglamento del Club Gallistico de Caracas.* Caracas: Tip. Londres.
Marvin, G. 1984. "The Cockfight in Andalusia, Spain: Images of the Truly Male." *Anthropolog. Quart.* 57: 60–70.
McCaghy, C. H. & Neal, A. G. 1974. "The Fraternity of Cockfighters: Ethical Embellishments of an Illegal Sport." *J. Pop. Cult.* 8: 557–569.
Mendoza, V. T. 1943. "Folklore de los gallos." *Anuario de la Sociedad Folklorica de Mexico* 4: 115–125.
Modi, J. J. 1911. "The Cock as a Sacred Bird in Ancient Iran." In *Anthropological Papers*, pp. 104–121. Bombay: British Indian Press.
Mosher, H. F. 1989. *A Stranger in the Kingdom.* New York: Doubleday.
Niederland, W. G. *et al.* 1967. "A Contribution to the Psychology of Gambling." *Psychoanal. Forum* 2: 175–185.
Nugent, W. H. 1929. "Cock Fighting Today." *Amer. Mercury* 17: 75–82.
O'Gormon, M. 1983, *Clancy's Bulba.* London: Hutchinson.
Olivares Figueroa, R. 1949. "Gallos y galleros." In *Diversiones Pascuales en Oriente y Otros Ensayos*, pp. 179–191. Caracas: Ardor.
Olmsted, C. 1962. *Heads I Win, Tails You Lose.* New York: Macmillan.
Parker, G. L. 1986. "An Outlet for Male Aggression: The Secret Fraternity of the Southern Cockfighter." *Tenn. Anthropolog.* 11: 21–28.
Parker, R. 1985. "From Symbolism to Interpretation: Reflections on the Work of Clifford Geertz." *Anthropol. & Humanism Quart.* 10: 62–67.
Parsons, G. E., Jr. 1969. "Cockfighting: A Potential Field of Research." *N.Y. Folklore Quart.* 25: 265–288.
Partridge, E. 1960. *Shakespeare's Bawdy.* New York: Dutton.
Paul, E. C. 1952. "*La gaguère" ou le combat de coqs.* Port-au-Prince: Imprimerie de l'Etat.
Peate, I. C. 1970. "The Denbigh Cockpit and Cockfighting in Wales." *Trans. Denbigshire Historical Soc.* 19: 125–132.
Pegge, S. 1773. "A Memoir on Cock-fighting." *Archaeologia* 3: 132–150.
Penrose, B. 1976. "Blood in the Suburbs." *The Listener* 95: 236.
Perez, O. A. 1984. *La Pelea de Gallos en Venezuela: Léxico, Historia y Literatura.* Caracas: Ediciones Espada Rota.
Peters, J. P. 1913. "The Cock." *J. Amer. Oriental Soc.* 33: 363–396.
Phillott, D. C. 1910. "Murgh-Nama." *J. Asiatic Soc. Bengal* 6: 73–91.
Picard, M. 1983. "En Feuilletant le 'Bali Post': A propos de l'interdiction des combats de coqs à Bali." *Archipel.* 25: 171–180.

Powel, H. 1937. "The Game Cock." *Amer. Mercury* 41: 185–191.

Rasch, J. 1930. "De Haan in het volksgeloof" *Eigen Volk* 2: 216–221.

Remouchamps, E. and Remacle, L. 1949. "Les combats de coqs." *Enquêtes du Musée de la Vie Wallonee* 4: 40–80.

Roberts, B. S. C. 1965. "Cockfighting: An Early Entertainment in North Carolina." *N. C. Hist. Rev.* 42: 306–314.

Roces, A. R. 1959. *Of Cocks and Kites.* Manila: Regal.

Roseberry, W. 1982. "Balinese Cockfights and the Seduction of Anthropology." *Soc. Res* 49: 1013–1028.

Russell, R. P. 1942. *Divine Providence and the Problem of Evil: A Translation of St. Augustine's De Ordine.* New York: Cosmopolitan Science and Art Service.

Saltore, B. A. 1926–1927. "Cock-fighting in Tuluva." *Quart. J. Mythic Soc.* 17: 316–327.

Sandin, B. 1959. "Cock-fighting: The Dayak National Game." *Sarawak Museum J.* 9: 25–32.

Sarabia Viejo, M. J. 1972. *El juego de gallos en Nueva Espaná.* Sevilla: Escuela de Estudios Hispanoamericanos de Sevilla.

Sarma, I. K. 1964. "The Ancient Game of Cock-fight in India." *Quart. J. Mythic Soc.* 54: 113–120.

Saubidet, T. 1952. *Vocabulario y refranero criollo.* Buenos Aires: Editorial Guillermo Kraft.

Saussure, C. De 1902. *A Foreign View of England in the Reigns of George I & George II.* London: Murray.

Scheltema, J. F. 1919. "Roostam, the Game-Cock." *J. Amer. Folklore* 32: 306–323.

Schneider, M. A. 1987. "Culture-as-Text in the Work of Clifford Geertz." *Theory and Soc.* 16: 809–839.

Scott, G. R. 1941. *Phallic Worship.* London: Laurie.

Scott, G. R. 1957. *The History of Cockfighting.* London: Skilton.

Serière, V. De 1873. "Javasche volksspelen en vermaken." *Tijdschrift voor Nederlandsch Indië,* 4th series, 2.1: 81–101.

Simmel E. 1920. "Psycho-Analysis of the Gambler." *Internat. J. Psycho-Anal.* 1: 352–353.

Smith, P. & Daniel, C. 1975. *The Chicken Book.* Boston: Little, Brown.

Soeroto, N. 1916–1917. "Hanengevechten op Java." *Nederlandsch-Indië Oud & Nieuw* 1: 126–132.

Spears, R. A. 1990. *Forbidden American English.* Lincolnwood, IL: Passport Books.

Stekel, W. 1924. *Peculiarities of Behavior,* vol. 2. New York: Liveright.

Tegetmeier, W. B. 1896. "Sport in Art: Cockfighting." *Magazine of Art* 19: 408–412.

Teixeira, S. A. 1992. *A Sementica Simbolica dos Nomes de Galos de Briga, Bois, Prostitutas, Prostitutos e Travestis.* Cadernos de Anthropologia, no. 8., Porto Alegre: PPGAS.

Tippette, G. 1978. "The Birds of Death." *Texas Monthly* 6: 163–165, 271–277.

Tudela, J. 1959. "Los gallos de dos mundos." *Amerikanistische Miszellen. Mitteilungen aus dem Museum für Völkerkunde in Hamburg* 25: 14–20.

Vandereuse, J. 1951. "Le coq et les ecoliers (anciennes coutumes scolaires)." *Folklore Brabançon* 23: 182–208.

Vatsyayana, 1963. *Kama Sutra: The Hindu Ritual of Love.* New York: Castle.

Vichot, J. 1970. "La Symbolique du coq." *Neptunia* 98: 2–13.

Vogeler, E. J. 1942. "Cock Fighting in Florida." *Amer. Mercury* 54: 422–428.

Walker, J. L. 1986. "Feathers and Street: A Folkloric Study of Cockfighting in Northern Utah." Master's thesis, Utah State University.

Watson, R. J. 1989. "Definitive Geertz." *Ethnos* 54: 23–30.

West, N. 1950. *The Day of the Locust.* New York: New Directions Books.

Wilkinson, R. J. 1925. *Papers on Malay Subjects: Life and Customs, Part III. Malay Amusements* Kuala Lumpur: F. M. S. Government Press.

Willeford, C. 1972. *Cockfighter.* New York: Crown.

Witte, J. De 1868. "Le Génie des combats de coqs." *Revue Archéologique, n. s.* 17: 372–381.

Wollan, L. A., Jr. 1980. "Questions from a Study of Cockfighting." *Bull. Center Study of Southern Culture & Religion* 4.2: 26–32.

Worden, S. and Darden, D. 1992. "Knives and Gaffs: Definitions in the Deviant World of Cockfighting." *Deviant Behavior* 13:271–289.

Wurdemann, J. G. 1844. *Notes on Cuba.* Boston: Munroe.

Selected Bibliography
Index

A Selected Bibliography:
Suggestions for Further Material
on the Cockfight

Baird, Lorrayne Y. "Pripaus gallinaceus: The Roll of the Cock in Fertility and Eroticism in Classical Antiquity and the Middle Ages." *Studies in Iconography* 7–8 (1981–
1982): 81–111. A remarkable survey of phallic cocks in Greek art and sculpture.

Cegarra, Marie. *Le Cercle, le plume, le sang: étude anthropologique des combats de coqs dans le
Norde de la France.* Paris: Mission du Patrimonie ethnologique, 1987. 279 pp. A
superb ethnographic account of the contemporary cockfighting tradition on the
Belgian-French border.

Cutter, Robert Joe. *The Brush and the Spur: Chinese Culture and the Cockfight.* Hong
Kong: The Chinese University Press, 1989. 255 pp. An impressively comprehensive
survey of historical and literary references to the cockfight in China from 517 B.C. to
the present day.

Danaë, Olivier. *Combats de coqs: histoire et actualité de l'oiseau guerrier.* Paris: Éditions
L'Harmattan, 1989. 253 pp. A magisterial worldwide survey of cockfighting including discussion of possible paths of diffusion.

Eck, R. Van. "Schetsen uit het Volksleven in Nederlandsche Oost-Indië (I. Het
Hanengevecht)." *De Indische Gids* 1 (1879): 102–118. A surprisingly good
nineteenth-century account of cockfighting in Bali and Java which includes a list of
forty-five official rules governing the conduct of cockfights.

Finsterbusch, C. A. *Cock Fighting All Over the World.* Hindhead, Surrey: Saiga Publishing Co., 1980. 465 pp. One of several general worldwide semi-popular surveys of cockfighting which includes extended discussions of breeding, diet, and care.

Fraser, Howard M. "The Cockfight Motif in Spanish American Literature." *Inter-
American Review of Bibliography* 31 (1981): 514–523. A survey of the literary uses of
the cockfight in works by a number of prominent Latin American authors.

Hawley, F. Frederick. "Organized Cockfighting: A Deviant Recreational Subculture."
(1982). Unpublished doctoral dissertation in criminology, Florida State University.
165 pp. An in-depth survey of cockfighters in the United States as a subculture,
based upon interviews and fieldwork carried out in south Georgia and north Louisiana. Appendices include D. Henry Wortham's thirty-page 1961 revised edition of
Modern Tournament and Derby Rules.

Lansang, Angel J. *Cockfighting in the Philippines (Our Genuine National Sport).* Atlag,
Malolog, Bulacan: Enrian Press, 1966. 218 pp. A partisan, personal manual on how
to raise and fight cocks in the Philippines.

Parsons, Gerald E., Jr. "Cockfighting: A Potential Field of Research." *New York Folklore*
25 (1969): 265–288. A useful programmatic appeal for fieldwork on the subject of
cockfighting which includes a detailed outline of topics to be investigated, an anno-

tated bibliography, and a partial list of U.S. periodicals devoted to cock breeding and fighting.

Paul, Emmanuel C. '*La Gaguere*' *ou le combat de coqs.* Port-au-Prince, Haiti: Imprimerie de l'Etat, 1952. 32 pp. A concise ethnographic account of cockfighting procedures in Haiti.

Perez, Omar Alberto. *La pelea de gallos en Venezuela: léxico, historia y literatura.* Caracas: Ediciones Espada Rota, 1984. 267 pp. A valuable compilation of information about cockfighting in Venezuela including a lexicon of cockfighting terminology (pp. 17–77), a history of the development of the sport in that country, e.g., its various codes of regulations (pp. 81–128), and a generous sampling of literary poems and short stories on the subject (pp. 129–253).

Remouchamps, Ed., and L. Remacle. "Les combats de coqs." *Enquêtes du Musée de la Vie Wallonne* 4 (1949): 35–80. A substantial, scholarly historical review of cockfighting in Belgium.

Sarabia Viejo, Maria J. *El juego de gallos en Nueva España.* Sevilla: Escuela de Estudios Hispanoamericanos de Sevilla, 1972. 149 pp. An important historical overview of the evolution of cockfighting customs and regulations in Mexico.

Sarma, I. Karthikeya. "The Ancient Game of Cock-Fight in India." *The Quarterly Journal of the Mythic Society* 54 (1964): 113–120. Documentation through textual evidence and tabular dice of the antiquity of cockfighting in India.

Scott, George Ryley. *The History of Cockfighting.* London: Charles Skilton, 1957. 204 pp. One of the better general historical surveys of cockfighting in England and elsewhere.

Soeroto, Noto, "Hanengevechten op Java." *Nederlandsch-Indië Oud & Nieuw* 1 (1916–1917): 126–132. An essay (with photographs) describing cockfighting in Java.

Vandereuse, Jules. "Le Coq et les ecoliers (Anciennes coutumes scolaires)." *Folklore Brabançon* 23 (1951): 182–208. A useful listing of former cockfighting practices among schoolboys in Belgium and France.

Witte, J. de. "Le Genie des combats de coqs." *Revue Archéologique,* n.s. 17 (1868): 372–381 A listing of classical texts, monuments, inscriptions, mosaics, and vase paintings which allude to or depict cockfights in antiquity.

Those interested in seeing a film or videotape devoted to cockfighting might wish to rent or purchase "The Feathered Warrior," a twelve-minute color interview with Troy Muncie in southern West Virginia. Muncie, a veteran cockfighter, discusses breeding techniques and traits deemed desirable in a bird. A prize rooster is prepared for a fight, with details including the placement of the gaffs. Produced in 1973 and directed by Ben Zickafoose, this short documentary is available from Appalshop Films, 306 Madison Street, Whitesburg, Kentucky, 41858. It can be ordered by telephone, 1-800-545-7467, or by FAX, 606-633-1009. VHS video rental is $50, purchase $95; 16 mm film rental is $55, purchase $195.

Another possibility is film-maker Jerry Barrish's "Cockfighting," a twenty-five minute color video showing the training of handsome cocks by Filipino-Americans as well as actual dramatic scenes of cockfights in the vicinity of Watsonville, California, in 1974. The script for the film was written by Danielle Steel. "Cockfighting" #38218 vhs is available for a modest rental fee of $25 from University of California Extension Center for Media and Independent Learning, 2176 Shattuck Avenue, Berkeley, California, 94704. The telephone number is 510–642–0460; FAX is 510–643–8683.

These two treatments of cockfighting are probably more suitable for classroom use than the commercial U.S. film *Cockfighter,* an eighty-three minute Metrocolor motion picture released in 1974 featuring Warren Oates as a professional cockfighter. Filmed in Georgia and directed by Monte Hellman, the picture's costars include Richard B. Shull, Harry Dean Stanton, Ed Begley, Jr., Laurie Bird, and Troy Donahue. The screenplay was adapted by Charles Willeford from his novel *Cockfighter* (New York: Crown Publishers, 1972), 247 pp.

Index